HUMAN ISSUES IN ANIMAL AGRICULTURE

NUMBER TWO:
TEXAS A&M UNIVERSITY AGRICULTURE SERIES
C. Allan Jones, General Editor

H. O. KUNKEL

HUMAN ISSUES IN ANIMAL AGRICULTURE

WITH CONTRIBUTIONS BY

WILLIAM P. BROWNE

STANLEY E. CURTIS

PAUL B. THOMPSON

TEXAS A&M UNIVERSITY PRESS
College Station

The paper used in this book meets the minimum requirements
of the American National Standard for Permanence
of Paper for Printed Library Materials, Z39.48-1984.
Binding materials have been chosen for durability.

∞

LIBRARY OF CONGRESS CATALOGING-IN-PUBLICATION DATA

Kunkel, H. O.
    Human issues in animal agriculture / H. O. Kunkel with
contributions by William P. Browne, Stanley E. Curtis, and Paul B.
Thompson.—1st ed.
        p. cm.—(Texas A & M University agriculture series ; no. 2)
    Includes bibliographical references (p.).
    ISBN 0-89096-927-2
        1. Livestock industry—Moral and ethical aspects. 2. Animal
welfare. I. Title. II. Series.

HV4757.K86 2000
338.1'76—dc21
                                                            99-053235

CONTENTS

TABLES

PREFACE

Agriculture and food systems throughout the world have undergone remarkable changes during recent decades. The agricultures of North America and other parts of the Western world have become industrialized. Advanced technology dominates agricultural production in much of the developed world; however, much of the world's food production is on small farms and units. Global population growth has been matched by increased global production of grain, but severe problems of malnutrition and famine continue to exist, probably due to issues of access and distribution more than economic ones. Human health, food safety, environmental integrity, global warming, and sustainability of agriculture and society have become major societal concerns. Scientific and technological infrastructures of agriculture and food and natural resources are being restructured in emphasis as well as content. This restructuring has impacted agriculture, food systems, and life on the farm. What is required are new fusions of human values and policy with science and technology.

These chapters are experimental ways of presenting components of a practical, philosophical extension of the subject matter usually termed the animal sciences. They have been and remain evolutionary in perception and content. They are not inclusive of all issues. Some major questions, those notably about the biology of the system, commodity programs, labor, occupational safety, water rights law, and other problems that are generally market issues, are not emphasized here. The reasoning is that interest in these areas can be found in other established applied disciplines and in-depth discussions are available elsewhere.

The roots of this effort are both personal and shared. They stem from an extended tenure in the administrative arena of an agricultural college during the time that nonfarmers began to raise issues about agriculture. What began as a traditional scientific approach soon turned to an interest in the invention of a new field of inquiry that was going on at the same time—human values in food and agriculture. That matured into a substantial interest in the assumptions, policies, and analyses of the whole systems relating to agriculture, natural resources, and human nutrition. We, however, defer neither to arbitrary critique nor to authoritarian defense. That bias also colors the writing.

This book is intended for students and scholars concerned with the animal and food sciences and natural resources as part of the animal sciences literature. Some information will not be new to students of agriculture, natural resources, political science, and philosophy; however, it is reiterated to form a more coherent piece. The premise is that science, including the social sciences, must be combined with ethical inquiry and education to gain the eventual capacity to sort out myth and reality in animal agriculture.

I owe a debt to many people who have shaped this book: the late O. D. Butler, who urged that we fashion an academic course on issues in animal agriculture; Paul B. Thompson, now of Purdue University, who reviewed the entire manuscript at various stages; Stanley E. Curtis of the University of Illinois and William P. Browne of Central Michigan University, who generously contributed to sections that were integrated into this book; Richard P. Haynes of the University of Florida and Glenn L. Johnson of Michigan State University, who provided my first opportunities to test the waters and write and speak in this intellectual arena; Deborah Tolman, who wrote the first drafts of two chapters; others who provided critical reviews of the drafts of one or more chapters: Mortimer Kothmann, Russell Cross, John Griffiths, Gary Smith, Bill A. Stout, J. W. Turner, Gerald Ward, Thomas H. Welsh, and Danny Turk; and the many students who read and responded to the essays that contributed to this study. I am especially appreciative of Lela Batcheler, Sherry Kelly, and Elizabeth Williamson, who transcribed the manuscript through its many revisions.

Finally, I am grateful to Bill Silag who reviewed the first complete manuscript and encouraged the effort to its conclusion.

—H. O. KUNKEL

HUMAN ISSUES IN ANIMAL AGRICULTURE

CHAPTER 1

INTRODUCTION

THE MATTER OF ISSUES

This is a study of issues in the context of a whole system of agriculture. An issue is an issue because we are uncertain of the truth, and uncertainties exist in science and knowledge. An issue exists because people have competitive, conceptual models of the matter and of what the principal guidance for agriculture should be. An issue exists because people have both needs and desires and often do not distinguish between them. An issue also may exist because some people derive power and presumed benefit from a dominance of their viewpoint.

Issues arise also because we each construct our own reality. Diverse attitudes are stated: Big is more efficient; small is beautiful. Food must be safe and wholesome; the family farm must have the public confidence for its own values. Developing countries must develop their own food production capacity; new international markets must be developed for farm products. Agriculture is a business; people engage in agriculture as a way of life for reasons that are not driven by economic justification. The world cannot sustain its agriculture if its present use rate of resources is not curtailed; efficient agriculture is dependent on industrial input. Fat from red meat may be harmful to human health; animal products are needed in the human diet so that people can survive. Various groups believe that inadequate attention is paid to the plight of the small farmer, the farmworker, women in agriculture, rural poverty, human nutrition, social justice, humane agriculture, the environment, energy, water, food security, and the sustainability of agriculture, a term that has come to include all of the above (Lynam and Herdt, 1989).

In a literal sense, advocates often are not talking about agriculture. They are using elements of agriculture as metaphors for their values, their points of view, and often, their preferred ways of life. Values often are matched with disagreements, and actions are not always guided by values. The agendas may be hidden.

People respond to the condition of the times, as do critics, experts, and scientists. If relative scarcity is the current condition, people tend to see the future in the same light. If supplies are in surplus and prices are relatively low, that then, is the predicted outlook. Agriculture, being inherently unstable, is subject more to cyclical visions of its future than are most other productive endeavors. The world, however, is undergoing significant changes in knowledge, technology, institutions, and attitudes. The time has come for a better way to see the future.

The integrating frameworks of agricultural and food systems are economic, ecological, and ethical ones. Agriculture is generally analyzed in terms of economic efficiency. The study of animal agriculture in this context is not a basic discussion of economic factors, but certain social, environmental, and health issues impinge on agriculture as factors outside the arena of economic values. These issues do have economic implications; in fact, it is often in the defense of the economic status quo that conflict and controversy emerge. Economic analyses of issues, however, are extremely difficult, and what may be left are ethical and ecological approaches, less satisfying or direct, but which nevertheless better serve our understanding of food and agriculture systems. Science, technology, and societal and ethical issues are entwined in decision making and problem solving in animal agriculture.

ISSUES IN ANIMAL AGRICULTURE

Examples of issues can be drawn from both plant and animal agricultures; however, special and different relationships exist between animal and crop agricultures and society. People view the issues in different ways.

Crop agricultures face issues such as those related to access to land and finance, sustainability of soil and water resources, intergenerational concepts linked to stewardship, food security, and trade relations. Animal agricultures face issues of health and diet, efficiencies of energy use, animal welfare, carrying capacities, and regulation that have different casts than crop agricultures. There are, however, obvious overlaps. Often, only the specifics of an issue are characteristic of animal agriculture. Animal agriculture can serve as the model for the study of issues pertaining to the entire food and agricultural system.

Unique to animal agriculture is the human–animal relationship. Through the centuries, animals and humans have formed partnerships (McDowell, 1991). In many parts of the world, an interdependence vital to the survival of both humans and animals has developed. In Western countries, animal agriculture is a substantial source of food and an integral part of the economy and society. Animal agriculture today, however, exists in a world in transition, one shaped by industrialization and consumer concerns, a societal interest in the environment and the well-being of animals, governmental interventions, the uncertainties of climate, and emergence of the global market for both feed grains and products of animal agriculture. Many in and out of agriculture are concerned about the safety of food and pathological risk. Some people would return agricultural production to a system more friendly to the environment, a move that has a certain political appeal.

The practices of animal agriculture have been progressively integrated with scientific and industrial knowledge, although the shape of this integration varies with the culture and economy. In much of the world, the empirical development of production methods based on firsthand experience continues to dominate animal husbandry (Byé and Fonte, 1993). There is a profound difference between the productional orientation in large-scale specialized agriculture in the United States and the strongly empirical and traditional approach that characterized animal agriculture in the United States prior to World War II and continues to characterize sectors of animal agriculture in much of the world.

ISSUES AND KNOWLEDGE

There is a return to the concept that critical knowledge is an important factor in the resolution of issues. The dependence of policy formation on scientific and integrative knowledge was suggested four decades ago by Don K. Price (1954): "long-range policy decisions do not depend on general political theory, but are frequently made (in effect) by scientists and technicians, working in professional associations or in universities or research institutions, who develop the basic ideas to which the practical politicians will turn in order to deal with the next emergency.

"The origins of policies are not found in party platforms or the pronouncements of political leaders. They can be traced in the discussions that take place among leaders in scientific and professional fields, in the research studies that such discussions stimulate, and in the consequent consensus among the professionals."

Today, it seems that policy consensus is based more on scientific than on shared moral values (Norton, 1991c). Advances in a group of enabling technologies—biotechnologies, medical technologies, materials science, artificial intelligence and robotics, and information technologies—promise to feed a new surge of technology for agriculture in the near future. In the process, animal scientists and professionals will be called on to integrate a wide range of disciplines, including the social sciences. Ruttan (1987) argued that research managers, scientists, and technologists have a clear responsibility to inform society as to the impact of scientific and economic policy, for example on: the choice of technologies; the distribution of income among laborers, landowners, and consumers; the structure of agricultural and related communities; the health and safety of both producers and consumers; the convergence of the market and societal costs, including environmental degradation; and the choices allowed to individuals.

Various disciplines differ in their ways of looking at humanity, the philosophy of their methods, how they structure the problem and how the research question is asked, and what the larger aim of the science is (Montgomery and Bennett, 1979). Diverse discipline-borne belief systems are also evident in the sciences related to agriculture. Biological scientists, agricultural engineers, and resource economists reductively explore the elements of the food and agricultural system and may, indeed, have the knowledge to allocate the research products efficiently (Norton, 1991c; Sagoff, 1993). Their science, however, may lack the broad integration to consider social and ethical issues. Social scientists are critics and their science may be adequate to explore the human interrelationships, but they may not be able to merge the human social system with nature. Ecologists, in contrast, may be developing a science that reveals what nature would be like without the human system (Norton, 1991c). None of these sciences may be adequate to capture the ethical intuitions about the interface of humanity and nature, but they are the intellectual resources on which we rely. The stage then is one upon which individual values and world views (i.e., our personal experiences, feelings, emotions, beliefs, morals, tastes, intelligence, and stores of knowledge) also play.

More knowledge will be needed, which should be both scientific and normative. New fusions of science with utility, utility with values, and values with science become the imperatives in animal agriculture.

THIS BOOK

This book is based on the conceptions of animal agricultures as food and agricultural systems, as human–animal interdependence, and as components of human ecology. Topics are based on ethical and societal as well as biophysical factors that are issues in food and agriculture in both developed and developing countries, with some emphasis given to the United States.

Part one, chapters 2–6, is intended to establish some of the bases for analyses of the whole systems of animal agriculture. To the extent that the principal issues can be examined on a level playing field of knowledgeable understanding, the analysis can be useful to animal scientists, social scientists, ethicists, and concerned interests.

Too often animal scientists will argue an issue from an incomplete understanding, and others who take different paths will have the advantage. In like manner, those who argue human values are often naive about biological and ecological realities. Perhaps this study can be useful to both groups. Thus, as understanding the issues is rooted in understanding whole systems, known and presumed factors in the animal agriculture system are examined. Discussions of values, moral philosophy, and ethical issues are placed early in the sequence. As issues are involved in the formations of policy or law and are often mediated, made worse, or made better through the regulatory and political processes, chapters relating to institutional matters are included. Political and regulatory factors frame the social and legal climate in which animal agriculture functions. These factors are often the mechanisms by which science, technology, and human values interconnect. Nutrition in this setting is human nutrition and is treated as a socioeconomic force. Biological and economic (market) factors are less developed in this book on the presumption that these are discussed in detail elsewhere, although clearly, nonmarket issues have economic impacts.

Part two, chapters 7–14, discusses the primary issues of the time. These chapters are primarily directed to dissect the issues, examining the knowledge about human values and uncertainty, as well as scientific and industrial knowledge. Issues are analyzed at three levels: the intellectual context of the issue, the methods of examining the issue, and the ownerships of the contending beliefs, arguments, and evidence. The intent is to present information and the analyses of many authors to maintain balance in reasoning about the issues; the conclusions reached are intended to open the mind rather than convince.

The issues are varied. They relate to the food-borne and environmental risks in animal agriculture. Questions are concerned about the sustainability of the production system. Issues are concerned about the impacts of the vagaries of climate and weather and of policies relating to the use of land resources. They focus on the allocations of energy and feeding a world's populations. They are concerned with waste management and land use. The inherent issues of the well-being of animals and the place of animal products in the human food system are important considerations. A final chapter is directed to those who seek new knowledge as to what they should do about issues.

This book is more descriptive than prescriptive, as it should be. Students, for example, should learn perspective, tolerance, and critical thinking, all of which demand interactive discussion. In the classroom, the outstanding teachers are those who present critical perspectives not available in the literature or in orthodox science classes. The issues presented here will always need such a wide-ranging touch of scholarship, whether in the classroom or the real world. The values of experience and varying points of view cannot be overestimated.

A WHOLE SYSTEMS ANALYSIS

Central to any consideration of issues related to agriculture, including animal agriculture, are the conceptions of the entire food and agricultural system, not of agricultural production alone.

The basic resources at the start of every food chain and natural resource system are solar radiation, carbon dioxide, mineral elements, and the land and water base. The amount of solar radiation that reaches the ground varies greatly from place to place, time to time, and season to season. These variations are reflected in the vastly differing crop and animal agricultures of the world, and the food and agricultural resources of the world are placed unevenly among nations.

Energy also enters the agricultural ecosystem in its stored forms, mainly as fossil energy. Human energy is expended directly as work or indirectly in management. Tools and instruments are used in the cycles of agriculture and most often require fossil fuel in their making and use. Livestock production utilizes biomass, some of which has been produced in systems using fossil and human energy. Food is harvested, transported, processed, stored, distributed, and cooked using energy sources that are finite. Thus, the natural food system with its trophic hierarchies (i.e., with animal agriculture) is matched and integrated with dependence on a nonrenewable resource-based system (Dahlberg, 1987).

What establishes the trophic relationships of humans to their food supply (i.e., whether animal intermediaries are used) are culture, the state of development of the food system, and the socioeconomic status of individuals, all of which determine the accessibility of food to individuals. Humans may choose their foods at different trophic levels. Some human populations (e.g., Inuits) consume diets high in animal products. Other populations (e.g., in southern Asia) have long existed largely on vegetarian diets. People may choose fish, which may have been nourished several steps removed from the primary photosynthetic plants; veal from animals fed milk; beef, poultry, and pork, which may be from animals fed grain or scavenge forage and household food wastes; or vegetables, fruits, and processed grain products.

Animals in the agricultural web spend their lives in different environments: farms and ranches, free ranges and confined housing, sties and pens, feedlots and battery cages, stalls and crates, and tethered or loose.

The natural flow of energy through the decomposer food chain also provides for the gradual breakdown and recycling of vital nutrients to green plants. Recycling, however, is cut off in many food chains. People may live close to production sites, on the farms, and near the oceans; but urbanization has moved a lot of people far from the site of production and food must be collected, processed, and transported. Waste is not returned to the site of production. Wastes accumulate, sometimes as pollutants, in one end of the system and the fertility of the soil must be replaced at the other.

Until recently, nutrition was considered mainly as a factor external to the agricultural system, with toxicology and food safety the critical issues. Today, however, human nutrition also targets the prolongation of the life-span. Each human has a *nutrition envelope,* a set of conditions set by heredity, the economic and cultural environment, eating habits and desires, and what has been eaten and drunk in the preceding lifetime (Lucas, 1988). Humans understand when they are sick. Now they need to know what constitutes the healthy person and the healthful food system.

The whole food system, not food, is key. Food as a segregative scientific or production problem is meaningless. So is animal production by itself.

Thus, we will argue that the focus on issues must be related to the whole systems beginning with the production systems and proceeding through processing, distribution, preparation, recycling, waste handling, storage at each phase, finance, trade, policy, regulation, and use for human life support. Our means of handling these diverse components and the issues and risks that they engender are our institutions, organization, communications, and legal frameworks.

CHAPTER 2

AGRICULTURAL SYSTEMS

World views about agriculture have changed substantially during the past decades, from agriculture being mainly a production function to being either (1) a much more complex, responsible management of resources (Bawden, 1986) or (2) a system of providing adequate, safe, and healthful foods to the population.

Social revisionists have tended to turn their interests in agriculture toward the sustainability of resources and values of rural community life. Those who believe that economic forces should be the main factor determining the system hold other visions for the structure of the food and agriculture system, visions that are often non-agrarian. The economic behaviors of producers and consumers, the markets, and economic policy are major areas of interest. Those who hold concerns about human health, mainly epidemiologists and human nutritionists, focus on the endpoints of food supplies and selection. Views concerning health and nutrition and those pertaining to resource and economic aspects of agriculture are not necessarily linked; however, linkages will likely be important considerations in the future and they may be facilitated by viewing production, use, and resource as an agroecosystem.

The common property of agroecosystems is that they each have a boundary-like interface, which distinguishes the ecosystem from its environment as well as from other ecosystems. Many elements cycle within the system, whereas energy and some elements move through the system. As generally recognized, the principal transformations in an ecosystem are the conversions of energy from the sun to chemical energy of tissues of living plant and animal organisms, the connected incorporation of minerals and organic matter from the environment into the biomass, and subsequent release of the energy through consumption, metabolism, decay, and burning.

Such a view is too simplistic. Communication and controls also occur within both natural and cultural ecosystems. Moreover, the environments across the earth are anything but homogeneous; there are significant locational, seasonal, and daily variations in solar radiation and rainfall. Soils and topography show wide variation, and these differences have given support to an enormous diversity of living organisms (animals, insects, microorganisms, and plants) in the environment. Altieri (1987) noted that each agricultural system has a unique mix of agroecosystemic determinants that shape the type of agriculture in a region or area or landscape. Each agricultural system is the totality of interacting individuals, populations and communities, and their environments. Simply put, animal agricultures occur in systems that include inputs, production, use of the produce of the system, and management. Animal agricultures operate within and are part of the economic and societal fabric of a country or region.

A critical difference between crop and livestock productions is that worldwide, relatively few animal species are used by humans compared to hundreds of useful crop species. Not only are fewer domestic animal species used, but for the most part, the same species of animals are used all over the world: cattle, sheep, goats, pigs, poultry, and camelids. Part of the reason is that special behavioral characteristics are possessed by domestic animals; they are relatively docile and capable of containment and breeding in captivity. In addition, the uses of animals are constrained by problems of psychological resistance and religious taboos. For example, the capture, slaughter, and conversion to meats of stray or feral dogs is wholly unacceptable to the people in the United States, but meats from both hunted and herded ruminant animals are quite acceptable.

The uses of relatively few species in animal agriculture mean that these species have to be adapted over a wide range of environments. As a result, they are inevitably used outside of the environment in which they evolved or to which they are adapted. In the process, domestic animals may have become wholly dependent upon humans and farmers have become nearly as dependent upon them (Budiansky, 1992).

CONTROL OF AGRICULTURAL SYSTEMS

Various agricultural systems differ widely in their biological and physical complexity, and in turn, human management of these systems (Snaydon and Elston, 1976). Rangelands are only slightly modified native ecosystems. Intensively managed systems such as greenhouse cropping or confined animal feeding operations are greatly modified environments. Modification of the agricultural system involves control and management of both physical and biological components. Physical control is designed to provide optimum conditions for the biological parts of the system, which involves environmental control as well as time- and site-specific stability. Biological control involves selection of the species and genotypes that are deemed most useful and the removal of species that are less productive.

This relationship may be visualized in a graphic form:

Control of biological components ▼	Urban areas
	Wilderness
	National forests
	Rangelands
	Planted forests
	Improved pastures
	Field crops
Complexity of ▲ biological components	Irrigated crops
	Greenhouse crops and pen-fed animals

Complexity of Physical Environment ▶
Control of Physical Environment ◀

(Adapted from Snaydon and Elston, 1976)

It is possible to achieve precise control of the physical environment, but less so of the biological components (Snaydon and Elston, 1976). Control of the physical environment and manipulation of the physical factors are part of the agricultural system and may include:

1. Supplementary irrigation and fertilizers.
2. Exploitation of the spectral transmissions of glass and plastic.

3. Protection against cold air movement, soil temperature modification by altering color and texture of the protective covering, and flooding with water.
4. Protection of animals in controlled environments.
5. Removal of wastes and odors.

Biological components have been controlled by humans to provide greater output to themselves by:

1. Determining the trophic level status of humans (i.e., changing from consumption of animal products to largely eating plants and vice versa).
2. Selecting species and varieties of both the plants and the animals consuming the plants.
3. Controlling the numbers of other species: pests, predators, pathogens, and competitors.

Methods of managing biological components are interdependent with each other and with environmental controls. Modification of the biological components of systems ranges from little in the hunting and gathering societies to considerable in the intensive crop and animal productions of industrial societies. The trophic levels of human populations range from almost completely vegetarian diets to almost completely carnivorous. The control of pests and pathogens ranges from zero to almost complete control in intensive agriculture.

VARIETIES OF AGRICULTURE

Agriculture is a composite of many different forms. Methods of production, harvest, and distribution vary greatly from one region or commodity to another, and each form is a matter of concern with respect to both the needs of people and the management of resources.

With respect to the relationship of people to agriculture, there are at least three general agricultural forms in the world, each of which has its distinctive interplay with the issues and values of agriculture:

1. The agriculture of the large commercial farm that takes on the characteristics of the business and industrial enterprise. Access to the land by the population is not a primary consideration in a society organized around large commercial farms. Neither is the value of private ownership and associated private rights and trespass emotions.

2. The agriculture depicted in the agrarian model in which sustaining the population in rural areas is a priority, the landscape of agriculture is important, and visible good husbandry is a goal. Ownership of the land may be an important component of the system. Among its values, this model of agriculture also embodies a pastoral vision of farm life containing a number of appealing features, perhaps more so to nonfarmers than the farmers themselves (Horwich, 1989). This category includes farms in the irrigated and stable rainfall, high potential areas of the developing world.

3. Low-resource, risk-prone agriculture, which in many developing countries sustains a substantial part of the population. Access to the land is a primary requirement for the livelihoods of a major part of the population (Chambers et al., 1989).

This categorization of types of agriculture differs from the three identified by the Brundtland Report (cited by Chambers et al., 1989: xvi–xx). The commission's categories were industrial agriculture, green revolution agriculture, and resource-poor agriculture. The industrial included smaller farms in industrialized countries which were subsidized or provided other inputs. We classify that group in the second agrarian type of agriculture in which personal and emotional ties to agriculture figure in the goals of the farmer. The commission's third type and our third type are coincident.

TRADITIONAL AGRICULTURE

Thousands of years of cultural change have led not only to the development of modern systems of intensive, mechanized agriculture, but also to a diversity of systems directed toward production of food for individual use or for sale and barter through local markets. These are the traditional farming systems, usually considered as forms of subsistence agriculture: pastoralism, shifting cultivation, permanent nonmechanized agricultural systems, polyculture, desert runoff agriculture, and hunting and gathering (Cox and Atkins, 1979).

Large numbers of the world's population depend on subsistence systems (Dover and Talbot, 1987). Systems of subsistence agriculture are thought to reflect a high level of ecological awareness, representing a kind of steady-state solution to problems of human life in a variable environment. They, however, also represent successive stages of agricultural development. The explosive growth of human populations and the spread of influences from industrializing societies are disrupting and displacing subsistence systems at an increasing rate. Traditional farming systems are, in the main, small and labor intensive, and often defenseless against incursion and crowding.

Pastoralist systems of subsistence agriculture are pursued on about one-third of the earth's grassland and savanna environments by about 100 million people (Crotty, 1980). These systems are characterized by the association of large numbers of people with herds of domestic animals. The purposes are to obtain sustainable yields of foods such as milk, meat, and blood, as well as animals for wealth and dowry.

Shifting (swidden) cultivation is now largely restricted to the tropics and is the crop agriculture counterpart to pastoralism. It is a farming system in which plots of land are cleared, cultivated for one or more seasons, and then abandoned because of the decline in productivity caused by the exhaustion of soil nutrients and a buildup of weeds and insect pests. The length of fallow may vary from one to three years or more, or even decades.

Both pastoral grazing and shifting cultivation depend on mobility, periodic mining of accumulated nutrients or harvestable food, and population densities that allow adequate mineral and vegetational resources to accumulate.

Until recent population and other pressures forced shortening of fallow periods, shifting agriculture was considered to be an ecologically sound agriculture. All traditional systems are being modified and displaced by forces resulting from human population growth. Rapid population growth sometimes forces more intensive manipulation: fallow periods are shortened, more land must be in production, greater yields are required, greater investments of energy, materials, and skill must be made.

Traditional agriculture is based on a legacy of farmer innovation and indigenous technical knowledge.[1] It has a much lower science and technological underpinning than intensive agriculture, and its needs may not be easily met by conventional research. Cropping patterns are not usually predetermined by design (Richards, 1989). A farmer's crop mix in each season develops as a performance, dependent on unpredictable weather, as an interplay of farming activities with the household's resources. Farming operations are embedded over time in the social context: "Last week we had to sell the cow to pay for mother's funeral." Options and coping skills are what matter (Chambers et al., 1989). Thus, traditional agriculture is not simple agriculture. Chambers et al. (1989) call it complex, diverse, and risk-prone agriculture.

INTENSIVELY MANAGED SYSTEMS

Most of the world's food supply, however, is produced by more intensively managed agroecosystems. Intensification does not necessarily involve mechanization. Agriculture also can be intensified biologically, by either increasing (polyculture) or reducing the variety of crops cultivated, increasing stocking level, and decreasing the time that fields are allowed to be fallow or pastures to go ungrazed.

Intensive agricultural systems usually have distinct boundaries. They lack spatial and temporal continuity, being neither self-regulating nor self-perpetuating. Successions of plants are usually prevented and detritus chains rarely have opportunity to develop fully. The plants and animals of intensive agriculture are products of intensive breeding programs with specific objectives that may be of little ecological importance. The individual components of intensive commercial agriculture are often critical to its existence and conduct.

Intensive systems have been so well accepted by the agricultural community that they are often designated as conventional or Western agriculture; however, an industrialized animal agriculture also has been created out of intensification. Industrial agriculture utilizes business and industrial techniques that depend on inputs from other industrial sources, and that have adopted scientifically based techniques and specialization in its operations (Byé and Fonte, 1993). The production process is segmented into simplified operations for purposes of control. The scientific base is generally clear. Specialization (i.e., knowledge in depth) seems also to emphasize the need to communicate technical knowledge and problem solving competencies. Industrialized agriculture, such as the modern cattle feedlot and poultry and swine production plants, are reductive in their operations. Management is hierarchical in its organization.

ALTERNATIVE SYSTEMS

A number of people—experts, scientists, activists, and interested citizens—are concerned that the intensified agricultural systems of today are not sustainable systems (Matson et al., 1997). One issue is that humans use or co-opt as much as 40 percent of the products of photosynthesis (Vitousek et al., 1986), using the material directly or indirectly, and cause it to flow to different consumers and decomposers. The material may be lost because of changes in land use. The result of the loss of these land-based resources may lead to extinctions of species and genetically distinct populations of certain plants and wild animals. The argument grows for alternative agricultural systems that are believed to be more sound ecologically than the conventional or industrial models, particularly in fragile environments. This thought extends to organic farmers in the United States and Europe. The challenge is to chemical and mechanized agriculture, and agroecology[2] becomes the watchword for the movement.

The literature relative to a scientific base for alternative agriculture is growing (Altieri, 1987; NRC, 1989a; Lockeretz, 1997). Dover and Talbot (1987), taking a more moderate view of Western agriculture than some, have argued that an ecological approach can begin to rectify the environmental degradation caused by both industrial and misplaced traditional agricultures. Soil quality can be improved by ensuring that plant or residue cover exists for most of the time by use of perennial plant populations in polycultural cropping systems. Mixed-crop farming systems including animal components can be important (NRC, 1989a). Energy efficiency may be sought in the design of the agroecosystem by systems that effectively recycle nutrients and cropping patterns. Stability in the system can be gained by prompt management actions and with methods that are available to respond to changes in the environment (e.g., weather changes, pest pressures). A sustainable agriculture is defined as meeting current production goals without compromising the future in terms of resource degradation or depletion (Matson et al., 1997). Other appropriate definitions may involve profitability that is environmentally and socially acceptable.

Animal systems may be devised on similar principles. Many alternative scenarios require the presence of animals (NRC, 1989a). Organic or natural animal products, meaning products out of animal systems that do not utilize pesticides, drugs, or other chemical adjuvants, can be devised and be competitive in a premium market. More space per bird or animal, reducing the conditions by which disease and parasites can enter or thrive in the environment, and very close supervision are considered to be requisites for production of organic animal products. Obviously, management intensity must grow with the size of the operation.

In the 1990s, the U.S. Congress began to recognize the scientific needs of sustainable agriculture with the passage of farm bills that emphasized environmental factors and facilitated setting standards for organic farm products.

Modern conventional agriculture and its scientific base have been criticized by advocates of sustainable agriculture for being destructive of resources and the cause of social problems (Altieri, 1987). On the other hand, the agricultural research establishment has chosen largely to distance themselves from the agroecologists. The debates seem drawn from the ends of an inevitable dichotomy of world views, a dichotomy that will challenge all scientists who would study agricultural systems. It has been the intensified cropping systems and swine, poultry, and farm fish production that have been responsible for a food system that has generally kept pace with population growth. Thus, the issues focus on the intensified systems, as they often are of greatest significance among the agricultural systems. Although intensified agroecosystems are typically managed in isolation from other ecosystems within a locale, the physical, ecological, and biogeochemical changes that may take place within them can have consequences for adjacent ecosystems (Matson et al., 1997). For example, the waste stream of confined animal production systems can contaminate groundwater and cause eutrophication in freshwater systems. Diseases such as salmonella can become concentrated and enter the food production process. The problems, however, are not necessarily inevitable. Broad implementation of strategies such as nutrient management, disease control, management of the waste stream, and site selection can lead to sustainability of intensive animal systems.

RISKS

The question may be asked if the manipulation of the biological components and the physical environment reduces the risks in agriculture. The ability to control, by definition, decreases risk; the risk would be greater when control is less. Traditional agriculture is surely risk-prone; however, in cases in which control is least and the biological components and the environment are most complex, the external inputs are minimal. Thus, the risk becomes less because there is less to risk.

The factors in this apparent contradiction may arise because as people develop the capacity to influence the food webs (agricultural systems) by introducing changes (control), they also encounter greater possibilities of making errors (Snaydon and Elston, 1976). In essence, increased control may substitute a more (or a less) error-prone condition for one that had been risk-prone. As people increase their ability to control, they increase the possibilities of making mistakes that may damage the environment or have other side effects. Arguably, the animal system that has been most vulnerable to criticism is that of anemic veal production. The animals are kept in confined quarters, fed liquid diets, and can be subject to managerial mistakes in a highly controlled system. A highly intense management can break down at any time.

The solution likely will be the further development of technology that reduces error. We have seen something of this in industrial poultry and swine production. As more knowledge is gained and technology is devised appropriately, errors can be reduced. Some people remain apprehensive, however, believing that the introduction of major new kinds of technology, such as biotechnology, may open the door to more unwanted side effects. Industrial animal agriculture may be constrained by society if this fear prevails.

CONSTRAINTS

Any system of agriculture is constructed within the socioeconomic constraints existent in a country; a key constraint is market demand. In developing countries, the creation of an economic demand for food is needed not only to reduce the constraints on human nutrition, but to create environments and incentives that increase both farm inputs and food supplies; however, in situations in which the human population density is high and increasing and the support energy is low, it is difficult to generate the needed economic demand (Duckham, 1976a; Stout, 1996). Rapidly expanding populations and/or more longevity mean that too high a percentage of the population will not be of working age but still need to be fed. Population pressure without economic development is an environmental constraint.

Future agricultural systems will likely be constructed to meet ecological constraints. Such constraints may be weather, weeds and brush, pests and diseases, ecological instabilities, as well as human population pressures. These constraints combine to limit the agricultural species that can be produced at a given site. The trend in the United States to distance large livestock production units from any human habitation (Marberry, 1995) is a modern example of an emerging population pressure. This constraint, however, may have been used also to deter the growth of large units as a means of reducing competition for small livestock producers.

Constraints can be mitigated or aggravated by the use or misuse of external technological inputs, derived in large part from the use of nonsolar energy. Such inputs, however, also depend on socioeconomic factors. Of the two classes of constraints, the socioeconomic may prove less tractable than the ecological. The economy has forced animal agriculture toward larger production units. Consumer demand, farm finance, international trade and embargoes, and restraint of competition may have effects that exceed those of new technology, particularly in the short term (Madden and Thompson, 1987).

ANIMAL AGRICULTURES

Livestock and poultry insert alternate and higher trophic links in the food chain between plants and people. This is particularly evident in industrial countries. The efficiency of livestock production is low in developing countries, although it has improved rapidly with the introduction of technologies related to poultry and swine productions and aquaculture. Animal agriculture usually is described as the use of two classes of animals: herbivorous (e.g., cattle, goats, sheep, buffaloes, camelids, horses, asses) and omnivorous (swine, poultry, fish).

Ruminant and other herbivorous animals use cellulose, the most abundant energy source in the biosphere. Characteristic of omnivores is their adaptability to almost anything that is available (Tudge, 1977). Carnivorous animals let other animals exploit the plants in the environment. Humans also lie in wait. The system allows a great deal of flexibility by letting other animals gather and store the food resources for people.

Similarly, ocean fish gather plankton and other ocean food resources; some on higher trophic levels are carnivorous, and thus exploit the environment for human consumption.

We can also characterize animal food systems by the structure of their productive environment (Brown, 1997): those heavily dependent upon natural systems, such as ocean fish, beef cattle, goats, sheep, and herbivorous wildlife; and those increasingly dependent upon technological development of the production system, such as swine, poultry, dairy cattle, and farm fish. The structures within these two classes are extremely variable and are changing.

Classic traditional pastoralism is a form of husbandry practiced by people who are dependent on ruminant livestock that graze largely communal pastures (Crotty, 1980). It is the oldest form of production after hunting and gathering. It engages hundreds of millions of owners and their families and hundreds of millions of cattle, buffalo, sheep, goats, and camelids. People in the Scottish Highlands make their living from sheep grazed communally (Crotty, 1980). Africa, with ten percent of the world's population, has one-fourth of the world's grasslands and one of each eight head of cattle in the world. Culture and the institutions of Africa are influenced by pastoralism.

The reversion of land from cropping to pasture while remaining under individual tenure and private ownership of range land has fostered a *capitalist pastoralism* (Crotty, 1980). The landed gentry of England, the ranch owners of North America, and the large individual holdings of South America (latifundia) have exploited pastoral resources under capitalist institutions. In particularly North America and Europe, livestock have replaced people as the population on the land. The ranches in South America and the land holdings in Ireland have replaced smaller numbers of people as they employ a larger number of people per animal unit than North America. The trend in the latter group is that the pastoralism will require less and less labor as time passes, but may produce little more animal products.

In preindustrial small-farm agriculture, livestock were and are mainly scavengers (Crotty, 1980). They use otherwise valueless resources—pasture, by-products, straw, household food wastes, and family labor—and convert these into useful products: draft, meat, milk, and eggs. As income increases, it becomes feasible to convert more expensive crop-produced feed into livestock products, and the system becomes something different.

As it became profitable to feed animals, the animal agriculture system included components beyond simply feeding the animal. An integrated system developed a mixed arable–livestock system commonly seen in the first half of the twentieth century in Europe and North America. This included integrated breeding–rearing–fattening animal operations. The range of required inputs widened: housing, veterinary support, improved agronomic technology for pasturage and grain, and eventually formula-mixed feeds and supplements. The principal residual now of the mixed arable–livestock operation in the United States and Europe is dairying. Some propositions toward sustainable agriculture reflect a renewed interest in a future return to this system.

In the main, intensive-confinement animal systems are the successor to the mixed agriculture. Technology is at its highest level of use. Dairy production has shifted from a dual purpose into an intensive closed system producing milk, cream, cheese, yogurt, ice cream, butter, and other products. Poultry production in much of the world is also consolidating into integrated production/marketing systems. Swine production may be concentrating into a smaller number of countries (Denmark, the Netherlands, and the United States) where intensive productions may further displace traditional systems as the source of meat in other pork consuming countries.

WHY AN ANIMAL AGRICULTURE?

There are multiple reasons why animal agricultures exist. Trenkle and Wilham (1977) have cited that animals serve as power; refuse scavengers; a means of storage grain energy after consumption; producers of fertilizer; a highly flexible food reserve; sources of fiber, leather, and biochemicals; and harvesters of forage from adjacent untillable land areas. Livestock thus can affect all facets of agriculture and many aspects of human life. Farm animals play a crucial role in the economy and social life of the whole world. In subsistence agriculture there is often a vital interdependence between humans and their animals.

A strong human appetite for animal products is evident throughout the world (Brown, 1997). Food products from animals are accepted as the bases of diets of people in industrial nations and some developing countries. Rising incomes generally create a rising demand for animal products. World productions of meat, milk, and fish for human consumption are estimated to total more than 800 million metric tons, and certain productions continue to increase.

In terms of the number of people in the world consuming animal protein, more than half of the world's population have depended on fish for their animal protein. The seafood catch, however, leveled off at about 90 million tons during the 1990s. Similarly, the production of beef escalated by a factor of 2.5 from 1950 to 1990, but has shown little increase since then. Fish and beef have been traditionally important sources of animal protein. Brown (1997) noted that with the slowdown, the world is turning to other sources: pork, poultry, eggs, and fish produced in aquaculture. Pork consumption per person in China is higher than in the United States. The share of poultry in the total meat supply has increased in both developed and developing countries. Egg production has increased rapidly in the 1990s, largely because eggs are not as dependent on refrigeration as milk and meat are.

Thus, the major sources of animal protein dependent upon natural systems (fish and beef) are being supplanted by systems dependent upon grain. Some, like Brown (1997), believe that the growth in grain-fed animal production may not be sustainable in the twenty-first century.

In summary, the hierarchy of purposes served varies (McDowell, 1980):

1. Animal agriculture in the United States exists for the purpose of *income*, the sale of meat, milk, fiber and eggs. It *uses nonarable lands*, serves as a *prestige factor*, and as a means to *generate capital*.

2. In developing societies, animal agricultures have served a different array of purposes. The primary purpose served is first the *reduction of risks* from cropping. Although land often is not individually owned, animals are privately owned and exchanged. Agricultural surpluses are invested in animals to *accumulate capital*. Animals serve to *render services:* traction, fertilizer, fuel, and heat in cold weather. They *satisfy cultural needs* and serve to *ensure status or prestige*. The lowest priority basis for animal agriculture in developing countries may be to *provide food* and *generate income*.

Farmers in developing countries frequently try to have their animals serve several objectives, whereas the U.S. production systems are centered on the most efficient method of producing a single product such as eggs, milk, or meat.

SYSTEMS AND ISSUES

Issues are bound up in the fact that animal agricultures exist as widely divergent systems throughout the world. Animal agricultures in the world differ more extensively from each other mainly in their cultural settings, socioeconomically and technologically, not in the species used or the basic products produced (meat, milk, eggs, hides, and work). Animal agriculture systems serve many cultural purposes and are subject to a range of views as to what they should be: intensive or extensive; sustainable, conventional, or alternative; a system of managing resources or a system of producing food and providing services; and whether corporate or farmer controlled.

Each system of animal agriculture has a unique complexity, which can be subject to systems analysis and theory; however, each system of agriculture—pastoral, traditional, mixed, intensive, technologically based, or industrial—has a human as well as a special economic and resource-based character. Inherent in each of the diverse systems is a unique and special relationship to humanity and society. When systems theorists ignore or shortchange human values, policies, and politics, they do not deal with the whole systems of agriculture.

NOTES

1. It is of interest that indigenous and local knowledge was in many respects, up until recently, the bases upon which higher education in U.S. agriculture was shaped. While science and research provided the technology, the intuitive ability of the person who grew up on the farm and had hands-on knowledge was counted on in most agricultural courses of study. Some faculty members in colleges of agriculture are disturbed that this traditional component of education has been greatly diminished.

2. The terms agroecosystem and agroecology should be distinguished. An agroecosystem would include all aspects of a given agricultural system and is defined by stated limits. The term may include intensive agricultural systems, subsistence or traditional agriculture, and even the rumen of a ruminant animal. The term agroecology has been increasingly co-opted to mean what is referred to as sustainable agriculture, alternative agriculture, or organic farming.

CHAPTER 3

ETHICAL AND VALUE ISSUES

How can we best learn how to realize what is of value?
—NICHOLAS MAXWELL (1992)

Animal agriculture exists in a pluralistic society, one in which it is inevitable for people to disagree over the rightness or wrongness of proposed acts. For example, an act regarded as right among farmers may be regarded as wrong in another group, or as morally neutral in still another. It seems that scholars concerned with food and agriculture and their sciences need to reflect on a variety of philosophical, moral, religious, scientific, and legal perspectives that often engender conflicting arguments. Agriculture and agricultural science and education may have to live with a fervor and ideological directness that will be important to many people. It also may be that laws and policy relevant to agriculture can be enacted in the years ahead only through ethical persuasion. This is the basis for the discussions in this chapter.

Agricultural production systems have enjoyed autonomy throughout most of U.S. history. Ethical responsibilities and humaneness have been intrinsic to farming and rural life; however, more and more considerations of fairness, questions of conflicts over rights and the resolution of those conflicts, and questions of virtue and integrity have entered the list of ethical demands upon agriculture.

Scientific and technological changes and the many issues of bioethics that focus on life and quality of life have created new problems. The issues in agriculture that now beg moral analysis and ethical practice are the industrialization of agriculture, the diminution of the family farm, the emphasis on production agriculture in contrast to the provision of food directed toward targets of human health and environmental integrity, the sustainability of the resources (soil, water, clean air) and agricultural people, equity among consumers and farmers, social justice for the poor and landless, the right of choice, the interests of nonhuman organisms, the apparent uncoupling of agricultural science and technology from ecology, and the current developments in science and technology, stimulated in part by biotechnology and other emerging sciences.

In this book, ethics refers to the philosophical inquiry into the principles of morality (right and wrong conduct, virtue and vice, good and evil) as they relate to conduct (Ladd, 1978). Agricultural ethics may be interpreted as the philosophical examination of the principles relating to the virtues and faults in the practice of agriculture and the operations of the markets and infrastructure of agriculture and food.

Ethics, as used here, does not mean the professional ethics that may be incorporated in ethical codes of conduct for professional agriculturalists. The social responsibilities of agricultural scientists and professionals, however, can be regarded as proper subjects of examination in the context of agricultural ethics. Ethics is not the same as law or jurisprudence nor is it concerned with custom or institutional practice and behavior. Rather, ethics refers to what law, custom, practice, or conduct should be.

Often, we in agriculture decide what to do in a practical manner. For example, animal agriculture has used nitrite as a preservative of meat; otherwise the meat would become tainted and those who consume it could die of bacterial toxins. For certain food preparations, there appeared to be no completely adequate substitute for nitrite. For awhile, we were told that people who consume meat preserved with nitrite may risk cancer, although subsequently, the basis of that argument was scientifically rejected. The use of nitrite has decreased, but the kinds of questions asked about nitrites are ethical areas which can be asked in other situations. Which risk is greater? How certain are we? How certain must we be before a decision is made?

Questions arise about moral constraints on decisions. How much autonomy can be allowed? With whom lies the burden of proof? Who has the power to decide and put decisions into effect? Should they have the power of decision and action?

What are the social and political implications of scientific advances? How does one allow for public supervision of certain parts of the scientific enterprise without crippling effects?

The development of moral and ethical issues in agriculture began with the writings of nonagriculturalists. The publication in 1906 of novelist Upton Sinclair's *The Jungle* sent media to the stockyards and stimulated the passage of food inspection laws. Rachel Carson's *Silent Spring* was published in 1962. Sensitivity to problems of the environment and their effects on human health, water contamination, and waste site problems are increasingly part of our daily television fare. Peter Singer's *Animal Liberation* was published in 1975, and the interests of animals have become a critical focus of medical research and animal agriculture. Wendell Berry's *The Unsettling of America* was published in 1977, and the structure of the farm became a subject of intellectual interest, as were the emotional interests elicited in 1939 by John Steinbeck's *The Grapes of Wrath* and the practical interests displayed by owners and migrant workers in an agricultural industry dependent upon seasonal labor.

Wunderlich (1990) classified most of the ethical issues pertaining to food and agriculture around four clusters: human and animal interests, conservation of resources, farm–industry organization and fairness, and food–people–planet. Included in these broad subjects are issues that create difficulty for governments and governmental policy as well as affect the basic needs of all people regarding health, equity, and quality of life. Concerns for the environment, the appropriateness of the developing agriculture system, and questions about the relevance of science and technology are also integrated in these clusters.

Such groupings also take on special considerations because they also can combine issues in conflict. For example, under the grouping of farm–industry organization and fairness, questions about who produces the food, controls the production, and where it takes place often matters more than what and how much is produced (Chambers, 1987). Human and animal interests and conservation of resources are sometimes summarized under the term sustainable agriculture, but a priority for some is not just sustainable agriculture, but sustainable livelihoods based on agriculture.

EXAMPLES OF DEVELOPING ETHICAL ISSUES:
FOOD–PEOPLE–WORLD ENVIRONMENT
AND FOOD PRODUCTION

Moral aspects of food and agriculture may have their roots in the base aspects of human nature. Thomas Hobbes's philosophical treatise *Leviathan* in 1651, pointed to the darker side: "The most frequent reason why men desire to hurt each other is that many men at the same time have an appetite to the same thing; which yet very often they can neither enjoy in common, nor yet divide it, whence it follows that the strongest should have it."

This basic human nature is often framed in terms of human greed. In the 1970s, many people in the United States and the rest of the world believed that the industrial nations should establish and hold a world reserve supply of grain for developing countries. Believing that the rates of grain consumption in rich countries were wasteful and that the primary limit in nutrition throughout the world was that humans could not eat what was not available, some people came to believe that if there would be a cutback on grain consumption in feeding animals, more food would be available for the malnourished world. The term world food crisis commonly was heard in agricultural circles and served as a flag for those in the United States who argued a need to perpetuate an agricultural system that produced surpluses of grain. The central point of the 1974 World Food Conference convened in Rome was that industrial nations have the responsibility to establish an adequate world food reserve.

In the 1970s, rich countries were blamed, as were their appetites. Lappé and Collins in their book *Food First* (1977) alleged:

With Food First self-reliance, industrial crops (like cotton and rubber), livestock feed crops, and luxury fruits and vegetables are planted *after* meeting the basic needs of all the people. In the United States, by contrast, . . . livestock production is, in fact, antithetical to getting maximum nutritional output from our land. Livestock is used instead to get rid of "overproduction" in a world where most people do not have the money to buy the grain they need. Livestock production thus consumes the production from over half of the harvested acreage in the United States. At the same time beans and grain products, competing with feed crops for land use, soar out of the price range of the really poor who rely on these staples.

It is hard for us Americans, brought up on corn-fed beef and milk-fed veal, to get the idea that livestock's unique role is to make food fit for humans out of the things we cannot eat.

By 1977, however, the World Food Council called attention to the substantial difficulties in fulfilling the World Food Conference goals. The worst fears of the World Food Conference were not realized except in parts of Africa. Crop shortfalls in the 1980s and 1990s occurred most severely and primarily in those countries in which there was political disruption: Ethiopia, Cambodia, Chad, Angola, Mozambique, Somalia, and the Sudan. Otherwise, grain supplies in the world became reasonably adequate in contrast to the situation between 1972 and 1975. In the 1980s, experts foresaw growth in demand (population and economic growth) for agricultural products and a system fed by technology able to meet the demand. Worldwide production of all major foods— cereals, legumes, vegetables, root crops, melons, meat, and milk—rose again in the 1980s by a healthy percentage, and food production in the developing countries outpaced that of developed countries.

Malnutrition, starvation, and disease, however, continue to afflict millions. Estimates are that 800 million are undernourished. Hundreds of millions of people are undernourished because they have no money to pay for food, even at today's historically low prices (Sagoff, 1993). The lack of infrastructure for a distribution system to get food to those who are in need is perhaps a greater constraint than personal income. Thus the moral issues remain related to problems of distributive justice, which concern the way wealth and resources are shared (Thompson et al., 1994).

Nearly abandoned in the 1990s is the concept of the easy solution of letting the surplus nations send food to the developing countries. That solution is not viable (Mellor, 1989). Food, unlike air and much of water, must be bought. Famines and hunger occur when people cannot buy food that in fact may be readily available, or when there is a lack of ability and resolve to move food to the places where needed (Dando, 1988).

Sen and Dréze (1990) have proposed that governments can do something about hunger and famine. Their message is that famines and chronic hunger are preventable, recommending monetary aid (cash-for-work) to the poor. They, as well as Mellor (1989), have argued that famines are much less likely to happen when a government is accountable to the people.

Food aid may be made available as a matter of justice. It is in the framework of the right to food that we also begin to see that moral philosophy transcends the emotional or opportunistic reaction. If the right to food is fundamental, the question follows if it is appropriate to frame agricultural issues in terms of food availability. If so, then the issues of agriculture become only production problems, and issues of responsibilities by government, farmers, business, and industry might be evaded. Moral obligation alone would justify giving highest priority to the task of overcoming hunger. The problems of getting the food system to end hunger are severe, however, and the structural roots of hunger go deep. Ultimately, the question of food security is a question of justice and equity (Sagoff, 1993). It relates not to the system of production or the capacity to feed a growing population, but to the ability of markets and the social system to make food available to the poor (Lappé et al., 1998).

Out of expressed concerns for the malnourished and hungry millions, however, some activist writers such as James Rachels (1977), John Robbins (1987), and Jeremy Rifkin (1992) continue to criticize animal agriculture. The industries and husbandries of livestock are challenged as being wasteful of land resources and fossil energy, feeding animals grain that otherwise might feed the malnourished and employing ecologically harmful methods of growing crops and animals. These allegations may be a part of other streams of moral issues. Increasingly, the issues of food security are being merged with issues of environmental impacts, but the issues raised by the activists may be also front for other agendas, such as animal rights and welfare or the campaigns for vegetarianism.

THE GOALS AND FORMS OF AGRICULTURE

The ubiquitous player in the balance between human needs and their food supplies and between food security and the environment is agriculture. Set in a distinctive culture, each national and regional agriculture has its distinctive goals and issues.

Schumacher (1973) wrote that the universal tasks of agriculture must have an encompassing set of goals:

1. "[T]o keep man in touch with living nature, of which he is and remains a vulnerable part."
2. "[T]o humanize and ennoble man's wider habitat."
3. "[T]o bring forth the foodstuffs and other materials which are needed for a becoming life."

He does not believe that a civilization that recognizes only the third goal can survive in the long term. Although the primary goal of agriculture is to produce, the agricultural process cannot be forgotten. Agriculture is an interconnected complex system of human activity. Farms do have social value; the resources of farms, human, aesthetic, and physical, are vital to the continuity of farms.

For Aiken (1982), the issues and goals for agriculture line up as profitable production, sustainable production, environmentally safe production, and a just social order to ensure the survival, health, and security needs of all members of society, including all members of agriculture. Aiken (1982) suggests that the first goal is not a pressing moral objective, but is a prudent one. These are all objectives that should be mutually compatible.

Following the theme of Aiken, we have fashioned a set of six major goals for the global agricultural science and educational complex to seek within the next decades. These goals, unlike many stated goals of agricultural science and education, strongly couple the futures of agriculture and human welfare. These goals are:

1. A food system put in place that can feed a world population that grows at the rate of a billion people each 11–12 years.
2. A diet that adds quality to life.
3. A diet free as possible of the risks of cancer, coronary heart disease, and food-borne diseases.
4. An environment and land resource protected against degradation.
5. An agriculture integrated into society's goals, both social and economic.
6. An agriculture that requires no one in it to live impoverished, either in livelihood or in spirit.

The bases for these goals seem obvious. Population growth in industrial countries has decreased and some developing countries such as China have attempted to curb population growth, although some other peoples have not. The world population now grows by 90 million people each year. Food demand will rise even more than predicted by growth in population; as people are lifted out of poverty, they eat more. Food production and commerce can surely become strained in the decades ahead, in spite of the recent history in which global agricultural production has kept pace with food production. The growth of crop yields in some regions may be slowing. The other side of the coin is that if people keep eating and multiplying and farmers keep on tilling and harvesting as today, the imperative of food will require more land, much from the natural resource. Encouraged by incentives, however, farmers will use new technologies to raise more crop per plot and more meat and milk per crop (Waggoner, 1994).

The food system also will be taxed to continue providing the variety and interest that people expect of it. A diet as free as practicable of the risks of cancer, coronary heart disease, and other diseases, however, is a worthy goal for the agricultural establishment as well as for the nutritional and medical communities. It is a goal of particular relevance to animal agriculture.

The call for environments to be protected against degradation is a reminder that a vast resource base is required for the world's nutrient supply; it is a fragile base of land, water, and air. Fears, however, are widespread that the attempts to make the resource more productive, to produce a food supply that is varied and looks good, or even to stabilize the resource, will load the food with invisible toxins that might diminish both health and the ecological relationship between humans and the land.

We are reminded that the agriculture and food system employs billions of people throughout the world, most of whom are in developing countries and a great many of whom are tied to production systems that require each farmer to farm a small acreage or fish out of a small boat. They often are forced to remain where they are because that is where they know how to work. Even though autonomous, the poor farmer may be underemployed or forced to live under dispiriting circumstances.

These are goals that call for moral reasoning. They reveal societal expectations in the decades ahead. They clearly would include agriculture, human health, human satisfaction, and the environment, but reality dictates that the road ahead will require much understanding.

These aspects, food–people–world and the goals and forms of agriculture, are evidence of changing values and issues. They are subject to different understandings but also to transitional conditions in the world: changing political structures, cultures, and values, relentless population growth, and new knowledge. They represent ethical problems, perceptions of values, and facts that should not be ignored. They will play their parts in the future of animal agriculture.

MEANINGS OF ETHICS

In common usage, ethics and morality have come to have the same meaning (Engel, 1990). Morality, however, refers to judgments and actions regarding what is right or good, while ethics refers to the reasoning that such judgments and actions require. Moral philosophy, often equated with ethics, can more properly refer to disciplinary thought about morality, moral problems, and moral decisions. One does not need to be a philosopher to be concerned about ethics, but one thus concerned about ethics must be willing to submit one's moral values and judgments to intellectual examination.

The meaning of ethics in the context of this book does not relate to whether or not a person has the characteristics of a morally good person or whether that person's behavior meets appropriate standards of morally acceptable behavior. Ethics, as used here, refers to the acts of describing, analyzing, and criticizing actions and to giving thought through statements or arguments for a certain position or recommendation on what one should do in a given situation (Thompson, 1985). The application of ethics includes both appropriate character traits and the skills of logical reasoning, in addition to good judgment and familiarity with both matters of fact and ethical values and virtues. Good judgment, common sense, can be improved through the philosophical study of ethical values.

Ethical issues in food, agriculture, and natural resources arise when we attempt to set policy, meaning to provide rules and principles to organize and operate within the implied agreement among all members of society. At issue is what rules and principles we are to adopt. As there are different perceptions and different unanswered questions, it is evident that there are different ways of answering the questions. One cannot successfully state and define ideas about what should be done unless one is committed to the view that differences of opinion in ethics represent logically contrary points of view (Thompson, 1985). One can agree to disagree with another and one can recognize that differences can result from different perspectives and values without taking the view that all is confusion and no right or wrong answer exists. Saying that there is no right or wrong answer or that it is a matter of opinion may be only an excuse for not wanting to think about one's own values in a way committed to an understanding of their validity. Ethics is partly a process of persuasion and debate and partly a process of enlightenment and self-development.

Ethics as a discipline is as subject to adequate or inadequate reasoning, accurate or faulty premises, and significant or trivial results as any other mode of human thought. Increasingly, however, there is need to try analyzing and establishing an experiential basis for our values and to see what the legal and social consequences are of adopting one rather than another alternative solution to our problems. Whenever a solution to a practical problem in animal agriculture is attempted, there is a need for ethical inquiry.

ETHICAL THEORIES

Moral reasoning relative to problems in agriculture will turn to both existing and developing theory (Fox and DeMarco, 1986). Construction of ethical theory is the basic research of ethics. Ethical theory can be used to examine the bases of policy and action and provide ways of thinking about the issues. Some of the traditional moral principles are:

DEONTOLOGICAL THEORIES. One of the oldest paradigms in the consideration of duties, Judeo-Christian ethics, views the ideal life of humans as obedience to the will of God. Judaic as well as Christian ethics were appeals to authority, although some authoritarian elements in Greek and Egyptian ethics exist. The idea is that what is right is the thing to do, not what one would choose to do. It follows that what one actually desires may differ from what is the right thing to do, but it is also maintained that the right thing is what one would choose to do if one followed one's rational thinking. Under this ethic, there are prohibitions that the morally good person would not disobey: deliberate killing of the innocent, including abortion; adultery; suicide; or obtaining punishment of the innocent.

Immanuel Kant (1788) holds that the requirements of morality always override all reasons for doing something counter to them. The first principle of moral reasoning is its universal applicability and the respect for persons. In post-Kantian deontological theory, the fundamental standard of a morally right act is if the rule under which one is acting can be universalized, and if one is acting so as to treat humans as ends in themselves, never only as a means to one's own ends.

Deontological theory emphasizes that it is the principle upon which an agent acts that is the morally decisive factor; however, whereas the ideal life is in submission to the will and command of universal imperatives and such imperatives are binding, whatever the consequences, a morally good person submits to one's own will and not that of another. The stress is on certain liberal values: freedom, dignity, self-respect, and respect for individual rights. John Rawls (1971) in a further development of the theory, conceived the ideal life to be lived necessarily both in cooperation and in competition with others.

The concept of duties is not limited to respect for human others and society. A sense of duty to the soil, plants, and animals is inherent in the biocentric ethic.[1]

RIGHTS. The focus of much recent moral philosophy has been on rights, as well as questions of duty, although the issues have been less well explored relative to food, agriculture, and natural resources. Rights are more than those guaranteed by law, although legislation is one way to acquire them. Moral rights are considered entitlements based on valid moral principles. They can be claimed even though a society fails to recognize, or is unable or unwilling, to assure them.

There are two very different forms of rights theory (Thompson et al., 1994). One takes a limited view of governmental duties; government has a duty to protect the life, freedom, and property rights, but no duty to protect people from their errors or compensate them for personal inadequacies. This has been termed libertarian theory, which sharply limits the scope of public policy. Governments should enforce laws against harmful acts such as assaults and theft and provide for the common defense, but otherwise keep out of citizens's affairs. Libertarian theory describes a social agreement focused on self-protection (Thompson et al., 1994).

The second rights theory includes the responsibilities of government to protect life, liberty, and property, but also the responsibilities to assure a minimum quality of life and equal opportunity. Termed egalitarian theories, they also have been called welfare theories, natural law theories, Rawlsian, or Kantian. Each view presents deeply different ideas of how society should be run. Libertarian theories limit the scope of public policy to certain negative rights; egalitarians are distinguished in that they find some positive rights (e.g., the right to fire protection and education) to be justified. In the egalitarian sense, every person wants to share in things that make a decent life possible—food, shelter, security, and some discretionary income—and these can be duties of government. In a sense, agriculture has received an egalitarian rights tradition which holds that people have a right not to go hungry when foods can be made available to them (Comstock, 1995).

CONSEQUENTIALISM. Consequentialist theories evaluate morality and policy based on the terms of the outcome instead of the principle under which the agent is acting. Since Jeremy Bentham wrote *Introduction to the Principles of Morals and Legislation* in 1789, utilitarian theory, one form of consequentialism, has been widely brought into policy making. The view of utilitarianism is that morality is based equally on the interests of the public at large. Its leading principle is to maximize benefit or reduce harm for all parties. The good is in the greatest happiness, satisfaction, or utility for the greatest number of people. Utility can be a variety of things such as happiness, pleasure, absence of pain, or monetary gain.

Agriculture has been the recipient of a utilitarian tradition that the best consequences come from feeding people by putting land and water into production (Comstock, 1995).

Utilitarianism does not view any individual as more important than another. It does not prohibit accumulation of wealth, but utilitarian views do not ignore the rights of all people or creatures able to share in the common good (Blatz, 1991). Bentham perceives it as an ordinary contract in which all agree to a set of benefits from policy, and agree on the price (Thompson et al., 1994).

Consequentialist theory can be expressed in a form of moral arithmetic: credits or debits, good or bad, benefit or harm (cost).

APPLICATION OF THEORY. Inquiry in ethics deals with the notion of validity, not necessarily of absolute truth. Results of ethical analysis cannot be verified. In fact, inquiry in ethics by competent persons with a wide range of experience can lead to the development of rival theories. This, however, need not diminish their value in the decision process. Different kinds of people make moral judgments of activities in agriculture. To move to the application of ethics into rival theories provides a much better hope of achieving coherence than not bringing actual experience into moral inquiry.

Theories come in different flavors with different labels (e.g., duties, consequentialism, and rights). There is no shortage of ethical theories (Blatz, 1991, 1992; Thompson et al., 1994). Theories, even rival theories, are useful as ways of thinking about ethics (Elliott, 1992). They are conceptual systems that provide a way of ordering the constructs of ethics. Ethics, however, is not a separate and distinct sort of thinking. It is a thread interwoven with other threads in the fabric of society.

Ethics is entwined in the customs, manners, traditions, and institutions of a people. A practice of agriculture is seen as ethically more desirable or not as it is put in the context of the way a member of society deals with society. If that is forgotten, we deal with a moral fiction instead of a responsible moral experience (Elliott, 1992).

MORAL REASONING

Ethics, like science, is inquiry; it deals with developing principles that indicate what actions are right or wrong, permissible, obligatory, or forbidden. These sets of principles ideally should embody a core of values that provide part of the base for decision. Ethics provides guidelines for directing correct behavior; thus ethics and the consideration of issues and values are preparation for decision. The more it is developed, the more effective and systematic decisions should be.

Marcus Singer (1986) posited that the development of applied ethics was possibly the rise of a new science independent of philosophy. This new independent subject exercises the skills of physicians, psychologists, lawyers, economists, sociologists, scientists, and others who normally would not think of themselves as dealing in philosophy.

More agricultural scientists and philosophers appear to be turning to considerations of ethics in agriculture. Rural sociology, agricultural economics, and animal science increasingly have become arenas for consideration of ethical application; the term ethics, however, may hold different meanings for nonphilosophers, largely because each holds a different set of values. The agricultural economist, for example, turns to policy: the purchase of land for its earning power, commodity rivalries, the inability to buy food, soil conservation for future generations, the U.S. farmer versus the rest of the world, persuasion versus compulsion in governmental farm programs. The rural sociologist turns to questions of social justice in the aims and structure of agriculture. The animal scientist is concerned with the issues of human management of animals and production of animal products as human food, with the intent that their solution will assist in decisions concerning animal agriculture (Cheeke, 1998).

Johnson (1986) had developed a problem solving framework which Hildreth (1982) simplified as:

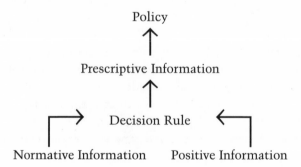

The process is iterative, requiring experience, trial, and error. It becomes interactive when more than one person is involved in defining and solving problems and carrying decisions. Two information banks are used, one including positivistic information and the other, normative knowledge.

Positive knowledge, according to Johnson (1986), is "synthetic knowledge that deals with characteristics of conditions, situations, or things in the real world." In positivism, as a philosophy, the emphasis is on knowledge gained by the senses (e.g., scientific and empirical studies). It undergirds much of the discovery research done by the biological and physical sciences and the subsequent translation into technology. Positivists rule out experiences of values and do not conceive value concepts as being objectively grounded; however, positivism in spite of its reputation for being objective and impersonal, is culturally dependent, judgmental, and subjective. Most research in the animal sciences has been guided by positivism.

Within Johnson's (1986) framework, *normative information* involves ethical inquiry about the goodness and badness of conditions, situations, and things, as well as "prescriptive propositions having to do with what ought not or ought to be done, whether the latter are stated as laws, recipes, regulations, social mores and norms, or ethical imperatives." Normativism (in the Johnson sense) designates the collection of philosophic theories concerned with answering questions about goodness and badness and rightness or wrongness. Normativism thus has many forms.

Both positive and normative knowledge are required for prescription. The pragmatic view is that the truth of value-free or value propositions depends on the consequences of using that knowledge to solve problems (Johnson, 1986).

REFLECTIVE EQUILIBRIUM

A working form of the integration of normative and positive knowledge, of ethics and science, is the ethic. Philosopher Norman Daniels (1980) wrote that an ethic is a theory reached via the method of wide reflective equilibrium, that is "a coherent ordered triple set of beliefs held by a particular person, namely a set of considered moral judgements (a); a set of moral principles (b); and a set of relevant background theories (c). . . . The agent may work back and forth, revising his moral judgements, moral principles, and background theories, to arrive at an equilibrium point which consists of the triple, (a), (b), and (c)."

An ethic is a moral theory in which (a) our considered intuitions have been brought into equilibrium with (b) our philosophical principles and (c) the scientific and other background knowledge. Comparative reasoning toward equilibrium is a legitimate method in science and law as well as ethics and policy making.

It is in ethics that we see that the construct of an ethic must face a test. Comstock (1995) pointed out that considered moral judgment, moral principles, and relevant background theories should all be independent sources of information. If we mix them up, or begin to mistake one of our intuitions for the deliverance of a science, then we may have reasoned in a circular fashion and the reasoning is flawed.

Comstock (1995) noted that in ethics, we go back and forth, revising our first intuitions in the light of other intuitions, general moral principles, and scientific information. Then our general principles are revised in the light of carefully considered intuitions and new scientific information. Our scientific information is revised when the number of different observations becomes so weighty as to cause scientists to jettison existing theory in favor of a new one.

Nutritional guidelines for Americans and endangered species listings are variants of the conclusions of an ethic reached by moral reasoning (Kunkel, 1996). Different chosen moral principles, such as libertarianism, utilitarianism, or the extension of these philosophical principles to animals, are apparent in the literature and can be presumed to bias the public view and perception of an argument. The danger in moral reasoning lies in confusing circular reasoning, an unsound method, with the sound method of comparative reasoning toward reflective equilibrium (Comstock, 1995). The danger exists when persons mistakenly allow their prejudices to determine their science.

Reflective equilibrium, like the scientific method, should be a dialectical process of belief formation, but it should not be circular. We suspect that many of the contemporary issues in animal agriculture would be less contentious if they were given wide reflection toward equilibrium.

Moral principles and judgment, however, are valuable. Neither naked scientific theory nor political theory will likely suffice alone. Intuitions will be stimulants and guideposts in resolution of an issue in animal agriculture. It is just that such intuitions should be brought into an equilibrium with relevant background theories. If they cannot, they should be admitted to be advocacies of social values and even personal interests.

VALUES AND ATTITUDES

Ethics is then a set of theories and moral values accepted by society. An ethic is a theory that is reached by way of a technique of wide reflective equilibrium (Daniels, 1980; Comstock, 1995). A value is a belief about the desirable, in terms of which objects, qualities, and principles are considered to be of value. An attitude is a mental position with regard to, or feelings and emotions toward, a fact or state. A belief system encompasses all three. Attitudes are not necessarily equatable with ethics or knowledge, although ethics might be used to analyze attitudes. It must be noted that we each carry our own attitudinal baggage. For example, we each are likely to have our own beliefs of what animal agriculture should be.

Attitudes may be beyond easy philosophical analysis (Madden and Thompson, 1987). Relative to the character and quality of agricultural technology, for example, the persisting agrarian tradition supported the concept of the family farm. Jackson (1980, 1987) argued that changing agricultural technology alters farming so as to rob it of its special moral significance and transform farming into "a corrupt enterprise." Modern technology may be seen as intrinsically wrong, taking agriculture away from the spiritual roots, an agriculture of smaller scale and more varied landscape. Biotechnology looms for some as creating environmental risks, but Rifkin (1983) argued that beyond risks, the applications of biotechnology to agriculture are morally wrong. Rifkin held that biotechnology applied in agriculture brings an ethic of self-interest into the control of agriculture, and that thinking and acting on this attitude of superiority will be destructive of moral values for human life. Ehrenfeld (1978) stated similarly that the manipulations of biological technology is an extension of human arrogance that deters a balanced and moral view of life and nature. Madden and Thompson (1987) evaluated Jackson, Rifkin, and Ehrenfeld as having based their judgments of agricultural technology upon "particular visions of human character and purpose. Their arguments turn upon the claim that these technologies are morally wrong because they tend to corrupt their users and to create character flaws not only among agricultural producers but throughout society as well. Any analysis of these arguments would have to draw upon religious and philosophical considerations of the broadest kind."

Bringing philosophy to an awareness of its normative role uncovers the values inherent in the past. Philosophy is criticism. It may attempt to be value-free (i.e., objective), but genuine inquiry must detail its choice of values. When we analyze ethical problems and values, we are able to choose the ethical principles, values, and beliefs that we think should apply to the problem and guide its solution. Elliott (1992), however, pointed out that we often see ethics not as a part of society, but as a kind of abstract position that society must accept, choose, or reject. This view is more likely to exist in the United States where a diversity of moral beliefs may be encountered. As in politics, the question of what one should do becomes that of what the best moral system is. In some aspects, such an approach can work. Policy making reflects the idea that the morally best course of action is morally the best in influencing decisions.

The idea that an ethic can be chosen, however, is also misleading. Elliott (1992) stated, "We do not—we cannot—choose our moral beliefs at will, and consequently a society has only very limited and indirect control over the moral values it embraces." In a democratic society, laws may be changed, policies reordered, and perhaps political institutions restructured (e.g., the Ross Perot phenomenon of 1992 and the Republican takeover of the U.S. Congress in 1994). Moral values, however, are the result of cultural factors beyond reach. They can be subject to scrutiny and change, but the broader aspects are difficult to move. Thus, while we make policy, we do not remake our values.

AGRICULTURAL VALUES

A rich literature is emerging in agricultural ethics. The principal journals that carry original papers in the field, *Agriculture and Human Values*, the *Journal of Agricultural and Environmental Ethics*, and *Environmental Ethics*, have become important to the considerations of animal agriculture. The papers, written by both philosophers and non-philosophers, each bear a commitment toward further understanding. The authors generally search for the issue or ethic. Characteristically, these papers are reflective of past values, but new issues are rising. What is evident is that all over the world, new ideals are pitted against the centuries-old utilitarian views of food and agriculture.

Dahlberg (1986) described how new ideals might affect values. He noted that the historic goals of the dominant and established agricultural groups in the United States have been drawn from anthropocentric values and Western understanding; however, an alternate position might be one receding from the Western value system and the entry of some non-Western thought. For example:

1. (a) The Western anthropocentric position is guided by values of rural conservatism and individualism that underlie desires for support of the family, income, and efficient production. (b) Valuing highly family and group self-reliance and the rural community turns the non-Western, alternate position goal to both family and community support. A desire for an integrated way of life might foster diversified farming.

2. (a) The love of nature in the Western tradition is expressed in stewardship of the land and a moral concern that may espouse a concern for world hunger. (b) Valuing harmony in nature, instead of just a love of nature, promotes conservation of energy, soil, and diversity of species.

3. (a) The national focus in the Western position is on economic growth, science, and technology linked to progress, and national power, which in turn set goal positions for increased production, cheap food, foreign exchange and aid, and urbanization and industrialization of agriculture. (b) The alternative national goals of safe and healthy foods, rural revival, and rural decentralization are seen as a national value system pointing toward sustainable economic growth, respect for nature and ecosystems, and cultural contentment.

4. (a) The Western anthropocentric international goal positions of elimination of hunger and agricultural and economic development flow not only from concepts of national sovereignty and planning, but also from expanding international markets and trade. The global position is seen as the need to balance food, resources, and population. (b) The international vision in the non-Western approach is one of a global village and greater national economic self-sufficiency. This value system might focus on elimination of hunger by increased governmental accountability, rural and ecological development, and cultural development. No model of morality, however, can be separated from its essential social nature (Elliott, 1992). The anthropocentric ethic is an embedded social institution in the United States and will not be easily influenced by some other system of evaluation (Paden, 1990).

Animal agriculture is a cultural institution, and cultural institutions change slowly. We do not know what changes will actually solve the problems or what changes will create other problems. Many of the issues of animal agriculture are the result of the ways farmers, ranchers, consumers, faculty, and scientists are educated, which reflect society's way of life. Many of the issues in animal agriculture develop because critics are trained as they are or have other interests. Each group has a different set of moral intuitions. This of course reflects the diversity in society, and society may ask animal agricultures to work within a new ethic or changed set of values that it has converted to political positions or market pressures.

To paraphrase advice directed at the industrial world, tomorrow's successful animal agricultural system can no longer afford to be a faceless institution that does little more than sell the right product at the right price (*Economist,* 1995). It will have to present itself as a person, as an intelligent actor that brings explicit moral judgment on its own actions and dealings with the wider world. Agricultural professional societies—at least the American Society of Animal Science, the American Society of Agronomy (1994), the Soil Science Society of America, and the Crop Science Society of America—have introduced discussions of agricultural ethics into their scientific meetings and publications. The gate has been opened, and agriculturalists as much as philosophers are discovering the mysteries of interest and values, and ethic and ethics, beyond the gate.

NOTE

1. Relative to environmental ethics, two value systems have emerged: anthropocentrism and biocentrism. Anthropocentric value systems emphasize moral justifications that describe human goods, virtues, or rights. Biocentric ethics grant equal or similar moral standing to some natural objects. Biocentric ethics argue for intrinsic values in nature that are equal to the intrinsic values of human interests.

CHAPTER 4

INSTITUTIONAL FACTORS IN ANIMAL AGRICULTURE

It is evident that every agricultural and food system operates within the arena of human activities and institutions. Food systems can be affected by changes induced by farmers, processors, or consumers. Many changes, however, are prompted by changes outside of the food system, that is, modifications in marketing, processing, transport, storage at each stage, and consumption of food products.[1] Almost without exception, technical changes are derived from institutional arrangements. All industrial countries support substantial research institutions to improve agricultural technologies involved in production, procession, distribution, marketing, and nutrition. Developing countries, to varying degrees, also are building research capabilities. Almost everywhere, there is some government support or intervention of agriculture in terms of controls to reduce animal and plant health hazards, education to enable people to respond to technological changes, and provision of part of the infrastructure (e.g., roads, fertilizer plants, inspection services).

Any agricultural system has its primary components, but the more intensive systems have well-developed infrastructures. Major components of the infrastructure are the marketing and supply systems, credit, expertise, and the generation and transfer of new technology. To these we can add incentive and the business structure in which agriculture operates. Obviously, part of the infrastructure is the institutional arrangements that are instruments of government policy.

The infrastructure of intensive animal agriculture in the United States and other developed countries is complex. Some aspects are governmentally developed; much is privately owned; much is shared with other industries. It has many components and its development follows and often must accompany the development of agricultural production.

The infrastructure of intensive animal agriculture can perhaps be visualized best by listing its components. Some of the more obvious components of the marketing system are:

1. Feedlots.
2. Poultry houses.
3. Dairy facilities.
4. The slaughter, packing, and processing industries.
5. Poultry processing plants.
6. Milk processing units, including ice cream and cheese manufacturers.
7. Food stores.

Less obvious are:

8. Health inspection services.
9. Identification services.

Other elements of the infrastructure include:

10. The tax structure.
11. Land ownership patterns including private ownership, governmental intervention of private ownership (land use and land reform), and non-agricultural firms (integrators and other handlers, foreign owners, federal lands).
12. Agricultural supply industries.
13. Agricultural biologics, drugs, and chemicals, including antibiotics, supplements, growth regulators, and metabolic modifiers.
14. Water rights, underground water, and water resources.
15. Marketing orders.
16. International trade: exports, imports, international commodity agreements, and the value of the currency.
17. Predator control.
18. Labor supply and expertise.
19. Energy resources: electric power, oil, gas.
20. Transportation: railroads, trucks, highways, truck and automobile manufacturers, waterways, air carriers.
21. Feed and grain brokers.
22. Grain elevators, feed manufacturers, gins.
23. Farm machinery: problems of standardizing farm equipment, hookups, hydraulic couplings, etc.
24. Credit: nongovernmental suppliers, banks, cooperative credit systems.

25. Regulatory agencies.
26. The educational system.
27. The research or scientific establishment.
28. Extension services.
29. Radio, television, media information systems.
30. The internet.

The very complex relationships of the agricultural system, both within and external, would assure one that issues exist. Conflicts of both interests and ethics are bound to occur in such an intricate web of institutions. As noted above, there are institutional factors that work through both the agricultural system and elements of the system's infrastructure.

This chapter turns to some of the institutional environments that both create issues and facilitate dealing with issues. Improvement of institutions as well as of human development are important considerations. For example, institutional factors are presented to serve as conceptual bases for understanding external factors that impinge on animal agriculture. These factors are education, governmental activities, social organization and structure, and the market.

EDUCATION AND EXPERTISE

A principal factor affecting animal agriculture is expertise; the quality of managers is important. Critical to change in human capital is the education of scientists who participate in change activities and staff health and other regulatory agencies. It also is necessary to educate unsophisticated producers, processors, distributors, and consumers on how to respond to changes in technology.

T. W. Schulz, 1979 Nobel laureate in economics, and his colleagues generally are given the credit for developing some of the central concepts about the functions of human skills and knowledge in U.S. and international agriculture (Johnson, 1986). His searches grew out of the difficulties in explaining changes in agricultural output in the classic economic terms relating to land, capital, and labor. Schulz (1971) saw that technological advance could be related also to human capital development through general education, vocational agricultural training, and extension work. The creation of new technology, new institutions, and investments to improve quality of life also require investment in education and on-the-job training to handle the new technologies and the need to operate in changing environments. Technological and institutional change come about as the result of activities of highly trained, innovative people. As technology becomes more advanced, the creativity, diligence, and entrepreneurship of such people must be augmented by the technical education of others.

Part of the education takes place in the general education system while other parts become highly specialized in technical colleges of agriculture and advisory (extension) services operated by governments or academic institutions. In the more developed countries, private enterprises also are involved in improving technology. They maintain research establishments and carry out extensive educational programs: in-house training, support of training institutions, and advertisement. The fundamental education (as well as skills training) of farmers and workers, however, may be the more important factor in agriculture. Schulz (1964) wrote of this in 1963:

Taking the long view, it is essential to see that the acquisition of new skills by farm people is also one of the primary new profitable inputs [into agriculture]. Though I have concentrated on new material inputs [in this discussion], and though they are necessary to a limited extent, the fruit from the advance of knowledge that is useful in economic endeavors is to a larger extent dependent upon new skills. The necessity for learning the skills that are required for modernizing agriculture brings us to the issue of investing in farm people. How to do this most efficiently is a matter about which we know all too little. . . . Crash programs are warranted under some circumstances. So are demonstrations designed to instruct farmers. There is also a place for some on-the-job training. But investment in schooling is in all probability the most economical way when one takes a ten-to-twenty-year view of the process. What this means is that the rate of return to the costs of schooling, especially at the primary level, is probably exceedingly high, higher than the return to the investment in any alternative ways of acquiring these new skills.

What is implied is that a highly flexible education that contributes to the ability of people to adopt the new skills needed is likely the most effective way of providing for the expertise needed in agriculture.

INDIGENOUS AND EXOGENOUS KNOWLEDGE. As with many issues and matters related to agriculture, a dichotomy emerges relative to the knowledge base. Anthropologist John W. Bennett (1986) argued that the academic approach to agriculture has spawned a conceptual dichotomy (the expert versus the practitioner of what he termed "indigenous" and "exogenous" knowledge), which has "led to the feeling that the expert knew more than the farmer, and that therefore the communication was from the expert to the practitioner."[2] By inference, exogenous knowledge is obtained through the use of science, and is therefore in some way better and more effective than the indigenous knowledge accumulated (and perhaps transmitted intergenerationally) by farmers who have learned by trial, error, and experience (Bennett, 1986).

Indigenous knowledge, as Bennett (1986) states, is culturally standardized expertise; it is most important when technological change is not sought. Exogenous knowledge becomes more important when change is sought in the shortest time possible, and in time may become indigenous knowledge. It should be noted that even in developed countries, gaps exist in exogenous knowledge and the fallback position is indigenous and experiential knowledge. The failure of some aspects of the system—be it in research, policy, extension, books and other material, or education to recognize the central position of indigenous knowledge in some agricultures—has elicited criticism and, at times, loss of respect for the system. The call for participatory research, the expressions of need to bring the world view of farmers into research and education, the historic lack of farmer support for the land-grant system, and the call for *appropriate technology* in developing countries all are evidence that agriculture is shaped at least in part by indigenous knowledge, which has resulted from empiricism (i.e., observation and experience).

Agricultural knowledge has changed. It is now and has been a combination of different forms of knowledge: indigenous, scientific, and industrial. In the process of change, radical breaks with the past have not occurred; however, the hierarchy of these forms has undergone progressive modification (Byé and Fonte, 1993).

Scientific knowledge is based on scientific principles, with the emphasis on expected effects of a method or technical object. It is based upon important discoveries in areas such as physiology, nutrition, genetics, and sociology.

Industrial knowledge is that of the work process rather than the agricultural production process itself. It is technological knowledge, science-based, but interpreted in relation to changes in the functions of agriculture in industrialized economies. It is also organizational knowledge of simplification, specialization, and segmentation.

Throughout technical changes in agriculture and food, the agricultural practices that have persisted have been progressively integrated with industrial and scientific knowledge. The extent to which this has occurred varies with the economy and the commodity. Throughout much of the world, empiricism, the convergence of experiences and improvement of production methods, continues to dominate animal husbandry techniques and the transformation of many food practices (Byé and Fonte, 1993). Thus both empirical and indigenous knowledge borne of economic practices and trade in food and agriculture, and the biological foundations of agricultural production, continue as central features of technological development, even through the recent decades of industrialization.

Higher education has provided much of the technical expertise used by animal agriculture. In many respects the institutions providing higher education in the agricultural sciences are increasing in diversity; however, the curricula for the sciences supporting animal agriculture at different universities have common features and provide much the same curricular content regardless of size and scope of the institution and geographic location. Individual course content may vary, but almost all institutions have courses in introduction to animal science, crop science or agricultural and resource economics, animal nutrition, genetics, breeding, physiology and/or growth, animal product technology, and production. At the graduate level, core courses at different institutions resemble each other.

The sciences in animal related curricula form a composite (Kunkel, 1992). They are important bridging disciplines, linking molecular biology, cell biology, genetics, nutrition, ecology, and economics to human populations and ecosystems on one hand, and connecting them to production systems and the economy on the other. Layered onto these aspects of the curriculum are changes, some of which deal with issues. Institutions of higher education once taught and researched the biological phenomena of production, the economic aspects of inputs in farming and ranching, and the commodity marketing system.

Departments concerned with animal agriculture now must deal increasingly with human nutrition and consumer concerns, international aspects, environmental integrity, sustainability, problems of distribution, social equity, and other contemporary issues. In recent decades, departments of animal sciences have shaped the contents of their courses from the results of experimental sciences, which largely replaced the empirical knowledge component that once dominated higher education in animal husbandry. Now, other concepts are beginning to augment what became traditional knowledge in mid-twentieth century. Education for animal agriculture may well include concepts of human attitudes, behavioral analysis, risk analysis, waste management, ecology, business management, and applied economics. Graduates will be facing a world having less social contract with science, a world in which there are competitive conceptual models (e.g., specialized versus conventional, intensive versus extensive) of animal agriculture.

A postindustrial agriculture may be in the making (Tweeten and Zulauf, 1998). It is knowledge-based and focuses on service activities (e.g., marketing, management, finance). Information systems are important, as is specialization by service. Niche markets are sought, and institutional interactions (e.g., environmental programs, taxes) are evident. The emphasis is less on large-scale mass production of homogenous products for a mass market. This model is the *microbrewery* of the 1990s, providing a rich array of firms engaging in a wider array of services. The educational requirements will be different, encompassing whatever it may take to prepare graduates with the skills to make appropriate individual decisions.

What is implied is that a highly flexible education, drawn on the range of possible careers and future directions of animal agriculture, is likely the most effective way of providing for the leadership needed in animal agriculture. What may be implied also is that higher education has the responsibility to educate other members of society about the issues surrounding animal agriculture and society.

Higher education for agriculture and the natural resources can be expected to undergo extensive reform in the twenty-first century (Kunkel et al., 1996; Kellogg Commission, 1997). It will join the larger universities to maintain the widest access to the benefits of a college education, and redefine itself as academic programs involved in the use of biological and ecological systems for the benefit of both humans and natural systems. Active learning will increasingly become the mode of education, but virtual education will supplement the process. Education will be dedicated to provide skills, attitudes, and values required for success in both work and life. It will respond to change and emerging needs more flexibly. It will follow different routes in different institutions, affecting animal agriculture by producing a cadre of leaders at the university level and a support base of technicians at the technical school and community college level, both of which may be required in industrial or service settings. Failing to change, departments of animal science, poultry science, and dairy science could become irrelevant in higher education.

GOVERNMENTAL ACTIVITIES

Governmental administrative capacity, skills and entrepreneurial capacities, and the values that humans, both as producers and consumers, attach to different kinds of food are clearly issues that affect animal agriculture. Many governmental activities will affect agricultures and the food systems and determine how they operate. Regulatory agencies regulate the conduct of the food systems as they produce quality and safe foods. Land tenure systems, agricultural subsidies, taxation of land, export taxes, import taxes, and trade barriers are obvious factors; trading arrangements and agricultural credit programs are others. So are politically motivated embargoes of exported agricultural chemicals, the use of which is banned or controlled in the country of manufacture. Irrigation complexes, quarantine and inspection services, marketing board operations, storage operations, and regulation of trucking can have significant effects on agriculture.

When technical, institutional, and human needs are recognized, they can be used to induce and administer changes in food chain and nutrient cycles. Decisions as to what changes are to be made by government units, private entrepreneurs, or consumers usually has been related to the degree that the economy is centralized in the country.

Indirect interventions by governments are largely educational processes. Science has come to occupy the commanding position in the knowledge industry (Bennett, 1986). Its influence has spread to all forms of human activity. Agricultural research has become the province of both governments, individually and in consortium, and the private sectors (business and industry). Knowledge resulting from research is the basis of both the technological foundations of the agricultural and industrial functions and the content of indirect interventions in democratic societies: financial incentives, subsidies, information, and guidelines.

Before World War II, attempts to improve agricultural technology were concentrated in the developed world or were made in the less developed countries by European nations to improve the production of export crops (rubber, palm oil, cocoa, tea, and sugar). After World War II, the approach was applied to domestic food production in developing countries by the Rockefeller and Ford Foundations and U.S., Canadian, British, and French technical assistance largely through the development of the International Agricultural Research Centers. These international research centers then fed information to national research agencies, which in turn carried out relevant research. Some transfer of technology also was accomplished out of the international centers through improved seeds and machinery design. The effectiveness of this approach is evident in the world grain production having kept pace with world population growth.

Direct intervention in developing countries includes improvement of seeds and planting materials, land reforms, production and distribution of fertilizers and plant and animal protection mechanisms, distribution of electric power and fossil fuels to use in producing food and establishment of domestic markets, and/or export channels. Also important are institutions for regulating commodity flows and prices.

It is evident that direct intervention also will become increasingly important in the industrial world, particularly as regulatory actions. There is great emphasis on improving and maintaining environmental quality as well as the production of human food. Appropriate interventions to manage agriculture better may have to await additional technical information on the risks reflected in safety of food and effects on the environment. Will society, however, wait for more information? Animal agriculture may have to come to terms with environmentalism, consumer advocacy, societal limitations on new technology, and new ideas before it may be intellectually, technologically, or scientifically ready to do so.

Conventional wisdom holds that the best policy is based on the best science. Science, however, is more than a body of facts and understandings; it is also a continuing process for discovering new information. Policy may not wait on the best science or the process. In life, if known facts are not available to guide our actions, human values and experience will fill the void. If the relationship of fact to biology is not understood, human values and beliefs will fill the breach. If decision makers are not versed in the methods and criteria of science, the testing of uncertain hypotheses increasingly will be done in public forums such as in the media, the courts, and the regulatory rule making process. Political processes may then replace scientific debates in development of policy. This suggests an uncertain future.

SOCIAL ORGANIZATION AND STRUCTURE

The ultimate infrastructure of agriculture is social organization and social structure. The two concepts can be distinguished from each other. Firth (1955) referred to organization as the day-to-day reactions of groups of people to the here and now needs in social and economic existence. Structure was defined as the slowly changing sets of expectations associated with status, prestige, rank authority, and power; these may be expressed in either secular or religious terms. Both concepts are embedded in the relationships of the agricultural unit to community and society.

Fundamental to considerations of infrastructures and organization are the matters of resources that the community can contribute to the agricultural unit and how the agricultural unit may obtain these and use them. Bennett (1986) visualized a box model in which exchanges or interchanges of resources and services occur. In the model, exchanges include not only material and economic phenomena but also social relations and symbols such as networks of kinship and friendship serving as channels for resources and as nuclei for celebration and ritual. In the inner core is the nuclear family household consisting of the: head or manager; membership of the household; budget; commissary; labor to maintain the household and its members; and the technology (i.e., the house, appliances, tools, conveniences, and so on). Also occupying the traditional inner core is the enterprise, with its manager to direct operations, capital to invest in production systems, labor to perform the task of production, physical resources (land, water, and shelter), access to sources of support including communications channels (extension?), political connections, and technology including machinery, energy, and seed stock.

These are set within a larger box, the *community*—neighbors, friends, kinsmen, organizations, sources of order and rationale, transportation and communications facilities—which has served both symbolic and practical needs. This organization then is set in an even larger box, the *national social structure,* which includes organizations and agencies, legal regulations and alternatives, political arrangements, the economic market, the media of information, and national values. To these, we might add the opportunities for collective action.

Animal agriculture is developing in a social organization that is increasingly different from that required for crop agriculture. For one thing, except for extensive ruminant animal operations, animal agriculture in the United States is becoming less and less dependent on the land except to produce feed crops or to provide distance from human residences. Bennett's (1986) inner box is changing. Management, capital, and labor are increasingly separated from the family households. The organizational trend in animal agriculture is an integrative one that has a business and marketing basis rather than a social basis.

Animal and crop agricultures are separating. Production units in animal agriculture, particularly poultry, swine, and cattle feedlots, are becoming more integrated with the market system. The trend is to bring producers, packers/processors, suppliers, and retailers into closer coordination. The organization of animal agriculture in the United States increasingly fits an industrial logic. Tradition and the nuclear family-controlled animal production, however, will remain longer in other parts of the world.

THE MARKET

Change in the agricultural system is partly a consequence of economic growth and development. As growth takes place in terms of per capita real incomes, dietary preferences of the people shift toward animal products and thence to fruits and vegetables. Then, generally, increases in the quantity and quality of food are demanded by the people. Economic growth and development, however, also foster changes in lifestyles, precipitating a desire for convenience and health concerns that can override the other patterns of food consumption.

The marketing organization and structure thus are important institutional factors impinging on animal agriculture. For example, more than two-thirds of the food dollar is spent for marketing service in the United States; some call that excessive.

Feedlots serve as integral parts of both the production and the marketing systems. These feedlots exist because soybean meal, corn, sorghum, and at times wheat, have become cheaper than the use of grasslands in the United States, thus reducing the cost of beef to the consumer. Such feedlots serve as a market assembly system that takes beef animals from diverse sources and prepares them for delivery to the packer. Large swine and poultry units are even more directly integrated into the marketing system.

North America has an effective marketing system. Some other countries, however, must rely mostly on direct sales from farm to consumer. These may be countries in which roads are poor and few, transport scarce, storehouses lacking, postharvest pest control inadequate, processors few, refrigeration nonexistent, and wholesaling a missing art.

A complex marketing infrastructure is essential in an urban society. It not only is essential in bringing to consumers the foods they want, but is essential to stimulating production of necessary food. The opposite side of the coin is that public perception of food needs also catalyzes marketing changes. Look to the rapid growth in the fast-food market in the United States. Moreover, the public perception need not be correct in order to affect greatly supplies and marketing. Some, however, want the opportunity to buy directly from the farmer. They want more of the food supply brought in from nearby farms to consumers, implying a preference for nearby farms.

Cultural factors and economic incentives are primary issues to which animal agriculture must continually adjust. For decades, the 10- to 12-year cattle cycle was the linchpin of economics relating to the livestock industry in North America. Beginning in the mid-1970s, the cattle cycle became subject to external issues and took on a new, indefinite structure. Part of the reason was the growth of large units, cattle feedlots and pork producing units, that restructured the production industries.

An increasing part of the reason was that Americans turned from beef and pork to chicken and fish, and many attempted to reduce the fat in their diet by reducing the consumption of red meat. By the mid-1980s, there was much to suggest that the market for products of animal agriculture was marching to a different drummer, playing a rhythm that incorporated an inexorable beat of nutrition policy and governmental regulation in flux and the public perceptions thereof. By the mid-1990s, however, the supply and demand for red meat stabilized and the cycle returned.

The modern livestock industry has been urged to fit current dietary guidelines rather than contest the diet/health hypothesis. The industry is responding. The meat and milk sectors set out on new marketing paths that essentially listened to what consumers were saying. Dairy product changes ranged from extra fortification with calcium to low fat and low lactose milk to *light* cheeses. The 1986 National Consumer Retail Beef Study providing data from the consumers and shoppers of Houston, Philadelphia, Kansas City, and San Francisco, determined that consumers often preferred the taste of beef, but price, leanness, and concerns about cholesterol and fat had become principal negative factors (Cross et al., 1986; Savell et al., 1989). When more trimmable fat was removed, the clients's health image of the beef increased and consumers purchased more beef. Industry's response was instantaneous. Several national or regional retail grocery chains implemented closely trimmed (less than 1/4 inch) or completely trimmed programs. Fat in meat display cases has been greatly reduced (Savell et al., 1991), and beef in particular has again become a meat of choice for both convenience and elegant dining. Smaller standard serving sizes, however, may dominate the market in the twenty-first century.

The presumption is that the production of beef and pork that is leaner and can fit health concerns is technologically feasible; trimming the fat has been a viable solution. It is suggested that appropriate genetic manipulation of the animals, manipulation of the diets fed to beef animals, and processing procedures can be developed to produce beef products that are palatable and low in fat content. The pork industry revised its production methods but took its own unique marketing approach. The reference to their product by the pork industry as *the other white meat*, implying the qualities of poultry and fish, is an imaginative marketing strategy, but also raises interesting ethical issues. These changes represent major changes in institutional concepts.

Nutrition and health information can be a powerful market force for food and agriculture, particularly now as part of the information is codified under the Nutrition Labeling and Education Act of 1990. The issue for animal agriculture, however, has become one in which judgment is not made based on the credibility of the dietary guidelines or the database for the guidelines; rather, it is if and how the policies and technologies of agriculture should reach for nutritional targets (NRC, 1989b; IOM, 1991a).

The changing animal agricultural system in the late 1980s was, in a sense, a capitulation to changing market forces, but it is probably one that relieves the industry of certain nagging issues; this is a new turn in the strategies of animal agriculture. In the past, policy has been used principally in the context of agricultural production and the marketing of commodities. The cattle and dairy industries, however, appear to be learning that it is easier to modify the product than to reset the production operation. With poultry and pork productions, the trend also is to modify the production function. The beef industry may follow.

The use of policy through the marketplace (food labels) and its attendant advertising also poses powerful mechanisms for agriculture and the agricultural sciences, the nutrition and welfare of the people, and the economic base of the community. Fat is trimmed from beef and potatoes are no longer fried in beef fat; however, a market for fat remains, largely in hamburger products, processed meats, and industrial feedstocks. If an acceptable substitute for fat is found and the fat market is greatly diminished, it is obvious that a whole new system of beef production might need to be devised. If so, that would require massive institutional changes in animal agriculture, government regulation of grades, ways of preparing foods, and the market itself. The demands of the people, however, change slowly; more accurately, after initial change, people often revert to older tastes and patterns of consumption. The market failures in the 1990s to gain wide acceptance of the lean hamburger is testimony to this point.

The marketplace is a harsh, inhuman institutional form. Yet with appropriate attention, it is possible for agriculture and agricultural science to co-opt it, cooperate with it, give it grist for its mill, or provide consumers with ways to interpret it. It cannot be brushed aside.

How to guide or live with the market may be the largest stage upon which agricultural research and education will play. Research institutions, however, will not limit the market with a stroke of the pen. They will run into the inertia of the community and the lobbies, groups with vested interests, entrepreneurs who are convinced that their products will promote better health, critics, and zealots.

We are also reminded that in some parts of the world as much as half of the food supply from plants and animals is lost between harvest and consumption. The marketing infrastructure is necessary to improve both production and nutrition in less developed countries. Where marketers are fewest and weakest, malnutrition is most common. The market and food distribution system is the last defense against famine.

One issue receiving attention is the use of surplus feed grains in animal production. This often is related to concerns about hunger and malnutrition, particularly as they occur in the developing world, and the issue also includes the use of nonrenewable energy resources to produce grain to feed animals. Decisions regarding exports of cereal grains and legumes and the market prices for these commodities, however, clearly influence the proportions diverted to animal production.

Many other cultural, political, geopolitical, and economic factors influence the final decision on the relative use of feed grains, and consequently, the production and availability of animal-food products. The U.S. grain embargo to the then Soviet Union in the 1980s, in retaliation to the Soviet incursion and occupation of Afghanistan, is an example of one governmental attempt to intervene in the food system of another country for geopolitical purposes. The embargo and blockade of Iraq in the early 1990s is another example. In the longer run, trade agreements, such as the European Union and the North America Free Trade Agreement, and monetary balances such as revaluation of currency may replace national policy actions as major external market-related factors perturbing animal agriculture.

CONCLUSION

As indicated at the outset, this chapter does not examine all of the institutions that can create or reduce issues for animal agriculture. What is discussed are illustrations of institutional factors. Education is seen as an enabling process for the functioning of agricultural systems. Government interventions include policy and direct interventions that impact the operations of food systems. Social organization and structure—and culture—are the settings in which issues often arise. The marketing system is judged as a highly prominent institutional factor in animal agriculture, and recent changes in market demand for beef are presented as evidence. Other institutional factors—lawmaking, planning, regulation, policy making, and research—are considered individually in subsequent chapters.

These examples provide an introduction toward an understanding that external institutional factors are the primary determinants of issues in animal agriculture. Contemporary issues in animal agriculture arise out of the confluence of societal factors, the agricultural systems themselves, and the institutional environment in which the system must function. This situation is complex and complicated. Putting the puzzle together requires coordination, improvements in the sources of progress, and service for all people. The definition of these requirements will become increasingly fundamental for animal agriculture.

NOTES

1. Consumption, or rather changes in the pattern of food consumption, produces a technical change through behavioral patterns affecting demand. For example, in 1976, 94.4 pounds of beef per capita were sold at retail outlets in the United States; in 1990, the figure was 64 pounds, and the consumption of poultry and fish increased concurrently. Poultry consumption was 50 pounds in 1980 and 61 pounds in 1990. These changes in consumption reflected demands that were not driven entirely by economic considerations of price, quality, and market availability. The animal agriculture industry had responded in its supplies of products.

2. Bennett (1986:369) suggested that the situation in which knowledge is perceived to flow from expert to farmer was ameliorated in North America by the institution of cooperative (agricultural) extension. An intermediary, or broker, role is played by a person educated in agricultural expertise but is also sympathetic to the farmer's practical knowledge and perhaps willing to learn. The indigenous–exogenous dichotomy appears more evident in the developing countries in which the extension broker may be less able to function effectively.

WITH CONTRIBUTIONS BY WILLIAM P. BROWNE
Central Michigan University

CHAPTER 5

LAWS, POLITICS, AND PLANNING
THE PROCESS OF POWER

Resolution of issues may be sought through oral and written debate, academic conferences, or discussions with various kinds of groups, institutions, and organizations. Philosophic positions may be stated and argued, but when positions are polarized, or simply when changes need to be made in existing rules of policy making, one or more of the protagonists may seek relief through legal instruments: legislation, court action, or regulatory rulings. In the final analysis, society speaks through these means, although academia and the media may serve to test the conscience of society before the legal means are invoked. Even in such stated positions, however, the spokesperson most likely represents a single view of one social group. No reason exists to expect that any proclamation represents a general societal perspective, even if raised by eminent professors or prizewinning journalists. This is the essence of politics.

In the United States, the visible political processes are often the ones highlighted by the media: the political campaigns, the election process, the treaties negotiated, the laws passed, and the appointments made and given consent. Lawmaking by Congress and state and local legislative bodies are the central element in the process of policy making. Laws are made there; the administration's discretion to act is allowed by the actions taken there. Many of the issues in agriculture derive from the policies, appropriations, and directives in legislative acts at the federal, state, and local level. The force of law is then implemented by the agencies of government, and interpreted and expanded when challenged by courts of law. What recently has been seen in the public media, however, are the processes of developing public policy, the operatives of private interests, and the sheer complexity of various stages of the processes. Witness the legislative and judicial battles concerning tobacco in the late 1990s.

In many countries, legislation as oversight of social problems is often integrated with the analytical and forecasting components of executive action, a process that is termed *planning*, but is more the pursuit of self-interest. The Congress, executive agencies, and even private interests share planning in the United States, and in the process of negotiating agreements, lend it less than a long-term perspective. The elements of planning differ in many countries depending upon the governmental structure. Approaches to planning depend on whether the country is a parliamentary democracy, centrally planned economy, or an oligarchy. As the case of the United States would suggest, the more that participatory democracy prevails in a government, the less likely the projection of policy matters, or the plans, will be long term. Democracy is subject to cyclic majority review on too regular a basis for there to be stability of plans. The extensive democratization emerging in the world since the late 1980s suggests that principles of planning are also undergoing revision.

LAWMAKING

THE U.S. CONGRESS AND OTHER LEGISLATURES

Many observers believe that Congress is more powerful than the president, a legacy both of constitutional heritage and the events of the Vietnam War and the Watergate scandal. An assertive Congress has set up its own Congressional Budget Office, and to reinforce its investigative arm, the General Accounting Office. The Congress is now less dependent upon the analysis and interpretations of the executive branch, although data collection is still an agency prerogative.

Legislative action is complex. Characteristic of legislative action is that it is often the follow-through on massive volumes of information which includes scientific data, facts, abstract ideas, and recommendations. Legislative decisions involve increasing detail, complexity, and sophistication. Yet at the same time, legislators are not forced to act on facts alone (Browne, 1995). They can react to highly emotionally charged issues that reflect the views of constituents or even lobbyists who play well on media themes.

Consequently, the initiative for legislative action is diffuse. It can rest with the executive office, a legislator or group of legislators, an organized interest, a lobby, or even an individual. It may be prompted by the *sunset* provisions of existent law. The process can be cumbersome, as with general farm legislation, or it can be swift. It, however, is less likely to be swift in the future if legislative contests involve large numbers of players. Farm legislation, for example, has utilized hours of hearings, hours of lobbying and *buttonholing*, consideration of a multiplicity of bills (each with its own concept), debates in committee and on the floor, considerations and discussions in conference committees, building coalitions and parliamentary maneuvering, floor passage, and finally, acceptance and signing by the president or governor.

INTERVENTION OF THE LEGISLATIVE PROCESS

The legislative process is a political process in which the images that constituents have are kept in the forefront. Legislators, as Fenno (1978) suggested, need to cultivate an acceptable "home style" that keeps them attractive to voters back in the district or state. Appearance is as important as what program, or even what issues, are within a program that legislators enact. The process, of course, is subject to the influence of friends, respected leaders, vested interests, and nearly any imaginable source of information that a legislator will value. Anyone can, under appropriate circumstances, have an input into lawmaking, if one has the persuasiveness or can employ effective people to be persuasive (interest groups, professional associations, business associations, lobby groups).

Intervention in the legislative process by interests begins before election. The concept of political support is that persons are elected whose political philosophy—and loyalty—are close to those who support them and help secure votes. The support comes because certain interests seek an active voice that will speak inside the appropriate house or committee for a specific cause. It is more than just votes that special interests are after.

The legislative process is affected, of course, by the way members of the legislative body behave, in subcommittee and in committee. Legislative behavior is affected by which bills are introduced as well as by what an individual member can do. The latter is leadership ability—a composite of committee assignments, seniority, legislative position, capability for parliamentary maneuvering, significance of the issue or problem under consideration, and political IOUs. Legislators will have or find varying amounts of each to aid moving the bill through the committee process and to the floor and chief executive. Intervention in the process, for better or worse, can occur in the adoption of rules of the house, a factor known widely as *institutional limits*.

Committee appointments are means of affecting the legislative process. Thus legislators often manage to serve on committees that reflect district or state needs, or even that of a special interest dear to a district. A political philosophy in control does not lose control simply following elections that may indicate changes in the political desires of voters. Single-issue politics and ad hoc coalitions often replace party loyalty. (In that sense, parliamentary systems in other countries seem to be more disciplined than legislative bodies in the United States, although discipline was more evident after the Republicans achieved control of the Congress in 1995.)

Growing influence in the legislative process can be observed in the legislative staffs. The congressional staff has grown rapidly in numbers and in professionalism (Browne, 1988b). They can process far more information than a single member, both from inside Washington and from back home. As a result, staff members are exercising substantial influence on the decisions congressmen and senators are elected to make.

External influence of the legislative process in a democracy can and does occur. The genesis of many of the issues relating to agriculture thus occurs in the making of our laws. Once a law has been enacted and implemented, changes are also difficult to make, even if the law has its own sunset provision. Too many people become stakeholders in the law, planning for action on the basis of its existence. Lawmaking, especially at the national level, is more cumbersome, more complex than often expected, and more important than often considered. Given the right circumstances, even unexpected rules for agricultural industries can emerge there, often uninspired by logic but fueled by emotion (Hansen, 1991).

INTERNAL POLITICAL TACTICS AND STRATEGIES

At least two aspects show up in analyses of the internal and external forces intervening in the political process, the internal political tactics that are used by both the bureaucrats and the politicians and the external and private (special) interests that influence the outcome of the process.

The writer Hedrick Smith (1988:297) stated that "[t]he common thread between the White House and Capitol Hill is that the shadow government of staff has gained power at the expense of those formally and publicly assumed to exercise power: Congress and the Cabinet." Numerous ties, ranging from informal contacts to issue and party connection, link staff together in ways that elected representatives, more tied to constituencies, are not.

For anyone interested in making contacts with legislators, direct access to the legislator seems curtailed (Browne, 1988b, 1995). Information is best handled when it is given to a committee or subcommittee staff member or the subject specialists in the office of the individual legislator who may be interested. The fairly rapid turnover of staff requires continued effort on the part of interested persons to maintain recognition.

Browne (1988b) cited long-term Washington observers as seeing four factors in the current situation:

1. Legislators generally sit on more committees and subcommittees than before and are likely to pay more attention to committee responsibilities.
2. Increasing numbers of lobbyists seek access.
3. Relevant data are more difficult to comprehend and interpret.
4. With increased congressional reliance on direct campaign efforts and the party less often an electoral intermediary, legislators are less available to lobbyists.

Constituents and work in the home district or state take up more of the legislator's time. Thus congressional staffs are the contact points for information exchange; they have become central to the analyses of issues, the reduction of workload, and the *protection* of the legislator.

THE DIFFUSION OF AGRICULTURAL POWER

Key committees in the Congress for agricultural matters are the House and Senate committees on agriculture and the agricultural subcommittees on the two appropriations committees. Congressional control of agricultural matters, however, is fractionated among more centers than ever before. Policy making centers for administration and oversight of agricultural affairs are equally scattered (Browne, 1988a). The industrialization of agriculture may be diminishing agriculture's special significance for lawmakers.

Historically, the focus of lobbying and organizational interests generally remains directed toward the commodity subcommittees of the House and Senate subcommittees on agricultural production, marketing, and stabilization (Browne, 1988b:55). These are the subcommittees that have drawn the interest of commodity groups, agribusiness groups, organizations interested in omnibus farm bill provisions, and even those groups favoring a more free market agriculture. They also draw the interest of those who have stakes of another sort: consumers, environmentalists, and even animal activists. Other subcommittees have similar constituencies and concern themselves with items such as credit, nutrition, marketing, foreign agriculture, and agricultural research. Thus, issues have proliferated.

Jurisdictional overlaps between committees and subcommittees complicate both communication and lawmaking. Some farm problems are dealt with by nonagricultural subcommittees with responsibilities for toxic substances, small business and family farms, labor, banking, trade, consumers, energy, agricultural taxation, estates, international regions, health and safety, public lands, water resources, and economic development (Browne, 1988b). When environmentalists, consumers, banking interests, multinational business firms, the U.S. State Department, or groups concerned with foreign debt, trade, and fiscal policy intervene in agricultural issues, they may well take their cases far afield from traditional agricultural policy makers. By so doing, they often can win by not engaging any of the traditional agricultural subcommittees or fighting old farm and agribusiness interests on their own turf.

Things, however, have not changed entirely. In spite of the growing complexity of other internal machinery for legislative and administrative activity, some more or less traditional elements remain operative (Browne, 1988b). Direct contact with legislators has become more difficult, but has not been eliminated. Friendship-based contacts and lobbying of legislators and advisors are still a fact of the present. The process is only less workable, and often best accomplished when an interest group cultivates a close constituent contact from back home, one who has or can easily get the legislator's ear.

PRIVATE INTERESTS AND PUBLIC POLICY

Agricultural politics are no longer simple. Reflecting the complexities of the food system itself, the diversity of interests in it is well institutionalized (Browne, 1988b:26–27). Interests, often group interests, represent each link of the system: suppliers, livestock and crop producers, markets and handlers, and consumers. Other private interests also intersect the food chain: business firms, labor unions, environmentalists and other public interest groups (conservation, health, consumer, environmental action, social justice, and animal protection interests), and religious groups. More recently, governmental agencies such as the U.S. Department of Agriculture (USDA), the Food and Drug Administration (FDA), the National Institutes of Health (NIH), and the quasi-governmental National Research Council (NRC), Institute of Medicine (IOM), and National Academy of Sciences (NAS) have become more activistic in their organizational style.

The politics and policy making of today are affected by far more players than even a decade ago. Browne (1988b) classified interested organizations as "producer organizations" (e.g., American Farm Bureau, National Farmers Union, National Cattlemen's Beef Association, National Pork Producers Council, United Egg Producers, National Wool Growers Association), "producer/agribusiness organizations" (e.g., National Cattlemen's Beef Association, National Broiler Council, National Milk Producers Federation, United Fresh Fruit and Vegetable Association), "agribusiness middleman organizations" (e.g., National Food Processors, Food Marketing Institute, International Association of Ice Cream Manufacturers/Milk Industry Foundation, National Independent Dairy-Food Association), "supplier/facilitator organizations" (e.g., Farm Credit Council, Fertilizer Institute, Independent Bankers Association, United Farm Workers, National Association of State Universities and Land-Grant Colleges, American Seed Trade Association), "public interest groups" and related organizations (e.g., American Farmland Trust, Environmental Policy Institute, Public Voice, Humane Society of America, Bread for the World, National Save the Family Farm Coalition, Rural Coalition, Farmworker Defense Fund, National Council of Churches), and "agribusiness and food firms" (e.g., Cargill, Giant Food, ConAgra, Monsanto).

Each group has its characteristic approach to intervention in policy making. The studies of Browne (1988b, 1995) appear to be helpful in understanding the process. For example, agrarian protest groups, those groups desiring sweeping reforms in food production or farm programs, often adopt an adversarial position. They emphasize a variety of issues, but generally condemn widely accepted agricultural practices and support strategies that are intended to force public officials to action. The farm groups in this category are organized around policy ideals of social justice, price parity, financial reform, or preservation of the family farm. Ideology such as anticorporate beliefs, antagonism to chemical use or mechanization of agriculture, protection of public lands, or relief of rural poverty is also an organizing and mobilizing force; however, ideology has had little or nothing to do with the motives of most of the farm protest leadership (Browne, 1987). They wanted changes in what they perceive from their unique positions and perspectives as flaws in agricultural policy.

Multipurpose interest groups—general farm groups, some commodity groups, trade associations, some large agribusiness firms—formulate policy statements and lobby on a wide array of administrative and legislative recommendations. They look at farm policy proposals to assess the possible impacts and often are seen as the major players in farm issues, in that they articulate positions on so much of relevance. Their focus is on wide-ranging lobbying efforts, but with limited staff and resources, they may spread themselves too thin and thereby fail to gain expertise on the issues they hope to influence. Single-issue organizations with specialized expertise, need for access to a limited number of policy makers, and focus on one item of interest are growing in number. The broad range of issues in the agricultural system of today demands broad attention, but one-on-one, it is often the single-issue organization that finds friends in Washington and thus advances its cause. Often junior members find the support of such groups to be avenues to congressional influence, especially if the cause is promotive or near and dear to central issues of agriculture (Browne, 1990).

Agribusiness also lobbies within the broader context of agricultural and food system policy (Browne, 1988b:114–17), which includes the superfund for environmental cleanup, the Federal Insecticide, Fungicide, and Rodenticide Act (FIFRA), product lobbying, trade regulations, and tax reform. Their priority concerns, beyond economic interests, focus on market expansion or protection. In some situations, trade associations such as the Food Marketing Institute (FMI), instead of a large firm itself, address the most controversial of issues. Trade associations, including such organizations as the National Cattlemen's Beef Association, offer a vehicle of a united front on an issue, expertise on the narrower issue, and a useful perspective on problems at issue. They are adept at working with the media. These groups (actually firms) often can be especially powerful by cultivating the *home-style* needs of legislators who need to look good in subsequent elections.

PUBLIC INTEREST GROUPS

A select number of groups that call for consideration of public instead of private interests attempt to influence policy making from what they argue to be a society-wide perspective. These groups, as briefly men-

tioned above, are sometimes identified as citizens groups and sometimes as nongovernmental organizations (NGOs). Browne (1988b)
termed them organizations with private views with a public interest.
The late political scientist Don Hadwiger (1982) called them "external-
ities/alternatives organizations" or "ex/al" groups. Such groups may
be directed to the unintended side effects of agricultural policies. They
are not concerned with profits, markets, and production as much as
they are with the undesirable effects to those who eat the food or are
employed by the system, whose backyard is contaminated, or who lives
near the operation. Policy problems that are held important in ex/al
concerns are conservation, environment, salt, saturated fatty acids,
cholesterol, animal welfare, animal rights, protection of plant plasmas
and landscapes, production and release of genetically engineered organisms, and pesticides and hormones in food supplies. These can be ral-
lying points for garnering sympathy, interest in the work of the group,
funding support, or even the lobbyist's next job.

Sapolsky (1986) noted that since Ralph Nader outmaneuvered General Motors Corporation on the automobile safety issue in the early
1960s, the United States has discovered that political influence is available to those who do not or cannot initially assemble an actual membership base for their activity. A constituency may already exist, as
Nader recognized, and the news media can mobilize dues payers when
it is needed. Sometimes such groups need no members, ever (Walker,
1991). They can rely on patrons, such as foundations or others with
large amounts of funding.

Each is a staff-led organization, and its board of directors is self-
perpetuating and not elected by a membership. Personalities of the
leadership are a principal factor in both what it does and the media
attention it generates. For example, some agrarian protest groups in
the 1970s and 1980s operated in the manner of public interest groups,
seeking greater power to affect policy by mobilizing a ready constituency. Using a "rowdy and randy message" (Browne, 1988b) in tandem
with effective organizing skills of the leaders and persuasive mobilizing
use of the media, early agrarian protest movements brought together
farmers already alienated by agricultural policy. The American Agriculture Movement of the late 1970s was one such coalition. Rhetoric,
however, can wear thin; massive mobilizations of irate farmers have
given way to more patient coalition politics (Lundgren, 1987; Tweeten,
1987). So it is with much of the ex/al movement at this time.

It may be that the market, or the regulation thereof in the implementation of congressionally mandated action related to nutrition labeling, will force the policy changes related to animal agriculture. What must be remembered, given the complexities of politics, is the similarity between the market and government. The market can and will be induced by the media and public relations specialists, just as government is moved by lobbyists as public affairs specialists. These forces often work together, seeking alternatives but also mutual support, sometimes employing the same specialist. The influential growth of the health food industry in the mid-1990s is a case in point. The Dietary Supplement Health and Education Act (DSHEA), the passage of which was influenced greatly by the health food industry, minimized federal control of dietary supplements. DSHEA simply took the matter out of regulatory hands.

THE PROCESS OF POWER

Policy in the United States, technically, is developed within the executive branch of government, formulated by congressional action, and implemented by the executive branch. Obviously, the lawmaking process incorporates elements of policy formulations from other sources as well. The system, however, does not seem to lend itself to a sustained and cohesive policy direction for almost any aspect of agriculture. It lacks the neutrality and objectivity to do so.

Single-issue politics seems to dominate the process, even when the need for broad review appears obvious to policy participants. There is a policy, or at least a set of programs; there is a Food Stamp program, an attack on disease, a special program on sewage, another on coastal waters. There are individual and continually changing attacks on individual pieces of agriculture. Although conceptually this may represent a flawed approach, realistically and politically, such tactics may be necessary in a government that is both pluralistic and democratic.

Historically, development in the United States has been planned only in the vaguest sense. There was a plan to give people the resources needed for agricultural development and to let them work at that goal. Beyond that, it was up to them, not withstanding the fact that the national political process is complex and suspect in its abilities to intervene to stop anyone or pick up those that fall through its cracks.

PLANNING

All countries, including industrial as well as developing countries, must develop institutions and political processes to handle the economic, social, and health problems of their people, and all must evolve a process of negotiation whereby society can balance and meet the differing needs of subgroups within the population. This is the planning process.

The process used to accomplish the development of food and agricultural policy in some developed and in most developing countries emphasizes planning. It is planning in a very systematic sense, assessing goals and thinking of the specific means of meeting them regardless of citizen disagreements. Planning is the way of governing in developing countries. Although planning remains dependent upon governmental philosophy, planning can allow for local initiative and local governmental participation to deal with varying circumstances of place. It, however, is never free of politics. The planning process is so reactive and highly negotiated that there is serious question, even in a strongly centralized government, if it really meets the diverse needs of the country and achieves the desired balance.

THE PLANNING PROCESS

The planning process can be best understood as the use of whatever forecasting and control mechanisms are needed by a country to cope with its numerous issues and problems (Duckham, 1976b). Planning, by design, identifies and also creates issues.

Ideally, planning is a dynamic activity involving the process of government decision. Steps are selected and formulated in accordance with goals and targets that recognize the hierarchy of needs for different sections of society. It is part of the overall political process, and is associated with direct implementation, social and governmental control, and extensive oversight.

Planning, in theory and practice, involves the identification, development, implementation, and evaluation of a range of policies and programs. The systems approach may be used. This approach, based increasingly on systems analysis, attempts to induce and administer changes both inside and outside the market structure and the ordinary administrative processes of government (i.e., the ruling institutions).

Planning follows the development of policy. Decision and financing follow planning.

Administration, or management, is the implementing factor and may be executive or consultative. Administration takes action through market manipulation, persuasion (demonstration, information, leadership), control, and enforcement (Duckham, 1976b). For agriculture and food, the target populations may be as much the consumers as the farmers. Middlemen are vital targets as well. The ideal system, as advanced by planning specialists, involves shifting of administration from the central authority through provincial and district authority to the individual decision makers, feedback of information about practical difficulties and local reaction to executive action, and local participation. The planning process involves the critical selection of the executive agency to do the job and the allocation of resources.

Planning has numerous purposes. Duckham (1976) noted that policy may be scientific or technical (e.g., for raising the energy and protein intake of humans or the control of a disease in the cattle population), strategic (e.g., for India to be less dependent upon surplus grains from the West and Europe), or downright political (e.g., to try to attract the votes of farmers or consumers). Agricultural planning, for example, may try to achieve change in the quantity and composition of products, the quantity and composition of inputs, or economic status.

Planning usually crosses sectors, linking agriculture to other economic and social components. If confusion occurs or if authorities cannot agree (e.g., on matters of nutrition in which there often may be as many solutions as there are nutritionists in the country), the issue may be ignored because planning is always done under a time constraint.

There may be conflicts among goals; to achieve one, the country may have to accept a negative impact on another social value. The issues are always complex. Institutionally, land-tenure systems, policies, and investments outside of the agricultural sector are at play. Agricultural sector planning can increase quantity and quality of food, but often will affect the income of farmers, a fact often forgotten. It can reduce or make worse the problems of low-income farmers.

Policy decisions, however, even in planned societies, often (nearly always?) are not made on the basis of analysis but on the basis of the political imperative. In almost all developing countries, whoever gains planner status is the crucial player. It is that planner who is concerned with determining the allocation of scarce resources, and the one who must be convinced. Policy makers, even if they adopt rigidity, still want to define the rules their way. Given the likelihood of planning to promote political stability in inherently unstable places, that desire is understandable.

Yet, even while being manipulative, planners develop certain ideals as the most effective means of control in pursuit of determined ends. Planning, in that sense, is an expression of the unique political will of the individual country, or of the dominant forces within it.

DEVELOPING COUNTRY ISSUES

Agricultural development in developing countries tends to proceed unevenly; however, the solution to tomorrow's food problem must come in large part from the problem countries themselves.

Too often, governments of developing countries have discouraged agricultural development through policies and actions. Many countries's economic development plans in the twentieth century have emphasized industry. The result was an allocation of resources out of agriculture, a patchwork of policies for agriculture, and an inadequate interaction of the agricultural sector in the overall developmental framework. Other negative policies have been insufficient allocations of resources to agricultural infrastructure and pricing mechanisms that fail to give farmers incentive to increase production, or cause farmers to withhold grain or sell to channels other than those intended by policy. There have been instances of a requirement to purchase locally produced inputs when prices are too high and quality is poor, or governments were led to believe that the world market had, and would continue to have, abundance of food at low prices and thus neglected agricultural investment.

Planning requires foremost that competent and well-trained people make and implement the farsighted document. The common heritage of many countries in the developing world has not been necessarily institutions and political theories as much as a shortage of educated people. The decision process, based on as much knowledge as can be mustered and minimal imperfect information, is the key to better management on the national level (as in a corporation or other firm). The question is how one gets there, given the uncertainties of politics in any nation and the natural inclination of those in power to seek survival of the regime.

EXTERNAL FORCES

The process of planning, and through planning, managing a country is as susceptible to external influences as the flexible and reactive political process and rule making in the United States. The difference lies in the fact that many such forces are external to the country, and well beyond its control. By selling grain cheaply in world markets, rich nations can lower world food prices and thereby encourage planners to subsidize food to urban dwellers, which is disadvantageous to farmers. With tariffs and quotas, the rich countries may deter investment in new industries in low-wage countries. World markets entice developing countries to export grain and thus create problems of food security for the poor.

This is just not a matter of economically powerful countries winning. Acting as financial regulator and guardian in the increasingly complex global system, the International Monetary Fund (IMF) and the World Bank have established themselves in the past as external regulators of the affairs of many countries (Lawrence, 1986).

The character of class difference and the balance of political forces within the ruling class play a key role in setting the degree to which external economic interests are represented in policy and planning. External forces can in turn become instruments that a national government uses to its own ends. The pathway for doing so, however, is fraught with immense difficulties, and requires in many ways a subjugation of natural instincts to the pursuit of self-interest in politics. That alone explains why planning has worked better in theory than in practice, why the former controlled economies of Eastern Europe and the former Soviet Union gave way, and why policy interests in the United States transferred little of their own political legitimacy to planners.

CONCLUSION

Legislative action in a pluralistic democracy such as the United Stated is influenced by a diversity of private interests as well as by political philosophy and constituent concerns. Many of those private interests are sustained by groups of people or patrons who may or may not agree totally with the special interest, but respond to the messages sent. Those who hold interests in the productivity of animal agriculture are but among the many, and the opportunity for conflict is high. Thus, the legislative and policy making process is central to resolution of issues in animal agriculture.

Intervention in policy making requires skill and influence. It requires knowledge of the system. It requires persuasiveness, time, and resources. It relies heavily on mass media.

The likely leveling force in the processes of power and politics is well grounded argument; however, the political process can replace the scientific process in setting policy. This less direct, more complicated route may be less error prone than the counterpart to the legislative process in many countries (i.e., the planning process), but requires the vigilance of interested parties.

Planning is a way of life in governing developing countries. The availability of a firm, long-term policy, authority and flexibility to coordinate and implement the policy, adequate financial and human resources, technical advice, effective communication, training and research, and a decentralized organization that allows people to be involved meaningfully, can bring a predictability not likely to be seen in democratic legislative policy making. The question is how does a country gain these advantages, given the uncertainties of politics in any country and the natural inclinations of those in power to continue to stay in power? Accountability of a government to its people is a critical, but also fragile, factor.

Planning also is subject to intervention, often by forces external to the country. The agriculture of planned economies often has little influence on policy. The response of an agriculture without power is not action, but inaction and little development. Perhaps, in that, there is a lesson for U.S. agriculture.

CHAPTER 6

REGULATION

An essential component of the whole system of food and animal agriculture is the regulatory process. Regulation is the extension of laws by executive action. The process may be changed in form and philosophic approach in the future as philosophies change in government and society.

The role of federal and state regulatory agencies in protecting citizens from risk to human health, safety, and the environment has increased dramatically since the 1960s. Agencies such as the Environmental Protection Agency (EPA), the Food and Drug Administration (FDA), the Food Safety and Inspection Service (FSIS) of the USDA, the Consumer Product Safety Commission, and the Occupational Safety and Health Administration (OSHA) have far-reaching legal powers. Customs is involved in the safety of imported foods.

Regulation is an attempt by the government to control the behavior of citizens, corporations, or state and local government (Meier, 1985). Regulation is but the governmental effort to limit the choices available to individuals within the framework of a democratic society. Some regulation is coercive, and much is accomplished by incentives offered by government. In the case of the Nutrition Labeling and Education Act (NLEA) of 1990, regulation provides for education and requires the knowledgeable consent of the consumer. In the case of the Hazard Analysis and Critical Control Points (HACCP) system, regulation is through directive and monitoring systems.

Regulation may provide for price control, franchising or licensing, setting standards, allocation of resources, providing incentives such as the USDA conservation program payments, promoting fair competition, and defining terms that may provide desired information about a product. Change of behavior is the objective, whatever the form.

Most regulatory laws are in fact short statements spelling out legislative intent and policy purpose in a road map fashion. They require implementation by an agency. That requires interpretation. Interpretation of legislative intent draws from the committee report (the fine print of the law) as well as the specific language of the law. Interpretation also may require scientific data, a sense of the reliability of such data, the effect of technological advances, recognition of social values, negotiation, and the authority written in the law. Each agency also has goals that agency employees wish to reach (Meier, 1985). When major disagreements occur, courts of law interpret and develop the precedent.

Rule making is the legal mechanism by which regulatory activities are promulgated. Rule making by U.S. executive agencies is dependent upon the delegation of power by Congress. Any rule making works under the constraint that the rule must be written with reasonable interpretation of the legislative intent. Restraint and limitations of authority may be written into law.

GOVERNMENTAL REGULATION

In the late 1960s and early 1970s, nearly two dozen new federal agencies were created. Federal legislation affecting animal agriculture passed or amended since 1970 regulating safety and toxic and ingredient substances include:

Clean Air Act
Clean Water Act
Egg Products Inspection Act
Endangered Species Act (ESA)
Federal Food, Drug, and Cosmetics Act (FDCA)
Federal Insecticide, Fungicide, and Rodenticide Act (FIFRA)
Federal Meat Inspection Act
Federal Water Pollution Control Act
Food Quality Protection Act of 1996 (FQPA)
Nutrition Labeling and Education Act of 1990 (NLEA)
Occupational Safety and Health Act
Perishable Agricultural Commodities Act
Poultry Products Inspection Act
Resource Conservation and Recovery Act
Wholesome Meat Act
Wholesome Poultry Products Act

Briefly, most of the restrictive legislation affecting animal agriculture can be classified as public protection legislation. The concept is based on the premise that many members of the public can be adversely affected by the activities of private and public operations, including farmers and ranchers. Balanced against this requirement is the need to assure that agriculture will have the necessary disease- and pest-control efficacy and market structure to meet the requirements of the nation for food and fiber.

The public is concerned about nutritional content of foods, residues, microbial contaminations, the effectiveness of the government inspection system, and now, biotechnological advancements. Food safety is a major issue with consumers. Additives, preservatives, and pesticides are matters that can instill strong public concerns about the possible consequences. Microbial contaminations are receiving greater attention.

Regulation also comes from another impetus: a society increasingly troubled about the humane treatment of animals, the preservation of endangered species, and the uses of animals in scientific research. Humane concerns for all sentient beings and the needs for healthy productive animals in agriculture can converge in the development of regulations and guidelines.

Animal agriculturalists argue that regulatory agencies should take reasonable and logical approaches to the development of new restrictive legislation. The protection of endangered species is at once a concern that is based on the belief that the loss of a species damages the human prospect and a concern that regulation could override the rights to private property. Those productively employed in animal agriculture often have used a simple economic principle to assist them with decision making, that as long as the necessary capital can be made available, inputs will continue as long as the revenue generated exceeds their costs. Although economic theory is clear on the principle, measuring all costs and all benefits is a difficult task.

PRIVATE SECTOR REGULATION

Regulation can be provided by the private as well as public sector. Such regulations are sets of standards established by associations and groups such as the American Oil Chemists Association (now AOAC International) and the American Association of Cereal Chemists. Cheit (1990) compared regulation through both private standards and government regulation and concluded that both have problems. Government regulation is frequently criticized for being time consuming, inflexible, unreasoning, and costly to agriculture. Standards set by the private sector, which can be increasingly important alternatives to regulation by governmental agencies, are assumed widely to be less careful of due process than government and often lax in their application. Cheit (1990) observed that setting private standards is prospective and ongoing, often intervening early in the life cycle of an issue and adjusting over time. Public regulatory efforts on the other hand are usually corrective and singular activities involving single issue standards without subsequent adjustments.

Animal agriculture has had a minimal involvement of setting private standards, relying instead on governmental functions to carry out regulatory activities, mainly on food quality standards (e.g., meat grading and standards, compositional definition of meat and dairy products, and wholesomeness and freedom from disease). Voluntary action by industry in cooperation with federal agencies may be increasing. The Quality Assurance Program for *Salmonella enteritidis* in egg production is an example of such cooperative efforts. The USDA's new approach to safety of the U.S. meat and poultry support, the HACCP system, went into effect in January 1997. Each company is responsible for developing its own system of addressing hazards in its operation. The burden of producing safer foods is shifted to industry, although the government conducts the verification.

POLITICS AND REGULATION

Meier (1985) stated regulatory policy as being dominated by two perspectives. One view sees regulatory agencies as having vast discretion; thus, they appear as a major force in regulatory policy. A second view suggests that regulatory agencies are dominated by an environment of interest groups, legislative committees, economic forces. and technological change. Both views have validity.

Many of the agencies created in the 1960s and 1970s were born of an entrepreneurial politics that built on a general antibusiness sentiment and specific instances of abuse (Wilson, 1980). These were not the traditional *captured* agencies that existed largely for the benefit of the regulated. These agencies generally chose "stricter and more costly standards over more lenient, less expensive ones" (Wilson, 1980). Cheit (1990) argued that as these agencies fell short of expectations, enthusiasm for the standards waned. Some government regulations became excessive and costly while others became time consuming and adversarial. Agricultural interests would likely agree with these sentiments even though the regulatory agencies are often seen by others as captured by agriculture (e.g., USDA).

The EPA engages in negotiated rule making; the FDA does not, although it seeks wide comment. Policy makers often act, or believe they must act, without the benefit of adequate scientific knowledge in order to make socially responsible decisions (Stenholm and Waggoner, 1989). Where the balance lies is a significant and pervasive question. Uncertainty often prevails in the regulatory area (Caplan, 1986). There are few uncontestable data in controlling toxic substances. It becomes necessary to act and make regulatory judgments on the basis of the best data available. The issues of environmental quality and the welfare of animals are even more complex and less the matters of science than of conscience, although often the problems are phrased in the language of science. These issues call into play feelings and images as well as actions. Those feelings and images, consolidated by public interest groups, can gain momentum and set a potential for new regulations.

Thus, rule making is subject to intervention. Executive orders can delay implementation of a regulation. Congress may direct a delay or moratorium of an action, requesting an independent scientific review. After long delay, inertia or impasse may follow. The courts are an arena in which a regulation may have to stand the test. In the final analysis, however, the agency may simply lack resources to pursue further issues. Lack of funding, perhaps, is the ultimate intervention.

It seems easier to thwart change in law than to actually influence a change.[1] For example, the 1958 Delaney Clause to the food additive law created consternation in the animal and feed industry when it first became law, and was responsible for the banning of diethylstilbestrol (DES) and chloramphenicol.[2] For four decades, the Delaney Clause proscribed the addition of any substance to food that in any way could be said to be carcinogenic. It remained with increasing rigidity. A court decision in early 1993, mandated that the Delaney Clause be strictly enforced (Abelson, 1993). A paradox arose. FIFRA governed residues on raw foods as they were not considered to be food additives. The FDA treated pesticide residues on processed foods as direct food additives subject to the Delaney Clause ban on carcinogens. Residues at safe levels on raw foods were exempt from further regulation by the FDA.

In August 1996, Congress suddenly enacted the Food Quality Protection Act of 1996 (FQPA). In the act, Congress partially resolved the

40-year-old regulatory problem—the Delaney Clause and its paradox. The FQPA amended the FDCA by removing chemical pesticides from the definition of food additive. This in turn removed chemical pesticide residues from the provision of the Delaney Clause. The FQPA, however, did not amend the Delaney Clause itself. The Clause remained untouched and continued to apply, with full force, to food additives, color additives, and substances administered to food-producing animals.

ROLE OF SCIENCE AND SCIENTISTS IN REGULATORY POLICY

Science and technology contributed to the need for regulating agriculture. They are now needed to set the standards for regulation.

In the years immediately following World War II, science and technology were first applied in some innocence and in an ethic that stressed individualism, self-reliance, achievement, and personal responsibility for one's fate (Christensen, 1984). Agricultural science, all science for that matter, was described as a value-free reach for truths. Although individual scientists may have had their own values, goals, and purposes, these were not seen to intrude into the value-neutral environment of science.

The end of World War II, with its dramatic conclusion driven by the atomic bombings of Hiroshima and Nagasaki in August 1945, marked the beginning of a search for other scientific values—humanitarianism, responsible uses of science, the good of society, trust in science, societal guidance of research, science and technology in the political world, assessment of technology—that scarcely had been thought about in earlier years. The perception of value-free science persisted in agricultural science until the environmental movement began in the 1960s and matured into a forceful lobby (Christensen, 1984). Even today, animal scientists may argue that regulation must be set by science, not emotion.

Scientists, however, are often challenged by a multiplicity of perceptions regarding the implications of scientific results. One expression of widespread feelings among agricultural scientists about their science is their banding together with farmers and industrialists to form the Council for Agricultural Science and Technology (CAST) to provide "summary information on scientific aspects of key national issues in agriculture and food processing to the government, news media, and the public." CAST now states that "as an educational institution [it] takes no advocacy stance on issues." Contributors take responsibility for the CAST reports that they write.

Although science is necessary to provide the instruments and the understandings that regulatory activities require, the scientists's own values, goals, and purposes have emerged as they participate in setting policy based on science (Kunkel and Thompson, 1988; Kunkel, 1996). Policy making is a second tier of interaction of scientists with each other and with the branches and agencies of government. In this environment, social scientists being the critics they must be, are often accorded special responsibilities for assessing outcomes and social risks.

The processes of policy making and science, however, are different. In science, the scientist is expected to approach his work with a single-minded purpose, seeking knowledge from experimental or empirical study with the singular intent of asking one question at a time and determining its truth. Policy making, the operation of government, on the other hand, almost always requires dialectic argument.[3] Opposing points of view are the stuff of formulating policy in a democratic society.

REGULATION OF BIOTECHNOLOGY

Emergent issues are directing the new interests in regulation. These interests are not in the intervention of rule making, but rather extensions of regulatory authorities. Biotechnologies, habitat of endangered species, and labeling of food products according to their means of production are now issues on the agenda for regulation.

Biotechnology was created in a world that had already lost its naive beliefs in the benefits of scientific progress. As soon as recombinant technology was devised, some perceived a potential for harm. Biotechnologies emerged, with powerful potentials and with value-laden envelopes. However great the promise or valuable the products, their exploitation quickly was encumbered by legal and regulatory uncertainties.

In the United States, three federal agencies, the FDA, USDA, and EPA, regulate agricultural biotechnology (Miller, 1994). There is no single law governing biotechnological research and commercial applications. A framework has been established and guidelines have been written; a patchwork of laws apply.

In the 1990s, and probably beyond, firms must seek approval for product research and commercialization from one to three agencies, depending on the nature of the product. It was then the product rather than the process that was to be considered; however, when regulation became involved, the process (i.e., the introduction of alien genes) was considered. With animals, it has been a case-by-case risk assessment. In effect, regulation is highly decentralized and each case is considered on the basis of whether it is a threat to health or to the environment, although, as with recombinant bovine somatotropin (rbST), fears of economic dislocation also had an impact on regulatory clearance. Some arguments for strict regulation have related to the deliberate spread of genetically transformed organisms, which is an international concern as well.

Under the existing legal framework, environmental releases of most genetically engineered animals are essentially unregulated. Some varieties of transgenic fish have extra copies of a fish growth hormone gene, and the FDA has considered regulating them as new animal drugs; however, the FDA has decided it does have the authority, although no statute covers the environmental impacts of commercializing transgenic fish.

Beginning in 1996, the stance in the USDA is to consider biotechnology as an interest of all components of the USDA, rather than isolate its regulation and promotion as a separate activity. The young biotechnology industry has matured, and issues such as trade rather than field testing and environmental ones became the key concern of regulators worldwide, with a goal of harmonizing regulations.

The promise of transgenic animals—faster growing, leaner, more disease-resistant animals—is what traditional animal breeders seek anyway. Genetic material was transferred between two species, a rabbit and a mouse, in 1980. Embryo transfer became a technological reality and cloning of sorts was achieved in the early 1980s. Cloning of cattle, actually embryonic duplication producing as many as eight identical calves, became a commercial reality. Transgenic mice are used regularly in biomedical research. Transgenic pigs and sheep have been produced.

Transgenic animals became a topic of heated national debate. Animal rights advocates claimed that animal patents would increase animal suffering. Farm groups feared concentrated control of the animal industries in the hands of a few large corporations and special benefits to the larger farms. Environmentalists said that the animals would upset the laws of nature. Religious leaders argued that such patents violated divine laws (Rollin, 1996).

In the future, transgenic animals will be created, although a broad debate on patenting life may develop. The critics of biotechnology may have increased the distrust of the American food system, raised the acceptability of anecdotal evidence as a call for political action, and delayed an application of science to animal agriculture. New animal drugs and vaccines, however, will be developed through biotechnology (Nicol, 1991). New understanding about the biologies of agriculture will emerge. Regulatory control will be exercised rigorously, and the research that develops genetic transformations may become the target of restraint. What the critics have achieved is a slowing of the process. On an international scale, the science was curtailed in some countries (e.g., Austria, Switzerland, and Germany) as governments responded to fierce public opposition, fanned by the *green movement*. In the 1990s, the situation intensified (Lang, 1999). What is now termed genetically modified organisms (GMOs) has become an international regulatory issue. The public and, hence, the regulatory systems of the United States and the European Union became very different and the bases of trade wars (Gaskell et al., 1999). The regulatory system in the United States is generally favorable to the development of GMOs; approval of genetically modified crops has been effectively curtailed in Europe. And, much of the rest of the world, mainly Africa, is engaged in attempting to set its own policies toward GMOs.

An important feature of the 1994 Uruguay Round of the General Agreement of Tariffs and Trade (GATT) was the increased influence that was given to the Codex Alimentarius Commission of the UN (Lang, 1999) in trade disputes over food standards. Codex was to arbitrate in difficult disputes on issues such as genetically modified foods as well as pesticides, additives, and growth hormones. The GATT set up the World Trade Organization and gave it the responsibility for implementing agreements on technical barriers to trade.

ANIMAL CARE

Care of animals in research has been regulated in part under the Animal Welfare Act, which is the responsibility of the USDA to implement. Institutions that wish to be eligible for U.S. Public Health Service (PHS) research and training grants in which vertebrate animals are used must file an assurance document with the agency. The institution must assure that it is following the guidelines in the "Guide for the Care and Use of Laboratory Animals" (NIH, 1985). Groups interested in animal agriculture research have banded together and developed a "Guide for the Care and Use of Agricultural Animals in Agricultural Research and Teaching" (Consortium, 1988). The guide has been revised (FASS, 1999). It is a voluntary guide issued as a companion to the NIH guide for laboratory animals.

Most animal welfare legislation and regulatory activities deal with the medical research sectors, but the issues for animal agriculture may be one of making sure that its house is in order. Barring even the continuing lack of direct regulatory action on agricultural animals in research and teaching, universities, colleges, and other agricultural research units are subject to visits, friendly or otherwise, by those caught up in animal protection issues.

Animal care is an obvious item on the agenda of animal welfare interests. Through the courts, they too have overturned a system, requiring the USDA to revise its standards. Most scientists believe that the USDA should continue to rely on performance-based guidelines that require animals to be healthy and content (Watson, 1993); however, animal activists (the Animal Legal Defense Fund and the Society for Animal Protective Legislation) argue that only engineering standards, such as cage specifications and duration of exercise, can prevent abuse. The courts agreed with the activists, implying that professional discretion is not to be trusted.

Whether regulated or not, an animal agriculture that raises the level of discomfort for livestock and poultry or accelerates the metabolic *engine* (e.g., with rbST) may have economic consequences as well as create an unfavorable image. Bruises, abscesses, and susceptibility to disease and diminished performance in the feed yard have been shown to be a result of an all too casual management of the animal before it is placed in the yard (Smith et al., 1992).

NUTRITION LABELING

The original intent of regulatory food labeling was to ensure that the consumer was not defrauded; it was mainly an ingredient labeling. Regulation of labeling of food is shared by three federal agencies: the USDA for meat, poultry, and egg products; the FDA for all other food products; and the Federal Trade Commission (FTC), which governs advertising. The intent of labeling has now been broadened to promoting the public health by providing information to consumers so that they can choose their foods for a better diet.

Major changes have occurred in the manufacture, processing, packaging, and distribution of food products since the passage of the 1938 Federal Food, Drug, and Cosmetic Act (FDCA). Changes in the regulatory mechanism, however, have changed only slightly, leading to inconsistencies and inadequacies. Although a joint FDA–USDA–FTC food labeling proposal was presented in 1979, the effect and the future of the proposal remained unclear until 1990, when legislative guidelines were developed and the Nutrition Labeling and Education Act (NLEA) was enacted into law. The NLEA is a truth-in-labeling law, the first comprehensive revision of national nutritional laws in two decades.

The emergence of nutrition guidelines placed emphasis on nutrition labeling together with ingredient labeling. Through the years, interest has grown relative to labeling that identified the amount of sodium, saturated, polyunsaturated, or monosaturated fats, or the amount of kernel oils making up the saturated fat, and the uses of such terms as *lite, light,* and *no* labels (e.g., no fat, no cholesterol) in making claims on food products.

The NLEA called for more information on virtually all foods. Unsubstantiated health claims are barred. The FDA was required to draft standard definitions of light, low fat, reduced calories, and high fiber, all terms that had been used indiscriminately to label food products. Major exceptions, however, include meat, poultry, and egg products which are regulated by the USDA. Restaurant food, prepared dishes sold in markets or delicatessens, and infant formulas are also exempt.

The FSIS issued nearly identical requirements for nutrition labeling of meat and poultry, resulting in a nearly uniform approach. A voluntary nutrition labeling is designated for single ingredient, raw meat and poultry products. Mandatory labeling is required for all other meat and poultry products, with the exception of certain products (i.e., those produced by small businesses, those used for further processing or not sold to a consumer, those in very small packages, those prepared for export, and ready-to-eat or multi-ingredient products processed at the retail level).

THE RIGHT NOT TO LABEL. Food labeling promises to become more complex with the entry of biotechnology in production of animal food products. In 1993, the FDA ruled milk products from rbST treated dairy animals as safe and indistinguishable from milk produced by untreated herds. A sign must be displayed in food stores stating, "FDA has determined there is not significant difference between milk from treated and untreated cows." Consumer advocates, however, remain suspicious of the product's safety. In 1995, Vermont introduced a new law that required, for the first time in the United States, a product containing a genetically engineered food product to be labeled as such on grocery shelves. Food industry groups challenged Vermont's law in court. The court concluded that consumer curiosity alone was not sufficient to justify requiring a product's manufacturer to publish the functional equivalent of a warning about a production method that had no discernable impact on a final product. This is in harmony with the FDA's long-term policy of requiring only meaningful and essential information on the food label.

FROM QUALITY TO SAFETY

One of the problems of implementing a comprehensive policy for food safety is that responsibilities are divided among agencies and congressional committees. There is no single, independent food safety agency, although the FDA and USDA routinely work together to coordinate food regulatory policy.

As the last decade of the 20th century began, the issues of food safety gained greater attention (Stenholm and Waggoner, 1989); however, the public concerns often were only of chemical contamination (e.g., pesticides, antibiotics, growth promoters). Food-borne enteric microorganisms (*Salmonella* spp., *Escherichia coli, Yersinia enterocolitica,* and *Campylobacter* spp.) present a more immediate problem (IOM, 1989; Ryder, 1990; Thompson et al., 1990). The ease with which *S. enteritidis* can enter the food chain has been underscored by data suggesting that instead of the usual mode of contamination through cracked shells by *Salmonella*-containing chicken feces, transmission was transovarial, with infection of the yolk before shell deposition (Telzak et al., 1990). That mode of transmission would not be blocked by the usual methods of egg decontamination. The FDA and USDA have implemented a Voluntary Model State Program for *S. enteritidis* Quality Assurance to survey the presence of the bacteria in flocks of hens. Eliminating raw or undercooked eggs from the diet is widely recommended.

The danger of undercooking as well as contamination was highlighted with the outbreak of food-borne illness in Washington State in early 1993. At least 100 cases (4 deaths) were linked to bacterium *E. coli* 0157:H7 in undercooked ground beef patties sold in some fast-food restaurants. As a result, the USDA issued food labeling requirements that advise consumers on cooking and handling the cooked product. *E. coli* 0157 infections, however, are a persistent problem and have international implications. In 1996, six deaths and over 200 *E. coli* 0157 infections were traced to one abattoir in Scotland. Cases of infection have been reported with unpasteurized milk and apple juice, the latter probably from fallen apples contaminated with animal feces. The USDA has set a zero tolerance for *E. coli* 0157 in ground meat.

The FSIS is the consumer protection agency of the USDA. It is pursuing a broad and long-term, science-based strategy to improve the safety of meat and poultry products and has adopted a farm-to-table approach that includes steps to improve the safety of meat and poultry products at each phase of production, processing, distribution, and marketing. For example, safe handling labels now are required on all raw products, informing consumers of the importance of proper handling and cooking in preventing food-borne diseases.

Significantly, the USDA proposed in the mid-1990s to reinvent the meat inspection system, which had depended on sight and smell. Adoption of the HACCP system by the whole of animal agriculture from farm to table was prominent. The premise was that the science was available to provide standards; the technology was available to accomplish the system (IOM, 1991b). The establishment of performance standards for industry and the requirement for appropriate controls at each stage were implemented. The initial initiatives were new sanitary procedures: new procedures for washing carcasses and for rapid cooling, and microbiological procedures for monitoring. The Food Code issued by the FDA in 1993 and subsequently revised, lays out the bases for improvement in handling meat and poultry. At the request of the U.S. seafood industry, the FDA has developed a HACCP-based program for seafood products.

The HACCP program is a science-based risk assessment and control system. It is a systematic approach to preventing food safety hazards by focusing resources at those points at which food safety hazards can be controlled. It is an alternative to general end-product testing (National Advisory Committee on Microbiological Criteria for Foods, 1997). Upon its introduction in the early 1970s, the HACCP approach to controlling food safety matters was adopted in the manufacture of low acid canned food products (Buchanan, 1990). As of 1990, regulatory agencies widely contemplated the incorporation of HACCP techniques into their programs (NRC, 1985; ICMSF, 1988; National Advisory Committee on Microbiological Criteria for Foods, 1990).[4]

The USDA's Pathogen Reduction HACCP Rule of 1996:

1. Requires an HACCP plan to be developed by all meat and poultry plants.
2. Sets pathogen reduction performance for *Salmonella*.
3. Requires all meat and poultry plants to develop and implement written standard operation procedures for sanitation (SSOP).
4. Requires slaughter plants to conduct microbial testing for generic *E. coli* to verify the adequacy of process controls for the prevention of fecal contamination.

One of the most debated issues in the implementation of HACCP regulations concerns how these regulations effectively replace the long-standing inspection procedures. In Canada, the implementation of HACCP allows the regulators to focus inspection efforts on critical areas and production process controls. In the United States, FSIS regulations establish a HACCP program in which food businesses are accountable for its safety, and government is responsible for setting standards, inspection oversight, and a strong enforcement program. HACCP clearly requires cooperation and communication.

CONFINED ANIMAL FEEDING OPERATIONS (CAFO)

Under the 1972 Clean Water Act, a confined animal feeding operation (CAFO) was defined as a dairy milking over 700 cows, a swine production farm with over 2,500 sows, or a beef feedlot with over 1,000 cattle. CAFOs are designated as point sources of pollution and are required to manage manure in accordance with a National Pollution Discharge Elimination System (NPDES) permit (Outlaw et al., 1997). As the EPA has not had sufficient personnel to issue and enforce individual CAFO permits, the authority to administer NPDES permits has been delegated to state environmental agencies in 35 states (Thurow and Holt, 1997). Improper manure management remains evident in a number of cases. As a result, improving the effectiveness of the CAFO permitting procedures will likely be a priority of state environmental agencies. At this writing, however, the EPA has issued plans to step in under the Clean Water Act and begin issuing rules on the largest livestock operations.

States have had expanded roles in crafting and enforcing the policies that frame options for environmental compliance by agricultural producers. Environmental regulations may be written as performance standards because flexibility can encourage technical innovation (Thurow and Holt, 1997). Environmental regulation that dictates the use of a particular technology or management practice tends to dampen incentives to innovate. Such innovation may be forced on large-scale farms concentrated in a small area that become large importers of feed such that nutrients in by-products accumulate more rapidly than can be applied to cropland (Martin and Zering, 1997). Previous livestock feeding programs emphasized productivity but increased attention is being placed on improving feeds to reduce sharply the surplus phosphorus and other minerals excreted by swine and poultry (Cromwell and Coffey, 1995).

The burden of regulations falls on the larger CAFOs, which in turn have made the investment to improve their waste handling (Thurow and Holt, 1997). Small-scale CAFOs are not regulated in many states. An assumption in regulation by permit is that large CAFOs pollute more than small-scale dairy and livestock operations, although there seems to be little evidence to support the claim.

Regulation of the waste stream differs from regulation of food products, biotechnology, animal care, and food safety. Outlaw et al. (1997) argued that there is almost no way to determine whether or not the animal product was produced under a production management that includes sound environmental stewardship. Consumers are not likely to know the difference and the market thus will not reward the producer. An exception, however, is developing. Integrated broiler, pork, and beef firms that sell branded products, or firms with marketing agreements that include environmental quality assurance as a stipulation, are highly motivated to avoid environmental damage (Martin and Zering, 1997).

ENDANGERED SPECIES

The Endangered Species Act (ESA) concerns habitat and implementation can affect some aspects of extensive animal agriculture. The ESA directed the U.S. Fish and Wildlife Service (USFWS), Department of Interior, to maintain a list of species that are either endangered (in immediate peril of becoming extinct) or threatened (likely to become endangered in the near future). The agency is directed to use the power of the law to halt any further endangerment, or it may "experimentally" attempt to establish the species in another locale. The ultimate goal is to bring species to "recovery," which the act defines as the point "at which the measures provided pursuant to this Act are no longer necessary." If a species attains recovery, the agency is supposed to remove it from the official list.

The scientific basis for the law's approach to protecting species has been considered as sound (Hyde et al., 1996). The Supreme Court has affirmed that altering an endangered species habitat is tantamount to harming the species and therefore could be prohibited under the endangered species legislation. This decision gave the Department of Interior the authority to continue its policy of banning destruction of habitat on private property. Although the decision was considered a major victory by the environmental movement, it also gave impetus to lawmakers intent on increasing individual private property rights at the expense of threatened or endangered species.

Congress delayed reauthorizing the ESA. Opponents claimed the original law cost the economy billions and violated the Constitution's ban on taking property without compensation. Supporters of the endangered species legislation argue that it is a vital safety net for an increasingly threatened biosphere. The ESA, however, had only modest success in delisting species (Hyde et al., 1996). The incentives for farmers and ranchers to cooperate in the task of preserving biodiversity did not exist in the original administration of the law. Under a provision of the ESA designed to ease tensions between landowners and environmentalists, agreements have been worked out that would allow landholders to build or develop property later if they restore tracts of land with improved habitat for the endangered species. Such Habitat Conservation Plans (HCP) became models of compromise (Kaiser, 1997), although they remain controversial (Shilling, 1997). Concurrent with the HCPs is the Incidental Take Permit/HCP process. Instead of threatening private property owners with fines or jail for harming endangered species, the agency would offer financial incentives, from tax breaks to future development rights, to owners who choose to protect species.

THE REGULATORY LANDSCAPE

For animal agriculture, the issues of regulation, regulatory standards, and risk rank high. In many respects, regulation controls how animal agriculture does its business. The regulatory mechanism in the United States, however, remains a maze of largely uncoordinated rules, standards, grades, inspections, threats, and labels.

In wealthy countries over the world, people increasingly say they are unhappy about the environment, noise and filth, odors, and the possibility that they are doing lasting harm to the fabric of the earth that their children will inherit. Sometimes they are just unhappy that their aesthetic senses are offended. They, however, are most worried that their bodies are inflicted with food that may not be conducive to good health, or that their water supply may contain molecules and organisms that somehow will damage the way of life to which they have been accustomed.

The regulatory landscape is likely to become more complex, because some problems are intensifying. State legislatures and local government entities are recognizing the special regulatory desires of their constituents. Iowa requires large livestock operations to keep their distance from people's homes. Yet some states also have passed right-to-farm laws that tend to shield intensive agriculture from nuisance suits and exempt them from odor pollution standards. At local levels, the perceptions of rights are highly selective.

The element that may permeate regulation in the future is risk assessment. In some measure, this is a different sort of cost-benefit analysis that affects both individual members of society and society as a whole. In any case, certain freedoms guaranteed by the Constitution, such as freedom of speech, religion, press, and so on, can be enjoyed extensively without reducing the rights of others, except when the law restricts them.

Regulations are the oldest and simplest way to control contamination and environmental damage, but a new force, the marketplace and consumer confidence, is also effective and from time to time has impacted the scene. The occurrence of Alar (chemical used to mature apples, now banned) in apples, diethylstilbestrol in meat from Italy, mad cow disease in Britain (and the subsequent withdrawals, avoidances, and bans) are cases in point. In most cases, however, the market impact was temporary, except that those cases may have left a legacy of distrusting the system.

This discussion has focused on the state of regulatory affairs in the United States. There are, of course, international dimensions that are not included here in deference to the limits of space and time; however, the international dimension of regulation is of consequence to agriculture in the United States as it affects international commerce, trade, and moral concern for the welfare, health, and safety of peoples in the world (Nicol, 1991; Beckman, 1996). The restriction on exporting agricultural chemicals banned or restricted in the United States and the European Union ban of imported livestock products from animals treated with hormones are cases in point. HACCP systems have been implemented in the European Union, Canada, Australia, and New Zealand as well as in the United States. Transmissible spongiform encephalopathies such as the bovine case in Britain face international regulation of trade. The final arbiter of international regulatory disputes is in fact the World Trade Organization.

Prior to 1995, the Congressional trend was to pass statutory reforms that included largely inflexible mandates, often with mechanistic solutions and aggressive deadlines. On the edge of the twenty-first century, however, risk assessment and regulation have become a high-profile issue for the nation. Interpretation of what is risk has become a national issue. The larger issue for animal agriculture is that more and more decisions have been taken away from individuals and this is perceived as a loss of liberty. Addressing risk and perceiving risk in a way that satisfies the perceptions and values of all of those interested is never easy.

NOTES

1. Few studies are available that outline the disciplinary differences and personnel views on policy development.

2. See Wise Burroughs's (1961) "Problems Concerned with Feed Additives." In *A Century of Nutrition Progress, 1861–1961*. Kansas City, Mo.: Midwest Feed Manufacturers Association. Burrough's highly charged comments are typical of the early reaction to the Delaney amendment.

3. This conclusion is by Dr. Alan Perreiah, Department of Philosophy, University of Kentucky (pers. comm.).

4. The principles of the HACCP are stated as follows (National Advisory Committee on Microbiological Criteria for Foods, 1997):

i. Conduct a hazard analysis. Prepare a list of steps in the process in which significant hazards occur and describe the preventive measures.

ii. Identify the critical control points (CCPs) in the process. These are the points in the process in which the potential hazards could occur and be prevented and/or controlled.

iii. Establish critical limits for preventive measures associated with each CCP. An HACCP plan might require a different pre-slaughter handling that reduces the population of *E. coli* 0157:H7 in the gut of the animal.

iv. Establish CCP monitoring requirements to ensure that the CCPs remain within limits. Monitoring is focused on keeping the process under control and preventing deviations from happening.

v. Establish corrective action to be taken when monitoring indicates that there is a deviation from an established critical limit.

vi. Establish effective record keeping procedures that document the HACCP system. The approved HACCP Plan and associated records must be on file at the establishment.

vii. Establish procedures for verifying that the HACCP system is working correctly. Verification is a process that reviews that HACCP Plan and ascertains that it is being carried out. It is a process that looks at trends and long-term implications. To verify, one might undertake strategic fecal sampling for key indicator organisms.

THE ISSUES

In the following pages, we take issues and controversies out of the whole spectrum of activities in animal agriculture and study their internal structure, meanings, and conflicts. Issues in animal agriculture are often specific to the use of animals, but they also reflect the global human domination of the earth's ecosystems. We live on a human-dominated planet (Vitousek et al., 1996). Animal agriculture is part of that human domination.

Issues in animal agriculture have emerged on the trails following certain incidents that became fixed in the public mind. They have emerged from the questioning of key individuals and groups and the emphases given to such matters by the media. Among such incidents was the proof of the carcinogenic activity of diethylstilbestrol, DES, which was a widely used growth promoter of beef cattle in the 1970s. Although not related to animal agriculture, the memory of the public outcry about Alar on apples produced in the Northwest remains a reminder of the unintended consequences of agricultural technology. Other incidents have been the regulatory battles surrounding recombinant bovine somatotropin to enhance milk production, the exposure of military personnel to Agent Orange and dioxins in the Vietnam conflict, the massive recalls in 1997 of frozen meat as a result of *E. coli* 0157:H7 contamination, and the specter of mad cow disease. Each case set in motion the demand for new policy to handle the issue.

In each case, it was argued that science and knowledge are essential for policy decisions if they are to last. Now we are beginning to factor in the realities of uncertainty into the knowledge base (Kunkel et al., 1998). We begin the study of the issues with such uncertainties; we call them risks.

The issues discussed in the following chapters illustrate the complexity of managing the whole systems of animal agriculture in the light of evolving knowledge. We have learned the biologies and economics of the animal agriculture technologies and continue to expand the biological knowledge base with tools such as molecular biology. We, however, face uncertainties as well when we attempt to put the biologies of contaminant pathological organisms, prion diseases, and animal well-being into perspective.

In each set of issues, we scan a range of human sensitivities and belief systems. We observe the perceptions of people within and outside animal agriculture. We respond to uncontrollable factors such as climate and weather. We look at animal products in the nutrition and health of human populations. We attempt to place the issues surrounding the care and use of our animals into sound public policy. Finally, the importance of scholarship and science in resolving issues is reiterated.

The key components of issue resolution are knowledge and trust. Inherent in the discussions that follow is the imperative that the uncertainties in our knowledge be acknowledged so that the public trust may be maintained. Inherent also is the imperative that we understand the genesis of each issue to deal with it in a responsible way. We, however, also must respect the plurality of views surrounding animal agriculture.

CHAPTER 7

RISK

Ulrich Beck (1992), a contemporary social theorist, character-ized the change in social organization since World War II as a shift to a risk society. Prior to 1940, much of what was happen-ing in Europe and America could be understood in terms of in-dustrialization. Production in all areas of the economy was being reorganized according to efficient economic and engi-neering principles. The primary social problems turned on a competition for future economic returns to land, labor, and capi-tal. Efficiency was promoted. That trend continued in agricul-ture during the development of scientific and technological abilities into the 1950s and beyond. Science was placed in a wholly positive and largely uncontroversial role in animal agri-culture.

Since 1950, the social problems in the industrial world were seen to be less and less a competition for future benefits and more and more as instances in which a person or group's action places another at risk (Thompson, 1997c). Some of the risk is economic, some health-related, some environmental, and some even psychological. The increase in the technical complexity of animal production and the rise of the risk society have created some of the most pressing issues for animal agriculture.

The issues in animal agriculture are matters of both reality and perception and of both probability of occurrence and con-text. The perceptions of risks as issues in animal agriculture stem from both descriptions of the factors that may pose a risk to someone (individuals or groups of people) or something (e.g., species, water, air, land resource) and descriptions of the public perception of the risk. The question of what constitutes a risk is important to animal agriculture in the context of its own resolution of issues.

This chapter turns to descriptions, perceptions, and philosophical construct of risk in animal agriculture. Values and interests in defining risks are considered. The principal issues of risks to animal agriculture relate to food safety. Pesticide residues are a primary concern of people consuming fruits and vegetables, but animal food products are viewed as sources of carcinogens, disease microorganisms, and unknown effects of biotechnology. The use of antimicrobials in animal agriculture is perceived as being responsible in part for the diminishing ability of antibiotics to control human disease. As a result of their natural constituents, foods can both bear risks and reduce the risks of disease. An emergent perception of risk for some is that some components of animal products contribute to the rich diet of Western societies and thus increases the risk of coronary heart disease, certain cancers, and the risks associated with obesity. (These latter issues are introduced here, but will be discussed in greater detail in subsequent chapters.) The final sections of this chapter are concerned with the evaluation of risks. It is suggested that alternate conceptions of risks are important as issues in animal agriculture.

RANGE OF RISKS

It has been argued that the United States today has a food supply that is as safe as any in the world (Kessler et al., 1992). That may well be so, but food safety has become a governmental public health emphasis. Consumers in America, as well as in Europe and in such places as South Korea and Japan, are showing growing concerns over their food supply. The known possible consequences of food contamination range from diarrhea to cancer. There are microbiological hazards, environmental contaminants, naturally occurring and contaminative toxicants and carcinogens, pesticide residues, and feed additives, all of which could penetrate the food we eat. The risk of diseases transmissible from animal to human through food is a newly recognized possibility. Natural components of foods as the foods are prepared and consumed pose risks, both real and imagined. Overuses by humans also may threaten the availability of antibiotics to control disease in animals and vice versa.

The issues of risk to society go beyond the food supply. There is concern about the social risks of new technology, particularly biotechnology (Thompson, 1997b). There is growing interest in the quality and sustainability of the environment. The special vulnerabilities of certain populations, such as children, call for reevaluations of standards of safety. Polarization of views, scientific disagreements, questions of the validity of data, and the inconsistencies of regulatory laws and rules also pose risks to both society and agriculture.

The issues relative to risk and safety pertaining to animal agriculture go beyond governmental regulation. There are questions of image that animal agriculture and food products may have with society. A variety of anxieties about animal agriculture are raised by some members of society, perhaps as a result of the growing separation of the populace from animal production agriculture. With the exception of companion animals, agricultural animals are considered less and less to be good neighbors. They are seen as polluters of air, water, and ground. Intensive agriculture is partly the cause. The biotechnologies that increase milk production may be seen as undesirable and mysteriously altering a food that has been a mainstay in the diets of children. The use of gamma irradiation to extend the shelf life of animal products creates concern simply because of its name. People associate irradiation with danger.

People have difficulty embracing the concept of risk unless it is translated into a simple context. Risk issues, however, are more complicated than they appear to the public and the government. Debates require elements of educating the public, media, and legislative bodies. Regulation will likely have to face questions of both doubt and certainty in science, and yet must maintain accountability. Regulations impacting animal agriculture will likely be swept along in any of the changing national climates of regulatory reform.

CARCINOGENIC AND ANTICARCINOGENIC SUBSTANCES

The development of the somewhat persistent perception that animal agriculture is a source of carcinogenic risk probably rests on the history of diethyestibestrol (DES). DES is a synthetic estrogen that was used to promote growth in beef cattle beginning in the early 1950s. DES also was used by women to prevent miscarriage, but evidence appeared in the 1970s that suggested a causal link between such DES use and a rare form of vaginal cancer in the daughters. DES, however, had received special Congressional exception in a 1968 amendment to the Delaney Clause (the DES exception). This amendment allowed DES use to continue into the 1970s, even though it was known to cause cancer in laboratory animals since 1938 (Kuchler et al., 1989). With the evidence that DES caused cancer in humans, the implant ban was finally imposed and use became illegal on November 1, 1979. DES manufacturers were not able to prove that DES met the *de minimus* risk standards of less than one in one million. DES is no longer used but animal agriculture has not been able to shake off the image.

Doll and Peto (1981) and Doll (1992) estimated that 35 percent of all cancer mortality reported in the United States is related to diet, with an uncertainty range of 10 to 70 percent. The National Research Council (NRC) Committee on Comparative Toxicity of Naturally Occurring Carcinogens (NRC, 1996a) has accepted the concept. The human diet contains both naturally occurring and synthetic agents that may affect cancer risk. Carcinogens and other substances can enter food indirectly as a result of their uses as animal growth promoters or feed additives and be regarded as additives to human food. Naturally occurring carcinogens, however, are likely to pose the most serious risks in reality, largely because they are less well characterized and, hence, less well regulated.

The Committee on Comparative Toxicity (NRC, 1996a) also concluded that in terms of cancer causation, current evidence suggests that calories and fat outweigh all other individual food chemicals, both naturally occurring and synthetic. In some populations, fat intake is correlated with the consumption of meat, a major source of saturated fats in the diet. In this aspect alone, the carcinogenic contribution of the diet is an issue for animal agriculture. Most dietary constituents, other than fat and calories suspected of impacting on human cancer (both naturally occurring and synthetic), account individually for a small part of the diet and may pose correspondingly low risks.

After reviewing the evidence to date, Ames et al. (1995) concluded that risks of specific cancers can be reduced by decreasing the smoking of tobacco, avoiding intense sun exposure and high levels of alcohol consumption, controlling infections, increasing consumption of fruits and vegetables, and increasing physical activity. These authors also suggest that reduced consumption of red meat may decrease the incidence of colon and prostate cancers.

Assessing dietary cancer risks requires considerations of both carcinogenic and anticarcinogenic agents. For example, a beefsteak probably will not have any significant level of a carcinogenic substance that could have been introduced into the animal by additives to feeds or by injection or implant. Cooked beefsteak, however, may contain traces of naturally occurring carcinogens drawn from the environment, including mycotoxins, arsenic, and dioxins that may have contaminated feed (NRC, 1996a). Heterocyclic amines may be formed during cooking the steak. Synthetic carcinogens may have leaked from packaging materials. Anticarcinogenic substances such as conjugated linoleic acid and selenium, however, are also constituents of the steak, and steak is only one food in the diet. Many other foods, foods of plant origins, also contain both carcinogens and anticarcinogens.

Epidemiological evidence is not consistent. Much of the available evidence on carcinogenic compounds is derived from experimental studies with animals, and may or may not be indicative of a human cancer risk. Also, these are conclusions that are drawn for cancer causation in the United States, which are not necessarily the same as in other parts of the world.

Residues of pesticides, hormones, and other synthetic contaminants of food are regulated as toxic substances or carcinogens. For many years, there was one public policy, the Delaney Clause, that governed additives presenting a potential carcinogenic risk. Another policy governed such materials that could appear in food as a natural contaminant or residue.

The Delaney Clause (U.S. Code 21, 348 [c] [3]) states that "no additive shall be deemed safe if it is found to induce cancer when ingested by man or animal, or if it is found, after tests which are appropriate for the evaluation of the safety of food additives, to induce cancer in man or animal." The Food Quality Protection Act of 1996 (FQPA) removed pesticides from the compass of the Delaney Clause, but left the policy untouched and applicable with full vigor to compounds administered to food-producing animals. As long as it remains the law of the land, the Delaney Clause eliminates our need to think about the issue. Any additive (e.g., injection, implant, feed ingredient, packaging contaminant) indicated as a carcinogen in an animal is prohibited without regard to the magnitude of the risk at human use levels and without regard to possible benefits.

In contrast, food containing a potential carcinogen, one that enters the food supply as an additive (e.g., aflatoxins and pesticides), is subject to regulation but is not automatically prohibited. It may not be sold if levels of the substance exceed a certain tolerance level. Any agent presenting a potential noncarcinogenic hazard, whether it appears in food as an additive or in other ways, is acceptable as long as its concentration does not exceed its tolerance level.

Barring direct evidence of carcinogenicity to humans, the standard is the detectable carcinogenicity to experimental animals, mainly rodents. When the National Toxicology Program decides on the rodent carcinogenicity of a substance, it places the evidence in one of five categories: clear evidence, some evidence, equivocal evidence, no evidence, or inadequate study. Those substances that produce cancer with clear evidence are considered as being most likely carcinogenic to humans, but the weaker rodent carcinogens may or may not cause human cancer; currently there is no way to tell which are human carcinogens without epidemiological studies of human populations.

Ames and Gold (1990) challenged the general bases of determining carcinogenesis using rodents (mainly mice and rats) as test organisms and maximum tolerated doses (MTD) to accentuate the statistical likelihood of detecting a carcinogenic quality in a substance. Their thesis is that many promoters of carcinogenesis increase mitogenesis, or selective growth of preneoplastic cells, increasing the possibility of a naturally occurring mutagenesis. Animal cancer tests conducted at nearly toxic doses of the test chemical for long periods of time, can cause chronic mitogenesis by causing chronic wounding. Critics also argue that rodent risk studies lack reproducibility (Hart et al., 1995). The survival rate of control rodents has fallen in recent years, due to an apparent genetic drift in test rodents and continued use of ad libitum food consumption protocols. As with humans, overeating has its own range of deleterious effects on health, bringing into question the studies of chemical risk.

Ames and Gold (1990) also emphasized that the human diet contains high levels of many naturally occurring carcinogens and concluded that synthetic pesticides and animal hormonal substances are trivial additions to the heavy load already consumed. Philosophically, however, we might add that although humans have tolerated or endured the dangers of natural carcinogens, analyses of expected risk raise the question if there is any reason why humans must tolerate or endure similar levels of expected harm due to human action (Thompson, 1990b).

A model for the regulatory assessment of carcinogenic risk may exist in a new approach of the EPA. In 1996, the EPA proposed revised guidelines for assessment of carcinogenic risk, derived in part from a report of the NRC (1996a). The document called for infusing modern molecular biological information, such as how a substance might alter DNA, into the agency's policy for estimating toxicity. The EPA had relied on experiments in which rodents were exposed to high doses of chemicals, a practice that has been a subject of considerable scientific and regulatory debate.

The theory is that as knowledge of the biochemical mechanism of cancer development grows, it should be incorporated in the regulation of carcinogenic substances. It is an attempt to ensure that the assessment of cancer risk reflects scientific knowledge and advances. Earlier EPA guidelines were based on a major assumption that all dose–response relationships were linear. Risk assessors may be encouraged to use also nonlinear methods to estimate toxicity at the low end of the dose spectrum. Thus, some carcinogens may be deemed safe below a certain point.

Animal agriculture will likely find the nonlinear approach to be easier to negotiate than the simplistic approaches of the past, if and when such an approach is allowed. The science, however, remains inexact. Continuing scientific development, new techniques such as molecular biology, will likely make the science more precise. Recognition of both the current uncertainties and the evolving scientific abilities seem necessary in the evaluation of carcinogenic risk.

NATURALLY OCCURRING CARCINOGENS. Given that the Delaney Clause remains in force, synthetic carcinogenic substances that may be used in the technologies of animal agriculture are also likely to be greatly limited, perhaps creating economic discomfitures in the industry but little actual threat to human health. Other issues, however, exist for animal agriculture. Naturally occurring carcinogens and those formed during processing or contamination of food and feed may be found in animal products.

CALORIES AND FAT. The issue of carcinogenicity of natural constituents has an impact on animal agriculture by implicating high dietary fat and energy intakes as risk factors in colon and perhaps breast and prostate cancers. The association of dietary fat with animal products extends the implication to animal agriculture. Other substances unique to animal products also may be involved. Regular consumption of red meat has been singled out as a specific risk factor in colon and other cancers and coronary heart disease (Kushi et al., 1995); however, the evidence of special risk factors of red meat, other than fat and calories and carcinogens that can be formed in cooking, is equivocal at this time.

MYCOTOXINS. Meat, eggs, milk, and other edible products from animals that consume feed contaminated by aflatoxins and other mycotoxins are sources of potential exposure. If a crop is stressed by drought or insect attack, it is susceptible to *Aspergillus flavus* growth and contamination by aflatoxin, a hepatogenetic carcinogen. If the contaminated crop is fed to animals, the animals can be contaminated (IARC, 1993); so can the food produced by the animal. Other mycotoxins may be involved as well. *Fusarium* toxins occur in corn. They appear to play a role in the pathogenesis of esophageal cancer in humans. Ochratoxin A, produced primarily by *Aspergillus ochraceus* and *Penicillium verrucosum*, occurs worldwide in many commodities, including pork products, and is implicated in urinary tumorigeneses.

Mycotoxins mainly contaminate grains, particularly if plants are stressed and storage is faulty. Animal products are not the primary dietary sources. Unfortunately, mycotoxins are ubiquitous; they can and must be minimized, but cannot be eliminated entirely.

DERIVED SUBSTANCES. Carcinogenic substances derived from naturally occurring substances have been reported in a variety of foods. The principal risk associated with carcinogenic derived substances in animal food products appear to be related to cooking, especially overcooking. Polycyclic aromatic hydrocarbons (PAHs) are produced by cooking. The most potent carcinogenic PAH, benzo(a)pyrene, occurs in charred meats, smoked fish, vegetable oils, tea, roasted coffee, and some fruits and vegetables (NRC, 1996a). Heterocyclic amines, also formed during cooking of proteinaceous foods, may be consumed at the highest levels by high consumers of meat cooked well-done. Preformed N-nitroso compounds may be present in foods cured by nitrate or nitrites. Cured meats and beer are the most important sources of nitrosamines. Humans also may be exposed to a wide range of nitrogen-containing compounds and agents that form N-nitroso compounds in the body (Bartsch, 1991). Residual nitrites in cured meats and fish can be a source. The maximum concentration of nitrite in bacon is set by law to be 120 ppm, but improved manufacturing processes have led to a steady decline in the concentrations of nitrate and nitrate in preserved meats. In fact, nitrate is rarely used in the United States.

Nitrates may contaminate water supplies for human consumption, particularly when supplied by individual wells and other sources. This issue for animal agriculture in this case is animal waste and pollution of water supplies.

The derived substances that seem to haunt animal agriculture because of their environmental ubiquity are the dioxins, a group of polychlorinated dibenzo-p-dioxins and dibenzofurans and related compounds, now identified mainly as by-products in numerous industrial processes and as substances formed during the combustion of chemical and municipal wastes. Dioxin and dioxin-like substances result from a wide range of industrial processes and incineration of wastes.

Exposure to dioxins is nationwide. The theory is that emissions result in dioxin falling on leaves of plants that grazing animals consume or portions of which are used as animal feeds. As dioxins are fat-soluble substances, EPA theory suggests that dioxins are concentrated in the fat of animals and their products.

The risk from dioxin is a continuing story. Citing a link between exposure to a dioxin and increased risk of miscarriage, the EPA banned the use of two herbicides, 2,4,5-trichlorophenoxy acetic acid (2,4,5-T) and Silvex, two herbicides that had been a mainstay in range brush control. Alternative substances are now used for these purposes. Epidemiological studies following the chemical plant in Seveso, Italy, in 1976, indicated that exposure to dioxin increases risk of cancer in humans (Bertazzi, 1993). Long before that, the war in Vietnam brought a loud denunciation of the dioxin-contaminated phenoxy herbicides, particularly as they were components of Agent Orange.

The limited use of phenoxyacetic herbicides now poses little danger to livestock and humans that use livestock products. Industrial contamination, however, remains an unpredictable problem. For example, the 1997 contamination of a site source of bentonite, which is used to prepare soybean meal fed to poultry, led to condemnation of the poultry product.

The dioxin issue is a matter of perspective. EPA policy statements suggest that exposures to dioxin may be sufficiently high among the population throughout the country that any further exposure could trigger a cascade of health effects, including effects on development and the immune systems. A 1995 EPA statement holds that each molecule of dioxin increases the likelihood of an adverse response (i.e., no threshold). Others dispute this assumption as alarmist. The risk is not clearly defined, but,the theory that animals may concentrate dioxin was handled with restraint. This is significant because it is a case in which perceptive animal scientists prevailed in questioning the theory on the basis of statistical reasoning.

ANTICARCINOGENS. The presence of anticarcinogenic substances in food must be considered in any evaluation of the dietary risk of cancer. Anticarcinogenicity has been associated with fruits and vegetables (NRC, 1989a; Block et al., 1992). There is evidence that some of the inhibition of cancer by fruits and vegetables is due to the nutrient vitamins A, C, and E, and selenium (NRC, 1996a). Other phytochemicals—fiber, flavonoids, plant phenolics, antioxidants, and others—are reported as anticarcinogens, although at high levels they may induce carcinogenesis. Substances such as lycopene, lutein, indoles, and terpenes are also anticarcinogenic agents.

Epidemiologic studies have associated low intakes of fruits and vegetables with increased incidence of cancer (Ziegler, 1991). Supplemental nutrients have not been as effective as a diet rich in fruits and vegetables (NRC, 1996a). Although direct evidence based on intervention studies in humans has not been reported at this writing, it is possible that diets rich in fruits and vegetables are associated with reduced risk of cancer because of the lower fat and calories associated with such diets. Studies with experimental animals, however, suggest that fruits and vegetables have inherent inhibitory characteristics (Birt and Bresnick, 1991). Conversely, animal products may be associated with higher risk of certain cancers as they make up substantial components of the diet and thereby reduce intakes of fruits and vegetables (Kushi et al., 1995).

Linoleic acid is the only fatty acid shown unequivocally to increase carcinogenesis in experimental animals, although the epidemiological with humans is inconclusive (Erickson, 1998; Zock and Katan, 1998). Conjugated linoleic acid (CLA) is the only fatty acid that has been shown to inhibit carcinogenesis in experimental animals (Ha et al., 1990; Ip et al., 1994; NRC, 1996a). This may be of some significance for animal agriculture. The major dietary sources of CLA are foods derived from ruminant animals such as beef and dairy products (Chin et al., 1992; Lee et al., 1994; Banni et al., 1996). CLA, effective as an anticarcinogen at levels as low as 0.05 to 0.10 percent, appears to act biochemically in a signaling mechanism and in prostaglandin metabolism. Relative to cancer prevention in experimental animals, CLA appears to be more potent than omega-3 fatty acids (Miller et al., 1994). Before products from ruminant animals are consumed in the diet with the intent to protect from cancer, however, the risks of fat in the diet should balance the choice.

FOOD-BORNE MICROBIAL DISEASES

Food-borne microbial diseases are being increasingly recognized as a major cause of morbidity in both industrialized and developing countries. Effective control measures are important throughout the entire agricultural and food complex. Pathogens can enter the food chain at any point from farm to consumer. In animal agriculture, control measures integrated in the production program begin with the births of animals that produce the meat, milk, and eggs; the health of the animal is a crucial factor. Microbial contamination, unlike residue problems, can often be controlled in the food service or in the household through careful storage, preparation, and cooking (Smallwood, 1989).

There are other possibilities of contamination sources. Animals are intermingled before slaughter. Cross-contamination of carcasses can occur on production lines. Human to human transmission of organisms can occur as people handle food in processing, food service activities, restaurants, and the home. Salmonellosis, campylobacteriosis, and toxoplasmosis result from cross-contamination of animal products. Evidence of bacterial transmission from farm animal origins to humans has been found in two genera, *Escherichia* and *Salmonella* (Telzak et al., 1990). It is such colonization of humans with pathogenic microorganisms that amplified the question of risk in using antibiotics during animal production.

Food-borne microbial diseases may exist in all sources of animal products, but certain microbial infections have predominant sources. Salmonellosis is a health problem in the United States. Many cases are caused by the serotype *Salmonella enteritidis,* which is associated with eggs and poultry. Other *Salmonella* species may or may not be associated with poultry. *Campylobacter jejuni* is associated with unpasteurized milk; the organism may be secreted directly by the cow into milk. *Vibrio cholera,* which has caused periodic cholera outbreaks throughout the developing world, is associated with contamination by human feces. *Escherichia coli* 0157:H7 seems to be linked mainly to undercooked hamburger meat contaminated at slaughter or to other foods that might be contaminated with ruminal contents or fecal material. Other forms of *E. coli* may contaminate processed meats, particularly fermented products. *Listeria monocytogenes* haunts soft cheese. *Trichinella* organisms are found in domestic pigs, often from small farms in which the hogs are fed unprocessed garbage. The disease is minor in the United States, but can be serious in countries with high pork consumption and little effort being given to determining the source. The list of microbial food-borne diseases continues to grow as methods of detection and diagnosis improve.

Perhaps the most visible outbreak of microbial contamination of food in the 1990s was the outbreak of *E. coli* 0157:H7 in January 1993.

Over 200 individuals became ill, and at least 2 died of the contact. Since that time other cases have been described in the United States and Scotland. The organism is spread through raw milk, raw or undercooked meat, and through person-to-person transmission by the fecal–oral route. Hamburger poses a special risk because its large surface allows bacteria to grow and to escape destruction if the meat is undercooked. Milk-borne *E. coli* infections are reported as a result of contaminated bottling and other equipment subsequent to pasteurization (Upton and Cola, 1994).

Throughout much of the literature relative to food safety, the place of the individual human in reducing risk both in food service and the home has received little attention until recently. Food-borne pathogens can be controlled to a large extent by proper handling by individuals. Failing to cook eggs or refrigerate foods, returning cooked meats to the container in which the raw meat was carried, and cutting salad vegetables on the board on which raw chicken was prepared for cooking, certainly create avoidable risks. A growing percentage of the U.S. population consists of persons lacking experience in food preparation and knowledge of safe food handling and storage methods.

Zeckhauser and Viscusi (1990) concluded that efficient risk management requires decisions of not only what to regulate and how stringently it should be regulated, but also who bears responsibility for reducing the risks. They claim that individuals should do more for themselves, paying greater attention, for example, to their diets. Governments and corporations bear their responsibilities. Zeckhauser and Viscusi (1990) suggest that governments "should focus less on microscopic contingencies, and more on human mistakes and misdeeds, the source of far greater risks."

Regulatory bodies apparently are doing more of that. The growing risks associated with food handling has prompted the USDA's Food Safety and Inspection Service (FSIS) to issue regulations mandating that statements on safe handling be placed on the labels of raw meat and poultry. These include:

1. Washing hands before and after handling meat.
2. Cleaning the surface carefully before using any meat handling area (e.g., for cutting bread).
3. Cooking all the way through.
4. Always storing ground meat in the refrigerator.

The consumer is the ultimate protector of food.

A larger issue was highlighted by the outbreaks of *E. coli* 0157:H7: How safe should Americans expect their food to be when they buy it and what responsibility should the individual have to handle and cook it properly? Critics claim and consumers believe that government and industry should be responsible for assuring that all meat is pathogen-free. Should we adopt a more reasonable goal of identifying pathogens and making sure the level is as low as possible? It may be said that if products are clean when they are brought into the home, abuse by the food handler should be no problem. As noted earlier, FSIS has proposed the mandatory adoption of HACCP procedures by industry and government inspection. Clean food, however, will require new technologies such as irradiation, which was FDA-approved in 1997 for beef and other red meats, pork, and poultry. A fear continues that irradiation may have practical problems, such as being considered a catchall technique that reduces emphasis of other essential sanitary measures (Food Safety Notebook, 1993). Until all the pieces are in place, food-borne microbes will remain a risk (Food and Drug Law Institute, 1997). The information available indicates that food-borne microbial contaminants of meat and poultry products are associated with as many as 5 million cases of illness and more than 4,000 deaths annually.

Diseases of livestock may have their human counterparts. Often, the evidence is not clear. For example, Johne's disease in cattle, a debilitating disease linked to *Mycobacterium paratuberculosis*, has a long asymptomatic period of two to ten years after infection. Crohn's disease in humans has similar effects. The linkage is not clear, but activists point to possible contamination of water supplies.

SPONGIFORM ENCEPHALOPATHIES

The risk of food-borne disease became amplified in the public mind in Europe when the British Ministry of Health released a statement in March 1996, indicating a possible link between mad cow disease, bovine spongiform encephalopathy (BSE), in cattle and a variant of Creutzfeldt-Jakob disease (CJD) in humans (Nathanson et al., 1997). It became a palpable risk, the dimensions of which could not be calculated. BSE was epidemic in Britain. Here was the possibility that eating meat from BSE-infected cattle could infect humans, a theory considered impossible until the 1990s, and still treated cautiously by many scientists. The risk to humans, in one fell swoop, was considered as being unacceptably high, but could not be stated precisely (Dealler and Kent, 1995; *Economist*, 1996).

Both CJD and BSE belong to a class of transmissible spongiform encephalopathies (Narang, 1996). All are caused by similar agents that produce spongy changes in brain tissue. Specific types include: scrapie in sheep and goats; transmissible mink encephalopathy; cat spongiform encephalopathy; chronic wasting disease of mule deer and elk; and kuru, Creutzfeldt-Jakob disease, Gerstmann-Straussler-Scheiner syndrome, and fatal familial insomnia, four rare diseases in humans (Kreeger, 1996). A linkage is fairly well established between BSE and the 25 CJD cases in Britain identified as a new variant of the disease (Bruce et al., 1997). These cases could be linked to BSE before the implementation of a specified bovine offal ban for human consumption in 1989. The ban excluded brain, spinal cord, and other organs with potential BSE transmission in human food.

Epidemiologic data suggested that BSE in Britain may have been caused by feeding cattle rendered protein from the carcasses of scrapie-infected sheep, although BSE may have existed at undetectable levels in British cattle prior to 1986 (APHIS, 1996). Meat and bonemeal products have been used in cattle for decades. Scrapie has a long incubation period and has been endemic in Great Britain for centuries. Changes occurred in rendering operations in the early 1980s; a switch was made from a technique that used a noxious solvent and high temperatures to the American Carver-Greenfield process, which operates at a lower temperature, but was thought to provide a product more easily digested than the earlier product. The putative agent for transmission of the spongiform encephalopathies is a modified protein (prion) produced from a prion protein found normally in mammals. Oral transmission of encephalopathic diseases is implied by the transmission of scrapie in sheep, BSE by cattle in Britain, and kuru in humans. This fact calls for great caution in feeding animal neural, organ, flesh, and blood products to other mammals.

ANTIMICROBIALS

Most antibiotics were developed for disease control, but the growth promoting effects of the subtherapeutic uses of antibiotics have been evident in animal production for five decades. Some antibiotics, however, have been developed specifically for enhancement of production.

Specific growth promoting antimicrobials now include bacitracin, bambermycin, lasolosid, monensin, and virginiamycin. Approximately one-third of the antibiotics are used in animals.

The issues surrounding the subtherapeutic use of antimicrobials (e.g., antibiotics) in animal feeds focus on their possible impact on human health (NRC, 1980, 1998) as well as continued effectiveness in the treatment and prevention of specific animal diseases. The issues include the potential hazards to human health from resistant bacteria and the toxicological and immunological consequences that might arise from antimicrobial residues in animal products. Difficulties are inherent in the studies attempting to establish and measure levels of risk. Scientific evidence indicates that the chains of events leading to antimicrobial resistant infections are complex; however, they are demonstrated events. Regulatory action rests on detection of residues by the USDA's FSIS, which sets tolerance levels.

Beginning in 1950, antibiotics and other antimicrobials have been used as subtherapeutic additions, generally less than 200 g/ton for two weeks or more, to animal feeds for gaining growth and feed efficiency. In recent years the practice of using antimicrobials for growth and efficiency has greatly diminished with cattle and poultry, but remains important in the production of pork and lambs. What remains, however, is the significant use of antibiotics for disease prevention, particularly in the early stages of the animal's life or in the feedlot, and therapeutic use that some critics claim would be less needed if animal agriculture would not crowd animals.

Animal agriculture and animal scientists face the understandings and misunderstandings of risk almost daily. When challenged with the question of risk in using subtherapeutic levels of antibiotics, animal scientists note that there has been no clear evidence that humans have suffered as a result of the practice over four decades (Hays and Black, 1989). The number of cases of human illnesses that can be traced to antibiotic resistant microorganisms in food animals is very small (NRC, 1998). A risk, however, remains and is calculable (IOM, 1989).

In 1989, a study by a committee of the IOM (NAS) updated the review with these conclusions:

1. There is evidence of extensive use on farms and feedlots of subtherapeutic concentrations of penicillin, the tetracyclines, and other microbials. Most of all, antibiotic use in farm animals and poultry is administered in therapeutic concentrations. About 70 percent of all antibiotics used in animal feeds is given for the purpose of disease prevention (prophylaxis),

and the remainder of this amount is administered for growth promotion. The percentage of antibiotics used for growth promotion has continued to decrease. (Note: The major responses at this time are with baby pigs and veal calves.)

2. There are extensive experimental data that microbial resistance can be transferred, particularly in the presence of antibiotic selective pressure. (Note: Mutation and selective pressure on the pathogens themselves is now regarded as the primary consideration.)

3. There is ample evidence of high levels of antimicrobial resistance among animal isolates of salmonellae.

4. There is no direct evidence that subtherapeutic uses of antibiotics in animal feed create an excess risk of disease or death in humans consuming products from treated animals; however, human exposure to enteric organisms (pathogens and commensals) of animal origin is extensive.

Ten years after the IOM report, it is evident that resistance in microorganisms develops with any continued use of an antibiotic (Hays, 1997). Through selection pressure, resistant organisms can proliferate to become a dominant portion of the complex bacterial populations in animals and their environment. Resistance develops whether the antibiotic use is for therapy or feed additives to enhance performance. A ban on nontherapeutic uses would not prevent the development of resistance as long as therapeutic uses exist.

In the field of human medicine, pathogenic bacteria are clearly becoming increasingly resistant to antibiotics. One or more organisms have become so resistant to the once wide array of effective antibiotics that only one available antibiotic, vancomycin, is usable (Jarvis, 1994). Excessive prescriptions of antibiotics for humans, failures to take the full prescriptive doses, the human ability to carry resistant disease microorganisms across continents by air travel, and failure or inability of industry to produce new antibiotics, all are likely more responsible than usage in animal agriculture for what may indeed become a crisis in human medicine (Latta, 1999). The use of antibiotics in animal agriculture and animal health, however, is a visible use. The fact remains that the use of antibiotics in animal agriculture is a practice that puts tons of antibiotics into the environment. The future may hold a total ban on those antimicrobials that are a principal resource in human medicine.

Resistance to certain antibiotics does exist in *Salmonellae:* ampicillin, chloramphenicol, streptomycin, and the tetracyclines. As these antibiotics are not used to treat salmonellosis in humans, the resistance is not considered to be clinically relevant. Moreover, there is evidence that the growth promoting effects occur even in the presence of resistance to the antimicrobials in coliform organisms. In countries other than the United States, the human and animal microbial ecosystems are intertwined (Witte, 1998). Microbial resistance in animals can readily cross boundaries, if the antibiotics used in animal husbandry are closely related to the antibiotics used in human medicine, such as the avoparcin (animals) and vancomycin (humans). Resistant *Salmonellae* and coliform organisms are shared by farmers and then may be spread to the population. Also, antimicrobial use in some developing countries is unregulated.

The issue is that a global spread can occur due to international travel and trade in food products. Salmonellosis is primarily a food-borne disease, mostly due to contamination by animal feces. Person-to-person transmissions are rare, which is in contrast to the infective sources of *Shigella* and *E. coli*. Salmonella comes from food that humans eat, not from other people. Thus, if salmonella become resistant, it is likely that the phenomenon will occur in animals, particularly poultry. For example, in Britain the resistance pattern of *S. heidelberg* in poultry is the same as in humans. Fluroquinolone, for example, is a clinically relevant antibiotic in the United States and its use is limited, but its use with animals is widespread in Britain. In Britain, there is also a marked increase in DT104, a multi-resistant *S. typhimurium*. Dairy workers are infected by contact with sick animals; bloody diarrhea occurs in dairy workers after cattle have bloody diarrhea. The livestock and poultry industries in the United States are not immune to the resistances developed in other countries with different regulatory controls.

The risk to animal agriculture now is that improper use of antibiotics with humans and animals will render them ineffective for subsequent use in maintaining animal as well as human health. Different approaches are being taken toward resistant microbes: alternative vaccines, new antibiotics, unraveling the molecular mechanism of resistance, and total control of animal fecal contamination of food; however, the microbes are tenacious. Bacteria can maintain resistance levels even if the antibiotics are removed. Faced with a potentially endless race to outsmart (or just keep up with) evolving microbes, American society will not let animal agriculture use any of the newer antibiotics. Animal agriculture and veterinary practice have a critical need for new alternatives because the antibiotics available for animal use are limited (Witte, 1998). For animal agriculture, a window of vulnerability, a time in which all microbes affecting animals resist all current drugs, may become the risk for the future. The critical issue is not just human health but therapeutic and prophylactic uses against diseases of agricultural animals. The questions looms: Is banning subtherapeutic use the ultimate answer to extended use? Or is frugal use the answer to both human health and animal production?

ANIMAL GROWTH PROMOTERS

Two incidents in the latter part of the 1980s raised again the issues of risk created by using animal growth hormones:

1. The ban by the European Union (EU) of all animal products produced with the aid of hormones.
2. The successful synthesis, through recombinant DNA techniques, of human insulin, bovine somatotropin (rbST), and porcine somatotropin (rpST). This element is part of the larger consideration of the risks of biotechnology.

Hormones and substances with hormonelike activities affect many metabolic functions, including increasing the rates of growth and the partitioning of nutrients. The hormones used in beef and veal production technically are anabolic agents (Kenney and Fallert, 1989). They channel nutrients into muscle growth rather than into storage as fat.

Anabolic agents include both naturally occurring steroids (those normally produced by animals) and synthetic steroid hormones. Of the anabolic agents approved for use in the United States, three fit the category of natural steroids: estradiol, testosterone, and progesterone (an estrogen, an androgen, and a progestogen). Two synthetic anabolic agents, trenbolone acetate and melengestrol acetate (MGA), are included. Zeronal, a xenobiotic hormone, is derived from the fungus zeralenone. High levels of hormone residues can produce carcinogenic activity in the human body, but they themselves have not been identified as carcinogens (Hoffmann and Evers, 1986). The World Trade Organization has overridden the ban by the European Union, but the European Union has remained defiant.

The FDA limits hormone residues in meat to no more than one percent of the natural daily level produced by the most sensitive segment of the population. For estrogens, the standard is set for prepubertal boys, who are the lowest producers of estrogen and should be the most sensitive to the hormone.

The animal's own (endogenous) sex steroids and their metabolites are natural constituents of food of animal origin. Hoffmann and Evers (1986) suggested that as a result of residue studies following exogenous application of endogenous sex steroids, it can be stated that the levels are within the physiologic range with only slight indication of elevated levels. The general belief is that the natural steroids are safe when properly administered. The book may still be open on synthetically prepared anabolic agents.

The risk rests, however, largely in the possible misuse of these substances. Differences between the United States and other countries in beef production (beef production in the United States is a more intensive agriculture), consumer organizations, and regulatory systems have intensified the dispute (Krissoff, 1989). The total ban in Europe was followed by widespread use of illegal drugs (e.g., diethylstilbestrol). It appears that more risk to public health follows illegal use than controlled legalized use of certain compounds.

In the 1990s, a special case of misuse emerged in the United States relative to the anabolic properties of the β-agonist, clenbuterol. The illegal use of clenbuterol in animals prepared for exhibition surfaced in 1995, involving steer and lamb entries at several livestock shows. Clenbuterol is a potent *repartioning agent* with the ability to stimulate protein deposition in striated muscle; simultaneously, via thermogenic properties, it increases energy expenditure and hence reduces muscle glycogen and body fat deposition (Mersmann, 1998; Smith, 1998). These β-agonists also can provide a protein anabolic response in humans that could enhance performance and have certain therapeutic effects in wasting diseases. The misuse had both legal and ethical implications. Clenbuterol is now legal in Canada and the United States to treat respiratory diseases in horses but not for use in food animals. Concerns over the abuse of clenbuterol in food animals in the United States have led to strict enforcement against illegal sales and use.

BIOTECHNOLOGY

The newest subjects that raise considerations of risk are biotechnology and the products of biotechnology, that is, genetically modified organisms (GMO). With research and development in recombinant DNA (rDNA) technology beginning to bear fruit, an effort is being made to forge a comprehensive regulatory policy concerning the biotechnology industry. Although most of the activity will likely concern regulating genetic transformation of microorganisms and microbial products and modified plants, application to animal agriculture will also occur. As with other new technologies, the risks of a biotechnology focus on unintended consequences (Thompson, 1997b).

As commercialization of biotechnology develops, the question is asked if products produced by genetic transformation should be treated differently from products developed by conventional means. Biotechnological development itself takes on varying dimensions of risk; however, most are likely risks similar to those that were (largely unknowingly) taken by agriculture each time a new technology was introduced into its operations. These were the risks of economic dislocation and structural change, as well as possible risks affecting health, environment, and sustainability of resources. The adoptions of new technologies in the past decades surely have changed the face of the earth as well as the rural world in the United States. Throughout the years since World War II, almost every technology developed resulted in fewer and larger farms. Today, society is demanding answers about the effects of biotechnology before it is applied. Voices of concern are heard about economics, human health, consumer concerns, practicality, environmental impacts, and rural life, as well as ethical and moral issues related to the new technology.

The public is less likely to be comfortable with the idea of transgenic animals than with genetically engineered crops. The transfer of foreign genetic material into animals (the development of transgenic agricultural animals) will likely have a fairly long scientific incubation period before it reaches practicality. The primary value of research on transgenic animals remains largely one for science. More immediate effects, however, can be expected from products of rDNA technologies that synthesize substances of biological and medical interest. The recombinant somatotropins and other peptide hormones are examples of such biologics. Genetically engineered and molecular vaccines are being developed. Enzymes and transgenic organisms for food processing and degrading environmental toxins are of intermediate potential. Novel plants with specific antigenic characteristics are beginning to emerge. The promise of the ability to accelerate the formation of new technology is widely accepted.

Recombinant bovine somatotropin (rbST) and porcine somatotropin (rpST) have been subjected to a very cautious regulatory system. Somatotropins are different from the steroid hormones used in animal production because the rDNA technology produced copies nearly identical to the natural peptide hormone. They must be administered by injection or implant; the digestive system digests the hormone. The same fate would seem to await any residues of the somatotropins in meat or milk. An issue is if there are unknown conditions under which consumers might indeed be exposed (Kuchler et al., 1989). Unresolved is the question about the possible adverse effects, if any, of increased levels of insulin-like growth factor-I (IGF-I) present in the milk of treated cows. Safety for humans, however, may not be the final consideration in the use of rDNA-produced peptides. The use of rbST to induce greater milk flow also results in the greater incidence of mastitis which accompanies any greater milk production, whether induced by rbST or intensive technology and breeding. That in turn could result in greater use of antibiotics. Anecdotal evidence also suggests shortened life spans of dairy cattle developed for intensive milk productions, with rbST or not.

The introduction of *ex ante* (before the time) economic analysis has raised new questions (Kalter et al., 1984). In addition to questions of food safety and quality, they turn to short-term effects, structural effects, and long-term effects (Kuchler and McClelland, 1988). A bottom line issue is which farmers, if any, will go out of business if the technology is adopted. How will the market be affected? Will consumers be the major beneficiaries? Will the environment be changed for the better or worse, or not at all? As DuPuis and Geisler (1988) remarked, the *ex ante* approach focuses on the institutional constraints that prevent farmers from taking advantage of new technology, rather than simply labeling non-adopting farmers as traditional or laggard. If technology is to be scale neutral, an institutional approach is called for that asks if the institution is prepared to help small farms compete in the era of new technologies. After three years of the availability of rbST for use with dairy animals, small dairy producers tended not to use it.

A new phenomenon has been used by activists: legal action and court orders. These tacks not only impose regulation but open the door to the imposition of different philosophic views on the course of research related to animal agriculture. In October 1984, two groups, the Humane Society of the United States and a critic of genetic engineering, filed suit against the USDA to stop experiments regarding the insertion of human genes for growth hormone into pigs and sheep. The justification was that the action violates "the moral and ethical canons of civilization," perhaps by leading to a precedent of further gene transfers that could disrupt the integrity of the animal species. The argument thus was drawn from an ethical viewpoint rather than from law or any perception of risk.

The major worldwide thrust of biotechnological efforts related to animals is in the development of transgenic fish. Some scientists regard such fish as a potential answer to the depletion of the world's fisheries and a practical way to increase protein intake for many malnourished people. Even if some fertile transgenic fish escape to oceans and freshwater bodies, the opinion is that the fish will not pose an ecological hazard. Others see the gene-modified fish as a potential threat that could permanently eliminate many species of other fish.

Laboratories around the world are working on transgenic fish. In many cases, fish are modified to grow faster than their wild or traditionally bred aquaculture counterparts. The new genetic transforms have demonstrated growth rates 20 to more than 1000 percent greater than the wild biotypes. Such transgenic fish, however, are wild types or nearly so and are fully capable of mating with wild fish. They could eliminate the diversity of wild populations. The risks may be a matter of context and viewpoints. Many countries may wish to maintain their wild populations and precautions are taken to prevent the escape of transgenic fish into the environment. Such escapes may be of less consequence in China, in which the environment supports few wild fish.

CLONING. The emergence of the cloned sheep, Dolly, in 1997, signaled the first successful cloning of an adult animal (Wilmut et al., 1997) and created the specter of cloning humans. The announcement created considerable apprehension and debate among international and U.S. governmental and religious circles; the focus was not on the risk to animal agriculture but to human society (Begley, 1997; *Economist*, 1997; Weise, 1997).

The issues of cloning in animal agriculture will be dependent upon the application of the technology. At the time, cloning Dolly was a remarkable scientific discovery that challenged the dogma that nuclear DNA becomes permanently inactivated as cells and tissues differentiate during the normal course of embryonic and fetal development (Fuller Bazer, pers. comm.). The clone, however, cannot be the same as the donor of the nucleus. The maternal DNA in mitochondria would be different. The environment in which the new individual would develop would also be different. The technology is expensive so that large numbers of cloned animals seem unlikely. Cloning, if it becomes useful for animal agriculture, will likely be limited to special uses. Moreover, embryonic duplicates (clones) have been available to animal agriculture for some time; new technologies, however, will be developed. The primary use may be directed toward development of transgenic animals. Applications using fetal fibroblasts have resulted in cloned calves (Cibelli et al., 1998).

The issues that cloning might present to animal scientists are those of animal welfare (the longevity and health of cloned animals is uncertain), consumer resistance to consumption of products from cloned animals, the spread of disease among genetically identical animals, and the trend of basic animal science moving from questions of efficient animal production to questions of fundamental biology that will benefit society in the form of biomedical science (Thompson, 1997a). A pervasive ethical question also remains regarding the human intrusion and intervention of animal reproduction (particularly in natural systems). Then again, intervention of the reproductive process has been the essence of pest control in agriculture.

As with other potential risks, a *fire wall* of legal restrictions might be built to prevent any harm that might result from cloning. As cloning will be so important to biological science in general, and animal science in particular, the elucidation of relevant scientific principles will surely be sought.

FOOD AND SOCIETY

Evaluations of risks must be done in the appropriate context. The increasing capacity to alter and augment the components of the human diet has improved greatly the nutritional level of the food supply. The question of dietary compositions in terms of foods, in contrast to terms of nutrients, takes on a new significance. For example, expanding populations of the world and major economic changes have an overwhelming impact and multiply the demand for food. This increase in demand has brought about a highly sophisticated technology in food production, not only in quantity but also in quality.

American society wants a large variety of foods throughout the year. To meet this demand, foods are imported. The alternative to importation of foods is to process and preserve. The processing and preservation of foods made available in the United States have less of a negative impact than preservation in countries such as China because these populations rely on consumption of foods preserved with agents that can initiate and/or promote the formation of stomach and other cancers (Campbell, 1994).

The availability of a wide range of processed and prepared convenience foods is of considerable assistance in feeding a family, particularly one in which the parent who cooks is usually at work during most of the day. Additives and packaging have been devised because we require our food to look appealing and have a pleasant taste. There are also economic forces. If corporations are to be viable, they must use equipment and resources in the most efficient way. There is therefore constant creation of new products for new markets.

Thus, the question of assessing risks cannot be considered in the abstract. The benefits and risks of food may be categorized as individual or public, voluntary or involuntary, and vital or non-vital. A vital effect is protection against the chance of starvation, illness, incapacitation, or loss of life. Foods may have medicinal roles, both therapeutic and preventive. Examples of disease-specific components of food and processing that provide benefits are those for pellagra in the 1920s and the increases of life expectancy through the decades. The past trends give confidence that the classical deficiency diseases (pellagra, rickets, scurvy, avitaminosis A, goiter, sprue), endemic causes of morbidity and mortality in the early part of the twentieth century, will not recur in developed countries.

The decreases in age-specific incidence and mortality figures for cancer and cardiovascular diseases in the United States suggest benefits of the current pattern of food usage, although attempting to relate these beneficial changes to specific measures is more difficult with such chronic diseases than with the rapid changes in the more acute conditions like pellagra or deaths from infantile diarrhea.

Today, the dietary benefits of plant foods over animal products are thought to rest in the beneficial constituents of plants (e.g., antioxidants, phytochemicals, complex carbohydrates and fiber, and protease inhibitors) versus the negative effects of dietary fat that some people believe has a practical association with the consumption of foods from animal origin. Although it is easy to focus on animal products in the diet as bearing risks, any positive or negative aspect of any food carries a relationship to the entire diet.

Consumers are showing increasing concern about hazards in their food supply. Attitudes toward foods are changing. Instead of searching for positive nutritional values, people are approaching food with the attitude of avoiding risk (Heimbach, 1987). If a suspicion of risk falls upon a food, it becomes a food to be avoided. The situation is often exacerbated by the amount of attention given in the media. Such attention has attributed a risk to consumption of animal products, although the populations that have consumed animal products are among those with the longest life expectancies (United Nations, 1992).

POLITICAL VALUES, INTERESTS, AND THE PERCEPTION OF RISK— WHO SHALL DECIDE?

The question, "How safe is safe?" is basic to the issue (Farrell, 1988). The Food, Drug, and Cosmetic Act (FDCA) and the Federal Insecticide, Fungicide, and Rodenticide Act (FIFRA) set the framework that balances the health and environmental risks associated with pesticides and food additives against economic and cultural backgrounds. The Delaney Clause of the FDCA, however, sets a zero or no-risk standard for carcinogens in processed foods. The *de minimus* risk standard of the FDA is less than one per million from lifetime exposure to residues in foods. Further revisions of law will determine which standards will apply.

In estimates of social risk one must deal with different issues and values (Christensen, 1988). First are the issues of the needs and wants of the public. Second are the issues of social values: history, philosophy, and politics. Third are the issues of fairness, legitimacy of institutions, programs, and systems, and public trust. Fourth is the focus on the idea of prevention. Fifth, we should consider how a change in program could affect other programs, although this vision of values may be naive in a real world.

Farrell (1988) described significant variations among interested groups as to which standards should apply:

1. Agricultural producers generally believe that the standards are at least adequate.
2. Regulators state that they are operating to the extent they can under law, but within constraints of resources allocated to them.
3. Consumer advocates are uncertain about safety standards, and argue that doubts about the risks that consumers face are justified.
4. Consumers themselves have a great concern that suspected or known cancer-causing chemicals are used in food production and that they pose long-term health risks.

Congressional action has stated that the DHHS and the USDA have joint responsibility for issuance of dietary guidelines in the United States. The fourth edition of *Nutrition and Your Health: Dietary*

Guidelines for Americans was issued in December 1995, jointly by both departments (USDA, 1995). External to the governmental, and the NRC and IOM's formal efforts toward nutritional guidelines, alternative concepts of dietary guidelines have been proposed that compromise the consumption of animal products. One of these is a set of guidelines based on a culturally determined diet, the Mediterranean diet (Willett et al., 1995). Such guidelines emphasize the use of olive oil as the principal fat, minimally processed fresh plant foods, and a consumption of red meat limited from 12 to 16 ounces per month. This diet has official standing only with the World Health Organization Regional Office for Europe. Whether such unofficial advice for dietary reduction of risk to health is a trend or a passing scene is not known at this time.

In turn, the defensive advocacy of the food industry has often been less than convincing. The response of animal agriculture to the growing concerns of society is not clearly developed. Part of the industry at least has responded to health concerns by accepting the principle that animal products can and should be *designed* to meet diet and health guidelines. A report of the NRC (1989b), *Designing Foods: Animal Product Options in the Marketplace,* calls for changes in the production and marketing system. The beef cattle industry appears to have accepted this principle and other parts of the industry are changing their products. Elements of the pork industry developed a production and marketing program directed at residue-safe pork. Not all of animal agriculture and its supporting industry agrees with such approaches. The practicality of designer foods against wide-ranging attacks on food safety is doubted. Consumer education is seen as an alternative approach. The active sentiment in the livestock industries is that irresponsible and inaccurate allegations must be defused; scientific validation is seen as the only valid basis for determining risk.

The animal agricultural industry and its scientific support, however, should not forget that a hazard *may* exist. That should be put in perspective, engendering neither unwarranted fear and paralysis nor willful oversight.

RISK AND DECISION MAKERS

Risks that are involuntary, artificial, or unfamiliar cause greater concern than those that are voluntary, natural, or familiar (Baker, 1990). People accept risks under their own control but do not easily accept risks over which they have no control. They are likely to accept a risk of natural carcinogens, but are less tolerant of human introduction of a similar synthetic substance into the system. They will more likely accept risks defined scientifically than those about which there is uncertainty. Issues of natural versus contaminants, known versus unknowns, and voluntary selection of a food versus involuntary exposure are inherent in conceptions of food safety.

Much of the public debate concerning regulation stems from failures to distinguish between matters of evidence and matters of values. Lowrance (1976) urged that such distinction be respected and openly identified. He termed it an issue of responsibility, the implications of which are important as one examines the roles of various persons in decision making. This issue remains today (Kunkel, 1996).

Lowrance (1976) divided decision makers into categories of assessors, advocates, and primary deciders:

1. "Assessors in principle try to maintain as much objectivity as possible keeping their personal opinions in subjugation while they shape questions, grade the reliability of pieces of evidence, chart options and plot the probable sequences of each of the options." Members of this group would include scientists.
2. "Advocates are less strict about keeping their subjective convictions in check; they openly and vigorously champion particular courses of action." Darby (1989) has suggested that some scientists who become advocates lose their objectivity.
3. "Primary deciders work from some base of power. After listening to both assessors and advocates, they make decisions that cause action to be taken: a Food and Drug Administration Commissioner making a ruling on a drug." Darby also suggests that scientists who become primary deciders may be influenced into making nonobjective decisions.

Institutions, as well as individuals, can play these roles. Barring legislative intervention, the authority of food safety and other regulatory decisions rests with the administrators of the regulatory agencies. The majority of these decisions will continue to be handled by the staff of a regulatory agency. The issues of consistency, fixing responsibility and alternatives, objectivity, efficiency, political acceptability, consistency with overall values of society, equity, and risk–benefit assessment lies heavily upon these decision makers. The process suggests that such decision makers should use the advice and guidance of representatives from a cross section of society, with appropriate technical panels designed to assess difficult policy issues in regulation and to recommend courses of action.

Courts often intervene, playing the role of authoritative decision makers, but there must be a concern about the ability of the judiciary to cope with the complex scientific and technical issues that come before them (Bazelon, 1979). Judges have little or no training in understanding and resolving problems of toxicology and other specialties or cases that often present questions engaged by experts for years without having reached a consensus. The problem is not confined to the judiciary. Legislators face the same perplexities. They also lack the basic knowledge at the core of important issues.

Scientists face the difficulty of being totally objective, while at the same time questioning the wisdom of leaving regulation to the scientifically untutored. Obviously, science and scientists have much to offer in terms of technique, expertise, data, and understanding. In reaction to the public's often emotional response to risk, however, scientists have been tempted to disguise controversial value decisions in the cloak of scientific objectivity, obscuring those decisions from political accountability. This is as true of animal agriculture scientists as of others. Commodity interests often take positions against what they regard as regulatory intrusions into their businesses, and scientists may be caught up in support of the commodity group.

CONCEPTIONS OF RISK

Risk is a commonly used word, but it cannot be appropriated as a technical term without inducing miscommunication (Thompson, 1990b). Risk is a word that classifies acts. It also describes future events. It implies uncertainty. It says something about what people do, sometimes on purpose and sometimes unintentionally. Drunk driving is an act that bears risks. Undergoing a seizure or being caught in an accident are events that also bear risks. People are held responsible for drunken driving but not for undergoing a seizure or being caught in an earthquake (Rescher, 1983).

Thompson and Dean (1996) noted that a formal definition of risk specifies formulas, data, quantitative relationships, and other terms that determine procedures for using the term risk in a specific context. Definitions are generally useful when the author, speaker, readers, and audience share the same basic conception. Thus, the development of methods to measure the relevant probabilities has led to risk analysis as an interdisciplinary area of scientific research. Scientists in this area of inquiry define risk as follows:

$$Risk_{def} = F[P(e), V(e)]$$

where e is an event or set of events, P(e) is an estimated or measured probability of occurrence for e, and V(e) is a function that assigns value to e. The term F is a function, variable with the application, that translates probability and consequence into a measure of risk. Risk is defined as a function of the value (utility) of events and the probability that the events will actually occur. The mathematical combination of utility and probability provides a basis for a theory of utility analysis (consumer choice). A mathematical combination of negativity and probability provides a basis for a theory of risk analysis. Utility analysis, however, may also identify choices in which a given outcome is available (Friedman and Savage, 1948). The expected value analysis of risk thus defines risk as a function of the probability and the expected value of future events (Thompson, 1990b).

Conceptions of risk, however, are not equivalent to definitions (Thompson and Dean, 1996). Much of the literature on risk proposes or presupposes a general conception of risk, then proceeds to offer a definition based on the conception without acknowledging the existence of alternatives. Risk, however, is a contested concept (Morgan, 1981; Douglas and Wildavsky, 1982; Plough and Krimsky, 1987; Shrader-Frechette, 1991). Different conceptions of risk lead to problems in assessment, evaluation, and communication of risk.

Thompson and Dean (1996), as a point of departure, offered two concepts of risk in diametrical opposition. At one extreme is a probabilist conception of risk. At the opposite extreme is the contextualist concept, which places probability on the list along with familiarity and other attributes. Thompson and Dean (1996) stated that it is unlikely that anyone holds either extreme view, but other conceptions can be mapped out in between them.

The probabilist takes probability as the essential characteristic of risk, usually presuming that risk also is characterized by a negative or unwanted consequence. For Starr and Whipple (1980), the fundamental core of risk analysis is a quantitative analysis. The analysis is a process based on collected data, anecdotal cases, and statistics, on which simplified models are invented to predict an outcome. Whenever the risk is an issue, different social factors and intuitions come into play. Intuitive risk assessment may not be considered a legitimate form of knowledge, but it possesses a great deal of influence in the political arena (Starr and Whipple, 1980). Somewhere in between the extreme positions, objective data on the political procedure and on scientific values or postulates may be used in the analysis (Shrader-Frechette, 1991). Technical assessment of probabilities are always employed, but other dimensions can be equally important for acceptability and communication.

The contextualist, for example, states that no single attribute is a necessary condition for the existence of risk (Thompson and Dean, 1996). In the contextualist view, some instances of risk involve no element of probability or chance. From this view, it may be possible to classify some instances of dread or mistrust as risks, but some element of change or uncertainty will always be present.

Thompson and Dean (1996) noted that weak probabilists of a different kind make claims based on a "preponderance of the evidence." A preponderance of the evidence operates in the legal community and implies enough probability to make reasonable claim about harm. Regulatory assessment may move in the same direction (EPA, 1996). In contrast, the scientific community's conception of risk appears to rest on the quantification of probabilities.

We believe that animal agriculture has been caught between the two conceptions of risk (Kunkel et al., 1998). As challenges were raised to animal agriculture, scientists often have sought out and attempted to take refuge in a negligible probability that harm would occur.

A contextualist approach also deals with the attribute of control which comes to the fore in talking about risk (Plough and Krimsky, 1987). People may raise concerns about risk as ways of expressing anxiety about loss of control without regard to the association between control and harm. In fact, scientists, by saying that science must rely on quantification of probability to interpret risk (implying that only scientists know probabilities and levels of harm), often frame their talk about risk issues in a way that sounds like an attempt to claim authority, power, and privilege (Thompson, 1995). Such talk is suspect, but also unsettling. The world has long passed the point that assumes agriculture can do without science. We suggest that specialists who work on risk issues can more effectively carry out their responsibilities if they remember that cooperative public solving requires genuine, honest communication.

CASE STUDY: A CONTEXTUAL EVALUATION OF RISK

Spongiform encephalopathies are fatal neurogenerative diseases. There is no treatment or cure. The infectious elements evoke no immune response and slowly accumulate. Although full consensus has not been reached, the dominant belief at this time is that the infective agents are prions or infectious proteins (Nathanson et al., 1997). They are practically invulnerable. They cannot be destroyed by cooking or freezing. Enzymes that degrade DNA and proteolytic enzymes of the digestive tract are ineffective. The infective agent can survive for years in the soil. The case of mad cow disease, bovine spongiform encephalopathy (BSE), presented governments, scientists, and cattle farmers with an unprecedented challenge, a risk that could be evaluated only within its unusual biological context.

Narang (1996) noted that the retrospective clinical evidence strongly suggested BSE appeared as a new disease and did not exist before 1984. The prevailing hypothesis is that the origin of the epidemic was food-borne infection, caused by an increase in the absolute numbers of scrapie-infected sheep entering the rendering chain, combined with changes in the rendering technology. The majority of animals became infected as calves through their feed. The disease became epidemic in Britain, with over 168,000 recorded cases by 1997.

Britain's record of handling the disease was mixed. Although the inclusion of ruminant-derived protein in ruminant feed was banned in July 1988, and the destruction of all animals showing signs of BSE was insisted upon in August 1988, these orders were not fully enforced. The meal was not sold, but supplies on hand remained and were used by farmers. The compensation plan for the slaughter of animals at 50 percent of market value for a diseased cow encouraged farmers to sell at full price on the market before symptoms became too obvious. Only in November 1989, did the government ban the use of certain bovine organs, thought to carry infective material (brain, spinal cord, and tonsils), in pies and sausages or other human food. The mechanical recovery of meat from backbones with some spinal cord tissue included was permitted until 1995. Yet for six years, evidence of BSE's ability to jump species (cats, a variety of zoo animals, marmosets, laboratory animals) was officially ignored. Ignored also was that each time encephalopathic diseases jump from species to species, the characteristics of the disease can change, including the host range.

It has been common practice for apologists of animal agriculture to proclaim that if there is no scientific evidence for a situation to exist, that the condition does not exist. For example, unequivocal scientific evidence that subtherapeutic usage of antibiotics in the United States has been detrimental to human health has not been obtained; therefore, it has been argued that such risk does not exist or is small. The probabilist concept of the risk would seem to support the argument, but the outbreak of 26 new variant CJD cases in humans during the mid-1990s (now 50 plus and counting) may place a different twist on such arguments. In the early 1990s, there was no scientific evidence that BSE is a human health hazard. Claims that British beef was safe to eat also could not be considered scientific when the question had not been tested and was perhaps untestable.

Thus, science could not provide the needed answers to provide even slightly the quantitative estimate of risk. What policy makers had to do was depend on circumstances and intuition to evaluate the risk, taking the contextualist route to evaluating risk. Essentially, this is what the British Ministry of Health belatedly did in 1996. It was what the European Commission did also when it banned the exportation of British beef and created crises for the British government and the Union itself.

The case of BSE should be a continuing study in risk assessment. The disease clearly became epidemic among cattle in Britain after 1985. Scientific evidence appears to focus on a probabilistic assessment of a feeding practice. The implications to human health could only be assessed in context. Could the infective agent be transmitted to humans through food, did human infection require other routes, such as through lesions in the skin, or was the new variant CJD an entirely human disease with its own dynamics? The context did not distinguish among them. Nor did science at the time, although evidence of the link now exists. Likely, the only way total assurance could be obtained would be the total elimination of transmissible spongiform encephalopathy from the cattle herd in Britain and elsewhere. Reservoirs of transmissible spongiform encephalopathies remain in sheep, deer, and elk in the United States. Do they hold humans or the U.S. livestock industry hostage or in jeopardy? One would hope not.

Unpublished reports suggest that chronic wasting disease in deer and elk may be also transmissible to humans. Three young people have died from a CJD-like disease and they were heavily associated with consumption of deer meat. As deer and elk share the range with cattle, the possibility exists that chronic wasting disease may eventually be transmitted to cattle. That possibility is only a possibility, as yet undetected.

CASE STUDY: A CONTEXTUAL EVALUATION OF GENETICALLY MODIFIED ORGANISMS

The year 2000 marks a growing skepticism of technology and increasing unease for the consumer and farmer alike. Consumers want to be assured about the origins of their food and farmers are questioning whether they can bear the expense of that assurance.

There are two components of communication risk (Groth, 1998). First, the expert policy-making community wants to communicate the substance and base of its decision. Second, the public, or those groups actively concerned about food safety and the risk management process, must communicate their own scientific interpretations. Scientists and regulators tend to focus on the quantifiable, probabilistic attributes of risk. The public tends to focus on the qualitative, value-laden aspects of risk, that is, on factors other than science. The context for each group is very different.

The human contextual aspects of risk assessment are highly visible in Europe. The European public, at the turn of the twenty-first century, has expressed a lack of confidence in the analyses of risk and the regulators. As time passes, this infection of doubt appears to be extending to the United States and other countries where public confidence in the regulatory system and science has been high.

The consumer backlash, that began with the BSE outbreak, has been extended in Britain and western Europe with repeated *E. coli* and *Salmonella* scares in the late 1990s. The way they were handled left a legacy of doubt and damaged regard of the regulatory system. The British public does not seem to be reassured that the government can make food safety decisions on their behalf. They are more likely to trust consumer groups, environmentalists, farmers and physicians.

The foci of debate now reaching the whole European Union are the risks that may be posed by genetically modified organisms (GMOs) in the food and feed supplies and the environment and by food products from animals produced with treatment by hormones. The issues include intellectual property, patents, and multi-national corporate control of the future of agriculture at one end and the right to know and make individual choices at the other end.

Thus far, there is no evidence that food from genetically modified organisms (say, crops with the Bt or terminator gene) are unsafe. Instead, public concern may derive from ethical, socioeconomic, and multi-national issues and lack of trust and consideration of the needs of small farmers of developing countries (Gaskell et al., 1999; Serageldin,

1999). These concerns have validity and should be taken into account. They become parts of the context of the risks of biotechnology.

Members of the European Commission, conscious of public pressure, argue that any food containing detectable genetically modified ingredients should be labeled. But American farmers, as have farmers in Argentina, Australia, Canada, China, Mexico, and now parts of Brazil, have been quick to adopt genetically modified crops. Disaggregating basic food and feed components are considered by the grain producing countries as no easy task, despite industrial efforts to divert unapproved crops from export channels. Trade negotiations in the future will no doubt be affected by the controversy.

Scientific consensus in Britain is that food containing genetically modified ingredients is safe to eat and that growing such crops is unlikely to have a worse impact on the environment than growing other crops (Nuffield Council, 1999). Desiring not to see the British biotechnology industry undermined by a barrage of negative coverage, the government has set in motion efforts to provide a strategic, long-term outlook in dealing with issues of genetically modified crops and food. A panel with both expert and public members was set up by the USDA to examine the effects of biotechnology from all angles: its creation, applicability, marketability, and related trade and inspection implications. There is also an underlying concern in the USDA action that biotechnology will "tilt the playing field" against the small farmer. Both Britain and the United States vow to open biotechnology regulation to greater public involvement. But, there may be an overriding factor: the patent and its ownership.

The ability in industrialized countries to patent, that is own, genes is a relatively new phenomenon in the world. The effects are uncertain in the future of agriculture. As the concept of intellectual property becomes a fixed element in issues related to biotechnology, the course of food and agriculture can be driven by the perceptions and goals in the laboratories and executive councils of global industry. Biotechnology has stimulated the interest of universities in patenting and income producing licenses. It has led to further privatization of agriculture research, fading the strict public/private separation of the past. It, however, is the advanced base of scientific knowledge and application.

All of this places responsibility on powerful industrial complexes that hold or control patents and intellectual property to reestablish trust and promote honest debate around the world on risk issues: environment, human health, and sustainability of the food system to protect the livelihoods of the worlds' poorest farmers. Biotechnological products or policies that limit the ability of farmers to grow their own seed will not be easily integrated into the traditional or indigenous forms of agriculture in the developing world.

Animal agriculture is involved. Genetic modification is now mainly an issue related to agronomic crops. But animal production in many countries is dependent upon modified crops for feed. The world is on the edge of serious entry of biotechnology in animal agriculture. There is a lesson for animal agriculture in the current controversy. Openness and accountability, and what is done for the sake of consumers and not just for efficient production, will be critical to public acceptance. Acceptance by the public or not is a risk for both animal agriculture and humans. The creation of genetically modified animals or biotechnological processes to improve the health of humans will likely receive public approval. The creation of modified animals for xenotransplantation, that is, as sources for organs for transplant into humans, may be rejected by many for ethical and cultural reasons.

CONCLUSION

Risks—and the conceptions of risk—are prominent issues in animal agriculture. They are the concerns of those in animal agriculture, the health professions, the activists, the legislators, academia, and the public. In the probalistic sense, risk assessment entails characterizing and quantifying the potential harmful effects of environmental substances on humans. Risk management, however, adds the contextual issues (socioeconomic issues) such as the costs to producers and the industry as well as the anxieties of the public.

The issue with chemical substances is the potential for misuse, but also that we do not know the mechanism of the genesis of cancer. Moreover, certain segments of the population, such as children, may have greater exposure than other segments to residues in foods. The principal issue with enteric and other food-borne microorganisms is that sanitation, manufacturing and slaughtering processes, food preparation and storage, and food service and home procedures can break down at any time. The issue with the uses of antibiotics in animal agriculture is that an irreversible flow of resistance to antibiotics in pathogenic organisms is occurring. The release of genetically modified organisms have a similar issue of irreversible gene flow. The issue with animal drugs is potential improper use or overdosage of hormones. In the case of DES, absolute bans failed to prevent its unauthorized use in Europe; a black market for hormones reportedly developed.

Now, the issues of standards for carcinogens and for food safety are gaining substantial attention. Highly debated is the proposal that economic considerations be made in setting the level of residues allowed on and in food. It is the unintended consequences that have stimulated the most debate over biotechnology (Thompson, 1997b). The unintended consequences of the use of rbST, which raised concern, stressed the social impact on the structure of the dairy industry. Unwanted impacts in the form of environmental impact, social dislocation, and economic or psychological stress are risks also and should be balanced against benefits of greater and more efficient agricultural production and the cost of food to the consumer. Unwarranted regulatory actions, however, pose risks to agriculture and consumers by diminishing agriculture's ability to produce food economically. These are risks difficult to measure. Until recently, the market had not measured costs and benefits for such unwanted consequences. As far as the market could tell, these were noncontroversial. The evident desire that milk products be labeled as being produced by rbST-free techniques or not, may reflect a change in attitudes.

The probability of an unwanted effect from a technology may be low, but when health and environmental risks cannot be avoided entirely, there is a frequent tendency for low probability risks to assume major importance in public debate (Thompson, 1997b). Such public attitude to low probability risks from (e.g., agricultural biotechnology) may seem irrational, particularly when compared to health risks associated with food-borne microbial diseases. Thompson (1997b) noted that those advocating fair practice place special emphasis on the impacts of human actions. People do not expect a naturally occurring microorganism to ask them if they are willing to be exposed, even when probabilities are high, such as they are in many kitchens. They do expect human beings who introduce a new substance or organism to inform them of risks, and to do so under conditions that allow a choice.

The activists, consumerists or environmentalists who cry danger also have responsibilities. Fiction, as well as reality, exists with respect to risk in maintaining human health (Foster et al., 1993; Whelan, 1993). Epidemiological evidence can be equivocal, but many litigations have been based on the conclusions drawn on such evidence. There is, however, a significant disparity between the ease with which a controversy related to a suspected hazard can begin and the difficulty in resolving the nature of the linkage, if any, between the suspected hazard and an effect on health (Foster et al., 1993). Admittedly, there is difficulty in determining the degree of certainty of any assertion, but assertion without some sense of uncertainty or probability carries with it a breach of integrity.

Can risk assessment be done democratically? The perception that it can stems from the observation that risk is managed through policy, and policy must be established with public participation in order to be relevant. Scientific questions of risk assessment, however, must be asked and methodologies must be improved. Some risks are more important than others, but as noted above, people are also more willing to inflict on themselves much greater risks than they are prepared to have imposed upon them.

How can public perceptions of risk be changed? Better public education is essential. Scientists can help assess the level of risks, if people trust them. Risk, however, takes on its ultimate impact when the human condition is fatal and emerges without warning. A fear of new unknown diseases is evolving, driven by the emergence of HIV infections, Ebola outbreaks, and BSE. Animal agriculture in Europe is entangled in the latter and it may become the case in the United States and elsewhere. No longer can it be assumed that if a risk has not been evident in the past, it will not become so in the future.

Assessment of risk, in the final analysis, may not serve society for the best. Assessment of risk asks the questions such as how much of a substance would be negligible risk. It does not ask what the alternatives to using the substance are. Society may be better served by the latter (O'Brien, 1993). What are our options in reducing the risk? How can we best institute precautionary behaviors? If society will not accept a practice or use of a substance or technology in any phase of animal agriculture, does science seek to open other acceptable avenues, or does science continue to painstakingly gather reproducible data for more acceptable assessments of the risk?

When we use the word risk, we establish a burden of proof. Calling something a risk calls attention to it. Public usage of the word risk is vague and unreflective. Risk must somehow be defined in more conceptual ways that frame terms and put them in the context of communication.

CHAPTER 8
FROM AGRARIANISM
TO SUSTAINABILITY

*In my boyhood, Henry County, Kentucky, was not just a
rural county, as it still is—it was a farming county. The
farms were generally small. They were farmed by families
who lived not only upon them, but within and from them.
These families grew gardens. They produced their own
meat, milk, and eggs. The farms were highly diversified.
The main money crop was tobacco. But the farmers also
grew corn, wheat, barley, oats, hay, and sorghum. Cattle,
hogs, and sheep were all characteristically raised on the
same farms. There were small dairies, the milking more
often than not done by hand. Those were the farm
products that might have been considered major. But
there were also minor products, and one of the most
important characteristics of that old economy was the
existence of markets for minor products. In those days
a farm family could easily market its surplus cream,
eggs, old hens, and frying chickens. The power for the
field work was still furnished mainly by horses and
mules. There was still a prevalent pride in workmanship,
and thrift was still a forceful ideal . . .*

*This was by no means a perfect society. Its people had
often been violent and wasteful in their use of land and of
each other. Its present ills had already taken root in it. But
I have spoken of its agricultural economy of a generation
ago to suggest that there were also good qualities
indigenous to it that might have been cultivated and built
upon.*

—WENDELL BERRY (1977:39)

AGRARIAN EVOLUTION

Perhaps no issue facing animal agriculture is more poignant than the issues of what agriculture was and is and might be. The world views of many in U.S. agriculture have evolved, from agriculture as primarily a production function to agriculture as a much more complex issue of managing resources. The issues for Wendell Berry, however, are the human factor and the community. "Neither nature nor people alone can produce human sustenance, but only the two together, *culturally wedded.*" (Author's emphasis)

The cultural integration of agriculture existing prior to World War II has been diminished by the intensification of agriculture in the United States and other industrialized nations. Agrarianism was rooted in eighteenth century European thought (Danbom, 1986). Its premise was that farmers and rural life formed the safest basis for a free society and a republican political system. Farming was thought to be the most elevated and moral of occupations because farmers produced the basic foods and fibers that all people needed. Farmers, shaped by nature, were regarded as more moral and wiser than urban citizens. As property owners and managers, they were independent, conservative, and freedom-loving.

Throughout the years between the time of Jefferson and now, the U.S. government held agriculture in high esteem (Danbom, 1986). It created a system of higher education that extolled agriculture: the land-grant university. It created the USDA and the state agricultural experiment station as a national system of agricultural research. It created a cooperative system of extending knowledge to the individual farmer and homemaker.

Those who sought a viable agriculture used the argument of doing something for the farmer. The farmer and the agriculturalist on the other hand, were not strongly interested in what was done in their name. An agricultural research system was created, more as a reflection of the emerging faith that science and technology, rather than politics or religion, were the means of individual and social advancement. It assumed that the current farming practices posed a threat to society so critical as to require public attention. Farmers began to be seen as people who had problems.

Historian David Danbom (1986) traced the transformation. The way farmers were viewed changed subtly: What was needed was for farmers to become professionals who would demonstrate their expertise by increasing their productivity and thereby serve society. That, however, was an urban and industrial judgment. As cities grew and became centers of wealth, power, and learning, both urban attitudes assumed dominance. The image of the farmer became increasingly unflattering. It was an urban image. From the sturdy yeoman farmer that Jefferson wrote about, the farmer was gradually transformed into a benighted hick, yokel, or kicker who did work requiring brawn, but little brain. The farm came to be seen as a place to escape.[1]

The supporters of agricultural research and education hoped to elevate the farmer through professionalization, but the people who aided the farmer and provided expertise (the researcher, teacher, county extension agent) became the professionals. The new institutions (colleges of agriculture, experiment stations, USDA) received little support or interest among farmers. Those farmers who wanted these institutions demanded practical, short-term gains. The traditional support base of the institutions became the professional farmers, chambers of commerce, bankers's associations, and agribusiness corporations. Even that may be eroding now as agricultural natural sciences mature and the problems of agriculture are changing from issues of productivity to public concerns for health, environment, quality of life, and economic stability.

Following Rachel Carson's *Silent Spring* in 1962, agriculture and its institutions came to be criticized for their reliance on chemicals and their apparent lack of concern about food quality, safety and nutrition, and for their emphasis on production at the expense of long-term ecological considerations. The energy and food crises of the mid-1970s led some critics to question if North American agriculture was sustainable. To these critics, the public institutions, particularly research institutions, were a major part of the problem rather than a part of the solution. The critics called for the preparation of a smaller-scale, more environmentally sound, less energy- and chemical-intensive, postindustrial agriculture; a new kind of agrarianism was described.

An increasing recognition of weaknesses and social costs of conventional top-down models of agricultural research and development has contributed to a rising interest in participatory and bottom-up approaches and concern for the sustainability of human and land resources for agriculture. The institutions of agriculture were scorned by others, such as Wendell Berry (1977), for helping to make agriculture more of a business and less of a way of life. Berry wrote "that [the smaller farms] were not cultivated and built upon—that they were repudiated as the stuff of a hopelessly outmoded, unscientific way of life—is a tragic error on the part of the people themselves; and it is a work of monstrous ignorance and irresponsibility on the part of experts and politicians, who have prescribed, encouraged, and applauded the disintegration of such farming communities all over the country."

Berry believed that agriculture had lost its dignity, its uniqueness, its satisfaction, and its ability to contribute to the larger culture and the community when it became more of a business. Abundance had come, but had it come through practices that threaten human survival?

Thus social changes in the 1960s and 1970s led to questioning conventional agriculture and the agricultural research establishment in the United States. Social injustice briefly became a priority problem. A new radicalism arose. Jim Hightower's (1973) book *Hard Tomatoes, Hard Times* struck at the land-grant college system as serving only the elite and corporate interests. Hightower claimed that small farmers, sharecroppers, farm laborers, and ultimately the consumer were harmed.

These new criticisms were rooted in the agrarian mode. Agriculture, they said, had inherent values and those values were diminished as farmers became more businesslike and professional. Critics believed the system had betrayed farmers. They asked the question, although it had been created ostensibly to preserve a special and valuable lifestyle, if the system in effect undermined that lifestyle.

Perhaps the system was unfairly criticized; it was dedicated to and had created a source of inexpensive and abundant food production for domestic consumption and export. The critics, however, argued costs: high costs to marginal farmers, agricultural workers, and rural communities; costs in soil and water resources; costs in making agriculture vulnerable in energy crises; and costs in developing a food distribution of long distances vulnerable to disruption. Critics called for a populist kind of agriculture, termed in various ways—organic, alternative, sustainable, or natural or regenerative agriculture—to be made the dominant form of agricultural production.

THE AGRARIAN ISSUE

Agrarianism, thus, is a recurrent issue in agriculture. Some authors, however, doubt that agrarianism can serve as a model or moral example. Madden and Thompson (1987) argued that agrarian themes have not figured prominently in any modern philosophical tradition of ethical thought.[2] Even if a new philosophical defense of agrarianism can be derived, it is difficult to see how the agrarian vision can support the modern commercial farm, a system that Berry admitted has gone far beyond the agrarian vision of people and the soil.

In many respects, traditional agrarianism has become rhetoric, not an issue. The family farm enjoys a special place in the American imagination (Madden and Thompson, 1987). For many, it is a symbol of national traditions. Yet agrarian tradition is now mixed with matters that are clearly issues: sustainability, use of fertilizers and hormones in agricultural production, soil conservation, agroecology, and participatory development. The agrarian model may be held as an argument that agriculture plays a role in society's social goals and, as such, agriculture must have social goals as well as economic ones (Thompson, 1986). In most of the United States, there seems little likelihood that the marketing infrastructure, which integrates agriculture with the world of business and human life support (grain marketing concerns, feedlots, the road system, supermarkets, the global market) will be diminished.

Is there then a justification for a new agrarianism? The answer would be a qualified yes. Perhaps, it is a fundamental integration of the individual with the setting that is agriculture. It is the need for community. It is a matter of self-reliance. It may be the reason why some graduates in animal science choose a career of taking care of cattle for other people. It is not only an aura. It also connotes responsibilities for those who work in the food chain: the supply of safe and wholesome food, the care of animals, the care of the environment (which includes soil, water, and air), the care of the resources, and the care of oneself. These responsibilities are consistent with what might be expected of twenty-first century agrarianism.

The most important issues flowing out of agrarianism, however, may be those resulting from the pervasiveness of the residual sense of it in the populace. Kirkendall (1987) touched on some of these when he wrote that "[t]he entire agricultural system, not just the farming sector, may decline, but working for its survival is the long-recognized importance of the commodities it produces. This element of agrarianism, if no other, still seems to have some ability to build support for American agriculture. It may persuade the appropriate people that they must do what they can to make or maintain a superior agricultural system."

The future is difficult to foretell, but the food and agriculture system is likely to divide itself into two components. One will be a group of niche agricultures (e.g., fruit productions, Christmas tree farms, organic farms, cheese makers, avocational poultry on farms, and even microbreweries) emphasizing products that have grown in public recognition and will survive. In this, a residual of agrarianism will exist. The other is the industrial or large commercial agricultural system that will evolve to provide an increasing fraction of the food supplies in developed countries. Huge livestock production units are displacing other commercial productions of pork and milk, as much as they have in poultry production and feedlot operations, largely by capturing the marketing system.

To many people it does matter that a form of agriculture is retained which gives status to the people who grow the food and tend the livestock. The persistence of the agrarian ideal in parts of the United States may be seen in the new small movement to community supported farms (M. Ostrom, personal communication). The community support and the cooperative nature of these farms are attempts by the larger community to retain farming as a way of life.

SUSTAINABLE AGRICULTURE

A development borne of modern agrarianism is the sustainability movement. Numerous issues have been folded under the tent of sustainable agriculture. Varieties of sustainability are implicit in a wide array of concerns about ethics, environment, economic and social equity, and appeal to a wide range of groups: environmentalists, food safety interests, food security interests, animal welfare advocates, animal rights groups, organic farmers, advocates of low inputs, regenerative agriculturalists, conservationists, and more.

There are also inconsistencies in this gathering of banners under the sustainability flag. Animal rights supporters would reject the use of animals. The concepts of alternative agriculture, a variant of sustainable agriculture (NRC, 1989a), see the use of animals as absolutely necessary for sustainable agriculture; livestock are seen as essential for sustainable family farm agriculture. The number of animals and the way they are handled, however, could be seen entirely differently from the world view that animals are commodities. Similarly, although sustainability is essentially an environmental ideology (Buttel, 1991), the movement seems to be maintained on its implications for consumption: food quality, health, and landscape.

Agricultural economist Vernon Ruttan (1990) has explored, with skepticism, some of the dilemmas of the broader concept of agricultural sustainability, stating that "[t]raditional agricultural systems that have met the test of sustainability have not been able to respond adequately to modern rate[s] of growth in demand for agricultural commodities. A meaningful definition of sustainability must include the enhancement of agricultural productivity."

Social and natural scientists who share common (pro-environment) world views see themselves operating as a sustainability community, concerned about agricultural sustainability and the agricultural–environmental relationships. Beginning in the late 1980s, increased political pressure was placed on the agricultural research system to develop environmentally sound agricultural systems. A variety of subsequent developments made a more ecologically sound agriculture a desirable goal for the research establishment (Buttel, 1991).

VARIETIES OF SUSTAINABILITY

Allen and Sachs (1992) identified three features that they believe have had the greatest impact on the sustainability movement:

1. The first is the belief—expressed by Wendell Berry, Wes Jackson, Marty Strange, and several dedicated organizations—that the preservation of environmental sustainability can be best achieved on the family farm. The belief is stated also that threats to the family farm come from the industrialization of agriculture, a loss of traditional values, increasing corporate ownership of agricultural firms, and a lack of an ecological approach in agricultural production.

In such emphases, however, the position of the farmer is usually not situated in the context of the global food system and changes by other players in the food systems, such as food processors, distributors or consumers, are rarely advocated.

2. A second policy force in sustainable agriculture are the proponents of safe, or organic, food. The current food production system is seen as unsustainable because it relies on pesticides and other chemicals that may pollute the soil and water, injure the environment, and endanger human health.
3. The third arena of activity is within the agricultural science establishment, the Federal Sustainable Agriculture Research and Education Program (formerly the LISA program), and special efforts in California,

Ohio, Illinois, and Iowa focus on scientific and technical solutions for developing sustainable agriculture. Allen and Sachs (1992) contend, however, that no overall analysis for sustainability is sought by the agricultural science community.

Although varieties of sustainability have created a Babel of stated interests, the broader concepts include food quality, food security, intergenerational concepts linked to ideas of stewardship, sustainable trade relations, and sustainability of the global biosphere. What began as a concept of the human on the farm is being broadened to a societal range of human organizations and institutions, the historic focus on production agriculture replaced by the perception of the entire food system.

ANIMAL AGRICULTURE

Considerations of sustainability provide arguments for strengthening and improving animal agriculture. The criticisms that animal products are the major sources of excessive fat in human diets, that the use of grain to fatten cattle is inefficient, that large units of intensive animal agriculture challenge the environment and are a serious nuisance to neighboring humans, or that ruminants contribute to greenhouse effects of methane by flatulence have a negative ring in consideration of matters of sustainability. Yet acceptance or rejection of any aspect of animal agriculture relative to its importance or its contribution to sustainability of agriculture is linked to one's value system. The low-resource, risk-prone agriculture of some developing countries may be too harsh a form to view it in terms of an agrarian ideal. Its animal agriculture has significant elements of stability and sustainability.

Williams et al. (1995) wrote that "[t]he songs of praise that emanate from the North and the South, from the feedlots of (the United States) and the semidesert of Somalia, from those who eat too much and those who eat too little are very different. . . . We must learn to understand the enduring relationship of people and cattle that has benefitted both for thousands of years. If we respect and build on the hard-won lifestyle of such people we might eventually arrive at development policies that help rather than hurt those at whom aid is directed."

What appears to be emerging, particularly in animal agriculture with its many forms, is the concept that participation of people in their development is equally as important as the concept of sustainability itself, as an initiative in social and agricultural change (Thrupp et al., 1994).

In the United States, inherent in the diversity of animal agricultures is a diversity of views of what will lead to a sustainable agriculture. Similarly, inherent in the diversity of scientific and scholarly disciplines that may seek the goal of sustainability is a variety of views of what sustainability is. Vavra (1996) described the pathway to sustainability as one based on ecological soundness that provides the essentials of vegetation cover, water-holding capacity, and lack of erosion to the landscape. Heitschmidt et al. (1996) proposed the concept of ecosystem to be fundamental to understanding animal agriculture. Sustainable agriculture is defined as those forms of agriculture that do not necessarily require exogenous energy. Long-term survival of the livestock industry is seen to be dependent on the continued availability of energy sources and increased revenue (to offset higher energy costs) and/or the development of new production technology (to increase the ecological efficiency of production).

The major threat is human population growth. Oltjen and Beckett (1996) emphasized the importance of ruminants in converting the renewable resources from rangeland, pasture, crop residues, and by-products into edible food for humans. Honeyman (1996), whose interests focus on swine production, suggested a model for a sustainable system in the United States that would include many modestly sized, independent, diversified family farms. Some farms would be large enough to allow specialization in modern swine production. The farms would be managed by owner-operators or long-term tenants who are good stewards of "land, air, water, soil, pigs, family, and community." The farms would be linked to networks for coordination and communication. Swine production would be management intensive, but with implications for a wholesome, balanced environment, healthy rural families and communities, profitable family-based swine and crop farms, and quality pork. In Honeyman's thinking, agrarianism and sustainability are equated.

ETHICS AND VALUES OF SUSTAINABILITY

The varieties of sustainability call for consideration of the philosophical problems associated with its different dimensions.[3] Thompson (1992) noted that the question of the normative or ethical significance of ecological balance often has been framed in terms of duties to nature or duties to future generations. These two ways of approaching the ethics of environmental issues have taken philosophers toward the debate between the ecocentric and anthropocentric ethical theories.

Two alternatives are expressed: Nature is intrinsically valuable, requiring that in some instances human interests be sacrificed to ecological values, or ecological balance is important because of its instrumental value for human use. This framework has proven fruitful for debates over endangered species and the use of public lands for recreation, mining, or as preserves. Thompson argued that it has proven singularly unhelpful as applied to agriculture. Ecocentric language can specify duties to respect or preserve nature, but gives little guidance with respect to environments in which agriculture has already replaced nature. Anthropocentric language can specify duties to conserve resources for future use, but fails to present any concept of ecosystem integrity as a moral obligation (Norton, 1991c).

New terms of sustainability may provide a framework. Thompson wrote, "Although contradictory notions of sustainability often arise as a result of divergent interests and social goals, a deeper philosophical ambiguity is the focus of concern here. Rhetorically, at least, the concept of sustainability presents a new way to frame the ethical questions about natural or ecological balance. *Sustainability presents an alternative to the ecocentric/anthropocentric dichotomy.*" (Author's emphasis) Although the meaning of sustainability is debated by different interests, it is a concept that can promise philosophical unity.

There is an irony in the search for sustainability (Thompson, 1992). One can presume a moral justification and a rationality that does not actually exist but act on that presumption with confidence. Paraphrasing Busch (1989), we can note that animal scientists have objectives— efficiency of feed consumption, milk or egg yield, a high lean to fat ratio and others—that must be chosen according to criteria which are basically ethical choices (although they may be constrained by practical matters).

The ethical nature of these choices, however, is seldom in the consciousness of the scientist. A scientist may also impose philosophically disputable values under the dress of scientific argument. Scientists may believe they are arguing matters of science, but in fact may be arguing beliefs. On the other hand, critics may also obfuscate by defining the dimensions of the system and selecting performance criteria in such a way that the ethical or political judgment is smuggled into an analysis without argument.

WHAT DO WE MAKE OF THIS?

The sustainable agriculture movement emerged in the 1970s and was strengthened in the 1980s as a challenge to conventional agriculture (Sachs, 1992). The major concerns were environmental problems, the increasing power of agribusiness, declining biological diversity, and specialization in farming. The movement also may have been a reaction of farmers to the severe economic problems of agriculture in the 1980s (Pfeffer, 1992), during which farmers sought to cope by reducing inputs.

Agrarianism and sustainability are issues that have common roots, although they may be divergent in their final outcomes. Agrarianism remains a human ideal, sought by some and ignored by others. Bonanno (1991) argued that the new organizational forms characterize a global restructuring of the agricultural and food system to a transnational-based system of production. Issues such as the continuous overproduction and the decline in the number of farms and agriculturalists in developed regions of the world have been linked with the persistence of a large agricultural labor force, inaccessibility of much of the population to food, and economic stagnation in the less developed regions.

The relevancy of the *agrarian question* has been eroded in advanced societies. The working populations of agriculture in industrial countries are small and decreasing. Farms have declined in economic importance in the food system. Relevance of the farm sector in political factors has been altered.

Another set of issues, the food and natural resource questions, has connected with the agrarian question. Overproduction has been typical of agriculture in advanced societies, but the abundance of agricultural production in Europe and North America has not been translated into uniform accessibility to food. Food is a commodity purchased by those who can afford it and its abundance is irrelevant to those who cannot. Labor released by agriculture is absorbed by alternative employment opportunities in places where these are available. If alternative employment opportunities are not available, the labor remains on the farm, often underemployed.

It is the perceived deterioration of the environment and the threat of running out of some resources by the usual practices of agriculture that has led to a demand for a sustainable agriculture. Most who envision such sustainable agriculture envision the diversified agriculture production of the past; a far-reaching revision of current agricultural practices is seen as needed to ensure the sustainability of the system for future generations. This belief went so far in Canada that the Science Council of Canada issued a recommendation in 1992 that the entire agricultural research system should focus on sustainable agriculture as the principal challenge.

This sense of the need for sustainability will likely infuse the discussions of issues in animal agriculture (Heitschmidt et al., 1996; Honeyman, 1996; Oltjen and Beckett, 1996; Vavra, 1996). The position, place, and conduct of animal agriculture will be seen by some as a challenge to sustainability of agriculture as a production system, a means of producing safe food, and way of life. Animal agriculture also will be seen as vital components of sustainable systems of food production and as important elements in the food security of populations, as well as in terms of a healthy symbiosis with the environment. Both visions will likely shape animal agriculture in the future.

It is also important to note that animal agricultures are not constants in the human and sustainability equations. Grain fed to livestock has been a flexible reserve of grain, varying with national and global supplies. Intelligent substitutions of knowledge (technology) can be made. Efficiencies of production can be improved. Animal products (e.g., poultry meat) can displace other animal products (e.g., red meat) in contributions to the human diet. Changes in climate can pose confounding factors; drought, floods, and extreme heat or cold can affect animal populations by altering feed supplies and costs or the viability of the animals. These suggest that structural changes in animal agriculture will occur in the United States. Such developments can be directed to both sustainable economic productivity of agriculture and a healthy environment. It is not simply productive agriculture or the market or the environment, but the interplay of these considerations that is the critical issue (Daly, 1995; Sagoff, 1995).

NOTES

1. This concept persisted into decades after World War II. Many agricultural scientists at work from the 1950s to the 1990s were among those who saw the farm as the place to leave. They, however, retained their farm background although they sought fulfillment in intellectual work rather than farming. A continuing interest in helping those who remained on the farm probably shaped the course of agricultural science more than any societal factor.

2. Thompson (1990a) suggested that Jefferson's agrarianism is quite different

from an agrarianism that points toward establishing rights to farm. Thomas Jefferson's attitudes toward farming were practical and politically motivated. Thompson noted that no right to farm appears in the Bill of Rights. Jefferson's commitment to farming arose from his judgment of its service to the revolutionary virtue of democratic citizenship. His persisting interest lay in the formation of a democratic state.

3. The reader may be interested in a detailed examination of the philosophical problems regarding the concept of sustainability. It is suggested that the reader turn to Thompson (1992), Norton (1991c), George (1992), and/or Blatz (1992).

CHAPTER 9

LAND USE

Nor shall private property be taken for public use, without just compensation.

—BILL OF RIGHTS

Among all of the contemporary issues in animal agriculture, the issues relating to human–animal interrelationships in using the earth's physical resources are moving front and center. Humans have spread over the world, reaching even the remote islands. In so doing, the human population has manipulated the distribution of life on earth (Vitousek et al., 1996). Among the significant redistributions have been the genesis, development, and amplification of animal agriculture in all of its forms.

The effects of spreading human populations and redistributions of life are economic and ecological: widespread changes in land cover and land use; alterations in the geochemical cycle of nitrogen (Smil, 1997) and other elements; displacements of animal and plant species by other species, including humans; and challenges to human rights to hold property. This chapter is about such issues. It is about both the conflicts and interdependencies between humans and animals for space, water, and air. To simplify, we titled the chapter "Land Use," but the issues imply more than a single focus.

The earth's ecosystems, both managed and unmanaged, provide essential life support services to both human and animal populations (Kunkel et al., 1996). These services range from food and human health, fibers, housing, and energy to decomposition of organic wastes, oxygen production, and maintenance of biodiversity.[1] As human activity expands and uses or encroaches ecosystems, it can also reduce the environment's ability to provide such goods and services. Polluted air and water and contaminated food will affect human health and welfare directly. The managed ecosystems—agriculture, forests, and waterways—are also more than biological systems.

VALUES AND INTERESTS

There are two major conflicts of values in the United States that impact the uses of land. One visualizes farming and ranching as ways of life with which industrialization clashes. The second is the conflict between both conventional and industrialized agriculture and environmental interests.

WAY OF LIFE. The first conflict is between the conception of farm stewardship and land as instrumental factors in food production and the ultimate substitution of technology for land and labor. It is a separation of the farm household from the farm management. It is also a matter of retaining a self-concept of people in agriculture as families who produce the means of their livelihoods under conditions of economic independence and personal autonomy (Thompson, n.d.). The traditional farm family sees the family farm as a place of connection with personal identity and self-expression.

The conflict has historical roots (Berry, 1977; Kirkendall, 1987). Thompson pictured Wendell Berry's (1977) vision of the transformation away from family farming this way:

Berry's ecology of the virtues links personal loyalty, family identity, and community solidarity. Traditional farm life assigns tasks to each member of the family, so that the husbands do the plowing and planting, wives tend to butter making and baking, children tend chickens and elders make quilts, jams, tools and tend to other farm needs. Each member of the family can see the importance of their work to the overall survival and prosperity of the family. The family is the source of production that sustains each member. Children learn that actions have consequences. This vision does not deny self-interest, as portrayed in the discourses of liberty, efficiency or opportunity, but now in the family farm, self-interest is turned to the virtue of family loyalty. In industrialized economies, by contrast, the relationship between work and prosperity is mediated by money. Family life requires cash that must be earned outside the home. Jobs are held to support the family, but the family itself no longer exists to perform work. Those who don't work—children and retired elders—do not form part of the integrated, self-sustaining production that defines family identity on the farm. As a result, the family becomes defined as a consumption unit. Production is severed from consumption, and the moral significance of land . . . disappears behind a veil of rights and needs.

The same transformation of the duties in family farming impacted animal agriculture. Farm flocks of chickens and poultry have become mainly hobby activities in North America. Pork production is increasingly transformed into large units in the United States and western Europe. The growing competition of larger dairy farms is deeply felt by the remaining small dairies in the United States. The exception is the small cow–calf operation that remains as a major component of beef cattle production, although there is a trend toward very large and very small units. Even among the family farms, the trend is toward specialization.

None of these, however, is an inexorable trend. The commodity sectors, particularly cattle and dairy production, may remain multidimensional. Industrialization has been undergirded by inexpensive livestock feed, formula construction of animal diets, the transport system, and in the case of the dairy industry, inexpensive irrigation water to produce alfalfa and other forages. Concentrated animal production has occurred where social, economic and political barriers have been minimal, but the reemergence of such barriers just might result in maintenance of some of the traditional dairy regions in the United States.

The trend toward separation of people from the land as a source of their livelihood, and of ownership from work, continues. Strange (1988) suggested that farmers are defining their interests individually in terms of their own well-being rather than in terms of the well-being of family farming. The goal of many of the remaining family farmers in North America is to own their own destiny, to have control over resources, and to have a capacity to change things for the better. Every farmer wants to own that first piece of land, then another, and perhaps another. The irony is that farmers who retire want to hold on to land, seeking others to operate it through rental or other arrangements.

Strange (1988) also suggests that the movement along the continuum from family farming toward industrial agribusiness is pervasive and incremental, affecting nearly every farm. What was once considered an adequately sized farm is now considered as being very small. In the process, it is difficult to tell when a farm has stopped being a family farm and has become an industrial firm. Aggressive owners of family farms may acquire additional land and other units. Ownership may change as the farm is incorporated and equity sold to others to gain capital.

The values associated with family farming traditionally have been used to legitimize agricultural policy formation in the United States and western Europe. The passage of the 1996 Farm Bill in the United States and the fiscal crises of the European Union, however, have tended to undermine the position of family-based agricultural units as a social force in advanced countries. In Europe, family farming is valued less as a model and more as a means to enhance the socioeconomic conditions of farm dominated rural areas (Bonanno, 1989). In the United States, income and land ownership become the goals. Those who have bought into industrial values are now the farmers with the most political power (Strange, 1988).

Although the diversified farm with its multi-crop and animal mixture still works, specialization will take its place as the dominant production system.[2] The small unit farm may survive when the income is maintained by off-farm employment, or in a contractual relationship supplying specialized products (e.g., chickens) to an industrial processing unit, or perhaps as a family small business filling a niche in specialty items (e.g., sausages, organic farming products, flowers and ornamentals, a place for recreational outing). The ranch and the horse breeding and training farm can fit the family undertaking. A nascent movement in a number of areas in the United States is community supported agriculture (Ostrom, pers. comm.). Community supported farms build coalitions with one another to develop and exchange practical knowledge, coordinate public outreach, pool material resources, and provide assistance to new or struggling farms.

We also can expect land to retain some moral significance (Thompson, n.d.). Whatever the form—crop, ranch, specialty, recreational, or whatever—farming the land can still integrate interpersonal loyalties and reciprocities into a life in which family, community, and region are important, and in which production and consumption are complementary to actions that reflect loyalties to specific individuals and groups. Land by itself, however, or even in the form of rural homesites, green parks, and landscaped facades, is not enough. It is the nature of human interrelationships and relationships with the land that count as virtue. Views of liberty, efficiency, and opportunity modify the meaning of the model of agriculture as a way of life (Leopold, 1949; Doyle, 1985; Comstock, 1987; Callicott, 1989; Thompson, n.d.).

ENVIRONMENT AND PRODUCTIVITY. The second significant conflict of values exists as environmentally oriented agendas clash with the productivist values of agriculture. The argument is that the land is sensitive. It can be hurt. Soil is a nonrenewable resource and so are some subterranean supplies of water used for irrigation. The pools of crop, poultry, swine, and dairy germplasms have been reduced greatly, although the productivities of plants and animals have increased markedly. The industrial revolution of agriculture in America and elsewhere, caught up in the diffusion, dissemination, and application of technology, has engulfed animal agriculture in many ways.

Agriculture in the United States is increasingly large-scale and increasingly specialized with a focus on productivity. For some moralists, the emphasis on efficiency and productivity has yielded an agriculture that is unsustainable (Berry, 1977; Doyle, 1985; Comstock, 1987; Strange, 1988; Callicott, 1989; Crouch, 1991): Soil erodes; irrigation water is not replenished; the microorganismic ecology of the soil is disrupted; chemicals are used; and nonrenewable fossil fuels are the primary energy driving the agriculture.

All farmers by definition—large or small, traditional, organic, or modern—create a different ecology, an agroecological system. All farmers may be subject to the ecocentric critique. Whether one reads ecocentrism strictly or liberally, such holistic approach is not the only approach to farming (Comstock, 1995). The rights tradition holds that people have a right not to go hungry when food can be made available to them. Utilitarians generally hold that the best consequences come from feeding people by putting land into production.

THE AGROECOSYSTEM ETHIC. The ecocentric argument, often used in critique of the agroecosystem, can be reconstructed to include these elements (Comstock, 1995):

1. Ecosystems are teleological systems.
2. The good of an ecosystem is judged by the goal toward which it is internally directed (i.e., its mature equilibrium state).
3. To destroy the mature equilibrium state or any part of the system that will prevent it from attaining its mature equilibrium state is to destroy the ecosystem.
4. Moral agents have a direct duty to ecosystems not to destroy them or any part of them, the destruction of which would prevent the equilibrium from reaching its mature state.

In the scientific view, there is no single mature state. Comstock (1995) noted that through time, a geographical location exhibits many states of mature equilibrium, "none of which can simultaneously exist with at least some of the others." The current state of any ecosystem may not be an equilibrium state. Nonequilibrium theory is replacing the equilibrium concepts as an ecological principle on which ecosystem function is based (ESA, 1996). Previous changes, some anthropogenic, may have created an unstable state, which may be a state that must be overcome rather than maintained. Here we are reminded of highly overgrazed and deforested lands that require more than being left abandoned.

Ecocentrists hold an intuition that nature is composed of intrinsically valuable biological wholes. As Comstock (1995) argued, however, ecocentrism cannot rest on intuitions. An ethic must bring its components—moral principle, moral judgment or intuition, and the relevant background information—into equilibrium. It follows that ethical systems also must be built on sound science.

What then should the agroecosystem ethic be? Perhaps it should be some combination of utilitarian and rights-based approaches in the Western tradition, but extended to protect the legitimate interests of individuals who have preferences (Comstock, 1995).

There is also a conflicting philosophical argument. Ecocentrists have a goal of reducing human impact on nature. This ecocentric thought puts mankind outside of nature and the evolution that is imposed on the natural system. The natural/artificial dichotomy presumes that humans have been imposed on the natural system; however, the basic premise of ecocentrism that human activity is not natural seems flawed. If humans have evolved, it follows that whatever humans do is also natural. The human influence is pervasive in all systems, including those that are designated as wilderness. The question is what are the best relationships considering both short- and long-term goals and concerns.

PRODUCTIVE USES. Broadly stated, people derive minerals, energy, food, fibers, and other natural resources of economic use from the environment. People potentially can deplete these resources or degrade the biological systems on which continued production depends. Natural resources are transformed by industrial activity into products and energy services that are used, disseminated, ultimately discarded, or dissipated, thus creating wastes that unless recycled, flow into the environment.

Also, issues related to food and access to food are more than pollution and contamination. There is a growing perception that the right to food be recognized both in concept and in practice as a universal human right. If there is a moral imperative, let it be this: The agricultural community, including animal agriculture, must incorporate sustainable food security for the world's poor and the health and safety of all people as overlaying missions to which their work is dedicated. This is the fundamental dependence of human well-being on land.

LAND USE, HUMAN RELATIONSHIPS, AND ANIMAL AGRICULTURE

Other chapters in this book detail critiques that argue that animal agriculture should be extensive and utilize forages rather than compete with humans for grain resources. Implied in this argument is a need for a direct connection of animal production to land, particularly in temperate and tropical climates. Ruminant animals do utilize vast amounts of feedstuffs that are not humanly edible and grown mostly on wide ranges of uncultivated land. In parts of the United States, however, the balance between the animal population and land is shifting toward concentrations of the animals.

As one travels through the countryside of some of the eastern European countries (e.g., the Czech Republic or Slovakia), one is struck by the absence of agricultural animals on the scene. They are there—cattle, swine, poultry—but confined, out of sight, off the land. They are being fed, reared, and maintained inside buildings or in other year-round confinement. This practice probably follows decades of influence by the former Soviet hegemony after World War II, and reflects the methods devised in Russia for severe winter climates.

Of course, the apparent absence of livestock from the land in eastern Europe is illusory. Livestock must eat and the feeds they eat are produced on the land. Livestock produce waste and the ultimate sink for these wastes is the land. Animal agriculture remains integrated with crop production. The animals are concentrated also, although at smaller scales.

In another part of the world, there is no relationship among people, animals, and land use more poignant than in Latin America's lowland tropics. Most of the cleared tropical forest becomes pasture (Hecht, 1993). In the transformation from high-biomass forests on the Amazon, both the environment and people are victims. Species of wild animals and birds are lost. Carbon is added to the atmosphere. Hydrologic patterns are shifted. Microclimates are sharply altered. Soils are degraded. Forest people are displaced. Their livelihoods are diminished to ashes.

Lowland tropical areas have seen a disproportionate increase in population as a result of aggressive programs of colonization, the advance of road and other infrastructural development, and concerns for national security (Hecht, 1993). The lowlands, however, do not play a large part in food supply. They are constrained ecologically, as are all tropical zones, by fragile soils and pests.

The suggestion has been made that the emphasis on cattle raising stemmed from the increased demand for inexpensive beef in North America. The infamous *hamburger connection* was alleged (Meyers, 1981; Lewis, 1991). Concerns regarding cattle ranching in Central America as a major factor in deforestation attempted to link it to fast-food beef consumption in the United States.

Nations and Leonard (1986) suggested that the beef cattle–deforestation dilemma is one of inefficiency, not the conversion of rain forests to hamburger. They claim, however, that even though cattle ranching cannot be blamed as the primary cause, deforestation is related to "economic progress." In fact, logging is often the first step in deforestation (Repetto, 1990). Logging often is followed by complete clearing of trees and a shift to cattle ranching and inappropriate agricultures. International market dynamics have little to do with the expansion of cattle production along the Amazon. If deforestation were primarily a result of the workings of commodity markets, the solution would be a straightforward reduction of demand, but beef imports from Latin America are generally less than five percent of the U.S. total beef imports. Demand for beef has fallen in North American markets. Yet deforestation continues.

Factors that marginalize small farmers in Latin America are at play (Hecht, 1993). The structural change in agriculture (reduced labor demand and transformed access rights to land), expulsion of peasants by violence, excessively small holding sizes, and mechanization make small farms less viable. Left behind will be the fate of the landless poor (Hyde et al., 1996). The precarious status of the landless, and not the loss of diversity and other forest goods alone, may be the most important result of deforestation. In this, animal agriculture remains implicated.

In Latin America and the Philippines, the aggregation of the better agricultural lands into large farms and estates pushes the growing rural population into forested frontiers and upper watersheds. The connection in Brazil that promotes concentration of land ownership is the soybean meal market for pork production in Europe (Carroll, 1991). Small farmers, once stable, became redundant and were displaced; they had to choose the city or the land in the Amazon, as an indirect result of the industrialization and concentration of European pork production in the Netherlands and Denmark and a resultant high demand for Brazilian soybean meal. Such a scenario suggests that other uncertain and indirect global trails exist relative to impacts of consumption of animal products, hardwoods, and minerals.

ANIMAL AGRICULTURES AND HUMAN NEIGHBORS

Landscape qualities are valuable to any community, rural or urban. Deterioration of the rural landscape or the city block is a factor that the inhabitants of a community find dispiriting. Maintenance of rural landscape qualities became a desired goal for the public good in both Europe and the United States.

By its own definition, environmentalism finds itself at odds with the industrialization of agriculture. Confinement of livestock may be a way of easing the environmental critique: out of sight, out of mind. The maintenance of open, varied, and biologically rich landscapes, however, also begs for carefully targeted and economically efficient policies to sustain land uses that provide the public good. Relative to some animals (e.g., dairy and beef cattle and horses), some communities do not wish their animals to be *out of sight*. They regard such livestock as environmentally sound and needed for the vitality of the community. They perceive pasture as the place for animals. Seasonal, pasture-based animal agriculture is visually appealing. It also is seen as a basis for viability of the community; however, it is a vision that sees a larger number of producers feeding cattle on pasturage rather than a smaller number keeping dairy cattle in confinement year-round.

In 1996, the issue was summarized in the popular media (*Economist*, 1996):

Take two cows. One is a marvel of high-tech farming. It lolls in the straw in a giant shed. . . . It has been bred by artificial insemination and vaccinated against a variety of diseases. Once a year it has antibiotics inserted up its teats. Round its neck is an electronic signally device which opens its personal feed bin. The animal produces over 25,000 lb. of milk every year, roughly twice as much as Britain's average dairy cow.

The other, nonchalantly chewing the cud on an organic farm . . . is surrounded by a circle of admirers. For today the farm is open to the public. Visitors, worried about the recent mad-cow scare, have flocked from miles around.

This cow was sired by a live bull, not a pipette. It eats no manufactured feed, and its blood is free from drugs. Crops grown on the farm are fertilized by its manure, not by some chemical cocktail. The trouble is that the milk is more expensive than intensively farmed milk. Many visitors may be inspired by the cow's back-to-nature feeling. Fewer will buy its milk.

The setting for this comparison is Britain. Milk costs may not be higher with extensively produced milk elsewhere. In fact, some studies indicate that a small herd pasture-based dairy in some circumstances in the United States can be profitable (Murphy et al., 1996; Washburn et al., 1996). Such studies also find that the economic and organizational incentives for small and medium-sized producers are different from those of large intensive producers. Many individual managers and owners of small operations will not adopt intensive management methods to increase profits, due to the extra management required and because a status quo is available (Stuth et al., 1991). When the status quo is no longer sustainable, the farmer will leave the business. On the other hand, corporations will adapt intensive (confinement) management schemes to increase profits. This dichotomy applies to much of animal agriculture in North America.

The relationship of an animal agriculture operation to its neighbors is based on perceptions: Is it a neighbor that is pleasant or at least innocuous? Does it support the local economy? Are the values of my property enhanced (or not diminished) by its presence? The importance of these perceptions seems to be increasing. A critical stage in the relationship has been reached with particularly pork production in some states (Freese, 1994; DeLind, 1995; Honeyman, 1996; Keeney, 1996; Satchell, 1996). Pork production, following the pattern of poultry production, has entered a phase of extensive industrialization. The direct use of the land is minimal, but the spillover (actual and as a figure of speech) extends beyond the site. In the intensive facility, thousands of pigs are reared in specially designed, environmentally controlled buildings (DeLind, 1995). The pigs never go outside, are separated by age and sex, and raised using the latest management and nutritional technology. Conditions inside are spotless. Employees take a shower each time they enter the plant. A sign guards the entrance, "Warning, Disease Control Area."

In the meanwhile, the number of farm-sized swine units has dropped precipitously (Kleiner et al., 1997). The economy of the local small town may be threatened when the large firm buys equipment and supplies from distant suppliers. Also, the industry is plagued with a burden: too much sewage and too much manure concentrated in one place. Estimates are that 1 ton of chickens will generate 9 tons of waste a year, beef cattle 17 tons, dairy cows 24 tons, and pigs 32 tons (Satchell, 1996).

The huge volumes of excreta generated by hog units are generally applied to land or stored in settlement and evaporation lagoons. There are odors and spills and perceptions of water contamination (Letson and Gollehon, 1996). Unless well constructed, the lagoons might leak or break. The nutrient-rich waste may be sprayed on land, but it can be overapplied. Pollution of waterways may follow. The claim is made, hopefully appropriately, that lagoon spills and random dumping of dead animals can be blamed largely on individual pork producers, not corporate producers and their contract farmers. The swine industry, however, is less able to blame careless operators on the escape of gases and aerosols from the operation. Odor problems have become real issues as large facilities are built. The smell factor alone, or certainly the fear of it, may increase the number of voters who want the factory hog facilities to go away.

New technologies are likely to be developed to reduce odors and prevent the fouling of waterways. In the meanwhile, society is dealing with the issues. Local groups are using the courts in attempts to block construction. States are requiring state-approved plans for disposal of manure across all classes of livestock: poultry, swine, ruminant feedlots, and dairies. In Iowa, large livestock facilities must keep a larger mandatory distance from people's homes. Missouri has set requirements for setbacks of structures and lagoons. In Iowa, Michigan, and other states, however, new laws and guidelines based on new techniques and technologies also shield conforming operations from local complaints and suits.

The disaccord between the human community and animal agriculture can be extended to rangelands, particularly the public rangelands. Here the community may be mostly transient tourists and nature enthusiasts, but that means only that the impression is carried to wider reaches of the national populace. The West is also experiencing urban flight into open lands. On public lands of the western United States, concepts of multiuse public lands are increasingly accepted (Vavra, 1996). Since 1960, public values assigned to rangeland resources have turned away from livestock grazing toward greater aesthetic uses, preservation, and animal welfare (Heady, 1994). Livestock production must be compatible not only with grazing capacity but also with the maintenance of such products and services as migratory songbirds, large native herbivores such as elk and deer, fish habitat, and the safe capture, storage, and release of precipitation. Values are assigned also to endangered species, old-growth timber, tramped down riparian zones, abandoned and broken fences, and what appears to the public to be malpractice.

Trust and sensitivity are needed. The human sensitivities in the community must be recognized as dimensions of land use that require continued attention in the face of changing animal agricultures (Liebhart, 1993; Lal et al., 1995; Honeyman, 1996; Oltjen and Beckett, 1996). We sense an emerging trend that people do not wish the close company of any animals for which they do not have the responsibility of care.

THE WASTE STREAM

The problems with animal waste intensified on the heels of a fast-growing intensive livestock industry: the U.S. poultry industries in the 1950s and beyond, the beef cattle feedlots in the Great Plains and West in the 1960s and 1970s, the U.S. pork production industry in the 1990s, and similar events in other countries.

Managing the waste stream requires the use of land. Each step of the U.S. food production process, beginning with photosynthesis, yields by-products or waste (CAST, 1995). They include crop residues, the waste generated in the feedlot and slaughter house, and the excesses of inputs such as fertilizers and pest control chemicals needed for sustained crop production. Waste occurs when any input is spilled or used excessively. Pollution occurs when inputs and wastes escape into the environment. Soil erosion is in fact a generation of waste in the food production system. Runoff from cropland contributes to suspended and dissolved solids and an increased biological oxygen demand in waterways.

Waste may create problems of air quality in confinement buildings (Honeyman, 1996). The combination of hazardous gases—carbon dioxide, carbon monoxide, and hydrogen sulfide—and dust may pose significant hazards to swine production workers. Manure and dead animals are always considerations. Noise, odor, dust, flies, and rodents can be nuisances.

Livestock waste is handled in a variety of ways. An economic and environmental synergism between crop and animal productions has resulted as animal wastes are used for fertilizer (Honeyman, 1996). If the land is handled improperly, environmental problems can occur

(NRC, 1996b). Poultry, swine, and dairy manures rich in nitrates and phosphorus have the potential for pollution, but nutrient control can be used to decrease nitrogen and phosphorus in excreta. Alternative treatment plans, intensive grazing systems, composting, solids separation, and biogas productions are additional methods. Dead animals can be disposed of by a rendering industry and subsequent recycling.[3]

Currently the problems are regional. Farms throughout much of the United States continue to integrate animal and crop production, even in areas of intensive animal production such as the northern central and Great Lakes areas (Letson and Gollehon, 1996). In other parts, particularly along the East and West Coast states, the balance is less favorable. The issue is whether animal producers control or have access to a cropland base to balance the manure production. Across all animal types, however, the structural change inherent in the trend toward concentrated and specialized production breaks the traditional link between manure and cropland for manure disposal. Large specialized farms in the Pacific, Delta, Southeast, and Appalachian regions of the United States produce most of the animals in these regions but have little cropland. This presents new challenges for management and policy makers.

Volumes of poultry and swine waste are being stored in settlement and evaporation lagoons. Lagoons require careful construction, and most importantly, continuous attention. Such lagoon systems do not have the controls and sophistication of urban sewage systems. As breakdowns in the systems occur and are reported in the media, such as the fish kills and threats to wetlands that occurred in the early 1990s in eastern North Carolina and Maryland, and as odors offend neighbors, waste handling will increasingly be subject to public scrutiny and reaction (Satchell, 1996). Technological solutions are probably the long-term solutions, if the large unit continues to be the mode of production. As noted earlier, however, zoning restrictions and regulation by state and local governments will likely be sought in areas in which the human–animal agriculture interface is intensified. Composting is an alternative, but a market for the compost is necessary. A shift back to decentralized production systems may be forced.

Technological developments can promote recycling efforts. Thus land can be used to modify the waste stream, take value from the waste in the detritus system, and assist in an environmental cleansing. This, in addition to production, will continue to be a major use of agricultural land, but resilience, detrital organisms, weather patterns, and water flows, all vary from site to site. Municipal type sewage systems are not a likely solution, as socioeconomic constraints limit such uses. Animal agriculture will have to continue devising its own systems. The ideas of how to do this are not new (Taiganides, 1977). Investigations continue, and solutions to the problems are imperative.

RANGELANDS, PUBLIC AND PRIVATE

Rangeland is land on which the indigenous vegetation is predominantly grasses, grasslike plants, forbs, or shrubs, and is managed as a natural ecosystem (Kothmann, 1995). Rangelands include natural grasslands, savannas, shrublands, deserts, tundras, alpine communities, marshes, and meadows. Forages produced on rangelands are not harvested or used directly by humans. Grazing by livestock and game animals constitute the primary economic use of the forages. Management is primarily through control of grazing, use of controlled burning, and brush and weed control.

As with other natural resources, the purpose and status of rangelands may be seen from different world views (Box, 1990). A used range, grazed and productive and in fair condition, may be seen by some as valuable to society. For others, such rangeland may be wholly unacceptable, particularly to those who wish the resource to be in excellent condition and less productive of livestock and wildlife. The condition of the range is highly visible to those who travel it. Overgrazing is particularly visible and can and should demand attention, although to some environmentalists, any grazing by domestic animals is overgrazing. Cattle ranchers with cow–calf herds own or manage almost 800 million acres of range and pastureland, or about 35 percent of the U.S. agricultural lands.

Two questions may be asked concerning the use of U.S. western public lands for animal production (Heady, 1994):

1. Should grazing be allowed on public land?
2. Will removal of livestock from the public land return the rangeland ecosystems to near pristine conditions?

The first question is clearly societal and normative. The second may be answered by the biological sciences, but is asked in the presumption that the answer will assist in solving social and normative issues. The controversy expressed in these two questions includes elements of biological and social sciences, decision making in the courts, national policy, and political conflict. A public call for the removal of livestock has been made, but thus far, drastic action has been avoided (Vavra, 1996). A third question must now be asked:

3. Do livestock producers have a responsibility to protect natural ecosystems?

The public rangeland question in the United States is one of maintaining a delicate balance of user interests and public perception. Power in the U.S. Bureau of Land Management (BLM) has been concentrated at the state director level and strongly embedded in state and local interests heavily influenced by the grazing industry (West, 1982). An allegation has been made that western water and grazing subsidies are classic examples of patronage politics at work (Durning and Brough, 1991).

Today, public rangelands are managed largely by the BLM and the U.S. Forest Service (USFS) under acts of Congress that require management for multiple uses. Private rangelands are controlled by the people who own them. Rangeland scientists generally believe that the future of grasslands is dependent on the provision of technical and expert information for institutional policy deliberations and for multi-interest group compromise (Heady, 1994). They are optimistic. For over six decades, improved vegetation and the stabilization of habitats have been recorded. Knowledge has accumulated relative to regrowth and survival of plants, optimization of grazing, and biological diversity. The cure, however, is incomplete. Many riparian and other range areas were abused by too many animals for too long a time. Riparian areas may be resilient but other range areas have not been.

Rangeland ecosystems continually respond to temporary changes in the physical and biotic environments (NRC, 1993a). The process of degradation involves the interaction of changes in biological, physical, and chemical properties of soils as well as changes in the vigor of plants, the species composition, litter, seed germination and seedling recruitment, total biomass, and other functions. Soil erosion by wind and water is a major factor in soil degradation.

The soil itself may be a principal index of the extent that plants, animals, and climate are knit together into the integrated whole (Ellison, 1949). Of the indicators, the soil's organic carbon content and available water-holding capacity may be the most important. Land, however, cannot be just said to be healthy, at risk, or degraded on the basis of soil characteristics. The distribution of litter, plants, and roots are also indicative of site degradation. All indicators must be taken together to evaluate the uses of range and other lands. No single index has sufficed.

Rates of recovery of degraded land can only be inferred, not predicted with precision; too few attempts to rehabilitate land have been made (Daily, 1995). Natural rates and paths of natural succession vary widely. Factors influencing succession on land abandoned after some combination of cropping and pasturage or after overgrazing are complex, but the severity of erosion, invasion of ex situ seed sources (such as may be carried by birds and animals), the rainfall pattern, and other factors are involved. Natural plant residents of range areas (juniper, mesquite) have grown amok in many areas of rangeland, squeezing out forage plants (Whittlesey et al., 1993). As a result, reclamation of degraded land will likely require human intervention to assure a rate and path of succession that would improve the land (Daily, 1995). Intensive management is likely to be more productive, particularly with lands that have not been stripped of topsoil, than recovery of self-sustaining ecosystems. Exclusion of human activity from an ecosystem, particularly one degraded by past disruption or misuse, can be the wrong approach.

We can presume that the current emphasis on environmental issues will be reflected in governmental regulatory activity. The shift of emphasis from point-source to nonpoint-source pollution of water will likely lead to regulation unless landowners voluntarily improve watershed quality. Reports of meetings and the formation of new alliances among ranchers, environmentalists, BLM range conservationists, and USDA range scientists suggest that discrete problems may be solved by local cooperation.

SOCIOECONOMIC IMPLICATIONS. The western U.S. livestock industry has a significant dependency on public lands (Field, 1990). Much of the land in western states is federally owned and there is insufficient private land to maintain the level of production without grazing on public lands. Grazing pressure may decrease in the future, however, as a result of attrition of the industry. The traditional method of operation is being challenged by higher fees, lender resistance, a mature market for red meat, and emphasis placed on balanced multiuse management that includes recreation, mining, timber, wildlife, livestock grazing, and preservation of species and ecosystems. The desire to displace livestock grazing may stem from the argument that livestock are continuing to damage public rangelands (CAST, 1996). The perennial public-policy issue is the contention that the fee charged for public-land grazing should be raised to the rental level charged for grazing private lands. Ranchers on public lands argue that the preponderance of data shows steady improvement in the condition of public lands since the 1930s and that ranchers must bear the costs of providing improvements (water and fences) on public lands.

PROPERTY RIGHTS

State laws relating to rights to agricultural lands, for the most part of the last half of the twentieth century, were related to ownership and protecting the family farm over corporate competition, not environmental concerns (DeLind, 1995; Stout, 1996). Federal regulatory laws, however, have focused on the environmental issues. Federal regulatory actions do affect property rights: the presidential designation of three million acres in Utah as a national monument in 1996, the Farm Bill of 1996 focusing on environmental issues of land use, and the Endangered Species Act of 1973.

To varying degrees, property rights include the rights to exclude others from one's property, occupy and derive beneficial use, convey, and bequeath (McElfish, 1994). No one, however, has the unconditional use of one's property. Property rights are not inalienable; they have never been. They are a creature of society and change as society changes (Frances Philbrick cited in Vaughn, 1994).

TAKINGS AND REGULATION. The Fifth Amendment of the Bill of Rights of the U.S. Constitution ends with the words, "nor shall private property be taken for public use, without just compensation." Thus the land reforms seen periodically in developing countries in modern times were cut off in the United States by granting a constitutional right (Carpenter, 1994).

Both environmentalists and land rights advocates agree that when the government seizes land (e.g., for roads and schools), owners deserve to be compensated. Then, the arguments diverge. The land rights movement maintains that regulation without compensation also strips the owner of a fundamental liberty. Environmentalists believe that many of today's ecological problems stem from ordinary activities of millions of people, not the actions of a small group of dirty industries. Issues revolve about regulations being applied to private lands. Facing the property rights activists argument are the environmentalists whose interests are in social goals and who hold to a fundamental rule that owners should not use their land in any way that harms the community. The property rights camp defends its position with the theme that the right to own and use private property is sacred.

Both sides have turned activist, a natural consequence for those with environmental interests, but an unusual position for farmers and ranchers. Farmers, however, are joined by developers, loggers, miners, oil and gas producers, and a legion of home owners resulting from development and the urban sprawl, making a group of special interests with a substantial political clout.

Until the 1990s, property rights activists fought their campaigns primarily in the courts while the environmental interests used the legislative means and local government to impose a variety of important environmental regulations. The U.S. Supreme Court, however, has established the principle that regulations can constitute "takings." The courts have examined takings and property rights numerous times, sometimes ruling that property has been taken and compensation must be paid or that the regulation in question must give way (Hamilton, 1995). In other cases, the courts have ruled that reasonable regulations of land, such as a requirement to implement soil conservation or efforts to protect prime farmlands from development, are not constitutional takings.

The legal protections for property rights have not changed, but the number and nature of public policy regulations that may have an effect on how land property can be used have clearly increased, whether it is in the form of environmental causes (e.g., those dealing with water quality) or resource conservation such as soil conservation programs (Hamilton, 1995). Hamilton further stated that "[t]he collective effect of these regulations appears to have had the effect of taking away private property rights, some of questionable value or controversial science (for example, the restriction on the use of habitat to implement the endangered species act) that has attracted many people to the property rights movement."

The attraction of the property rights movement to farmers and landowners may be a natural result of political frustration. The agenda of the property rights movement, however, may be more than the protection of private property rights (Hamilton, 1995). The movement also may be seeking ways to curb or roll back environmental rules through the legislative process by imposing new requirements for compensations.

ALLOWABLE USES. An important distinction in the takings issue concerns the difference between the actual exchange of property interest and the regulation that directs how an allowable use may be conducted (Carpenter, 1994; Hamilton, 1995). For example, a zoning ordinance that forbids the use of an area of land for a feedlot or swine production could be a takings issue. On the other hand, the requirement for a feedlot or other animal unit to have a permit if the number of animals exceeded a stated limit would not normally be a taking. Hamilton (1995) listed several limitations to the constitutional protection of private property:

1. Water quality protection, such as requiring a nutrient management plan for disposal of animal wastes.
2. The permit required to operate a feedlot, a means of regulating economic activities that can have an adverse effect on public health.
3. Limitation of grazing rights on public land as part of a grazing permit. The land is public, not private property, although long-standing agreements might be seen as tantamount to a grant for private purposes.

THE UNCERTAIN CASE—THE ENDANGERED SPECIES ACT. The issue of takings that was most uncertain in both legal and legislative circles was a 1973 amendment to property rights, the Endangered Species Act. The act broadly protects a species against harm in some way, including degradation of its habitat. Under the 1973 law, destroying endangered species or their habits is considered unacceptable, and a property owner does not have the right to engage in it (Goldstein, 1996). In conformity with legislative tradition, which ordinarily does not compensate one for not doing an unacceptable act, compensation was not provided for not destroying a species or habitat. Uncompensated also were protective measures that could range from limited management changes to land set-asides. Until the mid-1990s, the administration of the Endangered Species Act, although determined to be valid by the U.S. Supreme Court, created frustrations among property owners. The Clinton administration, however, recognizing the political sensitivity of the issues in the mid-1990s, began using habitat conservation plans worked out with property owners to administer the act. The incentive for landowners was the promise of no further encroachment and bother by the government. There, however, is little information concerning the effectiveness of the conservation plans

(Kaiser, 1997). At this writing, the content of a reauthorized Endangered Species Act is uncertain.

Biodiversity and genetic reserves are broad international values provided by specialized and local natural resources (Hyde et al., 1996). Protecting biological diversity, however, is difficult because neither plant nor animal species respects property lines. Protecting a few target individuals also does not guarantee either diversity or long-term survival of the species. The protection of biodiversity requires more than fences and permanent restrictions of productive end uses. The spatial problems as well as incentives in the ESA have not been solved.

RIGHT TO FARM

The flip side of the regulatory issue is the right-to-farm laws. Such laws in one form or another have been enacted by all of the United States. They generally are designed to provide protection to existing farms, including livestock operations, by changing the common laws about nuisance to give farmers a defense if they were there first (Hamilton, 1995).

The societal framework also is changing here. As a result of the increasing attention to property rights, neighboring land owners have objected to the right-to-farm laws and sued. They claim that the right-to-farm nuisance protection effectively removed the neighbor's property right to protect the property from the intrusion of odors or contamination of waterways. As intrusion of odors may decrease the value of land, particularly if a human residence is involved, the right-to-farm laws also may represent a taking.

Society through its legislators may promote laws that protect economic as well as environmental interests. In the case of right-to-farm legislation, a spatial separation may be mandated in association with the right to protection against nuisance litigation, as is currently the case in Iowa, Missouri, and other states.

THE MICHIGAN CASE. DeLind (1995) chronicled the development of the right-to-farm legislation in Michigan, which could be a case study of changing definitions. The legal case was initiated as a protest from residential neighbors that a large, corporately structured, total confinement, swine production facility was polluting the area's air and water resources, and that it was a form of animal agriculture detrimental to family-scale farming and destructive of the quality of life at the local level. Through township zoning ordinances, residents curtailed the local expansion of intensified swine units. Through lawsuits, they placed legal constraints on the way the operation could manage its manure lagoons and apply the manure to land. In the process, definitions changed and issues were reinterpreted. The victory of the facility's neighbors was blunted.

First, agricultural scale was identified as an issue. Intensive operations, particularly those corporately owned and operated, were cast as a qualitatively distinct form of agriculture.

Second, Michigan's Right to Farm Act of 1981, intended to protect existing farming operators from nuisance suits, held that a farm was exempt from certain environmental standards, particularly odor control, as long as it conformed to "generally accepted agricultural management practices" or it existed before a change in land use or occupancy of land within one mile of the farm, and before such change would not have been a nuisance.

Third, after a series of legal actions, there was growing doubt as to whether large, intensified livestock units could claim their operation was normal and traditional for the area. State governmental responsibility was also acknowledged. Conflicting demands were to be faced. It was no longer possible to ignore or deny the impact of agriculture as a source of pollution. At the same time, if the state was to become agriculturally competitive, then high volume, state-of-the-art enterprises had to be assured of a hospitable environment.

The central issue then changed from the question of if intensive units were a form of industrial agriculture, and thus subject to the same environmental regulations and inspections as any other industry, to the issue of protecting the right to farm, both as a generic right and as a specific legislation. The challenge to the right-to-farm legislation was interpreted as a threat to free enterprise. There was a blurring of class-based distinctions; all farmers were lumped into a single class of independent entrepreneurs.

Finally, the legal argument was made that "flagrant environmental abuses" were the transgressions of "a few isolated producers" (DeLind, 1995). Framed within the context of right to farm, the animal agriculture controversy was redefined as an individual, not a systemic, problem. It was a problem to be remedied with improved management and techniques and "good will," not structural reform. It melded an uncritical belief in free enterprise and free trade with an equally uncritical belief in family farming.

A precedent was not set as the emphasis was at local and state levels. The issues created by a new kind of agriculture (industrialized agriculture) and other social factors such as the collapse of smaller, owner-operated, agricultural enterprises and the right to own residential property, will likely persist. Students of animal agriculture should take note. This is an area of legal ferment, but is likely to be a local and individual state reaction, with focal points on risks to water supplies, the nuisance factor, and if such operations are in the best interest of the community. The right to do animal agriculture is challenged by the community, but the entry of the federal government into the fray does not seem far off. EPA strategy calls for aggressive enforcement of the Clean Water Act of the nation's largest concentrated animal feeding operations.

AGRICULTURAL-PRODUCT DISPARAGEMENT LAWS. Akin to the right-to-farm laws are a spate of recently passed agricultural-product disparagement laws, which provide the right for animal agriculturalists and other growers to seek damages if someone suggests that a crop is unsafe to eat. The issue is if such laws violate the first amendment to the U.S. Constitution guaranteeing freedom of speech. American journalists have long been allowed to say what they like, as long as it cannot be shown that they knowingly spread lies or acted with reckless disregard for the truth. Under food disparagement laws, the burden of proof is shifted. Anyone who says a crop is dangerous has to show that the claim was based on reasonable and reliable scientific data. Whether or not such libel laws are constitutional has not been tested in court at this writing.

IMPACT OF U.S. FEDERAL POLICY ON PRIVATE LAND USE

The history of U.S. federal policy demonstrates the powerful impact of vacillating policy on the use and integrity of whole regions of lands. In this, there is a history of mistakes and repeated reversals of policy.

Kothmann (1995) noted that most of the cropland in the mid-United States (the Midwest and Great Plains) was originally rangeland. The start was with the Homestead Act policy which required farming the land. That led to the Dust Bowl of the 1930s. Farming as practiced then was obviously an inappropriate use for much of the western lands. Spurred by drought and accelerated erosion of Great Plains croplands during the 1930s, the federal government purchased 5.7 million acres of highly erodible cropland and converted them back to rangeland.

Conservation was the goal. During World War II, the plough was again unleashed. Then during the drought of the 1950s, the government acted through the Soil Bank Program to convert nearly 29 million acres of cropland to perennial vegetation at a cost of almost $2.5 billion. After this program expired, most of the land was returned to cultivation. In the 1970s, it was "plough it up again." Conversion of rangeland to cropland accelerated. In the 1980s, under the Conservation Reserve Program (CRP), almost 34 million acres were returned to perennial vegetation. Each time, a cost was levied on the people of the country.

The first farm bill was passed in 1930, and these bills have been seen as a way to increase farm income, curb erosion, and support an active rural population. Support for crops turned into the production of surplus crops (food grains, feed grains, cotton, dairy, wool, and others) and less freedom to plan alternative crops. The 1996 bill completed a trend: a phase out of crop supports and replacement by an emphasis on conservation. Grassland, wetlands, and aquatic species benefitted. Wildlife has become a goal of most farm conservation programs, as well as water and soil conservation.

The legislation marked another marked change in agricultural policy, toward removal of agricultural price supports and placing agriculture almost wholly within the global market structure, while the public continued to pay for environmental benefits associated with farming and ranching. The legislation scarcely resolved all issues, but it established the importance of incentives toward environmentally sound agriculture. The nature of the political process related to agriculture, however, also changed. The conclusion is this: Agriculture in the United States will lobby more like other industries do. Agricultural committees of the Congress will become less significant. Subsidies sought will be in tax expenditures and relief from regulation. The landscape is likely to change, again.

LAND RIGHTS, INTERNATIONAL

EUROPE. The new structure of western European agriculture has paralleled that of the United States (Bonanno, 1989). It has become increasingly polarized, consisting of one band of small farms and another of large farms. The larger farms have declined in number, but control an expanded area of land and a greater proportion of agricultural production. The small farms in turn are decreasingly dependent on agricultural income and increasingly dependent on alternative income; however, the small farms and green areas persist and remain a characteristic of the European landscape. In this scenario, Europe as well as other advanced countries, will be faced increasingly with the existence of two very different agricultures: one that controls production and the general commercial end of the spectrum and one in which farming as an apparent way of life is maintained.

Additionally, the increased political power of environmental groups has placed environmentalism as a central political issue in several European countries (Bonanno, 1989). The green movement has acquired significant electoral power in national as well as European Union (EU) elections. Future agriculture in Europe will depend largely on solutions adopted to address environmental problems.

These trends, however, are slower to develop in Portugal, Italy, and Greece. In Portugal, latifundia dominate in the south and small farms in the north (Bonanno, 1989). The crisis in Portugal is inefficiency and underproduction. Limited amounts of irrigation and protective agricultural policies have been characteristics of Greek agriculture. The farms in southern Italy are small, but agricultural units are larger and more efficient in the north. European agricultures and land uses are diverse among the countries and characterized by cultural, political, and social variations. A common agricultural policy, however, exists in the EU and the problems experienced by each individual country are curiously similar.

DEVELOPING COUNTRIES. Land-rights rules are particularly complicated in developing countries. An NRC report concluded that the greatest barrier to implementing sustainable practices in developing countries are not scientific or technical (NRC, 1993a). As in industrial countries, the barriers are social and political.

In many parts of the developing world, farmers do not own the land they cultivate. In some countries, farmers have lost ancestral territories to commercial interests. Without long-term tenure, they may exploit the land only for short-term gain. They fail to obtain loans because they do not own the land they farm.

Livestock, land use patterns, and human activities remain entwined in the arid and semiarid regions of the tropics and subtropics. Williams et al. (1995) described the interrelationships:

Farmers . . . , where resources are scarce, the soil thin and marginal, and the rains unpredictable, have found a way to survive by keeping livestock. Settled stock-keepers live in small scattered groups because marginal lands will not support intensive, irrigated agriculture of the kind carried out in Europe. Nomadic herders move with the rains and the grazing opportunities and carefully husband their resources. On subsistence farms cattle supplement human muscle power by pulling plows and transporting surplus produce to market. Cattle consume resources that otherwise cannot be exploited: they eat grass and crop wastes rather than grain. Their dung is used as fuel, as building material, as fertilizer. Their milk is a major source of protein for children. Hides and surplus milk are sold to buy clothes and seed, to pay medical expenses and school fees. For pastoral people living in areas too dry for arable farming cattle and small ruminants are essential.

In some measure, these conditions reflect rangelands throughout the world.

The governments of developing countries, however, tend to view the pastoralist way of life as backward and incompatible with administrative objectives such as tax collection, economic development, and provision of health and education services (Williams et al., 1995). Hence, governments promote sedentarization (i.e., subdivision of ranches), and irrigated agriculture is advocated instead of mobility and trade.[4] This occurs even when sedentary agriculture is not compatible with the ecology of arid lands. Division of land into small blocks, each with one owner, destroys pastoralism. As a result, the escape from disease and insects becomes inherently more difficult.

Tradition guides land use patterns in most developing countries, but traditional agriculture loses space when it comes up against population growth, industrialization, and urbanization.

PRACTICAL CONSIDERATIONS

A key issue of land use should be sustainability and maintenance of future options of the land resource. A contemporary extension of the vision is that of the healthy agroecosystem (NRC, 1993a). The framework of the healthy agroecosystem can implement sustainability, which is now an anthropocentric goal. But health is defined in terms arrived at by scientific and social consensus in which there is a plurality of expectations.

An accepted indicator of the biological health of an ecosystem has been biological diversity. Biological diversity, however, does not define biological integrity. Diversity can be expressed simply in terms of numbers and kinds of animals, plants, and other items. It is a collective property of the system. It could also be a measure of the piecemeal conservation of the species as intended in the Endangered Species Act. It, however, does not necessarily tell about the comprehensive health or the biological integrity of the system supporting these species. If the health of the ecosystem is the goal, maintaining a habitat for an endangered species from encroachment may simply be treating a symptom, not a root cause of an unhealthy environment.

The capacity of an ecosystem to produce commodities and to satisfy values on a sustained basis depends on internal, self-sustaining ecological processes such as nutrient cycling, soil development, and the structure and dynamics of the plant and animal communities (NRC, 1993b). If a rangeland does that, it may be called healthy. Thus, the terms healthy or unhealthy are also applied to ecosystems as indicators of the proper functioning of ecological processes resulting in the production of commodities and values. However, as the National Research Council (NRC, 1993a) stated, "It is also clear that the evolution of rangeland health is a judgment, not a measurement."

Many cattle ranchers believe their ethic and practice to be compatible with environmentalism in that they see aesthetic values about the integrity, stability, and beauty of the environment to be important for sustaining the resource they own. In the Western tradition, the cattle ranchers's love of nature is expressed in stewardship and conservation of water, soil, grassland, and wildlife. They do not consider livestock farming to be intrinsically destructive.

A motivation toward stewardship should be productivity now and sustainability of the resource for children and family, but except for horse farms, the larger cow–calf operations (ranches) are unique among North American animal agricultures in that they have held prospects of intergenerational transfer of the resources as a general incentive. In this sense, a community of cattle ranchers has cast itself as embracing an ethic guiding their use of a substantial proportion of the land in the United States, without necessarily defining the components of the ethic.

An ownership factor is also embodied in the integrated brush (i.e., rangeland) management system described by Stuth et al. (1991). A hierarchical process is proposed:

1. In order for a practice to be implemented, an individual must first be able to maintain ownership of the property (i.e., make the land payment and maintain some standard of living for self and family [livelihood]).
2. To protect against catastrophic losses, there must be activities that re-

duce risk and stabilize income to assure a standard of living and maintain ownership (security).

3. It is only after these needs are met that the owner will consider expending revenues, generally borrowed to improve the ranch and meet higher order needs. Once the needs for ownership, family, and risk avoidance are met, then the individual or owner can consider capital expenditures for technologies or knowledge that are more profitable.

Property rights, the right to farm, the environment and the community become entwined in the practical uses of land.

CAN THERE BE A UNIFIED CONCEPT?

Land uses have been polarizing issues. Often a proposed land use or regulation of land use—be it an urban development, a set-aside for a park, a restriction of habitat destruction, conversion of forests to pasture, or concentration of animals in confinement—is opposed by one group or another. Economic interests are involved. The prominent criticism by media and intellectual circles of land use practices is on ecological grounds (Loker, 1996). The concentration of land holdings and intensive animal agriculture is criticized on the grounds that they violate agrarian and farming traditions and the rights of other property owners. Can such conflicts of such disparate views be resolved?

The value of the ecosystem and biodiversity is a nonmarket valuation. Shogren and Crocker (1995) stated that the first step in nonmarket valuation is eliciting the knowledge of the services provided by the set of resources to be valued. Second, nonmarket valuation must provide opportunities for people to reveal their preferences for the resource relative to other goods (e.g., environmental image versus a grazing operation). Third, hypothetical valuations over a range of services can capture such preferences. Finally, real money with real decisions over repeated market experience will improve the precision of nonmarket valuation. Then, with time we can learn what becomes important to society relative to the uses of land.

Borrowing from Angermeier and Karr (1993), we note that inherent in the consideration of land uses are concepts of community and ecosystem. Community perspectives are grounded in biological (agricultural) changes and focus on the dynamics of the distribution, abundance, and productivities of plants and animals. Community has a human component. Ecosystem perspectives are based on thermodynamics and focus on flows of energy and materials through and around organisms, soil, and human inputs. Integration of both perspectives can provide a new view of ecological transformation and the human use of land.

Thus a more penetrating perspective of the ecosystem, including the agroecosystem, might be provided by the perspective of the human, biological, and physical integrity of the system. The language of integrity demands the inclusion of human thought. Systemic integrity may be an essential precursor of sustainability. As with sustainability, the definition of systemic integrity can take different forms, perhaps with the emphasis on community rather than ecosystem.

Relative to connecting agriculture to the concept of systemic integrity, Angermeier and Karr (1994) wrote that "[e]ven the value of many artificial, human generated elements (e.g., agricultural landscapes) depends on naturally evolved elements and processes, such as nitrogen-fixing bacteria and soil formation." Because of the pervasive effects of human actions, however, it is often difficult to characterize naturally evolved conditions.

Systemic integrity cannot be measured by biological integrity alone any more than it can by productivity alone. One influential concept of biological integrity is defined as "the capability of supporting and maintaining a balanced, integrative, adaptive community of organisms having a species composition, diversity, and functional organization comparable to that of natural habitat of the region" (Angermeier and Karr, 1993). This definition, however, will not work for an agroecosystem. Comparability to the natural habitat of the region is a weak argument for the systemic integrity of an agroecosystem.

As with biological integrity of a landscape, agricultural productivity and environmental integrity of a landscape deal with processes. Systemic integrity focuses on the organizational processes that generate and maintain elements of diversity, ecosystem health, and productivity, not the presence or absence of specific elements. The process can be informed by science and influenced by governmental policy. The process invariably is laden with the human attachments to land.

Kay (1993) noted that systems analysis always begin by considering spatial and temporal scales and hierarchy. "Are we concerned," Kay asks, "with integrity of a landscape, a forest, a particular species or all of these? What are the important processes which make up the system?" To answer such questions, one must separate the things we think important from those we deem unimportant.

Now having proposed a unifying concept, the integrity of the ecosystem, we are faced with the obvious problem. The appropriate definition of agroecosystem integrity is not at hand. All this means that there is no preferred observer (Kay, 1993). We have to take care that the system is explicitly specified in terms of scale, hierarchy, boundaries, environment, and time frame. The issues of importance are the contextual perspectives for the evaluation of integrity. The concept of ecological integrity does not exist outside of human value judgments (Serafin and Steedman, 1991). The definition of integrity of the ecosystem is dependent upon human values (i.e., the goodness or desirability of the state being sustained). That definition will require a certain scholarship, debate, and societal acceptance before it can serve as a guide to animal agriculture, land use, and the maintenance of environmental quality. One thing, however, seems evident. Human impacts are applied at landscape scales. This implies that management prescriptions should be focused at the same scales. Thus management of an animal agriculture operation on a landscape (e.g., floodplain, riparian zone, farmland, rangeland, concentrated animal feeding operation) would need to add perspectives founded on both the broad social concern and the long time frame to its commodity- and harvest-oriented perspectives.

NOTES

1. Ecosystems provide a variety of goods and services and carry out a diverse array of processes. The list below is derived from a listing by the Ecological Society of America (ESA, 1996). Goods refer to items with monetary value in the marketplace. Services are valued, but rarely bought and sold.

Ecosystem goods:

> Food.
> Forage or grazing.
> Construction materials.
> Medicinal plants.
> Wild genes for domestic plants and animals.
> Tourism and recreation.

Ecosystem services:

> Human health.
> Maintenance of hydrological cycles.
> Regulate climate.
> Cleansing water and air.
> Carbon dioxide absorption, oxygen production.

Pollination.
Generation of soils.
Storing and cycling essential nutrients.
Absorption and detoxification of pollutants.
Beauty, inspiration, scholarship.
Noise, annoyance.

Ecosystem processes:

Hydrologic flux and storage.
Biological productivity.
Biogeochemical cycling and storage.
Decomposition, detritus.
Maintenance of biological diversity.

2. A caveat is required as to the trend from diversified farm to specialized farm. Organic farming has adopted the diversified farm model and is growing in significance. Organic farming is a lifestyle choice as well as a production system and may be increasingly the choice of farmers of the future.

3. The use of recycled animal products or rendered products in the diet of ruminants may be restricted to reduce the risk of transmissible spongiform encephalopathy. See chapter 7 for a consideration of this risk.

4. The policies promoting sedentarization in the poorer countries of the world reflect similar policies in the United States during the nineteenth century with the passage of the Homestead Law. The pastoralist image was then the negative image of the cattle barons.

ANIMAL AGRICULTURE AND CLIMATIC FACTORS

The vagaries of climate and weather significantly and clearly affect the human relationship to agriculture. The story has been recounted many times in human history. In their haste to avoid widespread famine, Ethiopian farmers replanted their crops in July of both 1985 and 1986 after scheduled but scanty rains occurred for the first time since 1981. In August, those crops withered and died. Crop failure exceeded 80 percent along the Red Sea, and 50 percent elsewhere in the country, only to contribute to the ensuing famine. On the other side of the Pacific, Australia had endured the driest summer in two centuries. Huge brush fires ravaged the countryside while crop, livestock, and property damage approached $3 billion. Nineteen African countries, many in the continent's southern portion, endured property and crop damage of over $1 billion. Cattle, sheep, and goats died by the thousands. India, Sri Lanka, and Indonesia endured human deaths and millions of dollars in crop damage from drought. The summer of 1998 was a period in which floods inundated communities in the northern United States and drought, heat, and wildfires plagued Florida and Texas. Cattle on Texas pastures and ranges survived with emergency hay distributions. As scientists now assess the severity of a sub-Saharan drought that has persisted beyond the 1970s, questions arise as to who or what was the cause of the effects on the people, their livestock, their crops, and the environment (Nicholson, 1983).

When environmental questions are raised about animal agriculture, they are no longer just the narrow, although highly important, matters of concern such as the handling of wastes, contamination of water supplies by microbes and nitrates, and odors, which are limited by regulation and should be handled by the technology. Environmental justice is a larger issue in environmental protection and sustainable development. The theme that seems to connect such issues to all varieties of animal agriculture is climate.

The issues of climate and the environment loom as large for animal agriculture, and are the most globally sensitive issues. Fossil hydrocarbons are converted to carbon dioxide as grain is grown to feed animals. The flatulence of domestic animals contributes methane to thermally active gases in the atmosphere, although the significance of this is a matter of debate. Tropical deforestation, a loss of an important part of the world's carbon sink, has been linked to an increase in livestock numbers; overgrazing reduces carbon storage in grasslands and savannas. Moreover, science-based technology and modern agriculture in developed countries depend on high-energy technology on fertile lands with access to good quality rain- or irrigation water. Because populations in some poor countries are increasing faster than their domestic food production and because the pressure on prime land is increasing, the growth of animal agriculture and, perhaps the growth of agriculture, is limited to marginal areas and to those animal agricultures (poultry, swine) for which land requirements are minimal.

THE ISSUES

Climate affects animal agriculture in four major ways (Watson et al., 1996):

1. Through the impact of livestock feed grain availability and price.
2. Through impacts on livestock pastures and forage crops.
3. Through the direct effects of weather and extreme events on animal growth, reproduction, and health.
4. Through the distribution of livestock diseases.

Multiple issues in animal agriculture surround and are embedded in these relationships to climatic and weather factors. Many issues, however, involve human decisions that are beyond the conduct of the agriculture:

1. The impacts of climatic variation are widespread, and in some places they are felt deeply. Climatic variability yields uncertainty. Insecurity follows uncertainty as its effects result in disasters for humans and animals. Climatic variability becomes a critical issue when policy makes the hu-

man condition worse. Climatic events—droughts, wind storms, floods, freezes—trigger famines, which generally do not develop unless they are potentiated by human activities, error in governmental policies, war, and/or greed. The famines in Ethiopia, the Sudan, the Sahel, Kurdistan, Somalia, North Korea, and other countries in the 1970s through the 1990s were vivid examples of the interplay of drought or floods and human failures.

2. The effects of climate on animal agriculture are largely direct. The yearly productivities of cropland and rangelands vary widely from year to year, and drought and floods are common recurrences. For a developing country, however, livestock can be a better hedge than crops to extreme weather events such as drought (McDowell, 1980). Animals are better able to survive than cultivated crops; they have a lower sensitivity to climate change. Thus, animal agriculture can serve as a buffer to the effects of variable crop production, reducing risks and utilizing grain in excess of human food needs. Governments, however, may intervene. The historic case is that of the Soviet Union in the 1970s, in which policy changes in 1971 led to importation of substantial amounts of grain by the Soviet Union to avoid the necessity of heavy livestock slaughter (Tarrant, 1989). That led to the historic depletion of grain surpluses in the United States in the 1970s and a perturbation in animal agriculture not easily forgotten. Today, instead of importing grain to feed animals, Russia imports beef and poultry meat directly.

3. The thousands of cattle breeds developed over the millennia, like their owners, have adapted to extreme climates and poor nutrition (Williams et al., 1995). They have evolved resistances to disease and pests and are able to survive with little water. They are an essential part of the livelihoods of people in severe climates.

4. The agricultures today, however, exist in very dissimilar ecosystems. Where winters are severe, cattle are housed indoors because of lack of pasture and because they do not thrive in cold conditions (Tarrant, 1991). Yet in the Nordic lands (Finland, Iceland, Norway, Sweden, Russia), farmers are particularly dependent on animal agriculture. Sheep and goats can tolerate a wide range of conditions and are able to thrive in areas too arid for cattle rearing. Hardy goats can survive even in dry rangeland that is not able to support very much other life (signaling the deterioration of the rangeland). Aspects of animal production can also signal variations in climate. In eastern Europe and other places in the world, milk production is sensitive to the availability of feed for dairy cattle (Tarrant, 1991). Any shortage of feed shows up in reduced milk production well before animals have to be slaughtered.

5. The issues relating to animal agriculture include the questions of resilience of some agricultural systems to natural variability in climate. The increase in grain production through past decades with the help of technology, has been accompanied by increased uncertainty of climatic effects on grain production (Tarrant, 1987) and may be faltering (Brown, 1995). Year to year variability in yields has widened in recent decades. Efforts that focus on increased efficiency of agricultural production may lead to goals that contribute to inflexible production systems that are not well buffered against the uncertain effects of climate. One thing certain about the world's climate is that the efficiency of climatic predictions for years and decades remains low.

6. The common reaction in animal agriculture is to protect the animals against the vagaries of weather, seasonality of climatic effects, and climatic and cultural differences in various parts of the earth. Such protective considerations may flow into economic considerations, the cost and availability of human labor, and matters of convenience that lead to significant confinement management, and hence, issues of animal welfare. This may be seen particularly in countries of the former Soviet Union and eastern Europe.

7. Inherent in the relationship of animal agriculture and climate are issues of anthropogenic climate change (i.e., the enhanced greenhouse effect). Of the principal greenhouse gases, carbon dioxide, the chlorofluorocarbons, and nitrous oxide are the result of industrial and socioeconomic forces. The levels of greenhouse gases have grown significantly since preindustrial times, methane by 145 percent (IPCC, 1990; Houghton et al., 1996). Animal agriculture is linked to some of the increase in the production of carbon dioxide as a result of excessive grazing of rangeland. The contributions to the carbon dioxide load from increased plant culture to provide feed is a factor. Deforestation has greater significance. These, however, are the smaller contributions compared to industrial and transport production of carbon dioxide. The future significance of global warming to animal agriculture probably lies in the effects on agriculture itself in the tropics and subtropics.

8. The principal climate-related ecological problem posed by domestic animals is overgrazing in arid and semiarid areas. This was a common sight in the Great Plains of the United States in the drought periods of the 1930s and the 1950s, and has been seen in Africa and other developing areas in recent decades. National policies, as well as long-held culturally driven practices, can exacerbate or ameliorate climatic pressures on grasslands. At its most extreme, desertification may spread and never be reversed. Despite what would appear to be ample opportunities to match highly productive crop varieties with suitable climatic characteris-

tics, there has been a tendency throughout the world to expand the area of cultivation of a relatively few popular (and profitable) commodities and varieties. New agricultural areas are being carved from natural ecosystems. The two principal areas currently being invaded by agriculture are the lowland tropics and the warm deserts in which the temperature and long growing season offer possibilities for high productivity. Environmental degradation is most likely to occur in the warm climates.

WEATHER, CLIMATE, AND ANIMAL AGRICULTURE

Weather is a phenomenon that is considered over a few days. Climate summarizes weather conditions over a longer period of time. Climate includes many weather types but is not limited to a weather pattern; instead, climate encompasses many facets of weather with complex interactions. Climate includes elements such as temperature and rainfall, as well as other factors such as the surface receiving incident energy, part of which is reflected away, part is absorbed, and part is transmitted. Depending on the physical characteristics of the medium that receives the insolation, different climatic scenarios will be produced whereby the composition of the vegetation is controlled and the structure of the ecosystem is established (Griffiths, 1976).

Agricultural managers use both available land and capital to reduce the impacts of adverse weather and climate. Specifically, managers of animal agriculture can temper the impact of unfavorable weather with construction of buildings and shelters for animals. Other strategies to minimize climatic hazards to agricultural production include genetic selection that can produce animals and plants more tolerant to a region's environment, location of concentrated animal feeding operations, or management practices that reduce disease and pests. The migrations of nomadic people constitute a tactic to mitigate effects of seasonal as well as climatic variation. Indigenous animal and crop systems often form a natural buffer to variations in food supplies caused by climatic variations. The great migrations of wild animals over earlier ecosystems, however, are not duplicated in domestic animal production.

VARIATIONS IN WEATHER AND CLIMATE

"Climate processes are all the individual physical processes that separately contribute to the overall behavior of the climate system. They are also the interactions and feedbacks among the individual processes that determine the response of the climate system. They are also the interactions and feedbacks among the individual processes that determine the response of the climate system to external forcing, including the response to global anthropogenic forcing." Thus the 1995 report of the Intergovernmental Panel on Climate Change describes the basis for variation in weather and climate (Houghton et al., 1996).

Griffiths (1976) stated succinctly that "[c]hange is a fundamental characteristic of the atmosphere on all time scales. Investigators have shown temperature varies greatly during a few seconds and during hundreds of thousands of years." Issues for agriculture, however, stem mainly from the changes occurring from year to year and in an intermediate time frame (e.g., the changes over more than two or three decades) rather than immediate weather change. The issue of global warming and global anthropogenic effects is a concern of an even longer range. Climate modelers generally agree that the chaotic character of the climate systems rules out predictions at a particular point in time in the future but believe that it is possible to perform long-term predictions of the change in average statistical properties of the weather (Bengstsson, 1992; Palmer, 1993; Shackley and Wynne, 1996).

The largest scale of atmospheric movement, termed the general circulation, transports energy through the atmosphere from the equator to the poles (Cox and Atkins, 1979; Roberts and Lansford, 1979). The air, from some distance north and south of the equator, moves upward, poleward, then downward and toward the equator. The general circulation pattern can be conceived best as originating in the equatorial region in which the almost constant insolation heats surfaces and the air above them. Warm air rises and spreads north and south. At latitudes of about 25 to 30 N and S, some of the air begins to descend; upon reaching the surface, part is returned to the equator and part continues toward the poles, resulting in two great bands of surface winds. Because there are only small variations in pressures around the equator, the tradewinds (easterly winds below the 30 latitudes) are remarkable for the constancy of their direction (Griffiths, 1976). In the temperate zones where west winds predominate, frequent movements of pressure systems, particularly lows or cyclones, perturb the direction. The temperate zones's patterns present a wavelike motion around the poles known as the circumpolar vortex, or jet streams. Directions of wind and temperatures change as frontal systems move with the prevailing westerlies.

Rising air produces clouds and precipitation. Vertical motion of the air that is consistently downward produces little rain. Tropics near the equator have a generally high rainfall pattern. The deserts of North America, the Sahara, and many other arid regions are located in the high pressure regions of the horse latitudes (i.e., latitudes 25–30 from the equator).

Three major factors can make substantial changes in the patterns of atmospheric movement and precipitation:

1. Land masses heat and cool rapidly, while oceans gain or lose heat slowly (Roberts and Lansford, 1979). The land heats and air above it expands. This produces a low pressure area and winds move inland. When the land cools—at night or in winter with the larger land masses—the wind turns to blow out to the sea from the land. The largest land masses, such as the Asian subcontinent, produce monsoons, as winds reverse with the season. When spring and summer come, the air over land becomes warmer and lighter, and winds sweep inland, bringing torrential rains. In winter, the air over Asia grows cool and dense, and it spreads toward the oceans. Dry periods follow. Areas other than Asia experience similar wind reversals (i.e., monsoon effects) and these include the Gulf and western states of the United States, eastern Africa, and central eastern Australia.

2. As Griffiths (1976) pointed out, the atmosphere and the oceans are the basic media for redistribution of solar energy, and hence, determination of the macroclimates of the world. The ocean absorbs radiation through a thick layer and daily variation at the surface is generally less than 1 C, in contrast to land where a day's variation may be as much as 50 C. Water flow is generally at right angles with wind flow. As a result, off the coasts of Peru and California, the winds blow generally parallel to the coast and cause a water flow offshore. As the surface water is swept away, deeper and colder water wells up, substantially affecting the climate of the shore zone. The Gulf Stream and the north Pacific current bring warm winters to Europe and western North America.

3. The interactions of ocean currents and the atmosphere that appear to have the greatest impact on the stability of agriculture are the natural phenomena of the El Niño Southern Oscillation. The eastern Pacific is characterized by a region of high atmosphere pressure, while the western Pacific is a low pressure area. Winds blow from high pressure to low, so tradewinds usually flow from the South American coast westward toward Australia and Indonesia. These tradewinds coax the warm surface water along the coast of Peru toward the west. This changes the circulation of the Pacific Ocean Basin, which covers a third of the earth's circumference.

In the absence of El Niño and its cold counterpoint El Niña, the eastern tropical Pacific is cool and dry and the west is hot and humid. During El Niño, the surface water inexplicably seesaws in response to changes in the surface winds that drive the ocean conditions. El Niño is now associated, tenuously in some instances, with ecological and economic disasters and unusual weather patterns over various parts of the world: flooding in Louisiana, Florida, and in 1993, the Midwest; widespread drought in southern Africa, Sri Lanka, southern India, the Philippines, Indonesia, and Australia; and rare hurricanes in French Polynesia, Hawaii, and California, reportedly as El Niño occurred. Studies have linked individual El Niño warmings to months-long climate shifts around the world, such as unusually warm winters in Alaska, western Canada, and the northern United States.

El Niño, unlike global warming, is probably not caused by human actions. Its effects, however, are determined by where humans have built their houses, feedlots, and roads, by population levels and locations, and by the interdependency of industrial society. Understanding El Niño likely offers one of the best means of predicting climatic events and acting on such predictions. Technical accuracy remains an impediment to the use of forecasts. But equally constraining are a number of nontechnical, institutional factors. The institutions to act on forecasts have yet to be developed.

CLIMATE AND TRADE IN GRAIN FOR LIVESTOCK

Variability in world cereal yields and the resulting food production is a growing issue (Tarrant, 1987). Tarrant (1987) claimed that the mean (average) and variance of a range of biological populations are linearly related, which implies that if crop productivity increases, variability also increases. Mean yields of cereal grains are increasing, but absolute variability is also increasing. On a world scale there has been a remarkably linear increase in yields of all cereals through time. Along with these increases in yields, increases in variability have followed from country to country and from year to year. Relative variability among countries is increasing as technology is applied unevenly. Inequalities in food production are increasing. As yield and production increase, national concerns about problems of variability in production from year to year are also important (Tarrant, 1987).

Simply put, if livestock herds in Russia—where fluctuations are apparently relatively greater than in any other major cereal producing country—are not adjusted to the size of the cereal or other feed crop harvest, annual variability becomes a determinant of the size of the needed imports of meat and grain, the size of the necessary grain buffer stock, or both (Tarrant, 1989). As production increases, annual variability will increase as well; however, absolute variability (regional and annual) is higher than can be economically and practically handled by buffer stocks. Tarrant (1989) noted that imports into the former Soviet Union in 1989 were close to port-handling capacity and therefore limited the size of the buffer stocks. Now, Russia and other former countries of the Soviet Union import the meat directly.

Tarrant's tenets convey two messages. One characterizes a fragile agricultural system that is unable to regain its original resistance or original yield. The other, which follows closely, contends that dependence on such an agricultural system may lead to devastating consequences such as famine. In other words, the differences in grain productions among countries are increasing. As such, spatial and temporal variability affects grain available to animals, and hence, the sustainability of animal agriculture. This has been especially the case in high grain consumption countries such as Russia, and to some extent, the United States.

RISK AND UNCERTAINTY AND MANAGEMENT OF THE ANIMAL ENVIRONMENT

Risk and uncertainty exist in agricultural systems in which weather is a factor. Although uncertainty is not calculable, risk can be measured. The greater the economic value of the operation, the more the factor of risk is considered, and the more intensive the management effort likely will be in the attempt to reduce risk.

Protection against risk varies according to the type of agriculture practiced. Animal systems are affected through the reproductive pattern; beef and dairy animal populations with long gestation periods and low fecundity increase only slowly and require less protection, while populations of swine, and especially chickens, expand quickly and require shelter. Losses during severe weather stress, however, are more easily replaced with chickens than with beef cattle.

Extensive systems such as cattle operations on open grasslands usually involve minimal inputs. Decisions on stock and stocking rates and on grazing patterns are determined by the number and size of pastures and on the distribution of water. Construction of animal shelters and the production and storage of emergency feed supplies reduce risk from weather and usually reduce the variation in output. Fully enclosed and environmentally controlled shelter systems, now common for poultry and other livestock, are energy- and capital-intensive management steps to much lower vulnerability to weather.

The advent of intensive management systems not only has increased the significance of environmental factors in animal agriculture, it also has changed the relative importance of the different environmental factors and the nature of the strategies that are used to attend to animal–environmental problems (Curtis, 1983). Confinement intensifies the association of the animal with its environment and limits the animal's opportunities to seek more favorable surroundings. Thus, although the animal is more protected from environmental vagaries by controlling its environment, the cost of providing the protection may further limit the animal's freedoms. This can create discomfort and/or images of discomfort, and to some critics, these are not distinguishable. Society may see such systems as diminishing the animal's welfare, creating an undue dependence on antibiotics and medications, restricting the markets that family farmers can use effectively, and polluting the environment by producing large quantities of concentrated, unpleasant, or noxious animal wastes.

In extensive animal production, there is a tendency to fit the management systems and the animals themselves to the natural environment (Curtis, 1983). In intensive animal production, control of thermal and light factors are the dominant features, but important also are social and behavioral factors and disease elements. Although it is considered important to adapt management and animals to the environment, there must be attempts to adapt the environment to the animal's needs in intensive systems.

GLOBAL CLIMATE CHANGE

If the interests of the well-being of the environment are the basis for energy policy, then global climate change may be the major concern. Atmospheric carbon dioxide protects the earth by ensuring that not all the warmth that arrives as sunlight is radiated away. There is growing consensus that abundant supplies of carbon dioxide, methane, nitrous oxide, and artificially made hydrochlorofluorocarbons and hydrofluorocarbons are overstuffing the supply of this protective covering (IPCC, 1990; Houghton et al., 1996). The Intergovernmental Panel on

Climate Change (IPCC)—a collection of thousands of scientists and other experts who advise the United Nations—argues that the evidence for anthropogenic climate change recently has become stronger (Houghton et al., 1996). The IPCC report, however, is also cautious, stating only that the "balance of evidence suggests a discernible human influence on global climate. The half a degree of warming suggested by the land-based temperature records might just be due to natural variation."

The global warming issue remains full of controversies. Scientists skeptical of the greenhouse gases theory, do not deny that such gases can trap heat (Michaels, 1990). A heated debate has raged, however, over whether measures to ward off climate change are worth the price or not; any climatic change due to the greenhouse effect will be slow in making a real difference (Zurer, 1991). In assessments for policy makers, climate scientists usually give a range of estimates for the temperature response at the earth's surface to a doubling of carbon dioxide levels (Shackley and Wynne, 1996). The estimated range is from 1.5 to 3.5° C, suggesting substantial uncertainty. The uncertainty, however, is not the result of experimental error but the result of using deterministic climate models that use different sets of assumptions.

Uncertainties do not negate the value of attempting to make long-term predictions. They simply suggest that producers of scientific knowledge regarding climate have a difficult task ahead of them (Shackley and Wynne, 1996). Users of the knowledge on the other hand, tend to perceive the knowledge as more certain. Critics and other policy actors may interpret uncertainty in conformity with their own assumptions about the implications.

ANIMAL AGRICULTURE'S IMPACT ON CLIMATE

Lyman and associates (1990) cite worldwide agriculture as contributing 14 percent to global warming. It appears to be a growing contributor, particularly as developing countries mechanize their agriculture and increase their use of synthetic fertilizer.

The contributions of agriculture to the greenhouse effect also include nitrous oxide from microbial action on chemical fertilizers (used in intensive agriculture in industrial countries and in *green revolution* agriculture in the developing countries) and methane, a by-product of plant and animal culture (Lyman et al., 1990). Incomplete combustion of fossil fuels, escape of gas from coal mines and natural gas fields, forest burning, burial of garbage in landfills, and termites are major contributors to methane emissions. Agricultural sources are mainly flooded rice paddies and wetlands and ruminant animals. Methane is normally removed from the atmosphere, but increased carbon monoxide, largely from vehicle exhausts, reduces the natural cleansing.

The potential rise in methane production due to anaerobic fermentation by microbes located in the rumina of ruminants and in the lower digestive tract of all animals is a stated concern (World Resources Institute, 1996). Methane is 20–30 times more efficient than carbon dioxide at trapping radiation, and its concentration in the atmosphere has been increasing more than one percent a year (WRI, 1996). Fifteen percent of the change in radiative forcing from 1980 to 1990 is calculated to be the result of methane (IPCC, 1990). *Worldwatch* estimates that as livestock account for 15 to 20 percent of global methane emissions, livestock account for 3 percent of the global warming (Durning and Brough, 1991). Johnson and Johnson (1995) reported estimates that are about 20 percent of global sources of methane is due to enteric fermentation (mostly cattle) and animal wastes.

Byers (1990) stated that current assessments indicate 7 percent of the methane produced globally is from beef, dairy, draft, and collateral (e.g., sacred, hobby) cattle worldwide. Byers (1990) estimated that other ruminants (including both domestic and wild nonruminants) produce an additional 3.7 percent of the total. Animal wastes decaying anaerobically are estimated to contribute 2.7 percent. Humans contribute 1 percent of the total.

Critics urge limiting the contribution of cattle methanogenesis to global warming and changing the earth's climates, largely by greatly reducing animal numbers (Durning and Brough, 1991). Byers (1990) argued that technology has a positive effect. Byers's (1990) models suggest that of the 7 percent global methane attributable to cattle, 3.6 percent is from cattle in developed countries other than the United States, 2.9 percent from cattle in developing countries, and 0.5 percent from cattle in the United States. Technology is available to reduce methane emissions (grain feeding, ionophores), but even eliminating all cattle and sheep in the United States would make little detectable difference in atmospheric warming in the decadal time frame. Fermentative production of methane, however, is a loss to the animal. The value of strategies to reduce methane production by domestic ruminants may lie in the improved efficiency of production, not in reducing the contribution to atmospheric warming.

OVERGRAZING AND DESERTIFICATION

Rangelands (grasslands, savannas, shrublands, deserts, and tundra) occupy 51 percent of the global land surface and contain about 36 percent of the world's total above- and belowground biomass (Watson et al., 1996). They sustain millions of people and animals. Rangelands support half of the world's livestock and both domestic and wildlife populations. Carbon dioxide increases are likely the result of reductions in forage quality because of maturation and unsustainable land use practices such as inappropriate plowing, excessive fuelwood use, and particularly, overgrazing (Watson et al., 1996). The effect of overgrazing is damage to a fragile ecosystem, leading to erosion of soil and decreasing livestock carrying capacities (Cooke, 1980).

Desertification usually follows reduction of meager vegetation after exposing the ground surface cleared for cultivation, left fallow, or trampled by animals (UN, 1978). Desertification usually occurs during times of drought in areas of naturally vulnerable land subject to pressures of land use. It is a patch destruction, in which patches of denuded land link up to extend the process to wider areas. It is a subtle process.

Critics, recalling perhaps the harm done by the overgrazing of rangelands in the past (in the southwestern United States during the droughts of the 1930s and 1950s and the cattle drives of the nineteenth century), focus on the degradation of public lands in the western United States: The U.S. Bureau of Land Management (BLM) has been responsive to the grazing industry constituency, inferring that the livestock industry is the culprit (West, 1982; Durning and Brough, 1991).

Dregne (1977) estimated that ten percent of the arid west has been subject to severe desertification in part because of overgrazing. Continued rangeland abuse is alleged. Lyman and coauthors (1990) remind that humankind has historically created deserts and wastelands by cutting down forests, overgrazing rangelands, or failing to leave agricultural lands idle long enough to replenish fertility. When vegetation is reduced, the light colored soil is exposed; this increases the reflectivity of the landscape. When more sunlight is reflected, the land becomes somewhat cooler. Air passing over this landscape is heated less and tends to rise less. As a result, cloud formation decreases and so does rainfall. Lower rainfall prevents regrowth of vegetation, reflectivity is further increased, and the deserts expand. Animal agriculture is implicated in such desertification by contributing to the reduction of vegetation.

The Sahel has become a useful laboratory for studying elements leading to desertification. Beginning in the 1960s, Sahelian farmers were encouraged by their governments to settle. Government projects designed to encourage permanent settlement consisted of constructing thousands of boreholes and wells throughout the Sahel. Reluctant to follow rainfall, nomadic tribes established themselves and their herds near the wells year-round. These factors not only reinforced each other, but led to significant degradation (i.e., desertification). The change of the African nomadic farmers to sedentary tribes led to the possibilities of four problems (Sinclair and Wells, 1989):

1. Livestock no longer had access to the high quality but ephemeral food supplies in the drier areas of their range.
2. The year-round grazing resulted in the death of the grasses and the collapse of the pasture (overgrazing).
3. As described above, human populations have increased as a result of improved health care and education, while access to land has decreased through settlement and the incursion of permanent agriculture.
4. Livestock populations, already above carrying capacity for a sedentary system, further increased as a result of improved veterinary services.

Denudation originated near the wells, and as more wells were dug, circles of trampled barren land fused. Today, the African people and their dependency on the modified rangeland reflect a classic case of the loss of resilience—the failure to tolerate any reduction in rainfall. Where cattle herds and people may exist on sparse and overgrazed vegetation, the slightest decrease in rainfall can create a crisis (Sinclair and Wells, 1989). Schlesinger and co-workers (1990) also noted that it is the large herds of domestic livestock that mostly disrupt the tight connection between soil and plant processes leading to the decline in cover in semiarid grasslands. The conversion of degraded grasslands also is aided when cattle disperse the seeds of desert species.

Arid and semiarid lands cover about 45 percent of the earth's surface. Schlesinger et al. (1990) argued that although these lands contribute a small amount of the net primary productivity of the biosphere, the flux of dust, catastrophic runoff events that result in high concentration of suspended solids in rivers, the reduction in the recharge of soil moisture, the invasion of the land by shrubs, and soil erosion following the expansion of arid land at the expense of semiarid land have impacts that can extend far beyond the arid and semiarid lands. This will be an important issue for animal agriculture in the decades ahead.

CONCLUSION

Agriculture is the principal climate-sensitive industry in many countries, although fisheries, forest products, and the insurance industry follow closely. An industrialized country with most of its economy supported by climate-tolerant industries is little affected by the vagaries of El Niño or by potential global warming, except for energy costs involved in cooling and heating buildings and disruption of transport by river floods. Developing countries, however, face another set of issues; droughts, floods, and variation in growing season due to rainfall patterns and thaws and freezes dictate the productivity of these agriculturally dominated societies.

Animal–human relationships manifest climatic responses in developing countries. In subsistence cultures, there is a high degree of interdependence between humans and animals (McDowell, 1980). Animals are a hedge against crop failure in places where financial institutions are not available and land is not owned. They are the investment for surplus funds. Animals may survive where crops fail to grow because they can eat feed other than crops. If drought and disease become severe and animals die, humans may die also unless intervention occurs. This fragile relationship in developing countries also requires attention as to its sustainability. Land degradation is the first problem for livestock policies in developing countries (Durning and Brough, 1991; Daily, 1995).

Animal agricultures in developed countries, however, are not immune from climatic phenomena. The productivities of agriculture, including those of animal agriculture, can be affected by long-term changes in climate as well as sporadic, widespread droughts. Decisions made in world trade can affect the costs of animal production. Wide variations in global demands for grain can have geo-climatic origins. Society's concern for animal welfare may override the attempts to neutralize the stresses of climatic variation and weather.

Relative to global warming, most feel that prevention deserves first priority. Preventing greenhouse gas emission should delay the onset of significant global warming or slow its advances and reduce its magnitude. Many policies could be proposed with a prevention strategy. Five elements, however, have generally received the greater consideration (Mintzer et al., 1989):

1. Increasing the efficiency of energy production and use.
2. Switching from carbon-intensive fuels such as coal to hydrogen-intensive fuels such as natural gas.
3. Encouraging the rapid development and use of solar and other carbon-free energy sources.
4. Eliminating the production of most chlorofluorocarbons and developing the means to recapture those now in use.
5. Reducing the rate of deforestation.

These elements are echoed in IPCC reports (Houghton et al., 1996; Watson et al., 1996).

In the face of such massive considerations, animal agriculture seems to be on the sidelines (Flavin and Tunali, 1996). It is significant that in these recommendations and those emanating from international conferences (e.g., Rio de Janeiro in 1996), little emphasis is placed on the contributions of animal agriculture. Climate-related issues of agriculture, except for deforestation and overgrazing, have received little attention in national and international policy; that may remain the case. Perhaps the issues of global warming will be mainly grist for the mills of those who have had or now have other agendas— the reduction of animal agriculture on philosophical grounds (Lappé, 1982; Robbins, 1987; Durning and Brough, 1991).

All of the issues themselves are large enough to demand the attention of those in the traditional sectors: farming, industry, science, education, and policy. These are not issues for only critics.

WITH CONTRIBUTIONS BY PAUL B. THOMPSON
Purdue University, West Lafayette, Indiana
AND STANLEY E. CURTIS[1]
University of Illinois, Urbana

CHAPTER 11

THE WELL-BEING OF
AGRICULTURAL ANIMALS

Early on, humans and their ancestors were hunters, gatherers, and scavengers. Some five to ten thousand years ago, humans and animals became interdependent; animals were domesticated. Animals evolved throughout history by natural selection, in which the fittest (in Darwin's terms) passed their genes to their offspring. When humans began to domesticate plants, they took weeds and planted them in areas under control and began to select what was the fittest for their needs. Some animals— docile, ever youthful in behavior, perhaps seeking protection— were given that protection and made part of human domestic development (Coppinger and Smith, 1983). Humans took control of the biological reproductive success and made use of the animals and plants. So began the ultimate modifier of habitat on the planet: the invention and spread of agriculture (Budiansky, 1992). A natural relationship was established with animals. The human heritage and present condition, both physiologically and culturally, became deeply dependent upon animals for food and other needs.

Animals have played important roles in the course of civilization (Cole and Garrett, 1980; Spedding, 1984; Campbell and Lasley, 1985; McDowell, 1991). They were first a source of food for humans. They became part of the culture and were involved in the religious experience of humans. They provided power for draft, clothing fibers and skins, fertilizers, medicine, and household fuel. Animals became a means by which humans could store food for themselves when season and drought deprived them of plant foods (Rappaport, 1967).

Animal culture has been woven into the fabric of North American agriculture, beginning with the second voyage of Christopher Columbus who imported the first seed stock. The shape and scope of North American animal agriculture have been determined by the desire for meat, eggs, and dairy products and the cultural–economic structure of American society as certainly as they have by the adaptive and climatic features of the land.

Meat has importance in the diets of people in all developed countries. Iceland and Japan are among the world leaders in the per capita consumption of fishery products. The United States, Israel, Hong Kong, and Singapore consume poultry meat in the largest quantities. The U.S. beef and veal per capita annual consumption puts Americans third among the beef eating populations. European countries rank high in the consumption of pork. Eggs and milk are substantial dietary components in most Western countries.

Livestock and poultry also make an important contribution to the food security of developing countries (FAO, 1992). Demand for meat and milk increases with increasing incomes and urbanization. Animals, however, also provide production inputs into crop agriculture. Animal draft power extends the area that can be cultivated by a person and allows the use of heavy soils. Animal power lifts water for irrigation and provides transport. Animals provide fertilizer; they graze cropped areas or gather food away from cropped areas and are brought to sleep on village fields. They reduce variability in incomes and food supplies.

Stephen Budiansky (1992), popularizing the work of Coppinger and Smith (1983), has offered a simple and intriguing thesis on the relationship of domesticated animals and humans. In his view, domestication was an evolutionary adaption accomplished through the process of natural selection—animals chose domestication as a strategy for evolutionary survival. Whether this is true or whether the selection was natural is questionable, but domestic animals in their current state are dependent upon humans, and farmers, ranchers, and herdsmen are nearly as dependent upon them. That above all places responsibility on humans, knowingly or not, to strive to decrease cruelty to animals on the farm and in the laboratory. The issues, however, do not stop there.

The pasture and farmyard view of animal agriculture was publicly accepted for most of the history of this country (Rollin, 1989; Thompson, 1993a). Agricultural uses of animals, with the exception of overt cruelties such as branding or dehorning, were largely ignored. Farmers and ranchers for the most part enjoyed a positive image. Animal agriculture was rarely critiqued. As Rollin (1989) noted, the majority of those concerned with animal welfare were and probably still are consumers of animal products. At mid-twentieth century, however, animal agriculture was transformed.

The discoveries of all the known human vitamin and mineral requirements and the effects of antimicrobial dietary supplements in the first half of the twentieth century, led to the development of successful formula feeds for what had been farmyard animals: cattle on pasture and poultry dependent upon barnyard manure and swine on swill for vitamin B_{12}. With the development of an infrastructure, the feed manufacturing industry, *extensive* culture of livestock was replaced in many aspects by intensive production systems. Many animals were placed in smaller areas. Mechanization replaced labor. The industrial model replaced the traditional farm. Many people, troubled by the departure from the traditional, comfortable view of the farmyard, wondered if animals suffered under such conditions, and some in society came to believe that it is practically impossible to use animals without some form of cruelty. Rollin (1990) described that belief: Most animal suffering at human hands grows out of such decent motivations as increasing knowledge, curing disease, increasing efficiency of food production, protecting humans against toxic substance and so on. Correlative with this realization has come a demand for the control of suffering in areas of animal use which previously enjoyed laissez faire, notably toxicity testing, animal research, and animal agriculture.

Thus, this chapter begins with the arguments of intensive animal agriculture and biomedical and agricultural research. The prominent place that moral philosophy plays in the animal welfare–rights movement is examined. A distinction is made between the philosophical theories of consequentialist welfare and of rights, and the practical resonance of this difference is noted. The history of the animal rights movement and its significance is discussed. The need for attention to the issues by animal agriculture is stressed.

INTENSIVE ANIMAL PRODUCTION SYSTEMS

Most people in developed countries and the large cities of developing countries choose not to grow food for themselves. Food production has become a business in which some members of society choose to engage. In the process of fulfilling the perceived goals of animal agriculture in the United States, productive, efficient, but intensive systems for producing animal products of high demand were developed. The movement of agricultural animals from pastures, barnyards, and muddy lots to confinement facilities accelerated markedly during the 1950s in the poultry and dairy industries and the 1960s in livestock production.

The competition for land and the development of land management practices was one force leading to intensiveness (Curtis, 1983). Raising animals extensively (open lots, pastures, and ranges from which animals forage part or all of their feed) required large acreage. Also, passing with the family farm were the low-paid workers upon whom extensive farming and ranching were based. The need grew to provide incentives to skilled employees. Thus animal producers expanded and specialized their operations in order to justify increased outlays for labor.

As a result of intensifying animal agriculture, cyclical and seasonal variations in production have leveled considerably. Housing eases the care of animals in contrast to the natural surroundings or crude shelters typical of extensive animal agriculture. Provision of a complete diet and clean water is facilitated. Predation of animals is prevented. Observations of individual animals is easier. The goal of managers is higher productivity and efficiency, and therefore, there is incentive to secure the well-being of the animals. Economic efficiency, increasing with economies of scale of purchasing, and marketing on schedule are made feasible in the intensive form of animal agriculture (Halcrow, 1980).

There is, however, another side to the story. Since the mid-1960s, concerned people have questioned the ethics of raising animals in such systems (Harrison, 1964, 1993). Since the mid-1970s, mainstream humane movement organizations in the United States have focused much attention on agricultural animals (Jasper and Nelkin, 1992).

The notions of stress and negative subjective experiences in animals have become the descriptors of diminished well-being in animals and other negative features in intensive systems. Michael W. Fox (1984) and Mason and Singer (1980) have been concerned with problems of inadequate veterinary care for sick and injured animals and for humane destruction, poor preventive medicine, and inadequate provision for animals's behavioral requirements. Crowding is a particular concern. Designs of farrowing crates and poultry cages are seen as a problem. Animals are perceived as being treated like *biomachines*, fed food designed in the laboratory, not by nature. Beef cattle in feedlots may lack shade, shelter, dry lying areas, and roughage in the diet. Dairy cattle are raised without bedding, and in the western United States, are kept lacking shade, shelter, and lying areas. Poultry can suffer from poor ventilation and climate control and most of all from crowding. Veal calves are raised in stalls or crates on slats, deprived of normal movements, iron in the diet, and forage. Animals are plagued with diarrhea and other diseases and ammonia and other irritating gases from manure pits. Trimming the beaks of birds is considered offensive. So are the methods of destroying culled chicks at hatcheries.

Hurnik (1993) summarized the most commonly mentioned concerns of animal welfare supporters regarding the well-being of animals in intensive production systems. In terms of dietary deviation from nutritional requirements, concerns are high density diets and insufficient roughage and extended feed or water deprivation. Regarding close confinement housing, the objections are to insufficient or no opportunity for daily exercise and bodily movements, uncomfortable or injurious floors, and inadequate control of the animals's environment. Overcrowding and excessive group sizes pose concerns of insufficient eating and resting space, the difficulties of establishing a social hierarchy, excessive production stress, and insufficient health care. Concerns pertaining to the insensitive handling of animals are the use of stressful identification methods and painful restraints and handling of animals. Transport difficulties are the stressful loading and unloading of animals, the mixing of animals unfamiliar with each other, long transport times. Stressful slaughtering methods complete the summary.

Because of their efficiency and productivity, intensive systems of animal agriculture are likely to remain on the American scene. The negative features of modern agriculture, real or alleged, widespread or occasional, emphasize an imperative to consider animal well-being in crafting the animal agricultures of the future (Hurnik, 1993). Failure in total quality management, including a quality of life for our animals, may multiply restrictions on animal agriculture.

USE OF ANIMALS IN RESEARCH

The issue of using animals in scientific experiments is a major concern of animal activists. It is also relevant to animal agriculture. The case against the use of animals in scientific research has been made many times, in many ways, and scientists have defended their use of animals with equal vigor (e.g., Miller, 1985; Fox, 1986; Will, 1987; Rollin, 1989, 1995). Scientists argue that the end of biomedical research—finding cures and treatments for human cancer, heart disease, AIDS, and other afflictions—justifies the use of animals in research. The result has been the continuing use of animals in all kinds of scientific investigations, but under progressively closer regulation by the federal government. Animal extremists do not believe that the end justifies the means.

The Animal Welfare Act of 1966 and its amendments authorize the USDA to inspect any facility in which animals of certain species (i.e., subhuman primates, dogs, cats, rabbits, hamsters, and guinea pigs) are being held for use in research or teaching. Up to now, inspection by the USDA has emphasized the physical conditions of a facility. In amendments to the 1985 Farm Bill, USDA authority was extended to certain aspects of the animal's psychological well-being. Environments in which subhuman primates reside must be enriched so as to increase the level of environmental stimulation the animals experience, and dogs must be removed from their cages and exercised daily. The general approach is to set standards by quantitative specifications (engineering standards) instead of performance-based standards, because of the difficulty of measuring well-being. The USDA, however, does not monitor the care and use of rats, mice, and birds used in research. The department also allows universities to draw up their own plans to carry out the requirements of the Animal Welfare Act.

The NIH requires institutions receiving any of its research or training grant monies to comply with certain guidelines for the care and use of laboratory animals (NIH, 1985). The NIH requires an institutional animal care and use committee (IACUC), the composition of which is prescribed in certain respects (e.g., the membership must include at least one veterinarian, one institutional employee who does not use animals in research or teaching, and one member of the community). This committee has specified responsibilities, including the review of every animal-use protocol to assure that the proposed procedure is humane prior to the submission of the research proposal to a granting agency, as well as semiannual, in-house inspections of the physical plant in which the animals reside. Although most animals used in agricultural research and teaching in the United States are not being used in NIH-funded projects, the NIH policy has often shaped the animal care and use for the entire institution. An agreement between the USDA and NIH allows the USDA to report infractions of NIH policy to NIH (Rollin, 1989).

Standards for agricultural animal research and teaching facilities have also been developed. In 1986, a consortium of 20 governmental agencies, industrial organizations, and scientific and professional associations appointed a group of nearly 40 animal scientists, veterinarians, and agricultural engineers to develop guidelines for the care and use of agricultural animals in agricultural research and teaching. These guidelines were published early in 1988 (Consortium, 1988) and revised in 1999 (FASS, 1999). The American Association for Accreditation of Laboratory Animal Care (AAALAC, 1991) takes the position that housing and care for farm animals should meet the standards that prevail on a high quality, well-managed farm. The consortium guidelines are recognized by the AAALAC.

Efforts continue toward decreasing the requirements for animals in science and product testing. Since 1986, an EU directive has instructed researchers to choose nonanimal methods if they are "scientifically satisfactory [and] reasonably and practically available." Techniques in molecular biology using microorganisms, cell-culture systems, monoclonal antibodies for medical diagnosis, and artificial constructs such as skin and computerized virtual systems are suggested as alternatives. Improvement in communication among scientists may help minimize numbers of animals, but biomedical and agricultural sciences will continue to ask questions that only live animal experiments can answer.

Issues of animal welfare permeate the new technologies used in animal sciences that have the ultimate purpose of increasing the productivity of animal agriculture. Perhaps the most powerful tools in the hands of animal scientists at the turn of the twenty-first century are the biotechnologies, including the newly discovered methods of cloning adult animals (Wilmut et al., 1997) and of embryos that have been transformed by genetic engineering. Rollins (1995, 1996) visualized the risks of potentiating susceptibility to diseases, unknown effects of new genetic material in animals and diminished viability of the animals. The specter of the "geep" and the rachitic pigs still haunts. Rollins (1996) urges a principle be followed in biotechnological research: "Animals should be no worse off than the parent stock would be if they were not so engineered, and ideally should be better off." Research in animal agriculture should benefit animals as well as humans.

POLICY PERCEPTIONS AND ANIMAL WELFARE RIGHTS

The policy issues are complex (Curtis, 1993). They involve:

1. Production of a basic need of humans—foods—for a population who are increasingly removed from any aspect of production.
2. A range of moral concerns about the relationships of humans and animals that are held by individuals in a pluralistic society.

3. Caretaking of agricultural animals in ways that are based on science and technological (industrial) methodologies.
4. The fact that producing foods of animal origin for human consumption is a commercial business enterprise.

Animal agriculture historically has been viewed as benefitting human beings. The traditions for the use of agricultural animals evolved in an era when animals performed a variety of tasks and fulfilled several basic human needs. In their traditional uses, domestic animals were managed in ways that best suited the family's ability to secure the diverse needs of daily life. Although this pattern still exists on many farms and predominates in developing countries, most farm animals in industrialized nations today are raised for the purpose of providing meat, eggs, dairy goods, wool, leather, and recreation for human use. Thus they are produced for their economic value. When used for the exclusive purpose of producing salable commodities, agricultural animals are often subjected to specific management practices (Curtis, 1983), some of which may be questionable in terms of the well-being of the animals.

The animal welfare movement today includes individuals who support the elimination of all commercial exploitation of animals at the one extreme, and those who call for rather modest reforms in the care of farm animals at the other. As already noted, animal agriculture became a focus of concern for participants in the animal welfare movement because changes in animal production techniques gave rise to questions about how animals fare in these novel, artificial environments. Rollin (1994) argued that the social consensus ethic for the treatment of animals is changing. He stated that the animal welfare ethic has become a mainstream phenomenon that calls for the preservation of the "husbandry and fairness which characterized traditional agriculture until the mid-twentieth century." His is a call to return to a more artisanal, less industrial form of animal production.

It is not clear that farm animals were always, or even usually, treated humanely in the past, but the novelty of certain contemporary animal production techniques has raised a question in the minds of many observers: How do the animals fare as they reside in intensive production systems? In their broadest form, concerns for farm animal welfare are based on the belief that morally significant impacts upon farm animals must be weighed against the interests of producers and demands of consumers.

DEVELOPMENT OF ATTITUDES. Jasper and Nelkin (1992) in their comprehensive history of the animal rights movements noted that most societies in the past, and even today, have held two different attitudes toward animals. One view is the intimate, *familial attachment* to animals kept in the house as pets; emotional attachment and sympathy are laid on such animals. The second is an *instrumental* view of animals which has coexisted with the first: Animals are resources to be exploited, hunted, eaten, milked, and even tortured for human benefit and pleasure.

The variants of this dichotomy, however, are several. Loew (1993), citing Kellert (1988), described a range of views from people with different interests in life. People who hold a naturalistic attitude about animals often turn to wildlife and the outdoors. Those with the ecological view see the environment as a system involving interactions of wildlife species and natural habitats. The primary interest of humanistic persons is placed on individual animals and companions. Moralistic people may or may not like animals, but they are concerned about the wrongful treatment of animals and oppose what they see as exploitation and cruelty. Attitudes of scientists relate to the physical attributes and functions of animals. Aesthetic individuals are interested in the artistic and symbolic characteristics of animals. Those who see the utility of animals are concerned about the practical and material value of animals. Dominative individuals derive satisfaction from mastery and control over animals, typically in sporting and hunting situations. Negative individuals avoid animals as a result of perhaps fear, perhaps previous life experience, or simply little real interest in animals.

Attitudes about animal welfare change. At one time, animals were commonly used as victims of torture for the mere amusement of human spectators. Philosopher René Descartes's well-known view that animals are merely machines, incapable of consciousness or feeling pain, was cited often to justify many practices that made cruel use of animal subjects as well as biomedical experiments that have arguably returned manifold benefits to humans.[2] Today, it is doubtful that any in animal agriculture but the most callous would hold the view of animals as machines.

Although many ancient and medieval philosophers and theologians praised the virtue of kindness toward animals, modern concerns about animal welfare probably can be traced to three eighteenth and nineteenth century sources. The utilitarian philosophers—with their emphasis on pleasure and pain and deemphasis of theologically based concepts of human nature and natural law—advanced the idea that suffering is the basis of moral decision making; it mattered little whether the being that suffered was human or not. The utilitarians's attack upon the sanctity of human privilege was supported by Darwinian views, which weakened the basis for any sharp distinction between the human and other animal species. Anthropomorphic literature and art, such as the novel *Black Beauty* and the film *Bambi,* generated broad popular support for an attitude of taking animal well-being seriously. These three forces came together in the formation of humane societies and activist movements, which have carried through to the animal protection movement of today.

The instrumental view of animals was largely maintained by those in animal agriculture and those engaged in research with animals. The emerging view in the United States may be a new urban view of animal life that is characterized by an elevated moral status of animals (Loew, 1993). It is a changing and values-laden view that extends to livestock, but Loew (1993) noted that urbanism can cut two ways; urban dwellers want inexpensive and safe food. Poverty and issues of race are intertwined so that the relative availabilities of inexpensive and expensive foods could become a racial issue.

Moral concerns about agricultural animals also stem from the agrarian perception of agriculture that persists in the urban population (Thompson, 1993a). The agrarian ideal stipulates that animals have a role in the integrated and diversified farm that is a model of a healthy human environment. This is evident in the imagery of animals in children's books. Clearly, such views are distant from the intensive animal agriculture that evaluates agriculture solely in terms of trade-offs between cost and benefit. Today, the agrarian ideal may be an anachronism, but the appeal of agricultural animals to most people stems from that ideal.

REGULATION AS A RESULT OF ETHICAL CONCERNS. Concerns for animal welfare also may be directed to animal producers, consumers of animal products, or regulatory policy makers. When directed at producers, animal welfare concerns are intended to emphasize personal moral obligations that individual farmers and ranchers have for assuring the well-being of their animals. When directed at consumers, appeals to animal welfare are intended to cause the consumer to accept a moral responsibility for any sacrifices of animal welfare that may have been made in bringing specific animal products to market (e.g., become a vegetarian).

There are many laws and regulations concerning acceptable practices for the production, processing, and sale of animal products. Although many of these deal with consumer protection and food safety, a concern for animal welfare has also been an enduring feature of U.S. law (AWI, 1978).

Farm animals have been protected against cruel treatment since 1641 in some parts of the United States (AWI, 1978). Humane laws always have enforced the principle that animal well-being is more important than the human freedom to engage in or benefit from lazy or sadistic treatment of farm animals. Laws that limit a farmer's treatment of animals to humane practices could be justified on philosophical principles stating why human freedoms or benefits are less important than the impact of human actions upon animals in some cases, and more important in other cases. The philosophical problem is to state such a principle. What is right and good for animals in general may not be what is appropriate for a cow, pig, or chicken in a specific context.

Because regulatory policies are never formed with the benefits of perfect knowledge or agreement of values, a second level of difficulty arises. A welfare policy for animal agriculture must regulate a wide variety of animal species and production environments. It must be sensitive to the facts that there is disagreement about the importance of animal interests relative to human interests and that the quality and quantity of information about what harms farm animals changes with time.

The political issue here is one of defining a regulatory process that even given the imperfections in our knowledge, will be fair to all contending parties as well as the animals themselves. There is one key philosophical issue: On what basis is direct moral consideration extended to farm animal interests and well-being? Why should we care about farm animals? The answer is important not only because it secures the motivation for moral concern about farm animals, but also because the particular answer will shape and guide the approach to regulatory policy in the future. If animal suffering is indeed coequal with human suffering, or if animals do have moral rights, if an animal is somebody—not some thing—then to be fair and to protect animals, the law would likely have to be extended far beyond its current scope.

MORAL PHILOSOPHY AND ANIMAL WELFARE
AND ANIMAL RIGHTS

Why should we care about farm animals? Most would agree because they are worthy of moral consideration. When one tries to further specify exactly why and how animals are worthy of moral consideration, however, there is immediately a need to choose between two conceptual paths of animal welfare and animal rights.

The issue of animal welfare is based upon the belief that the painful or distressing experiences to which farm animals might be subjected ought to be minimized at least and eliminated if possible. The focus of concern is on the experience of pain (in this context, pain might be construed rather broadly to include any form of physical or mental illness); the reason we should care about animals is that farm animals are sentient beings, and are capable of feeling pain (Kitchell and Erickson, 1983; Griffin, 1984; Rollin, 1989).

On the other hand, concern for the rights of animals is based upon belief that each individual animal is worthy of moral respect. People are worthy of moral respect in that they have value simply by virtue of being human, or to paraphrase Kant, because being a rational person is an end in itself, requiring no further statement of purpose. To be human is to have capacities for caring about oneself and others and to be able to act in ways that serve the interests of oneself and others. We respect one another by acknowledging these capacities and by making sure that all people are free to exercise their own will in pursuit of these interests, at least insofar as this exercise does not interfere with the freedoms of others. When we are entitled to demand the respect of others in pursuit of our own interests, we may claim to have a moral right. Moral rights (e.g., rights to life, liberty, and property) protect our ability to pursue our interests and exercise our freedoms in meaningful ways. It seems obvious that farm animals would not be entitled to all of the rights of human beings, but it is plausible to think that they, like humans, also act in pursuit of their own chosen interests. If this indeed is the case, animals are worthy of moral respect too.

PHILOSOPHICAL ETHICS

NATURAL RIGHTS. One key tradition in ethics locates the basis of moral duty in the fulfillment of the human potential. The concepts of human nature and natural rights have been stated in terms that self-knowledge is attained by contrasting the unique nature of human beings against the natures of inanimate objects and sentient creatures below humans and the natures of God and the angels—pure spiritual beings—above. Accordingly, people have dominion over plants and animals, just as God has dominion over human beings, by dint of their relative positions on a *Great Chain of Being*. Thus, the Great Chain concept set boundaries and indicated the scope of action within which the human will could have free reign by natural right, human right as it were.

UTILITARIANISM. The modern tradition of welfare consequential ethics owes much to the utilitarian writings of Jeremy Bentham (1789) and John Stuart Mill (1863). Their works were aimed directly at what they deemed to be pernicious uses of the concept of natural rights. Natural rights was claimed not only to justify human dominion over plants and animals, but the king's, and later the propertied class's, dominion over other human beings (Hobbes, 1968). The utilitarians were social reformers who wanted to found social ethics upon the concept of equality of interests rather than the mysterious, metaphysical concept of natural rights. In their view, there was no reason why the well-being of a king was more important than that of a peasant. The utilitarians also associated themselves with the broad intellectual movement that was committed to the demystification of human nature. For them, there was no reason why the suffering of human beings should be more significant than the suffering of any sentient being.

In combination, the two goals of social reform and demystification of nature led the utilitarians to formulate an approach to ethics that was divorced from the doctrine of natural rights. The system that they developed stressed the comparison of benefits and harms—the outcome or consequence of an action. In attempting to decide how one is morally obligated to act in a given situation, one should, the utilitarians advised, simply consider the consequences of the action. One should choose the option that has the best ratio of benefit to harm for all parties affected. The common sense of this decision rule (often called the utilitarian maxim) is a large part of its appeal; but one must know how to measure benefit and harm in order to apply it. The measurement of benefit and harm (or utility) has been a persistent problem that has occupied utilitarians and other consequentialists.

Bentham's solution to the measurement problem was to rely on hedonism—to equate benefit with the experience of pleasure (or satisfaction) and harm with the experience of pain (or want). The hedonistic criteria applied equally to king and commoner, to the poor classes and the propertied. Furthermore, Bentham had reason to think that pleasure and pain had a physiological basis; they were concepts of the world, and not of the spiritual or ethereal realm that to his mind muddied philosophical thinking. In setting the hedonistic criteria, however, Bentham had rejected the tradition of defining human nature in contradistinction to that of the brutes below and the angels above. In adopting a criterion that applied equally to the aristocracy and the working class, he accepted a criterion that would or could be applied to all sentient beings.

Mill and subsequent consequentialists such as Peter Singer modified Bentham's hedonism to account for the more refined and long-term sorts of satisfaction that can be experienced by human beings. The recognition of higher forms of satisfaction allows utilitarians to count some aspects of personal fulfillment and respect for rights as moral goods. They, however, are counted as moral goods not because it was natural for the upper classes to obtain them, but simply because, like a full belly and the absence of pain, they represented forms of satisfaction (of utility). Thus, although contemporary consequentialists have grounds to weight the well-being of humans more highly than that of animals, they must still balance whatever benefit an action may cause for humans against the harm it may cause for other creatures that are sensitive to feelings and are able to perceive (i.e., the sentient animal).

CONTEMPORARY PHILOSOPHY AND THE ANIMAL WELFARE DEBATE

MODERN UTILITARIANS. The writings of Peter Singer (1975) and Michael W. Fox (1984) represent extensions of Bentham's and Mill's concerns for suffering into the contemporary discussion of animal agriculture. Their argument consists of the two assertions that certain contemporary farming methods cause suffering, and that this suffering should be taken into consideration at all levels of decision: when a producer chooses an animal production technique, when a consumer purchases an animal product, and when a regulatory policy for farm animals is set. In each case, any suffering experienced by the animals is to be weighed against any benefits of the production system in question, including any dietary and sensory benefits that humans derive from using the animal products generated.

In Singer's (1975) calculations of these benefits, they are far out-weighed by the suffering farm animals experience while residing in intensive agricultural systems. He thus concludes that consumers are obliged to become vegetarians. In his view, this is not because it is wrong to eat meat but because our system of animal production makes it impossible to bring meat to the table without first subjecting the animals to unacceptable distress and pain.

Singer's vegetarianism seems soft in two ways. First, a change in the circumstances of animal production could lead to a change in the moral justification for vegetarianism. If one became convinced that production practices had been modified so they were no longer cruel, one would have no reason to abstain from eating meat. To the extent that a meat diet contributes to human health and happiness, one would have good reason to eat it. Second, Singer's vegetarianism is a means to the end of reducing animal suffering rather than an end in itself. As such, it is justified only to the extent that it is effective—to the extent that personal vegetarianism can be expected to reduce the suffering of farm animals (Singer, 1980). Vegetarianism could only be effective if large numbers of people became vegetarians (Regan, 1980).

In his other writings, Singer (1979) explicitly rejected the rights view and adopted the utilitarian stance in the treatment of nonhuman animals. He became a hedonistic utilitarian (Varner, 1992), admitting that in utilitarian terms, it is ethically justifiable to eat meat if the animals are raised and slaughtered humanely (Singer, 1979). For a he-donistic utilitarian, a painless death is evil only if the opportunities for pleasure are foregone; but if slaughtered animals are replaced by happy animals (the replaceable argument), then nothing is lost in he-donistic terms. Varner (1992) doubts whether slaughter can be, in-deed, painless.

MODERN RIGHTS VIEWS. The weaknesses in Singer's vegetarianism has led some advocates of animal welfare to take a harder line. Regan (1983) has done this by extending the concept of moral rights to in-clude nonhuman animals.

In Regan's (1983) view, having rights comes down simply to being a subject to whom experiences can happen. If it turns out that the properties by which human beings are said to possess rights are not uniquely human, then there is no reason to restrict rights to human beings. The animal rights argument concludes by affirming the exis-tence of animal rights and asserting human duties to respect them (Regan, 1983). If animals have a right to live—and it is difficult to imagine any meaningful notion of animal rights without a right to life—then we can never be justified in killing animals in order to eat them. Regan (1983) argued that the rights issue calls for total abolition of scientific research on animals, commercial animal agriculture, and hunting and trapping.

Varner (1992) summarized the view of Regan as thus: There is basically one moral right—the right not to be harmed on the grounds that doing so benefits others—and at least all normal adult mammals have this basic moral right. We should treat birds, and probably reptiles and amphibians, in a spirit of moral caution as if they have rights also.

If it is impossible not to harm someone who has moral rights, Regan (1983) applies two principles, both of which are measured in absolute terms. The worse-off principle applies when noncomparable harms are involved. The principle requires avoiding harm to the worse-off individual. Although death is death for any individual and is always the greatest harm, Regan reasons that death to a normal human being is incomparably worse than death to any nonhuman animal, because a normal human's capacity to form and satisfy desires is much greater. The second principle applies to cases in which comparable harms are involved and harm to the few is required over harm to the many. This principle would not seem to have application in considering human–animal relationships in animal agriculture.

ANIMAL WELFARE OR ANIMAL RIGHTS?: THE RHETORICAL DEBATE

There is a sense that one can believe in consequence or rights ethics in a way that is similar to religious faith: action-guiding and strongly determinate of one's moral judgments. Such beliefs, however, need not determine one's choice of words to describe the ethics of treatment of animals. Singer (1975) and Fox (1984) often speak of rights, although their philosophical position actually has little to do with rights. It may turn out that the best way to minimize suffering is to act as if people and other animals did have rights.

The language of welfare and rights is part of everyday talk for many people. Each word performs a certain job as we speak about our duties or responsibilities. In everyday speech, we often choose these words more for their logical consequences or elocutionary force than for any deeper philosophical view with which they might be associated. Therefore, it is important to take a second look at the way the animal welfare debate is expressed: in terms either of welfare maximization and consequential ethics on the one hand, or of rights and duties of respect on the other.

The logical implications for the way one can act can be summarized in terms of essential contrasts (see also Table 11.1):

1. Describing the situation in terms of consequences leads one to make a comparative judgment of options based upon relative costs and benefits; casting it in terms of rights puts emphasis on the act itself, without regard to other options that may or may not be available.
2. Concern for rights means that the judgment will be dualistic: right or wrong, permissible or impermissible.

Concern for welfare consequences opens the way for different degrees of good and bad.

1. As welfare judgments are comparative and admit different degrees of good and bad, ethical decision making is a maximizing process: finding the action with the best net welfare. On the other hand, rights represent a threshold which allows any act that violates no right but prohibits any act that violates any right.
2. Although rights thinking considers only one possible action at a time, it admits multiple moral solutions (e.g., there may be many possible actions that violate on one's rights and all solutions equally permissible). In maximizing well-being, however, there is usually one solution that best satisfies the requirements for moral action. As such, welfare morality calls for reasoning that is hypothetical in nature, while rights morality is relatively concrete.
3. Welfare maximization is flexible in that what is best today may be superseded tomorrow by an action that is even better. On the other hand, rights are absolute, and if something is wrong today, it will still be wrong tomorrow.
4. Because it is hypothetical and situational, welfare-consequential ethics is also highly empirical (i.e., a great deal depends on who is harmed or benefitted and to what degree). Conversely, although one cannot be ignorant of facts altogether when considering rights, deciding whether a right will or will not be violated is primarily a conceptual inference.
5. The direction of reasoning in welfare-consequential ethics is positive in the sense that one works toward the single solution that reveals what to do; it is negative when considering rights in the sense that one finds

what one may or should do by eliminating the things one may or should not do.

6. The concept of rights indicates a boundary condition under which one may act purely at one's own discretion (i.e., one is within one's rights) as long as the threshold that delimits the rights of another is not breached; there is no set limit or boundary under consequential ethics, but as one is weighing benefits and harms, decision making always involves achieving a sense of balance.

One can see how the logical characteristics of welfare and rights have an impact on animal agriculture by examining how the commonplace moral idea that animals should not be made to suffer needlessly would be translated into the language of welfare or of rights. Suffering carries over fairly readily into the notion of harm in utilitarian reasoning. Other things being equal, an animal welfare ethic demands that suffering be minimized; however, other things rarely are equal, so animal welfare must be weighed against the other costs and benefits of a food production enterprise. This may sound easy enough, until one actually tries to do it. It calls for the ability not only to measure the amount of suffering but also to compare that meaningfully with the cost of doing the thing in another way (or perhaps not at all).

At this point, for some, the logic of rights begins to look attractive as a fallback position. If we say that farm animals have the right not to be subjected to needless suffering, perhaps we can circumscribe a certain territory of permissible action and get on with the work. Although the ethic of suffering provides an obvious conceptual starting point for deciding what amount of pain is needless (e.g., any not outweighed by other morally significant impacts upon welfare, including human welfare), the idea of the right of an animal not to be subjected to needless suffering provides no obvious place to start.

In general, the rhetoric of rights will be used by those who wish to establish absolute permission or prohibition, once and for all, and this can be done without philosophical worrying about benefits and harms; however, partly because they are so sweeping and powerful, rights claims are more difficult to make acceptable to those who are not already convinced.

Talk of animal welfare, as opposed to animal rights, allows one to make relevant not only the degree of suffering that exists in a particular case but also other considerations (e.g., the potential benefits of foods of animal origin or the morally significant costs of minimizing the suffering of farm animals). On the other hand, it means that no amount

TABLE 11.1. LOGICAL IMPLICATIONS OF ANIMAL WELFARE AND ANIMAL RIGHTS

Welfare Consequences	Rights
Relative costs and benefits.	Right or wrong.
Different degrees of good and bad.	Rights represent a threshold.
Consider all available options.	Consider one possible action at a time, but permits plural solutions.
Reasoning hypothetical.	Morality is concrete.
Maximization flexible.	Rights are absolute.
Ethics highly empirical.	Deciding if a right is violated is a conceptual inference.
Positive: works toward a solution.	Negative: works toward eliminating things one should not do.
No set boundaries: decision involves a sense of balance.	Boundary under works at one's own discretion as long as rights of another is not breached.

of potential suffering is too small to be insignificant ethically, and every use of animals may become subject to bioethical evaluation.

PLURALITY OF REASONS AND VALUES

A focus on the dominant modern ethical theories—rights-based or consequentialist–utilitarian with welfare concerns for the consequences of action—may be insufficient as bases for ethical examination of animal well-being. Animals actually may be a part of the personal ethical lives of humans. There is also a primary, although not exclusive, moral concern for human others.

Exploring the ethical landscape of animal biotechnology, Donnelley et al. (1994) raise issues that have general application to animals in agriculture. These are not only, or even primarily, welfare issues. When seriously considering our ethical duties to animals, critics and agriculturalists usually consider only individual animal welfare or experiential well-being, particularly pain and suffering, and not the broader significance of animal and animate life per se. In the case of intervention into nature—biotechnologies or breeding animals for specialized purposes (dairy animals for high milk production, turkeys with large breast muscles, chickens with high egg production)—the very character of the animal is manipulated. The question might be asked if humans have the right to undertake such interventions, but they have done so for centuries.

The human use of animals and the intervention into their natural settings and ecosystems exist within the complex fabric of human communities and as part of the wider cultural theme of human interventions into nature. Thus, the full range of human interactions with nature constitutes an appropriate context for raising final ethical concerns. Paraphrasing Donnelley et al. (1994), we ask: What should be the ethically self-imposed limits, if any, of human interventions into nature? Does intensified animal agriculture have special features that mark it for special ethical attention? Do the scope, scale, and depth of the new intensive and biotechnological interventions constitute a new ethical principle? Should we be guided by a single moral reason and ultimate value, or are we obligated to respond to a plurality of reasons and ultimate values, not derived from one another and not easily coordinated?

Donnelley and coauthors (1994) asked if there was a morally significant difference between the new and the old practices, and what practices, new or old, were ethically legitimate. These questions require paying attention to the various aspects of human activity, the different values and obligations involved, and the differing interventions into animal life. There are moral claims of welfare, respect, justice, and the human and natural good at play in particular situations of animal agriculture practice and intervention, but the failure of these claims may shift significantly with the context. Gussow (1994) illustrated the point:

The first thing likely to happen in the unlikely event that humans gradually eliminate domestic animals is that there would be less food. Soils suitable for tilling could theoretically feed more people if they were used to grow human rather than animal food, but the elimination of animal agriculture altogether would not support more people. Despite the fact that modern animal agriculture is usually a sink for feedgrains, much essential food is produced in all parts of the world by ruminants, which can produce high-quality food from grazing lands that are not suitable for crop growing. Without ruminants, Coppinger et al. (1992) point out, grasslands would probably revert to brush and forests.

Moreover, the problems created by agribusiness's assault on the environment cannot be solved by giving up flesh. Logging in the rainforest would not be halted through the act of rich people giving up beef. . . . The waste of water in the American west will not be eliminated with the elimination of cattle feeding, nor will the overuse of western public lands, because both are encouraged by short-sighted ecologically illogical policies that need fixing . . . in the nation's capitol.

Moreover, on a global scale, vegetarianism for all is unecological. There are many sustainable systems around the world that produce animals and plants for human consumption in which eliminating animals would decrease both sustainability and food output. However, these systems are threatened by modern agriculture; they need protection, encouragement, and more research so that they can be adapted to modern conditions.

The several spheres of human activity are not sealed off from one another. There is always the temptation to intrude from the outside the context at hand and establish influence of one ultimate ethical value over the plural others, whether the value is human or animal welfare, respect, justice, environmental integrity, or the cultural good. All interventions in animal and human life involve moral concerns for humans as well as animals and for various aspects of welfare, respect, justice, and the human good.

We are reminded that the use and manipulation of living organisms, both plant and animal, with a concomitant and often radical alteration in their form and function has always been a part of the cultural existence of humans (Donnelley et al., 1994). A web of nature exists. All living organisms use or are used by other organisms. Singleton (1994) argued that "from procaryotes to humans, we are all only somebody's next meal. To believe otherwise is to reject a fundamental premise of modern biology."

Humans are aware of this web of nature. Through intervention in nature, humans have long altered the biological world around them. This playing with nature is largely responsible for the development of human cultures and civilization, and alteration of other organisms for human benefit has not always been detrimental to the individual organisms or species (Coppinger and Smith, 1983; Budiansky, 1992).

Intervention in animal life, whether medical research, biotechnology, or development of systems of intensive agriculture, is a powerful tool in modern society. Such interventions promise to transform health care, markets, and agribusiness. They present a new era of human existence and well-being although plural moral values exist concerning these matters. They come out of the several spheres or domains of human activity. Each sphere, whether farming and ranching, consuming food, doing scientific research, or living in a city removed from food production or whatever, has its perspective of the world. Each is moved by dominant values (beliefs, attitudes, and ethical values). Each involves an overriding notion of how life should be lived (Donnelley et al., 1994b).

The animal protection movement of today is grounded in the two major traditions of philosophy and the environment of a modern, industrialized country like the United States or the countries of western Europe. It will not likely go away (Varner, 1994b). The animal agriculture system is grounded in the major tradition, based on the web of nature, that humans and other animals must use other organisms to live and thrive. A food production system that includes animals also will not go away. Throughout the world and for much of the history of the United States, wild animals have been and are being replaced by domestic animals that provide food, fuel, fiber, and work (McDowell, 1991). Agricultural systems are being revised to feed the populations, improve the economies, prevent disease, and improve human health. Although none of these functions by itself would justify a cavalier view of animal treatment, they are forces that modify an individual's world view of human–animal interdependence.

There is, however, a philosophical diversity underlying the animal protection movements (Varner, 1994b). "Animal rights philosophies run the philosophical gamut from a utilitarianism which may be similar to that held by ranchers and farmers to an outright animal rights view." Varner (1994b) noted that some would agree that "certain kinds of animal agriculture are permissible," and even on a true animal rights view like Regan's, it is possible to endorse some uses of animals. Where are the boundaries of acceptability of an agricultural system and its treatment of animals? Animal right's views legitimately increase the burden of proof that science and agricultures should meet in the use of animals. Thinkers in animal agriculture need to sort out their reasoning to ascertain if what they do to animals is a genuinely important practice in the process of meeting human needs.

With a plurality of moral obligations, it would seem that no sphere of human activity and no ethical interest should be allowed to override the legitimate ethical obligation of the plural others (Donnelley et al., 1994). How do we reach an ethically adequate accommodation between rival values and their human advocates? Varner (1994b) has suggested that confrontation be replaced with genuine conversation and dialogue. Civility can also be a resource. Sanders and Jasper (1994) stated that arguments over concrete cases, taken in their context, will more likely lead to agreement than those over fundamental moral issues.

ANIMAL AWARENESS

There is a general consensus that animals perceive sensations, particularly pain (Griffin, 1976, 1984; Kitchell and Erickson, 1983; Rollin, 1989). Even today one cannot characterize animals's cognition or conscious mental experiences directly, although there are substantial arguments based on indirect evidence that animals possess conscious awareness of their experiences, that they have subjective feelings and that they think (Griffin, 1976, 1984; Dawkins, 1980, 1985; Duncan, 1993). Science may become instructive in these matters. The observations and experimental results on subhuman primates are well-known (Goodall, 1971; Patterson and Linden, 1981), but even chickens (Stone et al., 1984; Tauson, 1993) and pigs (Jensen and Algers, 1984; Algers and Jensen, 1985) are now believed to communicate thoughtfully with their respective social grouping.

What we do not know—and what needs to be learned if we are ever going to be able to answer certain questions in both agriculture and philosophy—is how much, if any, an animal suffers (i.e., experiences an unpleasant emotional state such as fear, pain, frustration, or exhaustion [Brambell, 1965]) beyond some (as yet undescribed) threshold as the result of specific experiences of interest.

ANIMAL STRESS AND DISTRESS

Fundamental to assessing welfare in a farm animal are answers to two questions, the second of which will be exceedingly difficult to answer (Dawkins, 1985): Does the animal have subjective feelings? What indicators reveal any such feelings? Knowledge of animals's conscious mental experiences can be gained only via indirect experimental evidence at this time, a sort of third-person observation; hence, any conclusion must be considered tentative (Griffin, 1976, 1984; Dawkins, 1980, 1990a). In other words, the question is not: Do animals have feelings? There is general agreement that they do. The question is: How does the animal feel, living in this or that production system? Our knowledge of the cognitive abilities of farm animals is limited (Curtis and Stricklin, 1991). Duncan and Dawkins (1983) have alleged the presence of "indicators that with careful experimentation we may be able to [use to] accumulate indirect evidence about animals's subjective feelings. This should be our ultimate aim. There are many problems but they are not insurmountable." Testing the preferences of animals is an evolving paradigm relative to determining awareness, but is a frontier in animal welfare science (Fraser et al., 1993).

An animal is under stress when required to make extreme functional, structural, behavioral, or immunological adjustments in order to cope with adverse aspects of its environment. Because animals differ in the ways they perceive and respond to environmental impacts, the same environment can be stressful to one individual but not to another. An environmental factor that contributes to the stressful nature of an environment is called a *stressor*.

When one measures stress in an animal, one is limited to measuring the effects of stress: the changes that the stressor causes in the animal or the responses that the animal invokes while trying to reestablish or maintain a normal internal state in the face of a stressor. Effects of stress on health and productive and reproductive performance are a primary topic of production-oriented animal science research. The more difficult step is interpretation. At what point does stress stop and when does distress (i.e., excessive or unpleasant stress) begin? What does it mean when an animal increases its breathing rate by 250 percent in one environment compared to another? Does a 65-percent increase in plasma glucocorticoid concentration indicate the animal is under extreme stress? If so, then how extreme?

The animal's environment is complex. The external environment is comprised of thousands of physical, chemical, and biological factors that surround an animal. Each varies over space and time. Yet despite fluctuating external conditions, the animal must maintain a steady state in its internal environment.

An *environmental adaptation* refers to any functional, structural, behavioral, or immunological trait that favors an animal's survival or reproduction in a given environment, especially an extreme or adverse one. A *strain* is any functional, structural, behavioral, or immunological reaction to an environmental stimulus. Strains may be adaptive or nonadaptive. Many strains enhance the chances of the animal's survival, but others are seemingly of little consequence. A *stress* is any environmental situation that provokes strain by an animal, and a stressor may be chronic (gradual and sustained) or acute (abrupt and often profound). Thus environmental stress provokes animal strain (Selye, 1952).

It seems to be a relatively simple task to subject experimental animals to a controlled stressor and measure a resultant change in some physiological, anatomical, immunological, or behavioral parameter, but an objective index of stress in terms of animal health, performance, and well-being has been elusive. Marked physiological change may indicate only that an animal is adapting successfully to its environment, not necessarily that it is succumbing to adversity. Thus stress seems to be more of a concept than a biological reality (Dantzer, 1993), and appears doomed to remain a concept until health, defined as a state of psychological and physiological well-being, can be translated into biological terms. Some even argue that research effort to determine stress is using resources that should be used for research that could better be used to improve the welfare of animals in agriculture.

DEFINITION OF ANIMAL WELFARE

The issue is a definition of animal welfare, which will determine the guidelines (and likely laws, policy, and regulations) for the care and use of domestic animals (Moberg, 1993). Definition also implies the eventual ability to describe the well-being of the animal.

If animal welfare is expressed in noncognitive terms (i.e., in terms of biological responses), these can be measured, or at least we should be able to measure them (Moberg, 1993). The biological cost of stress (i.e., the diversion of an animal's biological resources from their normal function) may be related to some pre-pathological state in which the animal is vulnerable to disease or reproductive failure or growth is impaired. Moberg (1993) suggested that such measurements can provide the bases for the evaluation of an animal's well-being put at risk under various management conditions. McGlone (1993) argued that only when the animals reach the pre-pathological state can we say that welfare is poor (reaching the state of immunosuppression is an example). This standard, however, seems insufficient.

Broom (1993) defined the welfare of an animal in terms of its state as it attempts to cope with the environment. A variety of measurements—the environmental factors (stress) that overtax an animal's control system; behavioral, physiological, or immunological measures that indicate coping is difficult; and suffering, which may be in addition to injury or immunosuppression—could be used to pinpoint a continuum from good to very poor welfare.

Duncan (1993) argued that although it may not be possible to give a scientific definition, the term animal welfare is useful to describe a distinct phenomenon, and concluded that welfare has everything to do with what the animal feels. The study of animal cognition is likely to be pivotal in the animal welfare debate. At present, our knowledge about cognitive abilities (awareness, thinking, and the like) is limited (Curtis and Stricklin, 1991). If cognition is to be studied, an integrated research approach appears needed (Mench, 1993).

Philosopher Bernard Rollin (1993) has stated that science, as carried out today and with its current value judgment, is not enough. He believes that we are entering a new phase for animal welfare science based on a new moral posture that requires scientists to study ways to make animals "happy" (not only not miserable) while permitting society to continue utilizing animals. He predicts that this will change our systems of production, housing, and husbandry to better fit the natures of the animals. Saying this, Rollin (1993) would impute a value system to science that may or may not receive the concurrence of scientists. Most scientists hold that measures should be carried out in as objective a way as possible, and then moral judgments about what is tolerable (or what makes for animal happiness) should be made afterward (Broom, 1993).

PUBLIC POLICY AND LEGISLATION

WESTERN EUROPE. Since the late 1960s in many western European nations, laws have been in force that regulate the way animals are cared for on farms (Harrison, 1993). The current movement dates back to 1964, when Ruth Harrison's book *Animal Machines* was published in London. In response to subsequent pressures from concerned citizens, including many humane activists, the British Parliament appointed a technical committee to "enquire into conditions in intensive systems of livestock husbandry" (Brambell, 1965). Soon, the United Kingdom's Ministry of Agriculture, Fisheries, and Food had formed the Farm Animal Welfare Advisory Committee (superseded in 1979 by an enlarged Farm Animal Welfare Council) to advise ministers on action to improve the welfare of animals on the farm. By 1968, the parliament had passed an act that provided for development and publication of advisory codes of practice for the housing and management of livestock and poultry in intensive production systems. The Farm Animal Welfare Council's first public statement listed "five freedoms" (Spedding, 1993):

1. Freedom from thirst, hunger, or malnutrition.
2. Appropriate comfort and shelter.

3. Prevention, or rapid diagnosis and treatment, of vice, injury, parasitic infestation, and disease.
4. Freedom to display normal patterns of behavior.
5. Freedom from fear.

During the 1980–81 session of Parliament, the House of Commons Agriculture Committee decided to update the Brambell Committee report. Like the Brambell Committee, the new panel condemned battery cages, veal crates and sow stalls, and tethers, which they "viewed with distaste" (Harrison, 1993). They stated that "[w]here unacceptable suffering can be eliminated only at extra cost, that cost should be borne or the product foregone."

In response to similar pressures from animal-protection communities in every nation of western Europe, similar laws have been passed and regulations promulgated in at least six other western European nations (AWI, 1978; Harrison, 1993). Keeping laying hens in cages is now being phased out in several nations; sows cannot be kept on a tether or in a crate in some countries; and keeping veal calves in individual crates is against the law in the United Kingdom. Interestingly, in western Europe the trend to regulating farm animal care is still confined to the northern, or affluent, nations. Nevertheless, both the Commission of the European Union and the Council of Europe are involved in international legislation and regulations related to farm animal welfare (Bendixin, 1980; Honduis, 1980; Spedding, 1993).

The most sweeping law in western Europe now is the Swedish law adopted in July 1988, under which cattle, pigs, and chickens are freed from intensive farming methods. Cattle have grazing rights, pigs must be given separate bedding and feeding places, and chickens have been freed from cramped quarters. The use of hormones or antibiotics as growth or lactation promoters is not permitted. Switzerland has mandated that egg production be done without battery cages.

The general belief of concerned individuals in Europe is that government has a responsibility to bring supply and demand for agricultural products into better balance: to create an agriculture that can coexist harmoniously with the environment, and to restrict livestock systems that do not offer the animal a life of comparative fulfillment (Harrison, 1993).

UNITED STATES. America is said to have had the distinction of being the first country to acknowledge the rights of animals by enacting statutory legislation to protect them from cruel treatment. In 1641, the Puritans of the Massachusetts Bay Colony voted to have printed their first legal code, *The Body of Liberties* (Leavitt and Halverson, 1978). Included is Liberty 92: "No man shall exercise any Tirranny or Crueltie toward any bruite Creature which are usuallie kept for man's use." Since that time, numerous state and federal laws dealing with the protection of animals, including agricultural animals (sometimes specifically), have been enacted (AWI, 1978). The most important federal statute with respect to humane treatment of animals, apart from the federal Humane Slaughter Act enacted in 1958 and amended in 1978, is the Animal Welfare Act, which was signed into law in 1966 and amended in 1970, 1976, and 1985. This act mandates the USDA to promulgate and enforce regulations pertaining to the care and use of animals in research and to the commercial transport of animals; the act as amended now specifically includes agricultural animals.

A major animal welfare legislation was the Food Security Act of 1985 (Tweeten, 1993). Federal legislation established rules for the care of animals for science but has not set animal welfare rules for farms (except in slaughter for poultry and "downer" cattle.) In recent years at both the state and federal levels, several pieces of legislation have been proposed that dealt more or less directly with the production of animals on farms. Although some of these bills and resolutions have attracted considerable cosponsorship, none has been enacted. Despite the fact that no significant legislation related to the regulation of animal care in production systems and on farms has been passed by either house of the U.S. Congress, numerous and various individuals and organizations have actively sought passage of legislation. This legislation would call for a congressional investigation of the methods and practices used in producing agricultural animals in intensive systems and enactment of appropriate laws and promulgation and enforcement of appropriate regulations in light of the findings.

Federal legislation introduced in 1989 and 1990 took an entirely different tack. A law has been enacted to protect farm animal and research facilities, making it a federal offense to enter, conceal oneself or remain in a research facility without the owner's consent, or to remove an animal or property with the intent to disrupt or damage the facility.

ANIMAL PROTECTION MOVEMENT

The early 1980s saw an expansion of animal rights groups and traditional welfare groups. Estimates vary, but by the end of the 1980s, the rights groups in the United States numbered in the hundreds and the animal welfare groups (many local humane societies) were counted in the thousands.

Leading humane advocates have taken individualistic approaches to their work. Consider the pioneer. The farm animal welfare movement started with the 1964 publication of *Animal Machines* by Ruth Harrison. In some ways, Harrison may have been as influential in stimulating concerns and public policy actions in the animal welfare movement in the United Kingdom and around the world as Rachel Carson was in the environmental movement that began with her publication of *Silent Spring* in 1962. Ruth Harrison considered herself to be a moderate, not an activist, in the sense that activism to her implied breaking laws and carrying out terrorist activities, which she felt to be destructive of the very cause it purports to help. Basically, she believed a that line had to be drawn regarding how to care for animals properly. Still, she recognized that every nation has an obligation to feed its people. She believed that this should be done with basic foodstuffs, and products for "pleasure eating" ought to come later. Harrison emphasized that, for her, the issue was less one of animal rights versus human rights than one of human responsibilities.

The history of the militant animal rights–welfare movement in the United States has been detailed by Jasper and Nelkin (1992). The movement began in the 1970s as Peter Singer's (1975) book provided an ideological frame of reference and spur to action. Questionable, unattractive research on sexual behavior using cats, involving what might be termed as mutilation (e.g., removing parts of the brain, severing nerves in the penis), at the American Museum of Natural History provided the target; Henry Spira provided the leadership. The research was discontinued, but the visibility of research with animals leading to expression of pro-animal values and protectionism spawned hundreds of organizations, and hundreds of thousands of followers have been recruited.

Of the many organizations, People for the Ethical Treatment of Animals (PETA) is among the most successful. It is controversial and perhaps the richest, and has encouraged public acts to demonstrate opposition to certain uses of animals (Jasper and Nelkin, 1992). In Defense of Animals (IDA) was founded in 1982, and its actions have remained nonviolent: civil disobedience, lawsuits, and disruptions. The Animal Liberation Front (ALF) was imported from Britain in 1979 and its alleged actions are often violent, destructive, and unlawful, such as destroying research equipment and information (Jasper and Nelkin,

1992). The Animal Legal Defense Fund, formerly the Attorneys for Animal Rights, established in 1984, works within the legal structure to promote liberation of animals. Jasper and Nelkin (1992) noted that these four prominent organizations employ diverse tactics, yet share a strong, explicit ideology.

The animal activist movement continues to undergo change. Since the mid-1980s, when public awareness and activist outrage rose over laboratory treatment of research animals, the movement has evolved to include various ideologies that embrace both moderate single-issue groups and radical groups (Jamison and Lunch, 1992). Sanders and Jasper (1994) have suggested that the success of a movement depends on the personal style of the leader, the financing of the group, the ability of the group to win symbolic victories, and the longevity of the group, which may give the group time to become more ideological and tenacious.

CONCLUSION: THE ISSUES

Jasper and Nelkin (1992) summarized the practical aspects of the rights–welfare dichotomy vis-à-vis animal well-being. Rightists, for example, emphasize the emotional life of animals. Whereas the welfare movement focuses on an animal's ability to feel pain, rightists insist that animals have a full, conscious life to lead, and therefore, humans cannot morally justify cutting that life short, even if they do so painlessly.

Any suffering an animal experiences at the hands of a farmer or rancher usually falls into one of three categories: abuse, neglect, or deprivation. Deprivation is a subtle form of cruelty, and thus the most difficult to assess. It involves the denial of relatively less vital resources, the actual requirements for most of which have yet to be established. When an animal's needs are not being met, its well-being is more or less jeopardized. A particular decrement in well-being, however, does not necessarily place the animal in an unacceptable environment; perhaps the animal simply experiences less—but still an ethically acceptable amount of—well-being. Whether or not farm animals residing in certain intensive production systems are suffering from deprivation is a major issue.

Agricultural animals may have a hierarchy of needs along the lines of Maslow's (1970) scheme for human beings:

1. First and most basic would be farm animals's physiological needs—for feed, physical and biological elements of the environment, and health care. These are relatively well understood and fulfilled.
2. Intermediate would be the animals's safety needs. Although important in animal agriculture, these safety needs are tended somewhat less rigorously than are the physiological needs.
3. Ultimately, the animals's behavioral needs would require attention. Many believe that behavioral needs exist, but scientific evidence has not been obtained widely. Without empirical data, knowledgeable perception and common sense are called for.

On any animal farm, achieving the highest level of animal welfare possible, consistently, is likely an impossible exercise. D. C. Hardwick formulated the idea that an ethically acceptable level of animal welfare exists over a range of conditions provided by a variety of agricultural production systems, not only in one ideal set of circumstances (cited in Duncan, 1981). This acceptable range of environments, according to Hardwick, comprises a "welfare plateau." On the welfare plateau, a relatively small environmental change might improve subtly an animal's overall well-being, but anywhere on the welfare plateau the animal is "as free of suffering as possible."

Producers strive to adopt the production system that will be economically optimal while providing the animals an existence as free of suffering as possible. This is the producer's dilemma; they must decide on which animal-production systems to employ, while constrained by humane concerns on one hand and the realities of doing business in a free enterprise milieu on the other. Any resolution today offered on the issue of animal well-being as it relates to commercial animal agriculture is qualified by uncertainties and open questions.

SCIENTIFIC ISSUES. Quantitative evaluation of animal suffering has proven elusive, but the matrix consisting of productive performance, pathology, physiology, and behavior provides a framework of researchable topics that promise progress in our understanding of animal well-being. An answer, however tentative and qualified, to the question of animal feeling (the animal's experience of satisfaction or want) is central to the whole matter of animal well-being. The question can be narrowed by focusing on the comparative impacts of alternative production systems, as the production system is most likely to be the target of regulatory action; however, even with such a restriction, the area of needed research spans all areas of animal science, ranging from basic scientific research on biochemical and immunological reactions to applied research on management practices and production technologies.

In addition to these issues in the animal and veterinary sciences, a host of topics in the agricultural social sciences also must be included in the agenda for research. Research on the economic impact to producers of animal welfare regulation is needed, reflecting both the increased costs of regulation and the effect that restructured markets would have upon producers. Although it is likely that consumers would pay higher prices for animal products if necessary, the extent and distribution of increased costs to consumers are unknown.

Also, there is a need for sociological and political science research on the animal welfare–animal rights movement itself. Leaders in animal agriculture only now are becoming aware of the philosophical values and tactical goals that differentiate activists and determine their respective goals (Albright, 1985). Some of the philosophical positions taken by parties to both sides (pro-animal agriculture versus pro-animal rights) seem uncompromising, but within the range of opinion, some convergence of interest can emerge, and indeed is emerging. The potential impact of animal well-being concerns on the future of animal agriculture should elevate these questions near the top of priorities for research and higher education in the coming years.

PHILOSOPHICAL ISSUES. Even among scientific issues, the question of how we evaluate animal well-being is the cornerstone for all others. In choosing to research the social and economic impacts of animal welfare legislation, for example, one makes a tacit commitment to the philosophical belief that these impacts can somehow be weighed against any impacts upon the animals themselves.

Research and regulation of animal well-being is inevitably couched within a range of beliefs and assumptions about ethics and moral responsibility. These beliefs and assumptions may be unspoken, perhaps even unrecognized by the participants themselves, but nevertheless shape the direction of the debate. Responsible science and responsible policy require scientists to state their philosophy as explicitly as they can, and to enjoin critics as honestly as they are able. Continuing inquiry into the philosophical implications of animal welfare and animal rights can illuminate the issue, even if it does not resolve it.

Dawkins (1990b) in closing a review of Richard Ryder's (1989) book *Animal Revolution*, summarized the situation:

The way humans treat nonhuman animals is a matter of great importance, but to many people issues such as whether we should eat animals or do experiments on them are not "startling simple" but difficult in the extreme. One man's view of these matters . . . will appeal to some, but probably fail to convince those for whom the moral issues are more complex.

POLICY. Any tendency to ignore either the scientific or the philosophical components of the animal well-being issue places decision makers in business, government, and research institutions in an ethically tenuous and ultimately indefensible position. Once the responsibility to address the issue has been accepted, some initial image of the interaction between factual, positive knowledge on one hand and value-oriented, normative knowledge on the other, must be offered to take the first steps in addressing the difficult policy choices of the years ahead. This image or view of an issue is, in a sense, a hypothesis on how to proceed. Like any hypothesis, it is open to revision as its weaknesses are recognized and it is modified to develop new strengths.

Jamison and Lunch (1992) suggested that as with other political movements in the United States (civil rights, feminist, environmental) the animal rights movement is likely to move in the direction of mainstream American politics and away from broad, systemic critiques of Western society. Motives may be beyond feelings for animals; they may be largely a symbolic expression of egalitarian, social, and political views concerning science and technology.

The animal rights movement, although abetted by moralistic eloquence, has had only limited sway on the routine behavior and preferences of most people (Jasper and Nelkin, 1992). Few Americans have been willing to give up meat, but to doggedly defend current practices of animal agriculture is to encourage further polarization. As Jasper and Nelkin (1992) have bluntly put it, "to denounce the movement as irrational, kooky, or terrorist is to miss the popular appeal of its moral intuitions and popular beliefs." When debate for one reason or another becomes polarized, it becomes extremely difficult to cultivate a middle ground.[3] It is easier to be an extremist. One can defend an extreme view to one's own people; even the other side expects and understands that it takes much courage to occupy the center ground.

This discussion may be seen as reaching for middle ground. We believe it is not, that it is rather more an attempt to emphasize clarification of the elements of the issues, an activity that seems to be an important antecedent to understanding if and where a center ground can exist.

Many in animal agriculture often hold a polarized view, but nevertheless can be seen as serving as a stimulus for change. The chances for consensus may appear to be slim, but the possibilities of convergence even without agreement may be possible (Sanders and Jasper, 1994; Varner, 1994b). If, however, animal agriculture is a silent constituency, even convergence of this sort will not be possible.

NOTES

1. This chapter is based on a manuscript originally written by Paul B. Thompson and Stanley E. Curtis for the workshop on Ethical Aspects of Food, Agriculture, and Natural Resources Policy, and is available from the Committee on Agricultural Research Policy, 223 Scovell Hall, University of Kentucky, Lexington, Ky. 40546. It has been rewritten in part, and edited as a chapter in this book.

2. Selections from the works of René Descartes have been translated and reprinted in a number of sources. One of these is in *Animal Rights and Human Obligations*, ed. T. Regan and P. Singer, 60–68. Englewood Cliffs, N.J.: Prentice-Hall (1976).

3. This is a comment made by Colin Spedding in a panel discussion at the International Conference on Farm Animal Welfare: Ethical, Technological, and Sociopolitical Perspectives, June 1991, Aspen Institute, Queenstown, Maryland. The proceedings of the conference are published in the *Journal of Agricultural and Environmental Ethics* 6, special supplements 1 and 2.

CHAPTER 12

FOOD AND SOCIETY

It is quite improbable that humans will ever create on any significant scale sustainable food systems that do not use animals and their products for either wool, fertilizer, draft power and transportation, biogas, or milk and eggs, or even for meat.

—JOAN GUSSOW (1994)

The importance of food consumption in determining health, development, and human welfare has been emphasized in contemporary nutritional literature (Mason et al., 1996). Malnutrition kills in synergy with infectious diseases; it is estimated that more than 50 percent of child deaths in the world can be avoided by eliminating malnutrition. Diet-related, noncommunicable chronic diseases are of increasing significance worldwide. Childhood malnutrition has a lifelong effect on human size, capacity for work, educability, and perhaps longevity.

Conceptually and systemically, the issues of food consumption, human health, the mores of society and animal agriculture are linked. Food acts as a boundary marker of identity. Culture works to define what will be eaten and indeed what society calls food. Animals provide a substantial portion of the world's food supply, more so in affluent societies than in developing countries. In many developing countries, however, the lives of people are entwined with their domestic animals. The issues are accessibility, dietary habits, cultural and religious forces, personal beliefs, and the socioeconomic status of individuals. Examination of these issues is the purpose of this chapter.

ATTITUDES AND CULTURE

Whether animal products are in the diet or not is often a matter of human attitude. In order to have an animal agriculture, which has a destructive harvest (i.e., one that involves slaughter of the animals), there must be a certain attitude in the populace. People must regard the animal as somehow subservient to humans. As a nation we have little aversion to eating chicken; who loves a chicken? We have difficulty killing dogs and horses because we regard them as friends, in some sense equal to us. Some Filipinos, on the other hand, exploit the dog, making the dog vicious for purpose of protection and also fattening and eating the dog.

Take children through a slaughter plant and see what happens to their meat consumption. Vegetarianism may also stem from a repulsion against killing animals, although there are also cultural bases for vegetarianism. The spread of vegetarianism has become a fundamental goal of believers in animal protection.

Animal muscle foods, on the other hand, may have provided humans with a sense of aggressiveness that might not otherwise have been present. The ancient Greek historian Polybius said, "Tyrants introduced meat into our diet so that they could have violent men at their disposal." Those who concur that animal protein is responsible for human aggressiveness would be apprehensive at the prospect of a meatless diet.

The cultural mediation of dietary patterns includes involvement of certain religious, moral, and ethical factors. These factors are at work today in different forms, ranging from the nongovernmental organization (NGO) movement for distribution of food to starving peoples to the dictate of an Islamic government that only meat from animals slaughtered in the Islamic tradition would be acceptable for import into the country.

Religions have their dietary edicts. Biblical accounts refer to killing the fatted lamb in the preparation of feasts. Fasts are associated with both codified and uncodified religions. These may pose important cultural–nutritional questions, particularly as fasts may be carried to an extreme. The aversion to carrion in the United States may have a logical public health basis, but probably is more a residual of Jewish, Christian, and Islamic prohibitions.

Perhaps the most challenging encounter of animal agriculture with religion will come from Hinduism and Buddhism (Palmer, 1990). A strong vegetarian ethic of Hinduism is derived from the belief in karma, the reincarnational, cyclical perspective that life is composed of souls that pass from human to lower to higher animal forms and to humans again. The Hindu viewpoint on nature is entwined with a reverence for life. The attitude is to use, but not kill, life. The cow is important to Hindus. A Hindu does not kill a cow, but the cow provides milk and milk products that are important dietary elements. Dung is a construction material and an essential fuel. In some places the cow or its offspring is used for plowing. Cattle in India may have owners and economic value. Cattle in India may be sold. The pressures against cow slaughter and beef eating, however, are being moderated by the increasing secularization of Indian life. Those Hindu Indians who migrate to other countries, however, may remain lifelong vegetarians (Sanders and Reddy, 1994).

A similar concept of cyclical flow through birth, growth, maturation, decline, death, and rebirth is found in Buddhist tenets (Palmer, 1990). Although vegetarianism is not a strict requirement for Buddhist communities, some sects give importance to not eating meat (Chapple, 1986). The viewpoint that all life is interrelated has been used to promote avoidance of meat. Jainism, Zoroastrianism, and sects in other Eastern religions stress vegetarianism (Barkas, 1975).

Religions can both be conservative and provide the framework for innovation. Thus cultures either prescribe or proscribe certain nutritional factors when certain foods are prescribed or proscribed. Yeast synthesizes amino acids and vitamins from inorganic nitrogen; yeast thus enhances the nutritional value of grain, whether the product is beer or bread. Which form, beer or bread, in which the fermentative enhancement of nutritional value is used differs with the culture. Foods may also have greater religious use when they have psychoactive properties (e.g., alcohol), but the control of excessive use is at the bases of the prohibition of alcoholic drinks.

Religious traditions can be the basis of transferring information about foods. The Jewish and Islamic religions have codes of detailed rules. Rules affect production by governing which species of animals are edible. Rules govern mixing of products of different species at a meal. Jewish rules govern holidays on which agricultural activities are prohibited. Rules require that the animal be unblemished and pure, ensuring both care of animals and conditions of storage. Rules set distribution: gathering of tithes and first fruits, and the handling of Kosher meat in which the rules of processing are elaborate.

Food habits are thus culturally determined and set by attitudes, and cultural habits and attitudes are not easily changed. The diets that people have traditionally accepted have been determined by a particular environment in which they live and the historical and cultural choices they make about acquiring, distributing, and consuming food. Neither physical nor cultural environments determine diet absolutely, but they establish a framework of dietary choices. Dietary patterns result from likes and dislikes and interactions of factors in the physical, biological, technological, social, and cultural environments.

FOOD HABITS DO CHANGE

Today, the major forces of change in food consumptions are the migrations of people, particularly from developing countries to the developed. Market analysts in the United States now recognize factors such as a growing availability of international foods, a shift to fruit- and vegetable-based foods, the Asian influence, adoption of California cuisine, importance of appearance and texture, increase in use of side dishes, and home growing. Additional factors of U.S. origin are smaller meals (*grazing*), growth in exotic white meats (e.g., catfish), microwavable foods, *healthy* snacks, and now the urge to treat oneself to an occasional break in the dietary discipline with a big steak. Food patterns of one country are also marketed to other countries.

The changes in dietary consumption in the United States are reflected in consumption (actually disappearance) data (Table 12.1). During the first 75 years of the twentieth century, a traditional pattern was established and placed meat in a dominant position in the diet of most Americans. Animal products (milk, meat, and egg groups of foods) provided major proportions of energy and nutrients at all ages, for both men and women. About 70 to 75 percent of the dietary protein in the United States came from foods in these groups. Up until the late 1970s, red meat (beef, pork, veal) increasingly contributed to the caloric intake. Overall, the average consumption of milk and milk products decreased during the 1960s and 1970s, but the consumption of cheese and yogurt has grown. The milk group remains an important supplier of energy, protein, fat, and carbohydrates, especially for infants, children, and teenagers. Generally, less protein is consumed by the elderly.

The 1996 USDA report on food consumption (Putnam and Allshouse, 1996) indicated that each American consumed annually on average, "63 pounds more of commercially grown vegetables than in 1970, 63 pounds more of grain products, 49 pounds more of fruit, 25 pounds more of caloric sweeteners, 16 pounds more of total red meat, poultry and fish (boneless, trimmed equivalent), 15 pounds more of cheese, 14 pounds more of added fats and oils, . . . 71 fewer eggs, . . . and 7 gallons less of milk. . . . Away-from-home meals and snacks captured 47 percent of the U.S. food dollar in 1994, up from 39 percent in 1980 and 34 percent in 1970. The percentage of disposable personal income spent on food declined from 13.9 percent in 1970 to 11.4 percent in 1994."

The consumption of eggs and the direct consumption of fat have decreased, although through most of the past three decades more fat was used, primarily in the preparation of fast-food products.

The consumption of bread, rolls, biscuits, pies, cakes, and cookies has declined from the 1960s to 1990s, but that decrease has been offset by a shift to other grain products such as pizzas, tortillas, and pasta. Vegetables and fruits maintained a portion of the diet of all people including infants and are increasing significantly today.

By 1977, the reported energy intakes of women in the age group of 23 to 64 years averaged from 1,515 to 1,615 kilocalories (kcal) per day; the energy intakes were about the same in 1985–86. Energy intakes for men of the same age averaged from 2,150 to 2,450 kcal. These levels of consumption are of particular interest in the light of recent estimates that place the national food supply at about 3,500 kcal per person per day (Table 12.2), leading Hegsted (1980) to pose the questions: Where does all that food go? How much redundancy in our total food supply is required to nourish adequately our population? How much redundancy in food supplies is needed to minimize or prevent undernutrition? The average actual caloric consumption of Americans of 1800 to 1900 kilocalories per day is not greatly different from that reported in many developing countries in which undernutrition and malnutrition are common. Few Americans, however, are hungry or suffer nutrient deficiency, and as obesity increases in the 1990s, it appears that more of the food supply is actually eaten.

THE FORCES OF CHANGE

The remarkable changes in food habits of the United States during the twentieth century can also be traced to evolutions in the interactions within the technological as well as social and ideological features of society (Connor, 1981; Capps, 1986; Senauer, 1986). Nutritional science discovered the elements of nutrition and thus permitted evaluation of the dietary pattern. Popular interest in nutrition heightened.

Animal flesh foods, including poultry products, remained a center-piece in the American diet, but new perceptions concerning meat developed in the 1960s and 1970s that placed food from plant sources in a more preeminent position. Prior to this time, and for many people today, the dietary pattern often was controlled by the work and social calendar. In the 1960s and 1970s, the pattern of food consumption became mixed up in the mood and social environment, the concern for pollution of the environment, the protest of a war conducted in Vietnam, and to other societal problems. Food in general, particularly the rejection of red meat, became a symbol of protest for many Americans. Concerns for the dietary relationships to health continued the trend into the 1980s and 1990s. Traditional food technology responded to produce a supply of food products deemed appropriate to a plant-based dietary pattern. The food system developed in response to alternative diets.

Throughout most of American history, food has been a center of social interaction, even to the point of elitism (Levenstein, 1988). At the turn of the twentieth century, there were tales about dinner parties of the rich. Sunday dinners were the pivotal social events of rural America. Now, such lunches and dinners appear to have become more moderate. Portions are smaller, except in steak houses; dessert is foregone, especially for lunch, although people have been observed to restrict the caloric content of the main portion of the meal and then eat the dessert as if there was no tomorrow.

By the turn of the 1980s, there was a different display relative to nutrition and food habits. John Brooks (1981), in an essay, wrote of an American cult of thinness that has coincided with a great rise in national affluence; thinness and wealth were regarded as concomitant values. Nutritional consequences became severe, ranging from possible frank deficiencies to the ultimate display, the disease termed anorexia nervosa. These are serious, sometimes fatal, conditions. Obesity and obese persons, however, remain in the population at higher numbers than ever before.

ECONOMIC ISSUES

Capps (1986) and Senauer (1986) suggested that changes in year-to-year food consumption patterns are typically more dependent on supply and price changes than on shifts in demand. Short-term changes in consumption reflect mostly changes in supply rather than changes in consumer tastes. From 1970 on, price changes may have accounted for much of the change in demand of meats. For example, over most of the period, poultry became a lower-priced alternative to red meat. Poultry, instead of fish, captured the decrease in red meat consumption.

The consumption of chicken has steadily increased since 1965, while the beef share increased until 1976 and declined thereafter (Putnam and Allshouse, 1996). According to Eales and Unnevehr (1988), changes in shares of chicken products can be explained by movements in relative prices and income, but a larger change occurred in the constant growth in demand for chicken parts, independent of relative price movements. Significant increase in the consumption of chicken parts and processed chicken may have been fostered by the growth of fast-food outlets (Wohlgenant, 1986). Note the buffalo wing phenomenon. The largest beef/poultry substitution was between hamburger and poultry, but the changes in preferences since the 1970s have led to the substitution of chicken parts for beef table cuts. Incomes have grown, tending to strengthen beef demand, but they have grown more rapidly in the higher income groups in which beef purchases are not very sensitive to increasing income (Putnam and Allshouse, 1996).

Changes in lifestyle have created changes as well. The percentage of single-person households more than doubled since 1950. During the same period, the proportion of more-than-two-person households decreased. Single-person and two-person households use more convenience foods per person than do more-than-two-person households because of time for food preparation (Capps, 1986). With more women working, breakfast habits changed, contributing to a decline in egg consumption. Consumers increasingly want the food they buy to be easy and quick to prepare. Thus thousands of convenience foods, particularly frozen items, mixes and ready-to-serve items are now in the marketplace (Capps, 1986). Great growth has occurred in the fast-food market.

Economists analyzing patterns of food consumption and expenditures also accept the premise that concerns for nutrition and health were embedded in changes in food patterns of the 1980s and 1990s (Schmitz and Capps, 1993). Concerns of obesity and the health factors outlined in nutrition guidelines and nutrition labels were factors leading to Americans moderating their intake of foods high in saturated fats, cholesterol, and sodium. The domestic consumption of fats and oils reflects a switch from animal fats to vegetable sources, predominantly soybean and corn. The belief remains that because of the impetus to reduce saturated fats and levels of serum cholesterol, the consumption of whole milk, beef, and pork have declined, although the consumptions of poultry and fishery products, low-fat milk, cheese, and frozen dairy products have increased (Capps, 1986; Schmitz and Capps, 1993). The analysis of Eales and Unnevehr (1988), however, could easily be interpreted to indicate that as *quality* table cut beef consumption decreased, it was replaced by *quality* chicken parts and fish. The advent of mandatory nutritional labeling of food products in the United States will likely maintain these trends.

Economics studies attempting to partition the effects of health concerns from the effects of prices, distribution of income, the aging population, and other factors have not been easy to obtain; however, studies of the kinds of exchanges (e.g., vegetable fats for animal fats), the survey of the beef market, and the claimed successes of pork industry's "the other white meat" campaign suggest strongly that health issues do in fact play a role in the selection of foods, particularly meats. Characteristic American diets, however, reflect remarkable variety, although there are exceptions that may be related to poverty (Senauer, 1986). The eating patterns of people in the United States demonstrate a complexity of human behavior and make it difficult to isolate individual behavioral factors affecting dietary intake.

FOOD CHOICES AND THE CONCERN ABOUT HEALTH

DIETING AND ALTERNATIVE DIETS. Dieting to lose weight is practiced by large numbers of people, especially females, but there is little evidence that long-term changes in diet preferences result. The surveys noted above suggest that Americans consume relatively large amounts of meat and sugar and use more refined than whole grain products and larger amounts of commercially processed than fresh foods. In contrast, the majority of the world's population today subsists on vegetarian or near-vegetarian diets for reasons that run the gamut: economic, philosophical, religious, cultural and ecological. Obesity, however, is becoming an increasing problem worldwide as nations undergo the nutrition transition (i.e., experience large changes in dietary and activity patterns; Popkin et al., 1996). The ultimate impact of this transition remains to be determined.

Since the 1970s, interest in dietary alternatives to the usual diet heightened in the United States. Some young people for the first time became vegetarians, adding to the numbers who had been vegetarian all their lives. Others following alternative diets include users of

TABLE 12.1. U.S. FOOD SUPPLY. TRENDS IN QUANTITIES OF FOOD AVAILABLE FOR CONSUMPTION PER CAPITA

Item	Per capita consumption[1]						
	1909–13	1929–33	1944–48	1970–74	1975–79	1980–84	1990–94
				Pounds			
Red meat[2]							
Beef	53.2	38.2	48.2	79.1*	82.8*	73.1*	63.0*
Veal	6.3	5.9	9.8	1.7*	2.3*	1.4*	0.8*
Pork	60.9	63.6	63.9	47.7*	42.4*	48.3*	46.3*
Lamb and mutton	6.2	5.8	5.4	1.9*	1.1*	1.1*	1.0*
Fish[3]	11.2						
Fresh and frozen		5.2	6.0	7.0	7.9	8.1	9.9
Canned and cured		4.3	3.8	5.1	5.0	4.8	5.0
Poultry							
Chicken	14.9	14.4	19.3	27.4**	29.4**	33.7**	46.3**
Turkey	1.1	1.6	3.1	6.7**	6.9**	8.4**	14.1**
Eggs	36.8	38.5	46.5	37.9	34.6	33.5	30.0
Dairy							
Fluid whole milk	265.0	270.2	317.4	205.2	168.4	135.4	84.2
Fluid low-fat milk	86.4	66.0	59.8	59.1	81.2	95.0	130.4
Cheese[4]	4.0	4.5	6.3	12.9	16.0	19.5	25.7
Cream	10.6	10.8	10.2	3.5	3.3	3.6	7.9
Frozen dairy products	1.2	4.4	12.0	28.1	27.5	26.7	29.2
Specialty products[5]	7.3	15.9	25.4	13.2	12.1	12.0	15.3
Fats and Oils							
Butter	17.3	17.7	10.7	5.0	4.4	4.6	4.5
Margarine	1.3	2.1	4.5	11.0	11.4	10.8	10.7
Shortening	8.3	8.7	9.3	17.1	17.7	22.9	23.0
Lard and edible tallow	11.6	13.3	12.1	3.8	2.8	3.8	3.7
Salad and cooking oils	1.5	5.3	6.6	16.7	19.5	23.5	24.9

(continued)

whole (minimally processed) foods and/or organically grown foods, as well as those who simply want to avoid additives. For many, the chief reason for adhering to an alternative diet is that they believe it to be healthier. Popular foods with those following alternative diets are whole grain products, leafy vegetables, fresh fruits, soybean products, raw nuts, wheat germ, brown rice, honey, yogurt, and dried fruits. Tofu has become a symbol for such food.

FOOD CHOICES AND HEALTH. Those who endeavor to change food habits for reasons of health must appreciate the fact that foods are heavily invested with symbolic, emotional, and cultural meanings. They must appreciate the cultivated tastes for certain food preparations.

One of many factors affecting food choices resides in an individual's belief system regarding the health or nutritional benefits or harm

TABLE 12.1.   U.S. FOOD SUPPLY.
(continued)

Item	Per capita consumption[1]						
	1909–13	1929–33	1944–48	1970–74	1975–79	1980–84	1990–94
				Pounds			
Fresh fruits							
Citrus	13.5	35.4	58.1	27.2	26.4	25.8	22.4
Non-citrus	116.2	90.3	73.3	48.8	54.4	61.2	74.6
Processed fruit & juice	NA	NA	NA	56.1	61.9	63.2	91.1
Melons	20.8	25.6	21.7	19.6	18.7	NA	22.6
Fresh vegetables	53.4	83.0	99.2	92.4	97.2	75.9[6]	105.0[6]
Processed vegetables	NA	NA	NA	106.3	105.1	102.6	130.5
Fresh potatoes	167.0	127.0	112.5	54.0	49.0	46.5	46.3
Frozen potatoes	NA	NA	NA	14.9	20.2	19.8	26.5
Sweet potatoes	21.0	19.2	13.8	5.0	5.1	4.8	4.3
Wheat flour & cereal							
products	287.0	222.6	183.2	134.9	141.8	148.2	191.5
Wheat flour	(216.0)			(111.0)	116.3	(117.3)	(139.8)
Corn products	(56.0)			(10.2)	11.8	(14.4)	(23.1)
Rice				(7.1)	(7.5)	(10.1)	(17.4)
Refined sugar	75.7	97.7	84.2	100.5	91.5	62.5	64.4
Syrups & sweeteners[7]	14.2	18.0	21.6	21.9	31.7	65.9	75.8

[1]Retail-weight equivalent. Based on U.S. total population and, except for 1944–48, includes armed forces overseas. Fluid milk and cream based on U.S. resident population, and fish on U.S. civilian population.

[2]Excludes consumption of game and edible offals.

[3]Edible weight.

[4]Product weight, excludes cottage cheese.

[5]Includes condensed and evaporated milk, and yogurt.

[6]Data for 1980–84 and 1989 excludes minor vegetables. Comparable figure for 1970–74 and 1975–79 are 65.0 and 68.4 lb., respectively.

[7]Corn sweeteners only after 1969.

NA: Data not available.

*Boneless, trimmed.

**Boneless.

Source: Putnam and Allshouse, 1996.

that may accrue from specific choices. Scientists and practitioners working in the area of diet and chronic diseases consequently focus their attention on ways to modify belief systems, to effect desired changes in food choices. In recent years, national campaigns have been launched to inform the public of suspected links between dietary salt (sodium) and hypertension; between dietary fat/saturated fat, cholesterol, and coronary heart disease; between dietary fats and fiber and certain cancers; and between certain antioxidant nutrients (vitamin

TABLE 12.2. NUTRIENTS AVAILABLE FOR CONSUMPTION, PER CAPITA PER DAY

Nutrient (unit)	1968	1978	1990
		Per person per day	
Food energy (kcal)	3,300.0	3,300.0	3,700.0
Carbohydrate (g)	379.0	387.0	452.0
Protein (g)	98.0	99.0	105.0
Fat (g)	158.0	157.0	165.0
Saturated fatty acids (g)	63.0	58.0	59.0
Monounsaturated fatty acids (g)	64.0	63.0	67.0
Polyunsaturated fatty acids (g)	24.0	30.0	32.0
Cholesterol (mg)	500.0	450.0	410.0
Vitamin A (RE)	1,430.0	1,500.0	1,420.0
Carotenes (RE)	470.0	580.0	6200.0
Vitamin E (mg)	12.7	14.6	15.7
Vitamin C (mg)	100.0	108.0	110.0
Thiamin (mg)	2.0	2.1	2.5
Riboflavin (mg)	2.3	2.3	2.6
Niacin (mg)	22.0	24.0	28.0
Vitamin B_6 (mg)	2.0	2.0	2.2
Folate (mcg)	270.0	267.0	296.0
Vitamin B_{12} (mcg)	10.2	9.8	9.1
Calcium (mg)	850.0	850.0	920.0
Phosphorus (mg)	1,470.0	1,460.0	1,600.0
Magnesium (mg)	320.0	310.0	350.0
Iron (mg)	14.7	14.8	19.3
Zinc (mg)	12.5	12.3	12.7
Copper (mg)	1.6	1.5	1.7
Potassium	3,510.0	3,400.0	3,540.0

Source: Economic Research Service, USDA. Food Consumption, Prices, and Expenditures, 1996. (Putnam and Allshouse, 1996).

C, vitamin E, selenium, beta-carotene and other phytochemicals) and coronary heart disease and some cancers.

The flag is now carried by the FDA, which established rules in 1994 implementing the National Labeling and Education Act (NLEA) of 1990. The labeling is intended to provide information on nutrients and fiber components that relate to coronary heart disease, cancer, osteoporosis, obesity, and high blood pressure. NGOs may join the campaign. The Center for Science in the Public Interest (CSPI) has been particularly diligent in studying the fat contents of various ethnic foods (as they are predominantly prepared in the United States) and publicizing their data to a public already sensitized to the level of dietary fat in the diet.

Some authors (e.g., Popkin et al., 1992) have suggested that public health messages focus too heavily on foods to avoid, that they do not give adequate guidance on how to plan and prepare meals so that Americans, particularly older Americans, can meet diet and health recommendations. This has not been rectified in the FDA rules and regulations implementing the NLEA.

Excessive consumption of fat is widely perceived to be the result of consuming animal products. Additional relationships link this excessive consumption of saturated fat with obesity and hypercholesterolemia. Dietary recommendations now focus on a reduction of the average consumption of calories from fat, from an average of 36 to 37 percent of the dietary calories to 30 percent (NRC, 1989c; IOM, 1991a). The recommendations focus on the reduction being wholly at the expense of the saturated fatty acids, which in turn calls for modification of the animal products in the diet. As a result, dietary advice by physicians often focuses on reduction of red meat as a primary way of reducing fat intake.

CASE STUDY: RED MEAT. The case of red meat, particularly beef, may provide an insight into diet/health related messages. The first version of the report of the Select Committee on Nutrition and Human Needs, U.S. Senate, "Dietary Goals for the United States" in 1977, and the 1979 Surgeon General's Report "Healthy People," (DHEW, 1979) suggested that Americans would be healthier if they consumed less red meat (i.e., beef and pork). The issue continued as people were told repeatedly that their principal source of dietary saturated fatty acids was red meat. Some of the guideline packages during the early 1980s in this country and elsewhere carried the admonition to eat less red meat. The message to many was that red meat was less healthful than other foods. The consumption of beef by Americans has declined considerably since 1978 (Table 12.1), although some reduction was the result of trimming the fat off the beef cuts.

It has been possible to analyze some of the parameters of the reduction in beef consumption. The 1986 National Consumer Retail Beef Study (Cross et al., 1986), providing data from four large cities in the United States, determined that consumers may have a preference for beef, but price, leanness, and concern about cholesterol and fat were principal negative factors. Testing the Fishbein and Ajzen model (Ajzen and Fishbein, 1980), Shepherd and Stockley (1987) found that attitudes were good predictors of consumption of foods associated with fat (meat, meat products, butter/margarine, and milk) in the United Kingdom, although social pressure had some effect. Nutritional education was not an appreciable factor related either to attitudes or the social norm. McIntosh and Zey-Ferrell (1988) extended studies to 400 women in Texas, on the assumption that women remained the gatekeepers relative to food selection. The influences of husband and friends, however, often countered the intent to consume less beef.

There are lessons that can be derived from the case. The first is that an attitude toward a specific food developed and persisted; a certain spectrum of knowledge was translated into attitude through repeated statements picked up in the media and through physicians. Second, the decision process in food selection is modified by the referent others (husband, peers, friends, and one's own desires and instincts that are negative to the decision) or by matters of convenience. Third, although the meanings were complex, the message was a simple one, and implied that alternatives—chicken, fish, vegetarian diets—could replace red meat in the diet. Even the current advertising program of the pork industry, touting pork as the other white meat, pays homage to the simple and residual nature of the message.

Beef remained a highly visible target of activists (Rifkin, 1992) and environmentalists (Durning and Brough, 1992). Although beef is not singled out by ethical vegetarians (Pluhar, 1990), vegetarians seem to be among the first to eliminate beef from their diet. Such movements, however, are not likely to add substantially to the discrimination against beef. Beef is increasingly a food consumed out of the home, a factor that suggests a positive image of some beef products.

BEHAVIORAL CHANGES

There is now a general public recognition that nutrition is important, but with the exceptions of those easily obtained nutritional aids such as vitamin supplements and appetite depressants, application of nutrition knowledge by the public has been shaped largely through attitudes toward specific foods: Saturated fat is translated into red meat and dairy products, but not necessarily into foods fried in or made with partially hydrogenated oils. Complex carbohydrates may translate into fiber and cereals, only sometimes into fruits and vegetables. Cholesterol-lowering diets translate into lowered consumption of eggs and beef, substituting fish and poultry, but little seems to be made of consumptions of high fat ice creams and processed cheese. The case study on beef suggests that the impacts of information (and misinformation) relative to the diet/health relationship have occurred largely as the result of the expression of that knowledge in a person's awareness and belief system.

Change in attitude—a person's predisposition to behave in a certain way—to a certain food seems to be the dominant factor in dietary change. People often translate general dietary prescription, such as "eat less fat," to specific injunctions, such as eat less beef, sausage, bacon, and luncheon meats (Popkin et al., 1992). Confusion and misinformation can exist when attitude is the motivating force. Rathje and Ho (1987), in the Arizona Household Refuse Study, noted indirect indications that individuals were buying red meats with non-separable fat instead of red meats with separable fat. As people bought fewer steaks, roasts, and chops for consumption at home, they may not have known that processed meats (ground beef, frankfurters, luncheon meats, and sausage) contain substantial amounts of fat.

People are concerned about diet and health but lack specific knowledge to act on these concerns in an effective manner. Perhaps some people do not wish to be knowledgeable in nutrition in order to eat well (IOM, 1991a). Dietary changes in older Americans from 1977 to 1987 showed that this group reduced their consumption of high-fat beef and pork, whole milk, and white bread and increased their intake of low-fat beef, pork, poultry, and fish, low-fat milk, and whole grain breads (Popkin et al., 1992); however, consumption of other important sources of calories and fat (high-fat desserts, butter and margarine) and of fiber (fruits, high-fiber cereals, and vegetables) changed little between 1977 and 1987.

THE MESSAGE AND THE MARKETPLACE

The availability of food in North America is determined by both accessibility and market demand for various foods. Demand and supply are interrelated. Consumption is described by demand. Supply is as much a matter of technology (e.g., storability, transport, import) as of production. Demand is a set of circumstances that results in consumption of different quantities. In the short term, if supply is low, prices go up and demand decreases. In the long term, however, supplies are generated to meet what people want to buy.

Obviously, the marketplace can be a formulator of change in food selection, and as such, can be part of the support system of any educational process. The market runs on images and reflects perceptions. The marketplace can change the image of food, but it also interacts with society. It is a reflection of how people feel about foods and which foods make people feel better (not necessarily with respect to health, but with respect to desires, impressions, and tastes). Convenience and quality form also a major, complicating set of factors. For example, the drop in egg consumption may have been a response to health-related images (e.g., the cholesterol factor) but the drop may also be a matter of the convenience element in home preparation (Deutermann, 1988). Those who breakfast at restaurants often increase their consumption of eggs. Eales and Unnevehr (1988) have suggested also that although awareness of health issues may be greater among consumers of high quality meats (which we believe to be the actual case), the shift from beef table cuts to chicken parts and processed chicken rather than some other foods, was likely caused by a growth in demand for convenience and some imaginative product development and marketing; however, the trends to consume more poultry, first stimulated by supply and price in the 1970s, were fixed somewhat by health concerns as well as convenience factors as the new eating habits developed in the 1990s (Putnam and Allshouse, 1996).

MALNUTRITION AND POVERTY

Concerns about too much fat, saturated fat, and cholesterol have little impact in the face of extreme poverty. Food, any kind of food, is the paramount consideration of the very poor.

Undernutrition[1] was recognized as a significant problem in the United States in 1969 when President Richard Nixon called for a White House Conference on Food, Nutrition, and Health (Mayer, 1990). Federal programs—the food stamp program, congregate feeding programs, and Meals on Wheels, the Women, Infants, and Children Program (WIC), and Social Security—subsequently worked well and by 1977, hunger essentially had disappeared as a social problem. The programs, however, began to slip somewhat; by 1989, there had been a return of large-scale hunger to the United States. By 1990, some program cuts were rescinded and over 30 million people are now covered by the food stamp program; many more, however, may be eligible. The federal programs, of course, stimulated a market for animal products.

The late Jean Mayer (1990) noted that the population at risk in the 1990s is very different from what it was in 1969 when a large number of elderly were poor. In 1989, with many more drawing Social Security payments, the elderly constituted only 12 percent of the population in poverty. Now, the special vulnerability of children must be noted. Nearly 40 percent of all poor people are children. Over a third of the households headed by women are at the poverty level. The food stamp program provides a nutritional base for children as well as the elderly.

The new factor, new because it is far more serious than in 1969, is homelessness and the cost of keeping a place to live. Families are living in cars or in welfare hotels. Many of the poor, however, have homes because they pay most of their incomes for shelter. In 1969, the average family set aside about one-third of their income for housing. For people below the poverty line, it was about 50 percent. In 1989, for people in poverty, about 80 percent of the income went for shelter. That, as Mayer (1990) stated, "squeezes out almost everything else, including the chance that the family will be decently fed."

Such forced reorientation of priorities means that the animal products being purchased will be those kept lower priced by a higher content of fat (i.e., less expensive cuts of meat such as processed meats, high fat hamburger, and free cheese out of government storage). Dietary guidelines become less important because of the imperative for the very poor to get something to eat. This also means that more children in the United States may be subject to undernutrition, although in milder forms than the undernutrition in developing countries. In 1992, an estimated 12 million American children consumed diets below the recommended dietary allowances (RDAs) established by the NAS (Brown and Pollitt, 1996).

VEGETARIANISM

Vegetarianism is a practice as old as mankind. It has occurred because of limited animal food sources for some people. It has occurred for religious and philosophical reasons throughout the developed world.

Dombrowski (1984) described ethical vegetarianism as an idea with a history of thousands of years. Held by some of the most prominent philosophers of Greece (Pythagoras, Empedocles, Plutarch, Plotinus, and Porphyry), the belief that it is wrong to eat animals died out for almost 1700 years. A renewed movement was born in the 1970s and has generated an enormous literature of books and papers in highly respected journals. This renewed philosophical movement has in turn spilled over into activist efforts in which nutritional factors (some real, some fabricated, and some zealously misunderstood) appear as justification (e.g., Robbins, 1987; Pluhar, 1992; Barnard, 1995).

Individuals who call themselves vegetarians vary from those who avoid only red meat but eat poultry or fish, to lactovegetarians (who eat milk and eggs but no flesh foods), to strict vegetarians (vegans, who eat no food of animal origin). Vegans are those who not only avoid all animal foods, but often use no other kinds of animal products such as wool, silk, or leather.

Although vegetarianism is a relatively recent phenomenon in the West, it has been practiced in Asia for centuries, especially by followers of the Hindu religion (Sanders and Reddy, 1994). Van Staveren and Dagnelie (1988) have described certain social movements which have been associated with vegetarianism:

The *ecological* movement is directed mainly to methods of food production that are harmless to humans and their environment. Growing grain for intensive animal production is considered detrimental to the environment and limits the access of poor people to food (Lewis, 1994). The diet is mainly lactoovovegetarian.

The *anthroposophic* movement advocates a way of life that searches for knowledge of humanity in relation to the direct environment and the cosmos. Participants in this movement use foods grown organically, use special herbs, and follow a calendar for sowing and the phases of the moon for harvesting.

The *macrobiotic* movement teaches a grain-based diet derived from the Chinese yin-yang principle. The macrobiotic diet has a vegan-like food pattern with very little animal product consumed after an infant has been weaned. The macrobiotic diet is similar to the typical developing country diet: low in fat, animal products, and cholesterol and relatively high in complex carbohydrates (van Dusseldorp et al., 1996).

Some religious groups have strong prohibitions against eating animal products. Some of these are cultist in character. Others are simply conservative in their beliefs.

For some, vegetarianism is a tactic for combating killing, pain, and suffering of animals (Frey, 1983). For some, vegetarianism is a tactic by which they hope to improve the treatment of food animals (Singer, 1975, 1980). There are some, perhaps including people from Asiatic origins, who consider eating meat simply an abomination and do not eat meat at all, regardless of whether or not the animal's rights have been violated (Frey, 1983).

A 1992 survey conducted by Yankelovich, Shelby, and White/Clancy and Shulman found 12.4 million self-described vegetarians, or about 5 percent of Americans (National Livestock and Meat Board, 1992). This is a larger figure than reported in the 1985 (3.7 percent), suggesting growth in the movement. Two-thirds of the surveyed vegetarians were women and tended to be slightly older and better educated than the general public. The respondents's definitions of the vegetarian, however, are unclear. It is reported that half agreed with the statement: "In order to satisfy my appetite, my main meal must include meat." Two-thirds said they ate chicken; one-third said they ate red meat. Forty percent consumed animal products at least weekly. Only four percent reported never eating animal products.

Vegetarians have generally higher caloric intakes than nonvegetarians. Mean body weights tended to be lower in vegetarians. Vegetarians also have lower intakes of protein, preformed niacin, and vitamin B_{12}, iron, zinc and thiamin than nonvegetarians (Harrison et al., 1988). All other nutrients are consumed, on average, at the same level or higher in vegetarian than in nonvegetarian diets.

Vegetarians are probably more health conscious than other citizens. Their death rates from all causes are below the national average (Burr and Butland, 1988). They smoke less. They have lower plasma cholesterol values, but the cause is not clear. Intakes of fruit and vegetables, which replace meat in vegetarian diets, have been reported to have an inverse relationship with plasma cholesterol (Burr et al., 1985). Seventh-Day Adventists, a conservative Christian group that originated in the United States during the nineteenth century, are prohibited from using tobacco, alcoholic beverages, and pork. They are discouraged (but not prohibited) from consuming other meats, fish, eggs, hot spices, and caffeine-containing beverages. The lower risk for ischemic heart disease noted in Seventh-Day Adventist men is probably related to their dietary habits, but also to the nonsmoking status, possibly their better exercise habits, and greater social support (Fraser, 1988; Snowdon, 1988).

The eating practices that promote health in the adult, however, may have detrimental effects on growth and health status of the infant and young child (Acosta, 1988; Jacobs and Dwyer, 1988). Large dietary intakes of fiber pose risks in infancy when the stomach capacity is limited. Unavailability of limiting essential amino acids and poor protein quality may result from excess fiber, food processing and storage, and poor metabolic retention because of inadequate energy (Sanders and Reddy, 1994).

The more liberal vegetarian diets (lactovegetarian and lactoovovegetarian diets) that include a large variety of foods can fulfill nutritional requirements (American Dietetic Association, 1993). It is within the vegan group that nutritional deficiencies have been more frequently described, particularly among children (Acosta, 1988; Sanders, 1988; van Staveren and Dagnelie, 1988; Dwyer, 1991). These, however, are often populations with extreme diets. Macrobiotically fed children are probably most at risk for deficiencies of energy and specific nutrients. The growth curve begins to deviate after weaning and there may or may not be a catch-up (van Dusseldorp et al., 1996).

Deficiencies of B_{12} are seldom reported in developing countries, perhaps because certain poor hygienic practices can easily reduce the incidence (Herbert and Coleman, 1988). More recently obtained data, however, confirm that young children in Western populations who virtually exclude food of animal origin, are at high risk of vitamin B_{12} deficiency (Dagnelie et al., 1989; Miller et al., 1991; Sanders and Reddy, 1994). Elevated urinary methylmalonic acid, progressive neurological degeneration, and short stature have been noted in children.

Well-planned lactovegetarian, lactoovovegetarian, and semi-vegetarian patterns can be satisfactory for children. The primary diet for children all over the world for the first six months is lactovegetarian (Jacobs and Dwyer, 1988). Later infancy, the time for transition from breast-feeding to table foods, poses a greater challenge for vegetarians, especially vegans, and children in some developing countries. During this period, risks of inappropriate diets and poor nutritional status are large (van Dusseldorp et al., 1996).

The inclusion of animal products, including meat, poultry, fish, milk and eggs, probably affords diets for children that require less planning and nutritional knowledge. Vegetarian diets require more attention (Dwyer, 1991). Dwyer (1988) has written, "Regardless of whether people choose vegetarian or nonvegetarian patterns with sound nutritional planning, they can reap health benefits."

THE ARGUMENTS OF ANIMAL AGRICULTURE

When nutritional science determined that certain essential amino acids were required in human and animal diets, a popular rationalization of the need for meat and other animal products in the human diet followed. Animal agriculturalists began to describe their business in terms of producing protein. In a myths-versus-facts framework, Frances Moore Lappé (1975) attempted to contradict justification for meat in the diet because of its "inefficiencies and our over-consumption of it." She listed eight "protein myths," which take on a certain sensitivity for animal agriculture, not because they may or may not be myths, but that they actually constitute a list of arguments which have been earnestly but erroneously offered by advocates of animal agriculture to justify animal products in the diet:

1. Meat contains more protein than any other food.
2. Eating lots of meat is the only way to get enough protein.
3. Meat is the sole source of certain essential vitamins and minerals.
4. Meat has the highest quality protein of any food.
5. Because plant protein is missing certain essential amino acids, it can never equal the quality of meat protein.
6. Plant-centered diets are dull.
7. Plant foods contain lots of carbohydrates and thus are more fattening than meat.
8. Meat-centered cuisine is overall more nutritious.

The truth is that one can refute any of these beliefs about the place of meat in the diets of people on the basis of current scientific nutritional knowledge. In fact, many advocates of animal agriculture no longer call forth any of these arguments, although the beliefs continue to be reflected in popular attitudes that people in the United States hold about foods. Adequate amino acids can be provided by both other animal products (milk and eggs) and by mixtures of plant proteins (Young and Pellett, 1994). Meat is not a sole source of any vitamin or mineral; it, however, is a rich source of iron, zinc, and vitamin B_{12} and several other water soluble vitamins (notably riboflavin, niacin, vitamin B_6), and in the case of pork, thiamin. Plant-centered diets need not lack taste, and complex carbohydrates without butter, oil, and cream are not especially fattening. Meat-centered cuisine generally requires less nutritional planning than plant centered diets, but that also is not an absolute.

To advocate animal agriculture on the basis of refutable arguments erodes the effectiveness of the advocacy. The current justification of animal agriculture given by advocates is that meat and milk products provide high quality protein, calcium, iron, zinc, and vitamins D and

B_{12}, and animals produce more high quality food than they consume. If one interprets this justification to mean that meat and milk are *the* superior sources of these nutrients, then the defense of animal products in the diet is weak. If one interprets the statement to mean that meat is *an* important dietary source of these nutrients that cannot easily (or acceptably) be replaced, that seems a stronger point to make.

On the flip side of the arguments that animal products are essential in the human diet are assertions against using these products. Vegetarian and animal rights movements aside, the following nutrition-oriented assertions have been made to discourage the meat-centered diet and are often collapsed into energy–environment arguments against eating meat:

1. The human is an animal whose digestive system is suited only to plant-centered diets.
2. High levels of dietary fat detrimental to health are the result of consuming meat and other animal products in the diet.
3. Red meat may have unique constituents that are carcinogenic (Willett et al., 1991).

Such assertions are also crossings into uncharted waters. The solutions offered by their proponents are often simplistic: eliminate red meat, particularly beef, from the diets. Such absolute banning of a food goes beyond the epidemiological evidence.

The meat-centered diets of many people are, in fact, high in fat and low in fiber, and these factors have long been associated with a risk of colon cancer (NRC, 1989c) as well as cardiovascular disease. People who eat generous amounts of meat, however, also eat less fruits and vegetables that may contain antioxidants and other anticarcinogens. Some of these risks of chronic disease are associated with dietary patterns that simply lack a variety of foods.

As noted earlier, the dietary pattern relative to the consumption of animal products has changed substantially in the United States since 1970 (Slattery and Randall, 1988; Putnam and Allshouse, 1996). The external fat on beef and pork has been trimmed extensively. The portions of meat eaten are smaller. Such significant changes in meat consumption make interpretations of epidemiological data on the relationship of chronic disease to health—such as the report linking red meat consumption in 1980 to subsequent incidence of colon cancer in women (Willett et al., 1991) and prostate cancer in men (Giovannucci,

1994)—difficult and less secure. Meat is not exonerated by the uncertainty of data, but neither is it indicted.

Animal agriculture, necessary or not, is part of modern human society. It is obviously desirable. Animals are part of the food web. People are not likely to be easily converted to vegetarianism in large numbers, although the forces of vegetarianism have been gathering strength.

THE ARGUMENTS ABOUT VEGETARIANISM

The arguments of vegetarianism largely have been carried on among philosophers. Moral philosophers Singer (1975) and Regan (1983) have led the philosophical offensive against human exploitation of non-humans, including the rearing of animals for their meat, suggesting that humans do not need animal flesh to live and thrive. The battleground for advancing vegetarianism, however, may be increasingly in the allocation of resources and the nutritional sciences (Durning and Brough, 1992; Rifkin, 1992; Lewis, 1994).

Ethically based objections to the use of animal products are frequently linked with the assertion that raising animals specifically for food is incompatible with sustainability of land resources. World meat production has quadrupled since 1950 as populations of affluent countries and the newly affluent of developing countries increase their consumption of meat. The growth in the population of domestic animals has been accompanied by developments that may not be sustainable. Both croplands and grazing lands are carrying increasing burdens.

The philosophical debate for veganism draws its force from the supposition that Regan's arguments for animal rights is sound (Comstock, 1994). Also, if it is wrong in general to kill an animal to eat its flesh, on what grounds is it justified to use an animal's eggs or milk for human ends? Spent birds and culled dairy animals are also slaughtered (Varner, 1994a).

Kathryn George (1990) has identified seven groups of people who could be nutritionally disadvantaged by strict vegetarian diets: (1) infants and children, (2) pregnant and lactating women, (3) older women and some older men, (4) allergic individuals and those suffering from disease that affects their ability to digest and metabolize foods, (5) undereducated individuals, (6) individuals in poverty in which selection of food is narrow and erratic, and (7) people who are physiologically not disposed to vegetarianism (e.g., women predisposed to osteoporosis). These indeed can be vulnerable groups. The vulnerability stems as much from practical factors, including the access to certain foods, as from unique nutritional requirements of the young, aged, gestating, lactating, or diseased human. George (1990, 1992) argued that as a result of this nutritional vulnerability, vegetarianism cannot be a moral obligation for many human beings. The documentation in her 1990 paper was arguably not very strong, but the question of if certain vulnerable individuals would face risks if required to eat a vegan diet is one shared by nutritionists (Dwyer, 1991).

In successive papers, Varner (1994a, c) and Pluhar (1994) moved from the philosophical issue (Regan's position) to a debate on the philosophy of nutritional science (i.e., whether the state of nutritional knowledge is such that one can hang a philosophical position on such a knowledge base). Varner (1994a) alleged that the nutrition literature on veganism is biased in terms of the way research on the subject is designed and in terms of the way scientists interpret the results of studies. He charged that nutritionists typically overestimate the risks to vegans of vitamin D, iron, and calcium deficiencies.

Pluhar (1994) and Varner (1994c) also defend their uses of nutritional sciences as bases for supporting the stance that adequate vegan diets can be selected and that George's concern of the risks involved are overstated. For example, the claim is made that concerns about the bioavailability of plant sources of iron are in part negated by studies of Chinese populations who consume primarily nonheme iron and have adequate blood levels of iron (see Chen et al., 1990). Vitamin B_{12} is discounted as a problem deficiency, largely because it is difficult to demonstrate in adults on a vegan diet. Claims also have been made by proponents of strict vegetarianism (PCRM, 1991; Pluhar, 1992; Varner, 1994a) that the data do not support the hypothesis that bone loss in adult women has a significant relationship to dietary calcium intake (e.g., Riggs et al., 1987). They contend that supplemental inorganic sources are as satisfactory as milk products, that the requirement for calcium is less than the amounts recommended in this country, and that high animal protein intakes are responsible for high loss of calcium.

Dairy products supply over two-thirds of the calcium in the diets of people in the United States. The vegan philosophical argument also questions if dairy products can be provided in a way consistent with treating animals in a humane way (Varner, 1994b). The linchpin in their argument, that dairy products are not needed in human diets, is that the prevalence of hip fracture is more common in the United States, Britain, and Sweden, where calcium intakes are higher than in other countries. To the vegetarian, the suggestion of Hegsted (1986) that the higher protein intake of omnivores causes an inefficiency in calcium utilization strikes a responsive chord. Indeed, Recker et al. (1992) have reported that the self-selected dietary calcium-to-protein ratio was a strong predictor of gain in bone mass among young women 19–30 years of age. These observations strike at the conventional nutrition wisdom, which states that osteoporotic risk is increased if peak bone mass is less than the genetically determined maximum at skeletal maturity. Decline in bone mass with age is a universal process in elderly women; peak bone mass at maturity and bone loss in later life are believed to be the two major determinants of bone mass in elderly women (Heaney, 1993). This peak bone mass largely has been achieved in the United States with the consumption of milk.

Confusion exists partly because malnutrition is biphasic. A diet with possible nutrient deficiencies for the young may provide possible benefits in protecting against chronic diseases. A diet fully adequate nutritionally for maximum growth in children may lead to increased risk of chronic disease in the adult. R. Peto (1992), a biostatistician of the Cancer Studies Group in Oxford, has offered this descriptive comment:

Over the past 40 years, life expectancy has improved by 20 years in the less developed regions and by 10 years in the developed regions of the world. Although the current rate of improvement is greater in less developed regions, the process has gone further in developed countries, such as Britain . . . where only 3% now expect to die before 40, still almost 30% do so before 70. Thus, in Britain death before middle age has been largely avoided, but death in middle age is still common, though it is largely avoidable: 80% of such deaths involve vascular or neoplastic diseases, for many of which better treatments and more effective preventive measures can be foreseen. . . .

Although the growing importance of chronic disease control has been stressed, the chief global health priority in the 1990's remains control of the main infectious diseases. In 1980 there were about 50 million deaths in the world, half in people under 35 years of age. Indeed, 15 million were under five . . . in early childhood about four million deaths a year were due to diarrhea, about four million to acute respiratory infections, and about four million to diseases that can largely be prevented by vaccination. . . . So, although easy control of infective disease remains the most important priority, the more successful it is the more people will survive to middle age, and the more important will become the control of the large avoidable causes of premature death from chronic disease, such as hepatitis B, blood pressure, blood cholesterol, and, particularly, tobacco.

With increased longevity, noncommunicable chronic diseases (coronary heart disease, cancer, hypertension, osteoporosis) became the nutritional problems of concern. Ethical vegetarians have attempted to draw argument from the positive effects of plant-based diets on certain chronic diseases, which are the main cause of premature death of adults (probably even in the poorest countries), disregarding the point that only populations with extended longevities suffer extensive chronic diseases.

There are hazards, however, of vegetarian diets for children (Sanders and Reddy, 1994). There are risks to the nursing children, the lactating mother, and the elderly. Risks include iron deficiency anemia, vitamin B_{12} deficiency, rickets, and a bulky diet that, for children, can restrict energy for the first few years of life. These pitfalls can be avoided but require the choice of appropriate, well-balanced diets consisting of a variety of foods and the use of nutritional supplements. Women and children, however, are vulnerable to malnutrition for both social and biological reasons (UN, 1992). The most vulnerable groups of people to nutritional deficiencies globally are women throughout their life cycle, infants, children (particularly newly weaned children in developing countries), and poor individuals in situations in which supplements are not accessible and the selection of food is narrow and erratic.

The principal deficiencies of largely plant-centered diets in many settings globally are calories and protein. If calories are deficient, protein is also likely to be lacking. The nutritional deficiencies created by widely used, mostly plant-centered diets lead to susceptibility to infection and stunting. The highest percentage of underweight preschool children occurs in association with the highest levels of poverty, which also is the characteristic associated with the highest rates of childhood death due to infections (UN, 1992). These are also in countries that consume mainly plant-based diets (India, Bangladesh, Pakistan, Ethiopia, and others) with low gross national product per capita. Whether this is a valid argument against vegetarianism or not is unclear, but it raises the pragmatic point that nutritional success is lowest in countries with the lowest consumptions of animal products.

THE ARGUMENTS OF NUTRITIONAL SCIENCE

The major nutritional deficiencies that activist vegetarianism has doubted are calcium, iron, and vitamin B_{12}, threshold nutrients for which the human body has developed complex and effective methods of storage. Measurement of the nutrient in the blood does not assess the status of storage, but these must have been in the diet at some time to be stored.

Bone, for example, is a massive storage system for calcium, and the metabolic deficiency of calcium cannot be demonstrated. If a person lives long enough, the time can come where the storage body (bone) runs out, wears thin, and breaks. Osteoporosis is a disease conditioned by the extent calcium is stored in the bone decades before the condition is apparent. The loss of calcium from bone in adulthood is multifactorial, with postmenopausal loss of estrogen related to the major loss. At all life stages, other things being equal, the higher the calcium intake, the stronger the skeleton (Heaney, 1993).

Studies of the relationship between calcium and bone density among middle-aged and elderly women in China (Hu et al., 1993) provide some insight into the observation that osteoporotic fractures are more common in the United States, Britain, and Sweden, where calcium intakes are higher than those in China and other countries. The comparison of women in five counties of China revealed that approximately 20 percent greater bone mass was observed among all ages of women in a pastoral county in which there was high consumption of dairy foods, compared to those in non-pastoral areas with lower calcium intakes (Hu et al., 1993). The results also suggested that differences in bone mass primarily result from the differences in bone mass at earlier ages rather than the differences in bone loss in later life. Bone mass, however, is not the only determinant of osteoporotic fractures. Daily physical activity, heredity, and body sizes may be important in understanding the discrepancy in bone fractures. Even if the hypothesis of Hegsted (1986) is valid that people who are adapted to high calcium diets are inefficient users of dietary calcium (as cited as an argument against any need for consuming dairy products), few if any nutritionists would recommend a diet for children with low calcium content to reverse the "addiction." Similarly, some proponents of vegetarianism have made much of the evidence that high levels of dietary protein will increase urinary calcium loss, implying that the consumption of animal products causes loss of urinary calcium. Excessive protein consumption is the issue, not the source of the protein (Heaney, 1993). Clearly, protein intake is a determinant of the calcium requirement, but the relationship of protein intake to calcium metabolism is biphasic; low intake of protein affects bone health, especially in the elderly. Insufficient protein can contribute substantially to the problem of bone fractures (Heaney, 1993).

The second specific nutrient questionable in diets of many who consume plant-centered diets is iron. The incidence of anemia is highest in developing countries (Scrimshaw, 1990). In practice, iron deficiency is most effectively ameliorated by heme iron (from meat) and by increasing the vitamin C content of the diet. Obviously, plant-based diets can be devised to provide adequate iron, but heme iron and vitamin C are both minor components in the diets of populations with the highest incidence of anemia. Iron deficiency anemia is the most common nutritional disorder in the world and affects over one-half billion people (UN, 1992).

Vitamin B_{12} deficiency is primarily a disease of the young and the elderly. Given a source of vitamin B_{12} when young, an adult could go on for years before showing any diminution in serum vitamin B_{12}. (Vitamin B_{12} deficiency in elderly people may signal a breakdown in the special absorptive mechanism for the vitamin.) In infants, vitamin B_{12} deficiency occurs mainly in those that are breast-fed by women who have become deficient in vitamin B_{12} through long-term adherence to a strict vegetarian diet (Fomon and McCormick, 1993; Sanders and Reddy, 1994). The serum vitamin B_{12} concentrations of such infants are in the normal range at birth, but body stores are low as evidenced by the early clinical appearance of macrocytic, megaloblastic anemia and neurologic changes in infants born to and nursed by B_{12}-deficient mothers. Children fed macrobiotic diets are at high risk of vitamin B_{12} deficiency if the diet is not supplemented. Admittedly, macrobiotic children reflect an extreme vegetarianism and data cannot be transferred to other populations. The existence of the deficiency, however, is practical evidence that the B_{12} synthesized in the lower gut is not absorbed. Humans must orally consume vitamin B_{12} for it to be absorbed.

Current knowledge indicates that dietary saturated fatty acids (SFA) and total fat intakes are critical elements in the risk of coronary heart disease, and total fat is an apparent risk factor in certain cancers. Relative to risk of coronary disease, all saturated fatty acids are not equivalent with respect to their effects on plasma lipoproteins and apolipoproteins. Lauric (C_{12}), myristic (C_{14}), and palmitic (C_{16}) acids are implicated as being hypercholesterolemic. They are regarded as primary components of animal fat. Monounsaturated fatty acids (MUFA) are considered to be neutral. Diets rich in trans-unsaturated fatty acids raise low density lipoprotein (LDL) cholesterol, but the issue may not be relevant in the United States because average intakes of trans fatty acids are generally low. Polyunsaturated fatty acids (PUFA) appear to decrease total and LDL levels of cholesterol. PUFA-rich LDL, however, are more susceptible to oxidation and other modification than MUFA- or SFA-rich LDL. The biologic significance of the oxidative susceptibilities is not clear. The antioxidant status of the host will influence the susceptibility of LDL to oxidative modification.

A low ratio of n-3 (omega-3) to n-6 (omega-6) polyunsaturated fatty acids result in thrombotic events that trigger coronary infarction. The cardioprotective effects of n-3 fatty acids are mediated by a number of physiological and biochemical mechanisms and may account for the reduction in cardiac arrest in those with higher long-chain n-3 fatty acid status and a protection against breast cancer in postmenopausal women. In contrast to the omnivorous diet, the vegan diet is devoid of long-chain n-3 fatty acids, which are commonly found in fish and fish oils and must depend on the inefficient conversion of α-linolenic acid to the long-chain counterpart (Conquer and Holub, 1996). Although vegetarians tend to be at an overall decreased risk for coronary heart disease, partly a result of their lower serum cholesterol values, their thrombogenic (blood clotting) risk factors may be significant (Pan et al., 1993).

Unraveling the complexities of carcinogenesis and anticarcinogenesis can lead to unanswered questions relative to the place of animal products in the human diet. Dietary fat and energy, regardless of source, have been implicated as carcinogenic factors. Components of ruminant milk fat, however, may be potential anticarcinogen agents (Parodi, 1997). Conjugated linoleic acid (CLA), a collective term for isomers of linoleic acid with conjugated cis and/or trans double bonds at positions 9 and 11 (or 10 and 12), inhibit certain tumors in animal experiments (Ha et al., 1990). Milk fat is the richest natural source of CLA. This is produced in ruminant animals as an intermediate in the biohydrogenation of dietary linoleic acid, which also yields the stearic acid characteristic of ruminant fat. CLA in butter varies with season and pasturage; for Australian milk fat and meat, some CLA values were two to three times high than comparable American products. An association between the consumption of cow and buffalo ghee, other CLA-rich products, and incidence of breast cancer in Indian women is suggested to be an interesting case-control study (Parodi, 1997).

NUTRITION POLICY

The development of nutrition policy aimed at indirect intervention has followed three general pathways:

1. The development of the recommended dietary allowances (RDAs), which were designed to provide the daily intakes of essentials of a nutritionally adequate diet to meet the known nutritional needs of practically all healthy persons (NRC, 1989e) in which growth, development, and resistance to disease are the targets.
2. The evolution of public advice proposed by scientists, private organizations, and public agencies relating to issues between diet and noncommunicable chronic diseases (American Heart Association, 1982, 1986, 1988).
3. The amalgamation to these two pathways, which appear evident in the nutrition guidelines of the future.

U.S. federal legislation now requires that the USDA and the DHHS review and jointly present dietary guidelines. Inherent in the political basis for that requirement is the desire by certain agricultural commodity groups that the guidelines be uniformly stated in government policy and that the guidelines also be positive for agricultural production, as well as for matters of diet and health. The fourth edition of *Nutrition and Your Health* was released in December 1995 (USDA–DHHS, 1995). The guidelines are as follows:

1. Eat a variety of foods.
2. Balance the food you eat with physical activity—maintain or improve your weight.
3. Choose a diet with plenty of grain products, vegetables, and fruits.
4. Choose a diet low in fat, saturated fat, and cholesterol.
5. Choose a diet moderate in sugars.
6. Choose a diet moderate in salt and sodium.
7. If one drinks alcoholic beverages, do so in moderation.

The rationale in setting these guidelines included the desire to update information and to focus on health, total diet in a positive way, and foods in total. There is an emphasis on maintaining one's weight. Some food components targeted are fat, sugars, salt, sodium, and alcohol. Although solid scientific evidence for the prescriptions regarding cholesterol failed to materialize, cholesterol continues to be targeted.

Since the late 1970s, the repeated advice reaching physicians, other health professionals, policy makers, and the public on risk factors for coronary heart disease carried a message that registered. The intake of foods high in cholesterol and saturated fats (e.g., eggs, fluid milk, and lard) has declined substantially. Adults have reduced their intake of beef and meats generally and have greatly curtailed their consumption of visible fats (Cross et al., 1986). Also, since the late 1960s, death rates in the United States from coronary heart disease have fallen steadily and markedly—by over 30 percent. Detection and better medical care have been partially responsible, but changes in lifestyle (in eating, smoking, and exercise habits) cannot be discounted. The general belief that diet and health are interrelated is now widely held and can be expected to result in further, significant changes in the dietary habits of Americans, even though the debates may continue. The food industry, including the animal food industry, has begun to bend the food system to produce products that are lower in fat, saturated fat, and sodium. The stimulus has been the change in the marketplace in response to public perceptions.

The general discovery of the possible importance of dietary antioxidants (vitamin C, vitamin E, selenium, beta-carotene, and other phytochemicals) in the prevention of cancer has resulted in a greater emphasis on fruits and vegetables in the diet. The use of one or more technologies to increase the partitioning of fat to lean remains a choice for the industry. Heroic reductions in dietary fat, coupled with other lifestyle factors, are reported to bring about regression of even severe coronary atherosclerosis after one year without the use of lipid-lowering drugs (Ornish et al., 1990). These are factors that will likely be reflected in nutritional standards in the future, but values and interests may continue to affect such standards.

New issues, now largely external to the process of setting nutritional standards, are used in attempts to introduce new philosophical views into policy. Some nutritionists argue a hypothesis that it is the intake of foods of animal origin, at the expense of foods of plant origin, that causes degenerative diseases (Campbell, 1994). A food guide pyramid based on Mediterranean dietary traditions (Willett et al., 1995) has been suggested by epidemiologists to emphasize plant foods, fruits, and olive oil as the principal sources of fat, low to moderate amounts of eggs, dairy products, fish and poultry, low amounts of red meat, and low to moderate amounts of wine. These new issues may be reflective of ethical (moral) vegetarianism or simply of a genuine belief that animal products bear components that are detrimental to health. Either way, a value system is served (Kunkel, 1996).

This additional consideration of ethical vegetarianism in the context of this study is the suggestion that members of the nutritional science community have interests and values of their own that are contrary to those of a vegetarian segment of the population. Both vegetarian and nonvegetarian scholars draw their supporting citations from the scientific literature. It is in the choosing of articles to reference that interests and values may be seen. Such writers, however, will also argue that the scientific community may be showing its own value system by failing to consider the needs of those who choose a vegetarian lifestyle.

The passage of the NLEA of 1990 signaled an ascendancy of the public health approach in policy and established policy making through regulatory decision. With the implementation of the NLEA, nutritional policy became in part an environmental economic policy, but the basic tension between optimizing outcome and safeguarding informed consent is residual with the food label. Nutritional labeling does not in itself speak the language of nutrition policy. Nutritional labeling permits the consumer to relate a food to one's interpretation of dietary guidelines.

THE ARGUMENTS OF ANIMAL AGRICULTURE—REDUX

The lessons of these cases—the arguments for animal products in human diets and the arguments for vegetarianism—are evident. First, the problems of validating any philosophical world view in scientific terms is a matter of including human values in interpreting the results of scientific experiments and studies; however, a principle holds. If philosophic argument is to be validated against scientific knowledge, the science must be responsibly interpreted. Knowledge need not be the truth to be useful, but it must be reliable knowledge. Serum levels of calcium, hemoglobin, and vitamin B_{12} may be measured truthfully, but normal levels may not be reliable indices of the nutritional statuses of individuals.

Second, the arguments in these cases have been directed to an industrial society (the United States) in which dietary habits supported by intensive animal agricultures and nutritional knowledge and a redundant food supply can facilitate dietary planning. Except for osteoporosis, deficiencies of energy and specific nutrients are rarely seen in the United States and other Western countries. Consideration is needed now to move to diets that provide adequate nutrients and that also account for excesses of fat, saturated fatty acids and sodium, and lifetime deficiencies of calcium, without diminishing the benefits to growth and healthy development. Touting a diet more plant-centered than is consumed now may make a good deal of sense in such an environment. By definition, vegans eat diets that are devoid of animal foods and must obtain some alternative sources of certain nutrients, including vitamins B_{12} and D (Dwyer and Loew, 1994). An industrial medical environment makes such alternative sources available. The nutritional arguments for animal agriculture soften in industrial countries. What remains are the economic and cultural arguments and the uncertainties in the knowledge base.

Populations in a large part of the world do not have the support base that exists in the industrialized world. Perhaps, it might make for better reasoning to find the means of increasing production of animal foods in those countries for both nutritional and socioeconomic reasons.

The issues surrounding human consumption of animal products settle on philosophical attitudes (of society as well as of individuals who may have positions at odds with each other) on if animal agriculture is justified on the basis of its nutritional benefit to humans and/or its socioeconomic benefits, if a food system can be devised that no longer uses animal flesh products that society will accept, or if animal agriculture truly serves society to the benefit of people. Rethinking its philosophical positions seems essential for the animal agriculture industry at this time when utilitarian philosophical thought (or attitudes) may be increasingly penetrating the mind-set of pluralistic populations such as in the United States. The old clichés will not suffice in the future, but persons holding differing philosophic views should also recognize that differing world views exist and be prepared to discuss them, not condemn them. The philosophical bases for vegetarianism are at issue as much as those for nonvegetarian diets.

In a larger sense, human health appears to be dependent upon a diversity of foods in the diet (Kant et al., 1993). The arguments for animal agriculture also become cultural and ecological. Once again, we refer to Gussow (1994):

It is unnecessary to promote meat consumption as an ecologically moral behavior, but it would probably be beneficial if everyone were to acknowledge the ecological appropriateness of omnivorousness. Those who are vegetarians may thus need to learn to live with yet another layer of moral ambiguity; it is quite improbable that humans will ever create any significant scale sustainable food systems that do not use animals and their products for either wool, fertilizer, draft power and transportation, biogas, or milk and eggs, or even for meat.

ADDITIONAL THOUGHT

Elimination of animal agriculture would severely reduce the food supply for humans, in spite of the allegations that some parts are wasteful and that increases in consumption of animal products may be part of the specter of the human race overwhelming the carrying capacity of the world. The nutritional messages that tend to be stressed today are the reduction in dietary fat, increase in fiber intake, and greater consumption of fruits and vegetables. A greater emphasis, however, should be placed on diversity of foods in the diet. That should be something that the animal industry should be willing to live with.

The values placed on foods become in fact values of the food system. Food systems have developed as a result of interventions outside of food: transport, urbanization, energy and mechanization, trade, and change in population demographics. Almost anything can alter a food system: religion, advertising, drought, labor problems, nutritional advice. All of these are transient. In the developing countries, and perhaps ultimately in developed countries as well, what people eat is what people buy or can buy. In the final analysis, the market dominates the food system.

Both food and sex are physiological factors that are intricately related with social mores and human behavior. Both food and sex have massive implications in all aspects of social life. Nutrition was not an issue in agriculture until efforts were made to link nutrition, dietary behavior, and health. Now the animal agriculture system has become sensitive to many aspects of the food system because eventually, changes in social life, including those of the severest kind, will be translated by the market. Food and society is an issue that should be attended to within the food system. Food systems are vital links in the human–animal relationship. Issues of food systems are being merged with other issues such as those of the environment. The factors in food consumption are but a piece of the puzzle, albeit a central piece.

NOTE

1. The American Institute of Nutrition (now the American Society for Nutritional Sciences) and the American Society of Clinical Nutrition initiated a task force on hunger and malnutrition (Dietz and Trowbridge, 1990). The task force initiated its activities by defining its terms:

Hunger is a recurrent, involuntary lack of access to food.

Malnutrition is a condition that results from an excess, imbalance, or deficit of nutrient availability in relation to tissue needs.

Nutrient is any substance provided from food that performs one of three functions: provides energy, promotes growth and maintenance of tissue, or regulates body processes. Examples may include constituents of food such as energy, protein, minerals, vitamins, water, and some constituents of dietary fiber.

Undernutrition is a form of malnutrition resulting from a deficit of nutrient availability in relation to tissue needs. One of the signs of undernutrition is inadequate growth in children. Undernutrition is accompanied by an excessive loss of lean body mass in children and adults.

Overnutrition is a form of malnutrition resulting from an excess of nutrient availability in relation to tissue needs. Energy overnutrition produces an excess of body fat, known as obesity. *Overweight* is a nonspecific term that relates to an excessive weight-for-height without specifying whether the excess is fat or fat-free mass.

CHAPTER 13

COMPETITION FOR RESOURCES[1]

The sordid lore of nicely calculated less or more.
—WILLIAM WORDSWORTH

With food, we are often on the brink of something that we do not understand. In the early 1970s, we saw massive breakdowns in the world food distribution system. The first major famine in modern times occurred in the Soviet Union. Drought occurred in the Sahel. The rains came afterward. All this frightened people.

All of this tells about carrying capacity, in which humans and animals are competitive, but the linkages and interactions are so great and diverse that one has to address the larger picture—the global food systems. Also, the issues are less pervasive than they will likely be in the future.

The primary resource currency of animal agriculture is the flow of energy through the system. The issues on energy, when related to animal agriculture, begin with familiar themes—efficiency of production, energy costs of the food system, and sustainability of fossil energy supplies—but then spill over into other channels that relate to competitions for resources: access of people to food; the use of renewable and nonrenewable resources for growing grain for animals; the effects of crop agriculture on soil erosion; groundwater contamination and other insults to the environment; and access of people to the land to ensure their own food supply. A range of issues exists because consumption of animal products is associated with the relative affluence of consumers and nations.

The world production of meat, milk, and eggs in the mid-1990s amounted to 200 million, 500 million, and 40 million tons, respectively. The production of livestock has increased significantly during the last two decades, particularly in the United States (poultry), China (swine), and the Far East (mixed livestock). Livestock production increased by 53 percent in developing countries during the 1980s (Pinstrup-Anderson et al., 1997), but the production of beef was unchanged from 1990 to 1996. The industrial countries that feed grain have one-fourth of the livestock and human population in the world, yet produce two-thirds of the world's meat and three-quarters of the world's milk. Feed grain use, however, is climbing in almost every country in Asia, and many countries are now importing beef, pork, and poultry directly (Brown, 1997).

Livestock production is also correlated with income growth (Pinstrup-Andersen et al., 1997). Production has increased where incomes grew rapidly and decreased in those countries where incomes stagnated or fell. Where strong income growth is expected (e.g., in China and Thailand), livestock production is expected to increase in the future. As incomes rise, direct consumption of coarse grain by humans decreases; wheat/rice consumption increases and then decreases, although wheat replaces rice at higher incomes; and meat consumption increases until the highest per capita income levels are reached and then decreases. In terms of global demand, the least to most preferred meats at the higher levels of income appear to be sheep/goat, poultry, beef, and pork. At the highest levels of income, poultry consumed in diet begins to rise rapidly, implying that beef and poultry are substitutes for each other. At highest levels of income, some people consume more vegetables and fruits.

Cultural factors modify such generalities. People in the United States spend more for beef but eat more poultry. Pork remains the choice in most of Europe and sheep are so in Muslim countries.

These productions and consumptions of animal products occur in the same world in which 700 million people are food insecure and for whom the food crisis has arrived, where one-third of the preschool children in the developing world are unable to grow to their full potential and face increased risk of death and disease. Are the reasons for these contrasts the unfair appropriation of food and energy resources by certain populations; are the causes poverty, high population growth, and limited access to education, technology, and land; or simply lack of income growth? Understanding the answers to such questions are important to the future of animal agriculture.

The general focus of this chapter is global and about populations. The analyses involved are twofold: the flow of energy within the system of animal agriculture and the issues of animal agriculture and food security. Threading through these issues is the debate of whether human capital and knowledge or the remaining natural resources will limit the carrying capacity of the world.

THE ORIGINS OF THE ISSUES

The issues of resource allocation were raised in the 1970s when a widely held perception prevailed that food crises in the world could be best reduced by rich countries sharing their food supplies with poor countries. This was the theme of the World Food Conference of 1974 (Library of Congress, 1984). Although this dire concept has been replaced by a realization that problems of distribution—incomes, foreign exchange, storage and transportation, governmental accountability—are far more important, the belief that developed countries have a responsibility set in motion a critique that animal agriculture in developed countries is and can be responsible for a shortage of food supplies for humans.

Lappé (1975, 1982) first questioned the allocation and use of resources in animal agriculture in her provocative volume, *Diet for a Small Planet.* Her questions and assertions were often ignored, as they might have been, framed as they were in ingenuous perceptions and unsubstantiated data; however, she also observed factors that are inherent in animal agriculture:

1. There is a caloric (energy) cost in animal agriculture.
2. The major nutrient contributions of animal products are protein and fat calories, both of which the average American consumes in excess.
3. Agriculture, including animal agriculture, exists as a human activity in the United States because of impelling forces beyond the production of human food: income, employment, quality of life, landscape, and power.

Lappé viewed these factors as representing wasteful practices and denying food to hungry people. Her thoughts were consistent with the international and philosophical thinking of the 1970s (Rachels, 1977); i.e., lower levels of consumption of animal products by the people in wealthy countries and a greater sharing of the production freed by a smaller animal agriculture was the moral thing to do.

Later, additional criticism expanding on perceptions of environmental costs, was directed to animal agriculture (Durning and Brough, 1991). In simplistic terms, the problem was the world's livestock population had grown too large. Such an issue does not diminish the premise that livestock have been, are, and will be of benefit to human well-being. It asks, given the inexorable increase in human population of the world and its demands on earth's resources, if due consideration should not be given also to the populations of animals as well. The theme is that "overgrown and resource-intensive, animal agriculture is out of alignment with the Earth's ecosystem." Admitting that livestock have been "boons" to the human enterprise and also wise investments, Durning and Brough (1991) raised the concern that livestock industries surged in country after country as soaring grain yields made feeding animals grain relatively inexpensive.

Lappé's (1975, 1982), Durning and Brough's (1992), and other arguments in the vein that animals are competitive with humans for resources are, of course, debatable, and they can be evaluated in the light of evidence. Brown (1995a, 1997), who is skeptical of the ability of the world to meet the future needs for grain for both direct human caloric intake and for indirect consumption in the form of livestock products, noted both the disparity of consumptions among nations and increased use of grain for animal production in the developing world. Grain use varies from a high of about 1,700 pounds per person in the more affluent societies to a low of about 400 pounds per person in low-income societies. Brown (1997) suggested that affluent societies lower their consumptions of meat, milk, and eggs. Brown (1997) also recommended that the steps needed to secure future food supplies includes stabilizing populations and climate (i.e., moving the world economy onto an environmentally sustainable path). As population grows and demand starts to outrun supply, grain prices rise. Some people will have to go hungry.

Some of the allegations relative to resources have been considered and answered earlier in this book, but these issues can be revisited profitably from the view of competitions between animals and humans for food and energy and a set of issues relating to the global carrying capacity.

Today, Lappé and coauthors (1998) are less pessimistic. Even with increasing production of food by animals, there does not seem to be a shortage of food. They claim that the millions who live on the brink of disaster in southern Asia, Africa, and elsewhere are deprived of economic opportunity by a "powerful few" and trapped in poverty by debt and poor pay.

TABLE 13.1. INPUTS AND RETURNS FROM ANIMAL PRODUCTION IN THE UNITED STATES

| Food product | *Product as percent of animal intake* | | | |
| | *Total energy and protein* | | *Human edible energy and protein* | |
	Energy (%)	Protein (%)	Energy (%)	Protein (%)
Milk	23.1*	28.8*	57–128**	96–276**
Beef	5.2*	5.3*	28–59**	52–104**
Pork	23.2*	37.8*	58.*	86.0*
Poultry meat	15.0*	30.0*	31.0*	75.0*

Source: *Bywater and Baldwin, 1980; **Oltjen and Beckett, 1996.

ELEMENTS OF THE COMPETITION

Humans are the focal link in the food web. Livestock eat grass and grain, and humans eat the meat and drink milk. So the relative conversions of grass and grain into meat and milk form a backdrop for issues of energy efficiency in animal agriculture.

Whatever their agenda may have been, some critics of animal agriculture evaluated the desirability of animal agriculture on gross caloric efficiency or protein intake/output relationships. Even today, such questions are asked (Oltjen and Beckett, 1996): Does the use of foodstuffs edible by humans (e.g., grains, protein resources, fat) in feeds for animals create a net loss of nutrients for human consumption? Does the use improve the nutrient quality or value of the product? What level of use is necessary or desirable?

Several factors have been evident since the 1980s (CAST 1984):

1. More humans can be fed per hectare of agricultural land used for grain production if humans eat the grain directly than if the grain is fed to animals, and humans then eat the animal products. Put on the basis of grain and other foods that are edible by humans, however, the caloric return shows conversion efficiencies that can be substantial (Table 13.1).
2. Economic forces play an important part in determining what is fed to livestock. Although cattle and sheep can subsist on fibrous feeds and do not require grain, much grain is fed to these animals in the United States and elsewhere because it is economically profitable (i.e., grain is abundant and prices are low).
3. With food animals consuming many products that humans do not eat, the efficiency of energy use from the biomass is increased.

4. Food quality and diet preferences are modifiers of the concepts pertaining to the efficiency of energy use.

It is a persistent dietary preference for animal products in the industrial countries and the growing demand for animal products in the developing countries that forces the use of grain in livestock production, and hence, the incentive to grow coarse grain.

Worldwide, about 40 percent of the grain is fed to livestock. The relative returns of human edible energy and proteins in different countries suggest that a variety of systems have been and are being devised to provide animal products. The United States has a substantial production of poultry and pork based almost entirely on grain. Although large amounts of grain are fed to cattle in the feedlots, the major portion of the U.S. beef production comes from grass. China, however, does not have vast rangelands and has turned to pork production (Brown, 1995a). Further increases in livestock production in China, whether in pork, poultry, or fish in aquaculture, may require importation of grain; however, the use of extensive production systems of livestock production and the use of by-products not edible by humans for animal feeds have their limits. The major production on terrestrial natural systems, beef, has changed little worldwide during the 1990s (Brown, 1997). The productions of grain-based animal productions (pork, poultry, farm fish) have continued to increase.

ENERGY IN ANIMAL AGRICULTURE

Humans modify natural ecosystems through agricultural activities in order to produce foods and fiber products. Energy must be expended to offset the processes that bring about natural change. Developmental changes in agricultural systems are subject to: direct and indirect inputs such as human and animal labor, animal manures and other biomass, and technologies, fertilizers, and power production and mechanization that utilize fossil fuels. Cultural energy is expended in agricultural systems to produce crops that in turn are consumed by humans (directly or after processing) or are used as feed for animals that provide food and services for humans. Although energy is expended in handling, feeding, housing, transporting, and marketing operations, the principal input of fuel energy into production animal agriculture is through grain and other cultivated crops that are fed to the animals.

The engine of energy flow in animal agriculture is economic activity. Although large numbers of producing animals are grazers or scavengers, feeding grain to livestock is an established economic and social factor in many countries. It has greatly increased the availability of poultry meat throughout the world. It has allowed the production of pork and milk products to parallel the growth of the population in the United States throughout the twentieth century. It has enabled the development of a beef cattle marketing system based on the feedlot, which fits the modern business of food distribution. Coarse grains for animal feed account for a major proportion of the world's agricultural exports. Grain is a symbol of both energy and food in global considerations of human and animal diets.

The energy flow does not end with production. Nor do the issues. Substantial amounts of energy are expended in transporting food to the cities. Some of the food energy is converted to human energy for life and work. A significant part, perhaps half, ends up in garbage and waste. None of the organic material and accompanying minerals is returned to maintain the fertility of the land and ocean. Urbanization has resulted in a massive shift of nutrients out of rural areas to the cities, diminishing the vitality of croplands, grazing lands, and fisheries (Nelson, 1996). This shift of nutrients is augmented by the concentration of livestock production in the United States (Gardner, 1997). As livestock operations have centralized, so has the expenditure of grain for feed.

CONCEPTS OF ENERGY ISSUES

Energy related issues in animal agriculture are embedded in at least four entirely different but eventually intertwining conceptions:

1. The first of these concepts is the *metabolic mandate*. The metabolic question tests the ability of the food system to provide the nutritional requirements of infants, children, pregnant women, lactating women, and other adults. A fundamental fact of natural reality is that all forms of animal life, including humans, must by nature use other instances of organic life in order to exist and to flourish (Donnelley, 1989).[2] *This interaction and capture of energy is a law of fundamental human existence.* In the process of development, human societies have become dependent on or have encroached upon animate others in order to exist. Animals as scavengers or as systems of agriculture enhance the ability of

a world population to gather, harvest, and use the products of photosynthetic transformation of light energy into the chemical energies of the organic substances that humans are able to digest and metabolize. Threading through the metabolic dictate are the issues of the dietary pattern: What animal product should be in the diet of humans? When is it not enough? When is it too much? Must there be a degree of parity in the return of calories in animal agriculture?

2. The second context relates to the evolved *food systems* and the energy required to operate them. In much of the world, animals serve humans as scavengers. Nonruminants use the wastes associated with human preparation of food, and ruminants, the plant materials areas not suitable for direct human consumption. Farm flocks of chickens and sheep, pens of pigs, and individual or small herds of cattle and goats are kept to use the products of the farmyard ecosystem. In the developed countries, these forms of animal production gave way to scientifically derived technologies of livestock and poultry management, first in the diversified farming system and then in specialized systems increasingly separated from crop agriculture. Production of income became the dominant priority in animal agriculture (McDowell, 1980). In the wake of this development, an increasingly industrialized system of feed production, feeding animals, and marketing the products developed, employing millions of people and still providing for a certain population base in rural areas. Millions of tons of corn, sorghum, oats, barley, and wheat are produced by an agricultural structure that intends these grains be purchased for animal feed. Economic and institutional frameworks are evolving to supply dietary supplements of animal products—meat, milk, and fish—to billions of people in both developing and industrialized countries. The energy requirement is both direct and indirect with fossil fuel a primary input. The principal issue in the context the food system is one of continued search for efficiencies, alternative animal feeding systems, and continued technological development; but economic forces—the price of oil and therefore prices of power and transport, trade, market price, and availability of grain—are now the more likely to control the energy inputs in animal agriculture. The primary, irreversible factor has been the substitution of fossil energy for human labor and animal draft in agriculture. Ward, citing data from Chancellor (1979), pointed out in 1982 that the cost of human labor and the near nonexistence of draft animals mandates that mechanized industrialized agriculture can be the only means of providing a food supply in the United States. The situation is unchanged today.

3. A third energy issue is bound up in the *heavy use of fossil energy* in industrialized countries. Inexpensive and easily obtained fossil energy

has fostered a lifestyle and set of amenities that people have come to expect: driving automobiles, riding airplanes, enjoying air-conditioning and warmth in season, purchasing fresh fruits and vegetables year-round, and consuming meat. The issues reflect the issues associated with the global production and use of energy—the sustainability of society, the collision of interests of developed and developing countries, plus the environmental problems, real or alleged, that are widely associated with civilization. Animal agriculture and the processing, transport, distribution, and preparation of its products consume but a fraction of the national energy budget but still share in the image of profligacy of affluent society; however, saving energy in developed countries, meritorious as it may be, may have little to do with increasing the energy supply in developing countries (Stout, 1996). The greater challenge is to make vastly more energy available in rural areas of developing countries.

4. The fourth question is that of *human productivity*. The attempts to quantify correlations between personal income and per capita intake of specific nutrients began with Orr in 1936. Correlations among low income, poor education, apathy, poor housing, high birth rates, low disease resistance, short stature and shortened life spans are found globally, but are even more evident in developing countries in which the poorest 40 percent of the population have an average of less than 15 percent of the total national income. Both undernutrition and overnutrition must be considered inefficiencies. One reduces human productivity while the latter implies a misuse of resources. The differences in energy in human diets may be substantially a matter of consumption of fat. Global dietary trends show increases in fat consumption, including animal fat, with rising incomes, but in general, the differences in fat intake among countries are explained more by food habits and local cuisine than by changes in income.

These four issues are intertwined in attitudes often expressed about animal agriculture and the debate about meat in the diet. The issues are dealt with imprecisely. Cost and benefits fall unequally on people and nations and are not easily evaluated.[3] They, however, are likely to be on the policy agendas of a number of countries in the coming years.

PERSPECTIVES ON ENERGY

Steinhart and Steinhart (1974) calculated the energy subsidy for various food crops in the 1970s (Table 13.2). Although their values represent the production efficiencies over two decades ago, the relative values

TABLE 13.2. ENERGY SUBSIDY FOR VARIOUS FOOD CROPS

Kcal of subsidy energy per kcal of food output	Type of product
0.02–0.05	Rice production with hand labor. Minimal draft power (China, Indonesia, Burma).
0.1–0.2	Hunting and gathering. Intensive rice production in Europe.
0.2–0.5	Extensive corn cultivation. Intensive soybean, potato cultivation.
0.5–0.9	Intensive corn cultivation. Family egg production. Extensive beef production.
About 1.0	Dairy farming on grassland. Coastal fishing.
2.0–5.0	Beef production on grassland. Industrial egg production.
10.0–20.0	Fishing. Livestock raising in feedlots.

Source: Steinhart and Steinhart, 1974.

are consistent with current conditions. The energy costs stand high for some systems providing animal products.

Nonmechanized agricultural systems—pastoralism, cropping systems that rely exclusively on human labor, and cropping systems that use draft labor—rely mainly on invested cultural energy that is biological, and therefore from renewable resources. The primary calories for draft animals comes from sources that cannot be utilized by humans, such as straw, tree leaves, and branches, banana trunks, and sugarcane leaves. It is of interest in the overall energy budget that draft animals in the world consume at least half as much of caloric and protein nutrients consumed by all of animals contributing to the world food supply (CAST, 1994).

Draft animals do not result in increased yields per unit of land greater than those systems that depend on human labor, but they make it possible to farm more land (Cox and Atkins, 1979). In cases of farming with draft animal labor, such as wheat farming in India, the investment of cultural energy becomes an exercise in trading calories of one type (those consumed by the draft animals) for calories that can be consumed by humans. Modern agriculture carries on this theme of trading calories for food.

Mechanized agricultural systems use energy from petroleum, natural gas and coal indirectly, and electric energy to manufacture agricultural machinery, fertilizers, pesticides, and other agricultural chemicals. These inputs plus direct usages of fossil fuels are used to operate farm equipment, pump irrigation water, and handle harvested materials. All these inputs represent the energy budget for agricultural production, but additional energy is required for transport, processing, distribution, preparation, and more beyond the farm gate. It has been generally accepted that agricultural production only consumes about three percent of the total national nonsolar energy budget (Ward, 1982; CAST, 1984). Food processing requires twice this amount, and the total food system requires more than five times this amount. The total amount of energy used in the food and agricultural system is estimated to be 16–17 percent of the total U.S. usage.

EFFICIENCY OF ANIMAL PRODUCTION

Although livestock provide resource-use roles other than food, increased efficiency of converting feed energy and protein into animal food products has been a central theme for improvement in animal agriculture. Some of the factors affecting the conversion of energy and protein are the losses that occur at each stage of the digestive and metabolic transformations from grass, hay, or grain into meat, milk, or eggs.

The level of feed intake is the single most important factor influencing feed efficiency conversion into animal products (Balch et al., 1976; Ward et al., 1977). All animals, regardless of age, require certain minimum amounts of nutrients or energy for the maintenance of bodily functions, inevitable heat losses, and expired gases. If energy is available in surplus of these maintenance requirements, then young animals grow. Thus the feed conversion ratio (wt. of feed:wt. of gain) improves with increased intake of food energy, making it economical to promote concentrated feed intakes. In animal agriculture systems in which feed grain is unlimited, the appetite and voluntary food intake are the only limiting factors. The productive capacity of the animal agriculture is maximized.

Over the last half century, considerable effort has been expended to develop improved strains of cattle, poultry, swine, and sheep to obtain high efficiency in both difficult and sheltered environments. The feeding system, however, determines the partitioning of nutrients into maintenance and productive growth or lactation. Various feeding systems can yield wide ranges of energy input per unit of protein produced (Ward, 1982). In an extreme case, Pimentel et al. (1973) contended that 122 kcal of feed energy were consumed per kcal of beef protein produced. Obviously, that was with a mature animal that gains weight only by fattening.

ATTITUDES

The food system requires that plants capture and convert light energy to chemical energy in the form of substances that can be digested and metabolized by humans and animals. The investments of additional energy supplied by fossil fuels make it possible to increase the productivity of the land, reduce the labor requirement, and provide concentrated sources of food. Questions are raised, however, if these inputs are sustainable for society in the future or if society should give these inputs special priorities (Daly, 1995; Sagoff, 1995).

Georgescu-Roegen (1973) argued that there are significant natural limits to growth on the basis of two premises. The first premise notes that there is always an energy deficit in any biological or economic enterprise. The second premise is that the usable energy used up to replace the deficit represents a fixed and dwindling stock. The first premise is generally accepted; the second premise is controversial (Sagoff, 1995). Are energy resources limited to a fixed and dwindling stock? Will not knowledge and technology replace energy sources and dwindling land? Many would like to believe that this last question can be answered positively, but the ultimate question is the world going to discover new sources of energy that can be safely used. Today, a prominent belief is that future projections for food production must be based on a limited and a more expensive fossil energy supply.

The issue of inefficiency is focused in part around animal agriculture because trends in feeding grain in global animal production give rise to questions concerning the length of time that nonrenewable energy resources will hold out. Questions are raised about the growing implication that large quantities of food will have to be produced in the future to meet the food needs of the growing world population. If energy requirements of agriculture were expanded in developing countries, as they are in developed countries, they could have an impact on their natural resources. Marcia Pimentel (1990) cited a scenario that illustrates the ultimate energy constraint. She wrote that if the current 17 percent of the total U.S. energy budget required for the food system, which is the equivalent of 1,500 billion liters of gasoline in the United States alone, were expanded to the world population of over 5 billion, it would take 7,500 billion liters of gasoline to feed the population for one year. She calculated that at such a rate of usage, if petroleum were the only source of energy for food production and if all known petroleum reserves were used to feed the present world population, the reserves would last less than 12 years. Obviously, this will not be the case.

What is implied is that an intermediate change of some dimension and some direction will be required. To achieve change, attitudes will have to be shaped. In turn, attitudes will shape the dimensions and directions of the change. Renewable energy sources for example are becoming less expensive with time. Wind power, solar energy, and even liquid fuels from biomass may prove available enough to moderate attitudes. Also, we can assume that policy makers in both the developed and developing worlds will respond, renewing their commitment to investment in agricultural research and development of technology.

The concerns for energy use may be directed at industrial producers or at consumers of resources. When directed toward producers, energy use concerns will likely emphasize environmental obligations (Crosson and Rosenberg, 1990). When directed toward consumers, appeals to lower energy use are intended to sway the consumer to accept a moral responsibility to conserve energy used in the production, transport, and distribution of products that contribute to the lifestyles in industrial countries. In an urbanizing world, growing some of the food in cities may make agriculture more sustainable (Pothukuchi and Kaufman, 1999).

FOOD SECURITY

It is the poorest people in the world who often are seen as competing for the grain fed to animals. The World Bank (1990) characterized 700 million people as living in extreme poverty. In addition to those who do not have enough calories to prevent stunted growth and serious health risks, another 500 million are between extreme poverty and poverty levels, some of whom may not have enough calories for an active life.

Ten to twelve million children under the age of five die each year in the world from affects of malnutrition and related infectious diseases. Death from disease—four million from diarrhea, four million from acute respiratory deficiency, and about four million from diseases that can be largely prevented by immunization—can be prevented and represent only in part a toll of malnutrition (UN, 1992). Wasting and stunting may affect as many as half of the children in countries of Africa. Protein energy and micronutrient malnutrition continue to affect large numbers of people in developing countries. Over 40 percent of the women are underweight and/or anemic. At least 1.5 billion people worldwide are probably affected by one or more nutritional deficiencies. The United Nations, however, estimates that the population of developing countries that are underfed (i.e., consume dietary energy inadequate to sustain more than light activity on average) has fallen substantially, from about one in three in 1975 to one in five in 1989. By such calculation, 700 million are underfed, but this number is less than at any time in the recent past.

A nutrition transition to higher caloric intakes is occurring in many developing countries, but the presence of starvation and hunger remains severe and apparently without end. Transitory food insecurity, which occurs when people are faced with a severe inability to acquire food as a result of sporadic misfortunes such as drought or civil strife, has gained visibility in the 1990s in such areas as Sudan, Ethiopia, Somalia and North Korea.

Food aid of internal or external origins often has been the first response to alleviate food insecurity. Food aid is of immense value in emergencies and famines and when opportunity is not developed, but too small of a surplus or carryover stocks generally have not been the cause of failing to alleviate transitory insecurity. The limiting factors have been logistical and/or political within recipient countries. Delivery of food to those who need it has not been an issue of availability of grain from the United States and other countries, but one of the conditions existing in the affected country.

The larger issue, however, is the prevention of deaths from chronic malnutrition and disease or even if the 700 million people in the world who are underfed can benefit from the action of grain growing countries turning from feeding animals to sending food to developing countries. If the world human population continues to increase at its current rate of about 90 million people annually (1 billion in a 11-year span), grain production to meet future needs will be pressed. Grain production, however, has kept pace with and exceeded population growth, although world stocks showed reductions in 1988 and 1989, largely as a result of drought conditions in North America and China and distribution problems with the 1990–92 drought in Africa. For most of the last decades in the twentieth century, surplus grain supplies grew, even in the face of growing world poultry and pork productions. Increased global supplies of grain alone, however, did not greatly affect the issues of food security in a number of developing countries

(Lappé et al., 1998), and the levels of surplus grain are no longer increasing.

The consensus is that problems of distribution—of family incomes, foreign exchange, nutritional knowledge, storage and transportation facilities, and relief programs—are the important to solving the world's hunger problems (Horwich and Lynch, 1989). Food security involves two factors: the availability of food and the ability of people to acquire it. The World Bank's (1989) report on hunger in Africa concluded that effective action to combat both chronic and transitory food insecurity must focus on a root cause: insufficient resources of families either to grow or to buy food. The problem is poverty, although in the 1990s, ethnic warfare in Somalia, Rwanda, Burundi, and Zaire, and floods and drought coupled with governmental mismanagement in North Korea, added to the toll.

Food production (not just food) is at the center of national development. Accelerated growth in the local food and agricultural sector is the crucial factor in the reduction of hunger. and added sources of energy will be required for that purpose (Stout, 1996). There is little evidence, however, that animal agriculture in developed countries threatens the food security of developing nations.

FOOD FOR HUMANS OR FEED FOR ANIMALS?

Brown (1995a) made the point that by far, the largest food reserve is the 37 percent or so of the world grain harvest, some 630 million tons in 1994, that is used to produce livestock and poultry products for human consumption. Market forces will tap this reserve if rising grain prices push up prices.

There is little evidence of the ultimate benefit to the hungry of the world that would result from a reduced consumption of animal products in North America. Any productive capacity for grain not used in animal production might be available for greater export of food grains to alleviate food insecurity in other lands, but it is more likely that the export would be controlled by market forces or by governmental intervention (FAO, 1983). Any advantageous effect of a reduced demand for grain to feed animals would be indirect: a downward pressure on grain prices. That effect will likely be short-lived (Parikh and Tims, 1989). Moreover, foreign grain distribution tends to reduce incentives for local grain production. Price regulation in the developing world often has removed financial incentives for local agriculture. The problem is purchasing power. Hungry people are those who often cannot afford to buy food. The recommendations of Sen and Dréze (1990) of improving the ability of people to buy food would likely increase incentives for local farmers to produce more food.

FOOD FOR HUMANS AND FEED FOR ANIMALS— THE DEVELOPING COUNTRY CONDITION

Lappé and Collins (1986) viewed the competition between growing crops for animal agriculture and food security in the light of another dimension of resource allocation. Hunger in developing countries, like rapid population growth, results from underlying inequities that deprive people of economic opportunity and security (Lappé et al., 1998). Hunger and rapid population growth are endemic to societies in which land ownership, jobs, education, health care, and old age security are beyond the reach of most people. Lappé and Collins (1984) pleaded that peasants be given access to better lands in their own countries, rather than being confined to marginal lands. They called for self-reliance, not food aid, and self-reliance in that context calls for access to land on which to grow their own food.

The studies of Barkin, Batt, and DeWalt (1990) are instructive, at least for our times. Their work documented that success in agricultural modernization in Mexico, leading to large increases in feed for animals and high-value crops for urban consumption and export, was accompanied by growing domestic inability to provide basic foodstuffs. They argued that exclusive reliance on either cash crops or feed crops is not in the best interests of people in most regions. Commercial production of feed grains may improve economic conditions in rural areas, but in many cases this leads to unavailability of traditional foods in local markets. Again, substitution of feed grains for food grains in production is viewed as a growing inequality of access to food. Access of people to land is not an issue in industrialized countries, but can be a serious issue in some developing countries.

PEOPLE–ANIMAL INTERDEPENDENCE

The interdependence between humans and animals in developing countries is strong. Animals serve to reduce risks from cropping, generate capital, render services (traction, fuel, fertilizer), satisfy cultural needs, generate income, ensure status and even property rights, as well as provide food (McDowell, 1980).

Livestock activities in many parts of the world are household activities. Livestock provide a large part of the cash income of the rural poor. Small and medium-sized private farms do mixed farming; subsistence farmers and peasant communities own between 60 and 80 percent of the cattle, sheep, goats, swine, and camelids in Latin America and the Caribbean (Quijandra, 1989). India has the world's largest population of cattle and buffaloes (McDowell, 1984). Africa is the second ranking continent in numbers of domestic animals, and China has the world's largest population of pigs. In the developing world, a primary function of livestock is a buffer between human populations and disaster. At the subsistence level, livestock constitute a standing reservoir of food that can carry the human population through at least a short-term catastrophe (Quijandra, 1989).

The developing countries contain 58 percent of the world's total land area, with 60 percent of the world's permanent pasture and 53 percent of the world's arable land. Holding more than 80 percent of the world's population, these countries also have about 65 percent of the world's cattle, 50 percent of the world's sheep, 55 percent of the world's swine, and 95 percent of the world's goats.

The symbiotic relationship between humans and animals is essential to human existence in developing countries (McDowell, 1980). Humans and domestic livestock and fowl mutually enhance survival and quality of life. Only a small percentage of domestic animals compete with humans for food resources. The vast majority, quite to the contrary, provide humans with the means to derive life-sustaining products. Although nonfood services provided by animals are substantial, the meat, milk, and eggs save many lives. During droughts in the past, in Tanzania and Ethiopia for example, when cattle died, people also died.

ALTERNATIVES

LIVESTOCK ALTERNATIVES. The most frequently suggested alternative to the current system of ruminant animal agriculture is a greater dependence upon forage resources. The world's natural system, however, has likely reached its maximum productivity. The average amount of beef produced per head of cattle per year in developing countries in which little or no fossil fuel or competitive feeds are used, is one-eighth that of cattle in the developed countries (McDowell, 1980). This suggests that maximization of total production of food may require certain amounts of foods edible by humans to be fed to animals, to gain the needed return on feeds that otherwise cannot be used by people.

Strategies to reduce beef consumption are unlikely to be effective unless societal views change radically. Meat and dairy product consumption responds to the interplay of supply and demand. If grain feeding were eliminated in a country, meat and poultry production would drop drastically and prices for the various products would increase greatly.

On the other hand, alternative strategies are available. Animals respond differently to constraints that the kinds of feeds available place on them (Bywater and Baldwin, 1980). For example, the range of alternate feeds is greater for beef animals than for dairy animals, which is greater than for single-stomached animals. Beef production strategies may involve: range, pasture/hay, pasture plus grain, or feedlots. In addition, Bywater and Baldwin (1980) claimed that if by-products and residues are not used by animals, the cost of other disposal would be an energy cost in itself and thus a credit to an animal system.

Grain fed to livestock has been a buffer to human food supplies. The historic case is that of the former Soviet Union where the policy reaction to poor grain harvests was to use livestock herds as a grain buffer by slaughtering them in times of feed shortage and building up herds when grain was available (Tarrant, 1989). Policy changes in 1971 led to importation of substantial amounts of grain to avoid the necessity of heavy livestock slaughter, and imports continued to rise. Ironically, the policy in Russia has changed in the 1990s. Recently, Russia has imported increasing amounts of beef in order to save its grain supplies.

As noted above, the grain now fed to livestock is the principal grain reserve in the world (Brown, 1988, 1995a). The use of grain in the production of livestock, particularly beef production, is highly flexible and price sensitive, both with respect to prices of inputs and prices of products; also, it responds readily to weather shocks or variations in export demands. Should little or no grain be fed to livestock, such flexibility would be reduced greatly. Conversion of grain to ethanol or some other use might be a buffer against climate and weather-driven fluctuations of grain for human food, but it is doubtful. The transportation sector in the United States is massive enough to utilize the ethanol supply generated from the grain now fed to livestock if the price of ethanol is competitive, removing the flexibility inherent in feeding grain to livestock.

AQUATIC FOODS. Stout (1990) suggested that the consideration of alternatives to excessive fossil fuel consumption includes the addition or substitution of aquatic foods as sources of protein, and hence is a solution to the world's food supply problems. Finfish are valuable nutritionally for vitamin B_{12} and a nearly correct ratio of amino acids, while low in saturated fat and calories and high in n-3 polyunsaturated fats (Rawitscher and Mayer, 1977). The limits of ocean productivity of fish, however, appear to limit this alternative (Brown, 1995).

From 1950 to 1960, the world's fish catch rose almost 150 percent, raising the hope that the seas would provide a solution to the world's food problems; however, an increasing amount of energy spent in fishing has not provided proportionately greater yields. Fossil energy used in fishing cannot be estimated by comparing boat types or the kind and amount of fish caught (Rawitscher and Mayer, 1977). There is a wide variation in energy used in harvesting seafoods to produce a kilogram of protein, a ratio of 117 to 1 for lobsters relative to sardines (Rawitscher and Mayer, 1977). Moreover, the energy used to bring seafood to the table depends also on processing, trade, home and restaurant preparation, and transportation (Rawitscher and Mayer, 1977).

Ocean fisheries have in general passed their peak production. Overall, the marine catch has stagnated, and while that has happened, the world population continues to grow about 1.6 percent per year. The current trends are rising prices, increasing exports from developing to industrial countries, and limits on the access to fisheries. The implications are severe for low-income people and subsistence cultures that rely on marine fish as a dietary staple (Weber, 1995). In addition, consumers in the industrial world are increasingly viewing fish as a source of nutrients that can have health implications, such as n-3 unsaturated fatty acids in the reduction of the incidence of coronary heart disease, as well as a luxury item.

Aquaculture (fish farming) is an old occupation. During the 1990s, it has been the fastest growing supplier of fish worldwide (Weber, 1995). As a result of the slowdown in the ocean catch, people have turned to fish farms for increased supplies. Aquaculture's contribution to the welfare and nutrition of people who have traditionally relied on marine fisheries, however, has been minimal. Marine aquaculture largely has fueled exports instead of increasing local food supplies.

The skills required for aquaculture are not those used in fishing; they are those of animal agriculture. Moreover, the criticisms of animal agriculture likely will be applied to fish farming: use of grain, coastal habitat destruction, and pollution.

PUBLIC POLICY

Resources have both instrumental and intrinsic values. Daly (1995) argued that after we have recognized the intrinsic value of the natural world, we then have an obligation to protect and increase that value. As we have noted throughout this book, and as others (Crosson and Rosenberg, 1990) conclude, the main concern of U.S. agriculture must turn from the capacity to meet long-term domestic demands for food and fiber to one of responding to the rising demand for environmental values in agriculture. This assertion rests on two propositions: that the demand for commodity values (food and fiber) will grow more slowly than the demand for environmental values, and that the supply of environmental values will rise less rapidly in response to increased demand than the supply of commodity values.

People in this world improve their situations in many ways but use energy inefficiently in the meantime (e.g., in running automobiles, heating houses). The food production system provides food that is desired by the human population, and it has certain energy costs. Will we curtail animal agriculture that uses less than 1 percent of the nation's energy budget in its production phase? The higher energy cost in the food system occurs beyond production. How much will people be willing to forego in terms of convenience, availability, freshness, and more, which are now supported by expenditures of energy?

Ward et al. (1977) calculated the fossil fuel energy use for beef production in 1976 to vary from about 5 to 12 megacalories (Mcal) per pound of edible beef. Per capita consumption in 1976 was estimated to be 129 pounds; in 1996, it was estimated at about 70 pounds of beef. As some reduction in the amount consumed was the result of close trimming of fat at the retail level, the 1976 calculations may be a fair approximation for today. The equivalent expenditure of 650 to 1,500 Mcal per capita for beef is equivalent to about 20 to 50 gallons of gasoline per capita, about what is needed to keep an automobile running one month.

Thus after all, the issue does not appear to be a serious energy question, but it may become an economic one. Are people likely to give up meat to keep the automobile going? That question no longer seems farfetched. Shelter and transportation have become as important as food in the priorities of the poor in the United States (Mayer, 1990). Herein may lie the eventual competition for energy resources should supplies of fossil fuel begin to fail: shelter and transport versus animal products and fruits and vegetables in the diet of an individual with limited resources.

The accepted premise today is that the resource bases are finite (Arrow et al., 1995). Discussions focusing on the ability of the earth's resources to provide adequate nutrition for additional billions invoke images of massive changes in diets to the vegetarian and emphasize the limits of resources to continue the past increases in grain production (CAST, 1994). Also, the environmental resource base upon which economic activity ultimately depends includes ecological systems that produce a variety of services. Thus, two principal solutions are proposed: that the diet of humans requires revision and that the ecological systems on which our economies depend must be resilient. Few analyses of the sustainability, however, predict the needs of animal agriculture as specific research needs of society. The power of knowledge appears to be viewed as a given.

CONCLUSION

In the face of a perceived exhaustive fuel supply, the issues to a large extent, are ones of lifestyles, human satisfactions, and human welfare, even as these impact animal agriculture. Behavioral, cultural, ecological, and economic conditions all play a part in defining the desirability (necessity) of animal products in the diet and the extent that nonsolar energy is expended to put them there. The current state of agriculture in the United States has determined that there be substantial energy requirements by the food system (Durning, 1990). Durning (1990) noted that the thousands of small farms, bakeries, and dairies that once encircled and fed the nation's cities cannot supply the supermarkets of today with sufficient quantities or uniform products to compete with the industrialized food system. There are also certain institutional developments, particularly the substantial diminution of the farm population, that seem irreversible.

At this time, none of the contemporary strategies to relieve world hunger calls for a conversion from the meat-centered diet of the United States to releasing grain for transfer to vulnerable populations. None of them call for the conversion of a substantial amount of the U.S. farming capacity from growing animal feeds to growing food directly consumed by humans; however, the substitution of cash crops for feed crops in developing countries, in which access to land is an important factor in the access to food, may require a diminished animal agriculture. In the long term, however, the inexorable growth in the world's population and the resultant growth in demand for food will place pressure in the future on grain usage to feed livestock and poultry, particularly if unfavorable climate and weather events strike major parts of world agriculture at greater frequency or if the increases in world grain production are not sustained by improved agronomic systems.[4]

The symbiosis between humans and animal agriculture is centuries old. Populations that consume animal products or fish have the longest life expectancies. For example, the substantial increases in growth, development, and life expectancy observed in Japan after World War II were associated with increased consumption of animal fat and protein (Matsuzaki, 1992). Animals are a reservoir of food energy at the subsistence level. The problems of the malnourished in the world are real and must not be ignored. Shortages of plant sources of protein, as in Africa, place absolute needs for animal products in the diet. The needs of the growing populations may require augmentation of animal agriculture in some countries. There is a continuing need to make both animal and agronomic agricultures more efficient and more flexible in their use of inputs.[5]

On the other hand, some aspects of animal agriculture may be equated with attributes of a civilization that is acquisitive and profligate. The consumption of beef is lumped with other aspects of a lifestyle provided by readily available fossil fuels. This, however, is an issue of luxurious consumption, if it is an issue, not a prohibition of animal agriculture.

The trade-offs are not well defined. Whether or not there is equality in the return of food calories for petroleum calories may well be a secondary issue relating to the long-term availability of fossil fuels, societal issues surrounding fossil fuels, and the environment. These are factors that should be faced in their own right.

Animal agriculture will be sustained by a reduction of resources needed to produce a constant or increasing flow of consumer goods and services through advances in science and technology (Sagoff, 1995). Those who were nurtured in the U.S. academic atmosphere also believe that. Will our research system, however, meet the challenge to provide human-made capital which augment the natural capital that we agree will be needed to feed the world in 2030? That is the issue of the final chapter of this book.

NOTES

1. This chapter was drafted initially by Deborah Tolman.

2. The philosopher Strachan Donnelley (1989) used the premise that because of the "metabolic rigors of organic being, animal individuals sustain themselves and their bodily wholeness only by encroaching upon other forms of organic life," as an argument in the context of the ethics of animals in scientific experimentation. That issue is not addressed in this chapter; however, the systematic philosophy of organic life sketched in Donnelley's (1989) paper can relate as well to ethics of animals as human food as to the ethics of animal experimentation.

3. See Matthews (1991) for a general discussion of energy and environmental problems.

4. See Toufexis (1990) in *Time* magazine for an example of a public presentation of the issues relating to the place of red meat in the diets of people in the United States. What is suggested is that disinterested study is needed in the many issues relating to animal agriculture.

5. The distinction must be made between the requirements of dietary energy in the diet for growth, reproduction, and health, and the overconsumption of dietary energy, which may lead to obesity, cancer, and other degenerative diseases.

CHAPTER 14

SCIENCE AND SCHOLARSHIP
REVISITED[1]

Can the animal sciences address the whole system? In the disciplinary sense, the answer is likely no. In a systemic sense, they must.

—THIS VOLUME

Many of the contemporary issues in animal agriculture were created by science, technology, and higher education of the past. In turn, scientific research, technology development, and education are viewed as the keys to solving the principal issues in animal agriculture. The common thesis is that the terms of science will either justify the position of animal agriculture or allow the crafting of an animal agriculture that will respond to concerns about the impacts on society, diet/health, and the environment (Cheeke, 1999).

As empirical inquiry contributes much to understanding agricultural issues, the structure of agricultural science will determine the success that science will have in solving the problems. Thus, the construct of agricultural research is a value issue in animal agriculture. It is doubtful, however, that the traditional disciplines of animal science can fully resolve issues by themselves. Systems analysis is also needed. So is intuition, experience, and common sense. In practice, however, policy consensus often is based more on scientific knowledge than on shared ethical and moral values.

Institutions of agricultural science and education are integral parts of the agricultural setting; they are primary agents of change in agriculture. Such institutions have sought more diligently than most to combine science and utility (i.e., to translate knowledge into technologies and policies as well as resolve issues) (NRC, 1989d).

Agricultural science, like its soul mate, medical science, is generally regarded as being dualistic: basic and applied, or as in medicine, basic and clinical. The applied facets of agricultural research are further divided as to purpose: descriptive, diagnostic, predictive, or prescriptive research. Historically, however, agricultural science has been distinguished in that it has helped define what agriculture should be. It has predicted—or attempted to predict—such matters as the market and use of agricultural products. It has prescribed ways of achieving an agriculture as it is perceived it should be. The issues are humanistic and substantive as well as scientific and technical.

Since their beginnings, agricultural and associated sciences have been directed largely toward the production of useful and practical knowledge. That direction was inherent in the authorizations of the Hatch Act but has existed for a much longer time. Since the early work of Liebig (1840), most research in agriculture and forestry has come from the surrounding agricultural and forestry cultures. Barnes and Edge (1982) suggested that agricultural research has been part of a large number of sciences that are oriented to specific human ends and objectives. Such goal-oriented research includes work in computer science, ecology, medicine, and engineering, as well as agriculture. Krohn and Schäfer (1982) have argued that agricultural science in the past has not provided insights into why agriculture functions, but rather constituted a design of how it should function. Thus, a perception developed as to how agriculture and food production ought to be organized, and scientists set out to construct the system. Substantial amounts of agricultural science seem to have been the construction of reality according to scientific methods and theories, directed by the changing goals of society.

Much of the history of research in animal agriculture has been dominated by a paradigm that focused on productivity and efficiency. Now, we are less sure what are the dominant goals of society for future agriculture should be, but these goals are likely to include accessible and sustainable food supplies, food safety, health, employment, clean water and air, a splendid landscape, a comfortable life with good food, and prestige and support to sustain the enterprise of agriculture.

The point is that the purpose for which agricultural science is undertaken will determine the kind of technology that develops or does not develop.[2] The kind of technology visualized as needed also determines the science. For example, the current interest in sustainable agriculture is one that sees a technological restructuring of agriculture. For animal agriculture of the future, the signs point to animal meat products (beef, pork, poultry) that have less fat but qualify for ready acceptance by the consumer, egg products with less cholesterol, milk products with less fat, animal agriculture systems that are more humane and use less grain per unit produced than they do now, and animal products that can be consumed without fear of food-borne disease.

It is the operational issues of research that are the subject of this chapter—issues pertaining to the integrity of science. Those involving fraud in science, self-deception, priority of discovery, allocation of credit, and plagiarism are not included in this study, as they are not unique to the science of animal agriculture.

DEVELOPMENT OF AGRICULTURAL RESEARCH IN THE UNITED STATES

Congress created the USDA in 1862 and gathered the small number of federally supported, agriculturally related research activities into the department (Danbom, 1986). In the same year, Congress passed the Morrill Act which provided land that could be sold by the states in order to create land-grant colleges that would teach subjects related to agriculture and the mechanic arts. Twenty-five years later, in 1887, Congress provided authorization and funding via the Hatch Act for an "agricultural experiment station" in each state. The motivating forces for these actions were summed up in the belief that government could and should take steps to encourage and direct economic development.

Historian Alan Marcus (1985) concluded that the enactment of the Hatch Act held both practical implications and symbolic value. It signified legitimization of agricultural science as an integral part of agriculture. It acknowledged the importance of the methods of science. The law also reflected the ascendancy of agricultural colleges as research institutions; however, the necessary scientific and personnel base needed for implementation did not exist. Aside from agricultural chemistry and botany, coherent disciplines did nonexistent in agricultural research. The system was forced to create new branches of science, probably before they might have developed otherwise (Rossiter, 1979).

Political realities dictated practical emphases in most of the universities, experiment stations, and the USDA (Danbom, 1986). These institutions attracted support from those who shared their outlook. They were mainly businessmen, bankers, and highly specialized and market-oriented farmers who tended to agree that the problems of agriculture were production problems, which often were specified in subsequent years as *the* production problem, whether an insect infestation, level of milk production, or mechanization. Concentrating on production problems, agricultural science narrowed its scope and became disciplined. Danbom (1986) stated that "by 1900, then, the agricultural research establishment had developed a habit of mind which made self-analysis difficult. Concentrating on increasing production, researchers failed to see the potential validity of other goals, or to recognize that their efforts might harm some in the agricultural community."

Agricultural science saw its most productive years in the post-World War II decades that yielded hybrid and high-yielding varieties, intensive systems of animal agriculture, completion of the revolution in mechanization, and unprecedented controls of diseases and pests, and hence, the halcyon years of public support for agricultural research. Even through those years, however, the agricultural sciences continued to draw their intellectual structure out of production animal and crop agriculture and horticulture and the family well-being.

The scope must be wider. There are fundamental shifts in science and technology, resource bases of the food chain, employment patterns, the marketplace, and the academic/scientific communities. The intellectual fabric of research that relates to food and agriculture ranges through the full scope of biological systems, including the infrastructures of food and its commerce and biotechnology. Biology, chemistry, and economics remain central to agricultural research, but increasingly, the *glue* became molecular biology, cell biology, information science, and the system sciences, which also form the foundations for the emerging technologies of food and agriculture. We now add moral philosophy to the list.

We see now that the clienteles of agricultural research are multiple. Few areas of the economy and society are untouched by the life sciences and their applications in agricultural research. The food system embraces both the human and the industrial complex. Ways of making a living and lifestyles permeate the agricultural and natural resource systems. Landownership and tenure are inherent in value systems surrounding agriculture. The vitality of the rural community is involved. Environmentalism is pervasive. Nutrition and the safety of the diet are a central concern. The renewal of the spirit and body through the natural environment is demanded by young and old. Social interpretations have become parallel imperatives of agricultural research and education (Johnson et al., 1991).

CONSTRUCTION OF SCIENCE FOR ANIMAL AGRICULTURE

Current animal science is dominated by reductive, specialized research, but four operational factors challenge the research systems (Kunkel and Hagevoort, 1994). First, the animal sciences have two sets of constituents. These are the scientific community and the external interests such as the animal industries, the processing and marketing systems, governmental agencies, and the consuming public. Second, the basic sciences important in animal science are shifting to greater emphases of molecular biology, metabolism, physiology, and systems and values studies; some of the new disciplines may not be sufficiently developed to solve the practical problems. Third, the base of experience and intuition of scientists, which the interconnection of specialized research and agricultural practice in the past had enabled so well, may not be available in the future. Fourth, as the disciplines shift, questions arise of how technological development can or should intervene in shaping animal agriculture of the future. We argue that addressing these factors requires integrative additions to the research in animal agriculture.

The concept of integrative scholarship has been legitimized in academic circles, largely flowing from Ernest L. Boyer's (1990) vision for higher education: "We need scholars who not only skillfully explore the frontiers of knowledge, but also to integrate ideas, connect thought to action, and inspire students."

Thomas Malone (1994) visualized the new paradigm of science in an extrapolation of Boyer's thoughts. Malone has written:

The aggregate of individual attitudes that reflect human knowledge and values . . . can be encapsulated in the concept of a *cascade of knowledge*. This cascade involves the discovery, integration, dissemination, and application of knowledge concerning the nature and interaction of matter, energy, living organisms, information, and human behavior.

The cascade of knowledge is not linear. Each of the elements from discovery through application has feedback to every other elements in the cascade. The wellspring of the knowledge stream is discovery (basic research) that extends the frontiers of human knowledge in the physical, biological, and social sciences, mathematics, engineering, and the humanities.

Our model of research in the animal sciences, we believe, is congruent with the concept of a cascade of knowledge, not so much as it is now, but as what it should be.

THEORETICAL PERSPECTIVES

Research in animal science as well as science in general is guided by the basic rules of problem-solving rationality (Popper, 1959; Maxwell, 1992). These rules are:

1. State and seek to improve the statement of the central problem to be solved.
2. Critically examine the various proposed solutions.
3. When necessary, and that is most often, break up the central problem into preliminary, simpler, subordinate, specialized problems tackled in the same way as in the first two rules.
4. Interconnect the attempts to solve central and specialized problems so that solution of the central problem may guide and be guided by disciplinary problem solving.

The scientific community does a very effective job of putting reductive research (rule 3) into action, but its performance on the other three is much less extensive, leaving specialized investigation as the overwhelming component of the research.

Reductionism in animal science, as in the biomedical sciences, is a reflection of the dominance of rule 3. The current operational reductionism in animal science is based on the belief that the properties or behavior of a composite system can be predicted from understanding the properties and behavior of the constituent parts studied in isolation (Schultz, 1996). Reductionism in animal science is perceived mainly as a method in which the attempt is made to hold external conditions constant and modify only one or two factors at a time (Rose, 1988). It is analytic reductionism.

Fractionated or extreme analytic reductionism, in any form, fails when it cannot describe the interactions of components in a complex system (Mayr, 1982). In fact, among biologists, resistance is growing to the idea that the most fundamental layer of nature holds the explanation for all the features of the higher layers (Williams, 1997). In research for animal agriculture, which operates as both a biophysical system and a human activity, analytically reductionistic research, by itself, faces difficulty if animal science is to concern itself with the issues of animal agriculture. What is needed is that knowledge flow from the molecular levels to the organismal levels, and the feedback. Also, a persistent need exists to integrate societal needs with scientific practice.

In the 1990s, investigations in the animal sciences remain predominantly within a hierarchy of biological sciences:

Human systems (including human nutrition).
Ecosystems.
Life systems (including intensive and extensive production systems).
Organisms.
Body systems (e.g., immune, reproductive, endocrine, gastrointestinal).
Cells.
Molecular mechanisms.

Research in what one usually terms the component arenas of animal science—biotechnology, nutrition and growth, physiology, genetics, animal behavior, food science, growth, and applied animal science—all of which are multidisciplinary, seems to be organized spanning different levels of the biological hierarchy.

Intervention in animal agriculture theoretically can flow from any of the biological levels (Kunkel and Hagevoort, 1994). For example, the repartitioning of fat and muscle to produce a leaner meat product could be accomplished through: studies at the molecular level (molecular genetic markers, anabolic agents), studies of the physiology of growth (hormonal controls), choosing different organisms (species), alteration of the production system, mechanical reduction of fat on the product, or the human choice to eat differently. Thus a single practical end can be achieved by working at one or more levels within the biological hierarchy. Which approach may be the most successful depends as much on a horizontal integration with societal factors as the scientific feasibility. Lawrence Busch (pers. comm.) points out that because intervention can flow from any of the biological levels, this implicates the different discipline or set of disciplines. To one who learns to trim the fat from meat on the butcher block, the solution is obvious. To one who learns molecular biology, the solution is equally obvious. The problem is that these things are not obvious. There are all sorts of practical and ethical implications as to which of these paths one takes and to what degree one goes down these paths. For example, an effective way of achieving repartitioning is the use of a β-agonist, such as clenbuterol, but regulatory restrictions do not permit that approach for practical purposes.

As sciences have matured and the hierarchy has developed, there has been a growing change in the questions being asked, away from those of the more fundamental level. Chemistry, for example, is an essential part of what is needed by biochemists and other biological scientists, but only a part (Rose, 1988). In making biological sense, biochemistry and molecular biology go beyond chemistry and are not reducible to it (Slater, 1988). Physiology is more than biochemistry and molecular biology and is not reducible to them.

In a similar line of reasoning, Coulson and Crossley (1987) devised a model to distinguish insect ecology from ecology. They argued that insect ecology embraces more than "an elaboration of basic concepts of ecology illustrated with examples from entomology." They consider applied ecology in hierarchical terms: the study of interactions and influences of insect populations and communities as ecosystem processes structured by the landscape. Necessary to the study of the composite system are both discovery at a fundamental level for the explanation and investigation into a higher level for interpretation.

Thus, the higher level in the biological hierarchy becomes an interpretive level, and in that sense is integrative; however, inherent in such a concept is the intuition that the scientist working at the higher level also has the task of making sense of the bits and pieces of the new knowledge that is accumulating. It is difficult, maybe impossible, to understand one level of a system's organization from a lower perspective in the hierarchy (Lenfant, 1996). Molecular and cellular biologists, for example, will not likely be the ones to integrate their science with societal needs. Scientists with a more holistic vision will reach out and incorporate molecular sciences into their interpretations; they also face the challenges of incorporating interests and values, which may seem to them as elusive as understanding molecular biologies.

Descriptions of some animal agricultural phenomena in terms of economics, ecology, developmental biology, biochemistry, and chemistry remain legitimate and important, but mainly as part of the explanation (Kunkel and Hagevoort, 1994). As animal sciences mature, they develop their own interrelationships, values, abstractions, and work boundaries (Krohn and Schäfer, 1982) and they improve their abilities to interpret. Over time, each discipline in a hierarchy of animal sciences, such as reproductive physiology or animal genetics, picks and chooses what elements of other sciences (including the social sciences) it wishes to incorporate for interpretation; in so doing, it develops into a scholarly self-sufficient domain. Contemporary animal science, however, is undergoing transformation. The mature disciplines are being replaced by the molecular biologies, and the animal sciences may be losing the ability to interpret.

The problem of interpretation becomes more complicated if its value to society is an issue. If one follows the model or premise that often the ultimate goals of research are problem solving (Maxwell, 1992) or demand driven (Busch et al., 1991), research in animal agriculture should also be placed in a hierarchy of practical or operational knowledge that is parallel to the biological hierarchy (Croft, 1985):

Anthrosphere (society, consumers, food chains, global markets).
Agrosphere (land resources, landscapes, human capital).
Strategies and systems of production.
Tactics of management.
Actions.
Validation of ideas and aims.

A third vertical integration may be constructed, oriented to moral aspects:
Global village.
National society and government (including laws and regulation).
Cultural determinants.
Attitudes and behaviors.
Beliefs.
Moral ethics.
Philosophical theory.
Human thought.

The experimental animal sciences seldom probe the functional or moral aspects, but the aims, goals, intuitions, and incentives of scientists and their institutions often flow from their perceptions of the functional hierarchy. The functional orientation implies inputs of clients. The moral orientation implies inputs of critics. Busch and coauthors (1991) argued that agricultural research reflects the influences of the clients although the research may first go through phases in which discovery and then theoretical questions control the research.

There is an obvious need for research—and education—in animal science to reach out beyond the boundaries of biological experiments into issues that are intertwined with society (i.e., a horizontal integration of the hierarchy of biological sciences with a hierarchy of practical and normative knowledge). That is not to say that animal scientists have not envisioned segments of agricultural science as being at once disciplinary, integrated, and applied. Animal scientists, for example, have moved to produce lower-fat products in response to perceived health needs of the populace (NRC, 1989b). They are at the forefront of adapting the principles of the HACCP program to the production of safe food products. It is to say that the reach into contemporary issues and functional systems should be a recognized research and education goal.

INTEGRATIVE STUDIES

The theme of our model of animal science is this: Both reductive and integrative approaches (i.e., both explanatory and interpretive elements) are needed. Reductive research and its driving force, competitive merit-review, provides for a high quality of science both in the animal sciences and the biomedical sciences. They are, as Malone (1994) stated, the wellspring of knowledge. Such mechanisms, however, do not provide assurance that an optimal value return will be derived by society from the investment in research (Cowling et al., 1996). More is needed. Eventual understanding of biological processes requires the integration of animal science knowledge from the whole spectrum of levels in each of the hierarchies. Knowledge obtained in the basic levels in the biological hierarchy should flow into the more complex biological areas and back again, and from the biological hierarchy into forming the manipulative knowledge of a functional hierarchy and be tempered by societal and ethical considerations.

Integrative studies probably requires individual scientists who can look at both the whole and the parts. Integration may be collaboration among multidisciplinary scientists and institutions, but integration also refers to the approach to the problem, the study prior to the experiment, the development of the design of the experiment with the need for explanation in mind, and the conclusions based upon understanding the central problem from which an experiment was drawn. Integration may refer to more complex designs of experiments. It also refers to the ability of scientists to interconnect fragmented research results and propose a possible answer to a problem higher in the hierarchy of sciences, which then can be tested.

Integrative research, by our definition, would be concerned with biological, physical, and social issues and ethical values and their interconnectedness in a particular context (Kunkel and Hagevoort, 1994).

IMPLEMENTING INTEGRATIVE RESEARCH

The integrative contexts in the animal sciences involve cells, tissues, and organs, cell-cell communication, body systems (e.g., metabolic, secretory, immune), organisms (microorganisms and plants as well as animals), organismal growth, energy flow, economics, and human health. Cellular function is basic to all biological systems. Organs and body systems are integrative of biological and systemic functions. Cell-cell communication is essential to remodeling any tissue or organ. Organisms are inherently part of the human life-support system, but as diseases and pests, they can be detrimental. The logic of organismal growth, reproduction, and survival is the essence of the productivity of animal agriculture and fisheries. Energy flow is central to concepts ranging from ecology to international productivity and distribution. Economics involves competition and business operations. Also, human health has become society's ultimate concern. These are systems combining the hierarchies of research in animal science.

The question arises, what approach could be proposed to describe integrative research in the animal sciences in an operational manner? If one assumes that the integration is systemic, that is, it involves a biological or functional system, at least two kinds of methodological inquiry are available. One kind might be termed a hard systems approach and the other a soft systems procedure (Wilson and Morren, 1990). A hard science approach uses integrative concepts and thinking during the problem identification phase, when the problem is defined, and a model of the relevant system is described. The problem is not reduced as in the manner of scientific problem-solving rationality (rules 1–3). Instead, the problem is sculpted to the requirements of an optimization.

In a soft systems approach, the focus is on problematic situations, including those in which there is human activity. The system is conceived after careful descriptions of the current situations are developed. Hard systems integration starts with a model, whereas soft systems integration creates a model.

In a hard systems approach, there is a preference for examining quantitative aspects of situations. Mathematical relationships are sought whenever possible. Computational biology can be applied to complex systems to yield progress in structural biology. The soft science approach is built on integration of disciplinary approaches to research. It emphasizes a multidisciplinary approach to biological, functional, and moral complexity.

In the hard science approach, external measurement of the integrative function is expected. In the soft science approach, internal feelings such as in health and illness are prominent. Both approaches will be useful in the theoretical and practical considerations of integration in the animal sciences.

PUBLIC INTEREST RESEARCH

Perhaps as an extension of integrative scholarship, the conceptions of new fields of research are emerging. One of these is public nutrition, a new term that contrasts with clinical nutrition. It is suggested that "public nutrition deals with population problems and public policies and programs to address these; clinical nutrition is already understood to deal with the individual. If the name were accepted, it could help to conceptually group activities now going on under different headings, thus improving synthesis and coherence" (Mason et al., 1996).

As suggested by Mason and coauthors (1996), public nutrition would include the following activities:

1. An understanding and a raising of awareness concerning the nature, causes, and consequences of nutrition problems in society.
2. Epidemiology (including monitoring, surveillance, and evaluation).
3. Nutritional requirements and dietary guidelines for populations.
4. Programs and interventions, their design, planning, management and evaluation.
5. Community nutrition and community-based programs.
6. Public education, especially nutrition education for behavioral change.
7. Timely warning, prevention, and mitigation of emergencies (including emergency food aid).
8. Advocacy and linkage with, for example, population and environmental concerns.
9. Public policies relevant to nutrition in several sectors, (e.g., economic development, health, agriculture, and education).

There is a good deal of congruence in these components with the concerns and issues in animal agriculture as we have presented them in this book. Public interest research activities specifically related to agriculture are:

10. Participatory research
11. Systems research and long-term studies.
12. Community-based, problem-solving research.
13. Team multidisciplinary (multicomponent) research.
14. Team interdisciplinary (integrated) research.
15. Independent interdisciplinary research.
16. Scientific public service.

The components of public interest activities focus both on issues and on methodologies of research and sustainable agriculture (e.g., nutrient cycling, control of pest populations, control of water movement, biological diversity). The vision is dependent upon both farmer and researcher knowledge (i.e., indigenous and scientific knowledge), implying some point short of industrial knowledge.

Elements of such scholarship in public interest research or in public nutrition can be at odds with mainstream science. The struggle is between the scientific methods as the means of scholarship and what is often termed *emotion* in the solution of problems. Many animal scientists have been prone to give little credence to conjecture (i.e., knowledge derived from nonanalytical evaluation), but the conflict also arises as a result of the perception of what the goals of public interest research programs should be.

UNCERTAINTY, RISK, AND INTEREST

Research in the public interest calls to mind those responses that animal agriculture and the animal sciences must make regarding uncertainty and risk. There are issues that relate to uncertainty: the possible existence of a risk, the severity of the problem, the need for more research and, above all, the interplay of judgment and evidence that underlies scientific and all other forms of decision making. In such matters, the issues are often interest laden, overriding, or encompassing the value aspects of the scientific decision. There is often a tendency to avoid references to the underlying realities. In fact, all knowledge may be held to be socially constructed and therefore interest laden (Miller and Reilly, 1995).

Although animal scientists utilize scientific protocols and statistical inference to remove bias and add confidence to their experimental results, the experimental study undertaken is influenced by the values of the discipline, scientist, and institution. This is a long-known factor in scientific research. Interests also come into play as funding sources, individual loyalties, commodity interests, and the philosophic leanings (education) of the researcher may constrain the objectivity of the scientist and scholar.

During the past several years, animal agriculture has had to cope with the reality of a wide range of risks and uncertainty. Assessments and evaluations of these risks, however, have required different approaches to handle the uncertainties (Kunkel et al., 1998). For example, the risk issue with growth promoters and recombinant bovine somato-tropin (rbST) is the potential for misuse. The issue of *E. coli* 0157:H7 and other food-borne microorganisms is that sanitation, processing, food preparation, and storage can break down at any time. The issue with transmissible spongiform encephalopathies (TSE) is that the dis-eases are fatal and uncertainty exists as to their transmissibility.

Scientific methodologies may be used to assess such matters as food contamination, the safety of rbST, and the transmissibility of TSE, but it is a difficult matter for a government to propose that the con-sumption of a pleasurable but perhaps harmful food factor should be reduced, particularly when the employment and prosperity of a large part of the nation depends on the production of such substances (Acheson, 1986; Miller and Reilly, 1995). Such conflicts of interest have been evident throughout the modern history of animal agriculture (Busch and Lacy, 1983), not only relative to food safety but to environ-mental issues, issues of social justice, employment patterns, and now the issues of focus in animal agriculture.

If there is existing scientific evidence or agreement of scientific committees (or scholarly advisory councils) that conflicts with ex-pressed interests, and the reports are suppressed by government, indus-try, or research institutions, the stage is set for public and media criticism, political defeat, litigation, and loss of public trust, should the suppressed evidence be revealed. True, suppression of findings may never be known, but if found out, the cost can be high. A government may rely on secrecy, but can an academic institution ethically do so?

The alternative is simply not do the research. If one does not look, the bad and discomfiting are not found. The philosophy is, "Don't look! Don't find!" (Michael Hansen, pers. comm.). This is an easier decision to deal with than the repercussions of the discovery of suppressed in-formation or deliberate omission from publication.

We have little documentation that decisions have been made to not undertake certain research studies or to withdraw support of research that might reveal unwanted knowledge in the animal sciences. Ru-mors, however, are heard; watchdog groups exist for such eventualities and advisory committees are bypassed. Decisions not to look have surely been made, even in our own institutions.

THE UNCERTAINTIES. The uncertainties in animal science that are of public concern often relate to risk. Risk may be defined by formulas that translate probability and consequence into a measure of risk, but conceptions of risk are not definitions (Thompson and Dean, 1996).

Risk itself is a contested concept, and the explicit recognition of competing conceptions of risk might clarify many contemporary issues for animal science and agriculture by providing different ways of looking at a risk.

We have noted earlier that the multiple conceptions of risk can be largely visualized as being dichotomous, for example, a positivist/relativist dichotomy described by Shrader-Frechette (1991) and a rationalist/subjectivist version by Hornig (1993). One position (rationalist) is a purely scientific concept involving data and quantitative analysis. Other positions are those of relativists who believe that risk is a subjective reaction to events encountered in social or personal experiences. Animal scientists cluster mainly at the rationalist end, without consciously doing so.

Thompson and Dean's (1996) proposed dichotomy is a useful approach. At one extreme is a *probabilist* conception of risk. At the opposite extreme is the *contextualist* concept. Important to this proposal is that other conceptions can fall in between.

The probabilist takes scientifically ascertained probability as the essential characteristic of risk assessment. Intuitive risk assessment is not considered by the probabilist to be a legitimate form of knowledge, although it may possess political influence.

The contextualist states that no single attribute is a necessary condition for the existence of risk, but some element of change or uncertainty will always be present. Probability is there, but it is no more important than any of the rest.

Weak probabilists, whose conception falls in between the extremes, make claims based on what may be called a preponderance of the evidence.

It seems that animal agriculture has been caught between the probabilistic and contextual, between rationalist and subjective conceptions of risk. Some animal scientists have been prone to give little credence to nonanalytical evaluations of risk as a legitimate form of knowledge. As strong probabilists, we animal scientists argue that quantitative risk data should relieve any public fear. Some in animal agriculture argue that science is *the* means of risk reduction (Rodgers, 1997). We may interpret the public's reaction to risks in animal agriculture as conjectures. Scientific research would be expected to refute or confirm these conjectures by providing robust measurement of probabilities. A contextualist, however, would not make the assumption that conjecture and intuition are simply poor substitutes for statistically verified measures of probability.

The practical use of such competing conceptions of risk may be tested against any of the risk issues in animal agriculture. In the initial work, we chose the transmissible spongiform encephalopathies as the case (Kunkel et al., 1998; chapter 7). Other risks, such as the uses of antimicrobials or the place of animal products in the genesis of certain cancers, in which uncertainty is present, might be subject to analysis by both context and probability.

It is at the level of high uncertainty that the philosophic methodologies may be increasingly called on for their contributions. The field, however, is immature and undeveloped. Thus, at this point, we are only speculative of the ways such methodologies will be used; however, we do know that the key to dealing with uncertainty is to acknowledge the uncertainty. It is more persuasive to acknowledge the existence of scientific judgment than to keep insisting that narrow probabilistic accounts are free from that judgment (Susanna Priest, pers. comm.).

IMPLICATIONS

The agricultural research community has not been well-served by stereotypes of research such as *basic* and *applied,* although both have often been carried out with vision for the future. Agricultural research may be no better served by such calls as for ascendance of *holistic* research, research for sustainable agriculture, or public interest research, unless the end points are defined or the scope of each is adequate to cover the range of inquiry in the future. Additional research dimensions are needed to couple biology to agricultural function and societal needs, and as new biological laws and paradigms evolve, they can be folded into a broadly defined integrative component.

Scientists in animal science, like other scientists, are emersed in the science about them. With each other, they share a body of theories and principles that form a complex network that defines a world view, or in Thomas Kuhn's (1996) terminology, a paradigm. They are comfortable, perhaps too comfortable, with their current world view. The same might be said for higher education in any field.

HIGHER EDUCATION. Rethinking a science in an integrative way changes the world view. The questions are changed. Changing the question changes the direction of research. In changing their assumptions, scientists can consider new possibilities that have been, thus far, unthinkable. This is a point that granting agencies need to think about.

Higher education for animal agriculture should also be seen as a continuum. Kunkel and Thompson (1996) described it as a continuum that reaches from basic biology, chemistry, and economics through production, marketing, human needs, and ethics to resource recovery and sustainability. We see a higher education for animal agriculture that has the responsibility to handle issues. Linkage to all areas, such as human health and environment, must be pervasive. If the linkages are not understood, then both animal scientists and environmentalists may well retreat to an isolated and insulated existence, unable to interface with the whole society.

It is likely that the educational process will be the initial arena for integrative scholarship. Some physiologists suggest that the appropriate changes in the academic process will enable the evolution of classical physiology into integrative physiology (Duling, 1996). In so doing, higher education will need more than courses that integrate knowledge, but should involve students (professional, graduate, and undergraduate) as teachers of themselves and of others. The essence of excellent education is not to tell the student what to think, but how to think.

In so doing, animal science may share its model with other disciplines in medicine and agriculture. Such integrations can serve national interests whether they are in food systems or in health and quality of living, as well as things scientific.

We suggest that animal science and other agricultural sciences be categorized as at least a trichotomy: disciplinary, integrative, and applied scholarship. We suggest that the disciplines in animal science include applications of moral philosophy.

Research and education for animal agriculture will also recruit from a shifting disciplinary base. In some aspects, it also may have to balance the entry of new disciplines (e.g., ethics, ecology, or molecular biology) that have not yet gone through the process of constructing theory relevant to animal agriculture with integrative studies. In this context, integrative scholarship may provide guidance for alternative solutions for intervention in animal agriculture.

ADMINISTRATION. An institutional response is needed. Better methods should be devised by the professional community and research institutions to encourage the scholar and scientist whose intellectual activities go beyond their contributions using the reductive scientific method. The reward system to develop collaborative research and integrative scholarship should be enhanced. Complementary changes in the education of animal scientists appear to be needed.

The need is to overcome professional barriers that constrain integrative scholarship and introduction of nontraditional disciplines. The well-administered, multidisciplinary animal science department requires its faculty to be up-to-date methodologically for scientific research, development of technology, analyses of policy and institutional choices and of rational choices by consumers, and building management systems and to be able to carry these concepts into the classroom. It requires that individual faculty member become sensitive to other disciplines.

Despite the apparent constraints related to organization and traditional staffing patterns, the potential for integrative scholarship and interdisciplinary communication appears to be increasing. The reasons for this include the development of the systems sciences, the infusion of the same powerful new scientific tools into a number of disciplines, and most importantly, the increased occurrence of informal networking among faculty members of different disciplines; however, given that individuals's values and personalities intrude into research strategies, the future of agricultural research and education may rest, not on administration, but on the faculty's intellectual visions and philosophical awareness which go beyond traditional disciplinary limits.

POLICY ISSUES. A good deal of agricultural science has stood on the thesis that it is a "theory about the most rational organization of nature to satisfy human needs" (Krohn and Schäfer, 1982). It has been less successful "as a science about the rationality about human needs vis à vis nature." What has not been dealt with well are potentially contradicting questions. Who is the system working for? Who are the people in "agriculture, food, and the natural resources?"

Whom should the system serve? It is more than the farmer and rancher, but farmers and ranchers are included: the small and the large, the family, and the corporate. The landowner is included, but are not also the landless? What of our economic and industrial needs? What of those who eat? That is all of us. What of the dangers and risks that animal agriculture now faces: transmissible spongiform encephalopathies, animal fecal transmission of pathogens, new technologies with unknown effects and on and on? What of our children, as resources are sustained or not, and their children? What of the fellow scientist and faculty member, the student, the high school and college teachers of agricultural science, and the extension agent? All of these require a constantly flowing knowledge base—factual, pragmatic, and normative. If we can truly know the extents of our clienteles, animal science could be more protective of humankind—and itself.

CONCLUSION

Fluidity and theoretical immaturity in the animal sciences characterize much of the current scholarship, but certain trends are evident.

First, a continuing goal of a substantial part of the system is that the science be excellent and incisive, of high quality, both in its conduct and its facilities. Limited by the growth of their traditional sources of support, agricultural and related sciences are moving into the mainstream of national science funding arrangements. That means not only a greater turn to basic biological sciences supported by governmental agencies, but also to a greater reliance on the growing industrial relationship for the support of problem-solving and targeted research.

Second, changes will occur in the assumptions that exist in the conduct of science. Disciplines and subject matters can be more broadly conceived epistemologically. Such breadth is developing in human nutrition, entomology, and other areas. It will do so in the animal sciences. Disciplines will incorporate different components of other disciplines as they develop. The boundaries of the institution's grasp of disciplines are determined by the knowledge, skills, and intellectual perceptive of the scientists and scholars recruited and retained.

Third, recognition must be given to the fact that not all questions can be answered by science. Empirical sciences are not the only valid knowledge base, but research that provides the information necessary for individual decisions (e.g., farm-scale production and marketing systems research) will likely succumb to increasing costs and the lack of students who are interested in such studies. Something more is needed: comprehensive professional and general knowledge and experience is suggested (Suppe, 1987). We have suggested the use of competitive conceptions of risk as a method of dealing with uncertainties (Kunkel et al., 1998)

Finally, society may increasingly determine what kinds of applied research will be allowed. Society will probably accept—and applaud—research on the genome, the means of creating genetic transforms, and the repartitioning of nutrients from fat to lean, but may ask serious questions when basic research to apply principles is undertaken. Will the public accept cloning of animals? What risks to animal and human health might be incurred? Which genes are chosen to be transferred? Why are they chosen? What will it mean to humans that the scientific bases of cloning are being worked out on animals? All these, however, may not be the larger questions that the animal sciences must face in the twenty-first century. Human issues represent a moving target. What was of major concern yesterday is of a lower level of interest today. As the twenty-first century begins, it is the specter of risk that has caught the interests of society. The context of preparing students for a risk society should be the focus of higher education in the twenty-first century.

The social process of animal science and the social institution of animal science research and education need attention. Breaking into the education of scientists may be the most appropriate way to begin the process. A new kind of scientist, trained in interdisciplinary sciences, may be required. Some sort of opportunity in systems education would likely be useful for all agricultural scientists. Disciplinarians who have also been educated in the decision-making processes should have many interesting opportunities for productive careers in the agricultural sciences.

The whole hierarchy of disciplines in biology and human studies provides a range of useful opportunities for intervention in animal agriculture. The choice of which intervention to use depends on a choice of purpose, but these are human choices based on human values. The different levels of intervention are not mutually exclusive. One can attempt to understand what is going on at a molecular level, at the systems level, and at a societal level at the same time. A diversity of disciplines must be made available to the research and education for animal agriculture. What seems to be needed is a diversity of institutions and disciplines contributing to animal science in the future and the professional acceptance of this need.

Can the animal sciences address the whole system? In the disciplinary sense, the answer most likely is no. In a systemic sense, however, they must.

NOTES

1. Material for this chapter includes parts published in journals: Kunkel and Hagevoort, 1994; Kunkel et al., 1998.

2. For purposes of this chapter, the term *goals* will refer to the goals *for* the research. Goals may be institutionally, externally, disciplinarily, or politically defined or driven. Goals for agricultural research, for example, might be for enhancement of a commodity-oriented research program (e.g., on dairy animals or poultry) of studies relative to a resource (e.g., on air quality effects, non-point contamination of water supplies, control of rangeland pests), investigations relative to a use (e.g., research in international marketing, human nutrition), or otherwise.

The term *mission* refers to the general purposes of the institution or program and may encompass the goals of the institution or for the effort.

The term *objectives* will refer to the objectives *of* the research itself or the research program. Such objectives may be, for example, increasing the yield of corn, producing a superior variety of crop, improving the nutritional quality of beef, developing a new means of genetically engineering a plant, or developing the understanding of a physiological phenomenon.

REFERENCES

(Entries of broader interest to the general reader are preceded by an asterisk.)

AAALAC (American Association for Accreditation of Laboratory Animal Care). 1991. *AAALAC accreditation program.* Bethesda: AAALAC.

Abelson, P. H. 1993. Editorial: Pesticides and foods. *Science* 9:1235.

Acheson, D. 1986. Food policy, nutrition, and the government. *Proc. Nutr. Soc.* 45:131–38.

Acosta, P. B. 1988. Availability of essential amino acids and nitrogen in vegan diets. *Am. J. Clin. Nutr.* 48:868–74.

Aiken, W. H. 1982. The goals of agriculture. In *Agriculture, change, and human values: Proceedings of a multidisciplinary conference, October 18–21, 1982,* 29–54. University of Florida, Gainesville, Humanities and Agriculture Program.

Ajzen, K., and M. Fishbein. 1980. *Understanding attitudes and predicting social behavior.* Englewood Cliffs, N.J.: Prentice-Hall.

Albright, J. L. 1985. Update of the animal welfare issue. Paper presented at the California Animal Nutrition Conference, Fresno, March 14.

Algers, B., and P. Jensen. 1985. Communication during suckling in the domestic pig: Effects of continuous noise. *Appl. Anim. Behav. Sci.* 14:49.

Allen, P. L., and C. S. Sachs. 1992. The poverty of sustainability: An analysis of current positions. *Agri. Hum. Val.* 9(4):29–35.

Altieri, M. A. 1987. *Agroecology: The scientific basis of alternative agriculture,* 29–45. Boulder, Colo.: Westview Press.

American Dietetic Association. 1993. Position of the American Dietetic Association: Vegetarian diets. *J. Am. Diet. Assoc.* 93:1317–19.

American Heart Association. 1982. Rationale of the diet-heart statement of the American Heart Association. Report of the Nutrition Committee. *Circulation* 65:839A–54A.

———. 1986. Dietary guidelines for healthy adult Americans. *Circulation* 74:1465A.

———. 1988. Dietary guidelines for healthy American adults. A statement for physicians and health professionals. *Circulation* 77:721A–24A.

Ames, B. N., and L. S. Gold. 1990. Too many rodent carcinogens: Mitogenesis increases mutagenesis. *Science* 249:970–71.

Ames, B. N., L. S. Gold, and W. C. Willett. 1995. The causes and prevention of cancer. *Proc. Nat. Acad. Sci. USA* 92:5258–65.

Angermeier, P. L., and J. R. Karr. 1993. Biological integrity versus biological diversity as policy directives. *BioScience* 44:690–97.

APHIS (Animal and Plant Health Inspection Services), USDA. 1996. *Bovine spongiform encephalopathy.* Veterinary Services Factsheet. Washington, D.C.: USDA.

Arrow, K., B. Bolin, R. Costanza, P. Dasgupta, C. Folke, C. S. Holling, B. Janssow, S. Levin, K.-G. Mäler, C. Perrings, and D. Pimentel. 1995. Economic growth, carrying capacity, and the environment. *Science* 268:520–21.

ASA (American Society of Agronomy). 1994. *Agricultural ethics: Issues for the 21st century.* ASA spec. publ. no. 57. Madison, Wis.: Soil Science Society of America, ASA, Crop Science Society of America.

AWI (Animal Welfare Institute). 1978. *Animals and their legal rights,* 3d ed. Washington, D.C.: AWI.

Baker, F. 1990. Risk communication about environmental hazards. *J. Pub. Hlth. Pol.* 11:341–49.

Balch, C. C., and J. T. Reid. 1976. Energy conversion into animal products. In *Food production and consumption.* A. N. Duckham, J. G. Jones, and E. H. R. Roberts, eds., 171–98. New York: American Elsevier.

Balter, M. 1999. Trade policy: Scientific cross-claims fly in continuing beef war. *Science* 294:1453–55.

Banni, S., G. Carta, M. S. Contini, E. Angioni, M. Deiana, M. A. Dressi, M. P. Melis, and F. P. Corongiu. 1996. Characterization of conjugated diene fatty acids in milk, dairy products, and lamb tissues. *Nutr. Biochem.* 7:150–55.

Barkas, J. 1975. *The vegetable passion.* New York: Charles Scribner's Sons.

Barkin, D., R. L. Batt, and B. R. DeWalt. 1990. *Food crops vs. feed crops: Global substitutions of grain in production.* Boulder, Colo.: Lynne Rienner Publishers.

Barnard, N. 1995. *Eat right, live longer.* New York: Harmony Books.

Barnes, B., and D. Edge. 1982. *Science in context: Readings in the sociology of science.* Cambridge: MIT Press.

Bartsch, H. 1991. N–nitroso compounds and human cancer: Where do we stand? In *Relevance to human cancer of N–nitroso compounds, tobacco smoke, and mycotoxins,* eds. I. K. O'Neill, J. Chen, and H. Bartsch, 1–10. Lyon, France: IARC.

Bawden, R. J. 1986. *Systems thinking and practice in agriculture: An overview. Systems approaches to food and agricultural problems,* 2.2–2.126. National Agriculture and Natural Resources Curriculum Project, Food and Agricultural Systems Task Group. New Brunswick, N.J.: Rutgers University.

Bazelon, D. L. 1979. Risk and responsibility. *Science* 205:277.

Beck, U. 1992 (orig. German 1986). *Risk society: Towards a modernity,* trans. M. Ritter. London: Sage Publications.

Beckman, C. K. 1996. Regulatory cooperation between the European Commission and U.S. administrative agencies. *Admin. Law J.* 9:933.

Begley, S. 1997. Little lamb, who made thee? *Newsweek* (March 10):53–58.

Bendixin, H. J. 1980. Role of the European Commission in animal welfare. *Anim. Reg. Stud.* 3:153.

Bengstsson, L. 1992. Climate system modeling prospects. In *Climate system modeling,* ed. K. Trenbeth, 705–24. Cambridge: Cambridge University Press.

Bennett, J. W. 1986. Research on farmer behavior and social organization. In *New directions for agriculture and agricultural research,* ed. K. A. Dahlberg, 367–402. Totowa, N.J.: Rowman and Allanheld.

Bentham, J. 1789. *Introduction to the principles of morals and legislation.*

* Berry, W. 1977. *The unsettling of America: Culture and agriculture.* San Francisco: Sierra Club Books.

Birt, D. F. and E. Bresnick. 1991. Chemoprevention by nonnutrient components of vegetables and fruits. In *Human nutrition: A comprehensive treatise,* 221–61. New York: Plenum.

Blatz, C. V. 1992. The very idea of sustainability. *Agri. Hum. Val.* 9(4):29–35.

* ———, ed. 1991. *Ethics and agriculture: An anthology on current issues in a world context.* Moscow: University of Idaho Press.

Block, G., B. Patterson, and A. Subar. 1992. Fruits, vegetables, and cancer prevention: A review of the epidemiological evidence. *Nutr. Can.* 18:1–29.

Bonanno, A. 1989. Changes, crisis, and restructuring in western Europe: The new dimensions of agriculture. *Agri. Hum. Val.* 6(1–2):2–10.

———. 1991. The restructuring of the agricultural and food system: Social and economic equity in the reshaping of the agrarian question and the food question. *Agri. Hum. Val.* 8(4):72–82.

Box, T. W. 1990. Rangelands. In *Natural resources for the 21st century,* eds. R. N. Sampson and D. Hair, 101–20. Washington, D.C.: Island Press.

Boyer, E. L. 1990. *Scholarship reconsidered,* 75–81. New York: Carnegie Foundation for the Advancement of Teaching.

Brambell, F. W. R. 1965. *Report of the technical committee to enquire into the welfare of animals kept under intensive livestock husbandry systems.* Cmnd. 2836. London: Her Majesty's Stationer's Office.

Brooks, J. 1981. The new snobbery. How to show off in America. *Atlantic Monthly* (January):37.

Broom, D. M. 1993. A usable definition of animal welfare. *J. Agric. Environ. Eth.* 6(spec. supp. 2):15–25.

Brown, J. L., and E. Pollitt. 1996. Malnutrition, poverty, and intellectual development. *Sci. Am.* (February):38–43.

Brown, L. R. 1988. *The changing world food prospect: The nineties and beyond.* Worldwatch pap. 85. Washington, D.C.: Worldwatch Institute.

———. 1997. *The agricultural link: How environmental deterioration could disrupt economic progress.* Worldwatch pap. 136. Washington, D.C.: Worldwatch Institute.

———. 1995. Facing food security. *Worldwatch* (Nov./Dec.):10–20.

Browne, W. P. 1987. Personality as power: Reconsidering Tweeten's sector argument. *Agri. Hum. Val.* 4(4):43–46.

———. 1988a. The fragmented and meandering politics of agriculture. In *U.S. agriculture in a global setting: An agenda for the future,* ed. M. A. Tutwiler, 136–53. Washington, D.C.: Resources for the Future.

———. 1988b. *Private interests, public policy, and American agriculture.* Lawrence: University Press of Kansas.

———. 1990. Organized interests and their issue niches: A search for pluralism in a policy domain. *J. Polit.* 52:477–509.

* ———. 1995. *Cultivating Congress: Constituents, issues, and interests in agricultural policy making.* Lawrence: University Press of Kansas.

* Browne, W. P., J. R. Skees, L. E. Swanson, P. B. Thompson, and L. J. Unnevehr. 1992. *Sacred cows and hot potatoes: Agrarian myths in agricultural policy.* Boulder, Colo.: Westview Press.

Bruce, M. E., R. G. Will, J. W. Ironside, I. McConnell, D. Drummond, A. Suttie, I. McCardle, A. Chres, J. Hope, C. Burkitt, S. Cousens, H. Fraser, and C. J. Bostick. 1997. Transmission to mice indicate that new variant CJD is caused by the BSE agent. *Nature* 389:498.

Buchanan, R. L. 1990. HACCP: A re-emerging approach to food safety. *Trends Food Sci. Technol.* 1:104–106.

Budiansky, S. 1992. *The covenant of the wild: Why animals chose domestication.* New York: William Morrow.

Burr, M. L., and B. K. Butland. 1988. Heart disease in British vegetarians. *Am. J. Clin. Nutr.* 48:830–32.

Burr, M., P. M. Sweetnam, and M. E. Barasi. 1985. Dietary fiber, blood pressure, and plasma cholesterol. *Nutr. Res.* 5:465–72.

Busch, L. 1989. Irony, tragedy, and temporality in agricultural systems, or, how values and systems are related. *Agri. Hum. Val.* 6(4):4–11.

Busch, L., and W. B. Lacy. 1983. *Science, agriculture, and the politics of research.* Boulder, Colo.: Westview Press.

Busch, L., W. B. Lacy, J. Burkhardt, and L. R. Lacy. 1991. *Plants, power, and profit: Social, economic, and ethical consequences of the new biotechnologies.* Cambridge, Mass.: Basil Blackwell.

Buttel, F. H. 1991. Knowledge production, ideology, and sustainability in the social and natural sciences. Unpublished paper presented at the meeting of the Agriculture, Food, and Human Values Society, Asilomar Conference Center, Pacific Grove, California, May 10–12.

Byé, P., and M. Fonte. 1993. Toward science-based techniques in agriculture. *Agri. Hum. Val.* 10(2):16–25.

Byers, F. M. 1990. Beef production and the greenhouse effect—the role of methane from beef in global warming. Unpublished manuscript. College Station: Texas A&M University, Department of Animal Science.

Bywater, A. C., and R. L. Baldwin. 1980. Alternative strategies in food-animal production. In *Animals, feed, food, and people,* ed. R. L. Baldwin, 1–30, Boulder, Colo.: Westview Press.

Callicott, J. B. 1989. Agroecology in context. *J. Agri. Eth.* 1:3–9.

———. 1989. In *Defense of the land ethic: Essays in environmental philosophy.* Albany: SUNY Press.

Campbell, J. R., and J. F. Lasley. 1985. *The science of animals that serve humanity,* 3d ed. New York: McGraw-Hill.

Campbell, T. C. 1994. The dietary causes of degenerative diseases, nutrients vs. foods. In *Western diseases: Their dietary prevention and reversibility,* N.J. Temple and D. P. Burkitt, eds. 119–52. Totowa, N.J.: Humana Press.

Caplan, A. L. 1986. The ethics of uncertainty: The regulation of food safety in the United States. *Agri. Hum. Val.* 3(1–2):180–90.

Capps, O., Jr. 1986. Changes in domestic demand for food: Impacts on Southern agriculture. *South. J. Agric. Econ.* 18(1):25–36.

Carpenter, B. 1994. This land is my land: Environmentalism is colliding with the rights of property owners. *U.S. News World Rept.* (March 11):65–69.

Carroll, J. E. 1991. First World diets and rainforest destruction: Exploring ethical issues. Unpublished paper presented at the meeting of the Agriculture, Food, and Human Values Society, Pacific Grove, California, May 10–12.

Carson, R. 1962. *Silent spring.* Boston: Houghton Mifflin.

CAST (Council for Agricultural Science and Technology). 1984. *Energy use and production agriculture,* 6–7. Rept. no. 99, February. Ames, Ia.: CAST.

———. 1994. *How much land can ten billion people spare for nature?* Task force rept. 121. Ames, Ia.: CAST.

———. 1995. *Waste management and utilization in food production and processing.* Ames, Ia.: CAST.

———. 1996. *Grazing on public lands.* Task force rept. 129. Ames, Ia.: CAST.

Chambers, R. 1987. Food and water as if poor people mattered: A professional revolution. In *Water and water policy in world food supplies,* ed. W. R. Jordan. Proceedings of conference, May 26–30, 1985, Texas A&M University. College Station: Texas A&M University Press.

Chambers, R., A. Pacey, and L. A. Thrupp, eds. 1989. *Farmer first: Farmer innovation and agricultural research.* London: Intermediate Technology Publications.

Chancellor, W. J. 1979. *Substituting information for energy in agricultural produc-*

tion and processing. Pap. no. 79-1531. St. Joseph, Mich.: American Society of Agricultural Engineers.

Chapple, C. 1986. Noninjury to animals: Jaina and Buddhist perspectives. In *Animal sacrifices: Religious perspectives on the use of animals in science,* ed. Tom Regan. Philadelphia: Temple University Press.

* Cheeke, P. R. 1999. *Contemporary issues in animal agriculture,* 2d ed. Danville, Ill.: Interstate Publishers.

Cheit, R. E. 1990. *Setting safety standards: Regulation in the public and private sectors.* Berkeley: University of California Press.

Chen, J., T. C. Campbell, J. Li, and R. Peto. 1990. *Diet, life-style, and mortality in China: A study of the characteristics of 65 Chinese counties.* Joint publication. Oxford: Oxford University Press; Ithaca, N.Y.: Cornell University Press; Beijing: People's Medical Publishing House.

Chin, S. F., J. M. Storkson, K. J. Albright, M. E. Cook, and M. W. Pariza. 1992. Conjugated linoleic acid is a growth factor for rats as shown by enhanced weight gain and improved feed efficiency. *J. Nutr.* 124:2344–49.

Christensen, J. A. 1984. Gemeinschaft and gesellschaft: Testing the spatial and communal hypothesis. *Soc. Forces* 63:160–68.

———. 1988. Social risk and rural sociology. *Rur. Sociol.* 53:1–24.

Cibelli, J. B., S. L. Stice, P. J. Golueke, J. K. Kane, J. Jerry, C. Blackwell, F. A. Ponce de Leon, and J. M. Rabl. 1998. Cloned transgenic calves produced from nonquiescent fetal fibroblasts. *Science* 280:1256–58.

Cole, H. H., and W. N. Garrett, eds. 1980. *Animal agriculture: The biology, husbandry, and use of domestic animals,* 2d ed. San Francisco: W. H. Freeman and Co.

Comstock, G. L. 1987. *Is there a moral obligation to save the family farm?* Ames: Iowa State University Press.

———. 1994. Might morality require veganism? Introduction. *J. Agric. Environ. Eth.* 7:1–6.

———. 1995. Do agriculturalists need a new, an ecocentric, ethic? *Agri. Hum. Val.* 12(1):2–16.

Connor, J. M. 1981. Food product proliferation: A market structure analysis. *Am. J. Agric. Econ.* 63:607–17.

Conquer, J. A., and B. J. Holub. 1996. Supplementation with an algae source of docosahexaenoic acid increases (n-3) fatty acid status and alters selected risk factors for heart disease in vegetarian subjects. *J. Nutr.* 126:3022–39.

Consortium for Developing a Guide for the Care and Use of Agricultural Animals in Agricultural Research and Teaching. 1988. *Guide for the care and use of agricultural animals in agricultural research and teaching.* Champaign, Ill.: Consortium for Developing a Guide for the Care and Use of Agricultural Animals in Agricultural Research and Teaching.

Cooke, G. W. 1980. Implications of the intensification of agriculture for ecological problems. In *Food chains and human nutrition,* ed. Sir K. Blaxter, 415–35. London: Applied Sciences Publication.

Coppinger, R. P., and C. K. Smith. 1983. The domestication of evolution. *Environ. Conserv.* 10:283–92.

Coppinger, R., E. Clarence, and T. Coppinger. 1992. Considerations for a sustainable society. *Land Rept.* 43:21–23.

Coulson, R. N., and D. A. Crossley Jr. 1987. What is insect ecology? A commentary. *Bull. Entomol. Soc. Am.* 33:64.

Cowling, E. B., J. T. Sigmon, and C. R. Putnam. 1996. Maximizing benefits from research: Lessons from medicine and agriculture. *Iss. Sci. Technol.* (Spring): 29–32.

* Cox, G. W., and M. D. Atkins. 1979. *Agricultural ecology.* San Francisco: W. H. Freeman and Co.

Croft, B. A. 1985. Integrated pest management: The agricultural–environment rationale. In *CIPM-Integrated pest management on major agricultural systems,* eds. R. E. Frisbie and P. L. Adkisson, 712–28. College Station: Texas Agricultural Experiment Station MP-1616.

Cromwell, G. L., and R. D. Coffey. 1995. Nutrient management from feed to field. Paper presented at the World Park Expo, Des Moines, Iowa, June 9–10.

Cross, H. R., J. W. Savell, R. E. Branson, D. S. Hale, J. J. Francis, J. W. Wise, and D. L. Wilkes. 1986. *National consumer retail beef study: Final report to the Agricultural Marketing Service.* Washington, D.C.: USDA.

Crosson, P. R., and J. J. Rosenberg. 1990. *Agriculture in a changing environment.* Disc. pap. ENR 90–01. Washington, D.C.: Resources for the Future.

Crotty, R. 1980. *Cattle, economics, and development.* Commonwealth Agricultural Bureau, 9 and 117. Old Woking, Surrey, UK: Gresham Press.

Crouch, M. 1991. The very structure of scientific research militates against developing products to help the environment. *J. Agric. Environ. Eth.* 4:151–58.

Curtis, S. E. 1983. *Environmental management in animal agriculture.* Ames: Iowa State University Press.

———. 1993. Future directions of science and public policy. *J. Agric. Environ. Eth.* 6(spec. supp. 1):133–38.

Curtis, S. E., and W. R. Stricklin. 1991. The importance of animal cognition in agricultural production systems: An overview. *J. Anim. Sci.* 69:5001–5007.

Dagnelie, P. C., W. A. van Staveren, F. J. V. R. A. Vergote, P. G. Dingjan, H. van den Berg, and J. G. A. J. Hautvast. 1989. Increased risk of vitamin B_{12} and iron deficiency in infants on macrobiotic diets. *Am. J. Clin. Nutr.* 50:818–24.

Dahlberg, K. A. 1986. Introduction: Changing contexts and goals and the need for new evaluative approaches. In *New directions for agriculture and agricultural research,* ed. K. Dahlberg, 1–27. Totowa, N.J.: Rowman and Allanheld.

———. 1987. Redefining development priorities: Genetic diversity and agroecodevelopment. *Conserv. Biol.* 1(4):311–22.

Daily, G. C. 1995. Restoring value to the world's degraded lands. *Science* 269:350–54.

Daly, H. F. 1995. Reply to Mark Sagoff's "Carrying capacity and ecological economics." *BioScience* 45:621–24.

Danbom, D. F. 1986. Publicly sponsored agricultural research in the United States from a historical perspective. In *New directions for agriculture and agricultural research,* ed. K. Dahlberg, 107–31. Totowa, N.J.: Rowman and Allanheld.

Dando, W. 1988. World food and regional famines: Problems and prospects. *Currents* 3(3):11–19.

Daniels, N. 1980. Reflective equilibrium and archimedean points. *Can. J. Philos.* 10:85–86.

Dantzer, R. 1993. Research perspectives in farm animal welfare: The concept of stress. *J. Agric. Environ. Eth.* 6(spec. supp. 2):86–92.

Darby, W. J. 1989. The nature of benefits. *Nutr. Rev.* 38:37.

Dawkins, M. S. 1980. *Animal suffering.* London: Chapman and Hall.

———. 1985. The scientific basis for assessing suffering in animals. In *Defense of animals,* ed. P. Singer. New York: Basil Blackwell.

———. 1990a. From an animal's point of view: Motivation, fitness, and animal welfare. *Behav. Brain Sci.* 13:1–61.

———. 1990b. Heroes and villains. *Nature* 343:521.

Dealler, S., and J. Kent. 1995. BSE: An update on the statistical evidence. *Brit. Food J.* 97:3–18.

DeLind, L. B. 1995. The state, hog hotels, and the "right to farm": A curious relationship. *Agri. Hum. Val.* 12(3):4–44.

Deutermann, J. L. 1988. Findings question notions about eggs. *Poul. Egg Mark.* (July):10–11.

DHHS (Department of Health and Human Services), Public Health Service (PHS). 1988. *The Surgeon General's Report on Nutrition and Health.* Publ. no. 88-50210. Washington, D.C.: DHHS, PHS.

Dietz, W. H., and F. L. Trowbridge. 1990. Symposium on the identification and prevalence of undernutrition in the United States: Introduction. *J. Nutr.* 120:917–18.

Doll, R. 1992. The lessons of life. Keynote address to the Nutrition and Cancer Conference. *Can. Res.* 54:2024–29.

Doll, R., and R. Peto. 1981. The causes of cancer: Quantitative estimates of avoidable risks of cancer in the United States today. *J. Nat. Can. Inst.* 66:1191–1308.

Dombrowski, D. A. 1984. *The philosophy of vegetarianism.* Amherst: University of Massachusetts Press.

Donnelley, S. 1989. Speculative philosophy and animal experimentation. *Hastings Ctr. Rept.* 19(2):15–21.

Donnelley, S., C. R. McCarthy, and R. Singleton Jr. 1994. The Brave New World of animal biotechnology. *Hastings Ctr. Rept.* 24(spec. supp. 1):S1–S31.

Douglas, M., and A. Wildavsky. 1992. *Risk and culture: An essay on the selection of technological and environmental dangers.* Berkeley: University of California Press.

Dover, M., and L. M. Talbot. 1987. *To feed the earth: Agro-ecology for sustainable development.* Washington, D.C.: World Resources Institute.

Doyle, J. 1985. *Altered harvest: Agriculture, genetics, and the fate of the world's food supply.* New York: Viking Penguin.

Dregne, H. 1977. Desertification of arid lands. *Econ. Geogr.* 53(4):325.

Duckham, A. N. 1976a. Environmental constraints. In *Food production and consumption,* eds. A. N. Duckham, J. G. W. Jones, and E. H. Roberts, 61–81. New York: American Elsevier.

———. 1976b. The inducement and administration of change: Practice. In *Food production and consumption,* eds. A. N. Duckham, J. G. W. Jones, and E. H. Roberts, 441–57. New York: American Elsevier.

Duling, B. R. 1996. Integrative physiology: A response. *Physiologist* 39:5, 11.

Duncan, I. J. H. 1981. Animal rights—animal welfare: A scientist's assessment. *Poul. Sci.* 60:489.

———. 1993. Welfare is to do with what animals feel. *J. Agric. Environ. Eth.* 6(spec. supp. 2):8–14.

Duncan, I. J. H., and M. S. Dawkins. 1983. The problem of assessing "well-being" and "suffering" in farm animals. In *Indications relevant to animal welfare,* ed. D. Smith, 13–24. The Hague: Martinus Nijhoff.

DuPuis, E. M., and C. Geisler. 1988. Biotechnology and the small farm. *BioScience* 38:406–11.

Durning, A. 1990. How much is "enough"? *Worldwatch* 3(6):12.

Durning, A. B., and H. B. Brough. 1991. *Taking stock: Animal farming and the environment.* Worldwatch pap. 103. Washington, D.C.: Worldwatch Institute.

———. 1992. Reforming the livestock economy. In *State of the world.* Worldwatch Institute. New York: W. W. Norton and Co.

Dwyer, J. T. 1988. Health aspects of vegetarian diets. *Am. J. Clin. Nutr.* 48:712–38.

———. 1991. Nutritional consequences of vegetarianism. *Annu. Rev. Nutr.* 11:61–91.

Dwyer, J., and F. M. Loew. 1994. Nutritional risks of vegan diets to women and children: Are they preventable? *J. Agric. Environ. Eth.* 7:87–109.

Eales, J. S., and L. J. Unnevehr. 1988. Demand for beef and chicken products: Separability and structural change. *Am. J. Agric. Econ.* 70:521–32.

Economist. 1995. Saints and sinners. *Economist* (June 24):15–16.

———. 1996. The BSE scare: Mad cows and Englishmen. The British disease. *Economist* (March 30):25–27.

———. 1997. Building to order. *Economist* (March 1):81.

Ehrenfeld, D. 1978. *The arrogance of humanism.* New York: Oxford University Press.

Elliott, C. 1992. Where ethics come from and what to do about it. *Hastings Ctr. Rept.* (July–August):28–35.

Ellison, L. 1949. The ecological basis for judging condition and trend on mountain range land. *J. For.* 47:787–95.

Engel, J. R. 1990. Introduction: The ethics of sustainable development. In *Ethics of Environment and Development,* eds. J. R. Engel and J. G. Engel, 1–23. Tucson: University of Arizona Press.

EPA (Environmental Protection Agency). 1996. *Proposed guidelines for carcinogen risk assessment.* Cincinnati: National Center for Environmental Publications and Information.

Erickson, K. L. 1998. Is there a relation between dietary linoleic acid and cancer of the breast, colon, or prostate? *Am. J. Clin. Nutr.* 68:5–7.

ESA (Ecological Society of America). 1996. *ESA report on the scientific basis for ecosystem management.* ESA, Committee Report. Washington, D.C.: ESA.

FAO (Food and Agriculture Organization of the United Nations). 1992. *The role of ruminant livestock in food security in developing countries.* Committee of World Food Security, 17th session, Rome, March 23–27. Rome: FAO.

FAO (Food and Agriculture Organization of the United Nations). 1983. *The state of food and agriculture, 1982-world review. Livestock production: A world perspective.* Agri. Series 15. Rome: FAO.

Farrell, K. R. 1988. Food safety: Finding a path to resolution. *Calif. Agri.* 4:2.

Federation of Animal Science Societies (FASS). 1999. *Guide for the care and use of agricultural animals in research and teaching.* Savoy, Ill.: FASS.

Fenno, R. F., Jr. 1978. *Home style: House members and their districts.* Boston: Little, Brown and Co.

Field, T. G. 1990. The future of grazing public lands. *Rangelands* 12(4):217–19.

Firth, R. 1955. Some principles of social organization. *J. Roy. Anthropol. Inst.* 85: 1–20.

Flavin, C., and O. Tunali. 1996. *Climate of hope: New strategies for stabilizing the world's atmosphere.* Worldwatch pap. 130. Washington, D.C.: Worldwatch Institute.

Fomon, S. J., and D. B. McCormick. 1993. B vitamins and choline. In *Nutrition of normal infants,* ed. S. J. Fomon. St. Louis: Mosby-Year Book.

Food and Drug Law Institute. 1997. Overview. In *Reaching food law and regulation: Information and strategies.* Washington, D.C.: Food and Drug Law Institute.

Food Safety Notebook. 1993. *E. coli* 0157:H7 in the news. *Food Saf. Notebk.* 4(3):27–28.

Foster, K. R., D. E. Bernstein, and P. W. Huber, eds. 1993. *Phantom risks: Scientific inference and the law.* Cambridge: MIT Press.

Fox, M. A. 1986. *The case for animal experimentation.* Berkeley: University of California Press.

Fox, M. W. 1984. *Farm animals: Husbandry, behavior, and veterinary practice.* Baltimore: University Park Press.

Fox, R. M., and J. P. DeMarco. 1986. The challenge of applied ethics. In *New directions in ethics,* eds. J. P. DeMarco and R. M. Fox, 1–20. New York: Routledge and Kegan Paul.

Fraser, D., P. A. Phillips, and B. K. Thompson. 1993. Environmental preference testing to assess the well-being of animals—an evolving paradigm. *J. Agric. Environ. Eth.* 6(spec. supp. 2):104–14.

Fraser, G. E. 1988. Determinants of ischemic heart disease in Seventh-Day Adventists: A review. *Am. J. Clin. Nutr.* 48:833–36.

Freese, B. 1994. Pork powerhouses. *Success. Farm.* 92(10):20–24.

Frey, R. G. 1983. *Rights, killing, and suffering: Moral vegetarianism and applied ethics.* Oxford, U.K.: Basil Blackwell.

Friedman, M., and L. J. Savage. 1948. The utility analysis of choices involving risk. *J. Polit. Econ.* 56:279–304.

Gardner, G. 1997. *Recycling organic waste: From urban pollutant to farm resource.* Worldwatch pap. 135. Washington, D.C.: Worldwatch Institute.

Gaskell, G., M. W. Bauer, J. Durant, and N. C. Allum. 1999. Worlds apart? The reception of genetically modified foods in Europe and in the U.S. *Science* 285:384–87.

George, K. P. 1990. So animal a human . . ., or the moral relevance of being an omnivore. *J. Agric. Environ. Eth.* 3:172–86.

———. 1992. The use and abuse of scientific studies. *J. Agric. Environ. Eth.* 5: 217–33.

Georgescu-Roegen, N. 1973. The entropy law and the economic problem. In *Toward a steady-state economy,* ed. H. E. Daly. Baltimore: Johns Hopkins University Press.

Giovannucci, E. 1994. Epidemiologic characteristics of prostate cancer. *Cancer* 75(supp.):1766–77.

Goldstein, J. H. 1996. Whose land is it anyway? Private property rights and the Endangered Species Act. *Choices* (2d quar.):4–8.

Goodall, J. van L. 1971. *In the shadow of men.* Boston: Houghton Mifflin.

Griffin, D. R. 1976. *The question of animal awareness.* New York: Rockefeller University Press.

———. 1984. *Animal thinking.* Cambridge: Harvard University Press.

Griffiths, J. F. 1976. *Climate and the environment: The atmospheric impact on man.* London: Paul Elek.

Groth, E. 1998. Discussion paper: Risk communication in the context of consumer perception of risks. Yonkers, N.Y.: Consumers Union of the U.S.

Gussow, J. D. 1994. Ecology and vegetarian considerations: Does environmental responsibility demand the elimination of livestock? *Am. J. Clin. Nutr.* 59 (supp.): 1110S–16S.

Ha, Y. L., N. K. Grimm, and M. W. Pariza. 1990. Inhibition of benzo(a)pyrene-induced mouse forestomach neoplasia by conjugated dienoic derivatives of linoleic acid. *Cnc. Res.* 50:1097–1101.

Hadwiger, D. F. 1982. *The politics of agricultural research,* 150–68. Lincoln: University of Nebraska Press.

Halcrow, H. G. 1980. *Economics of agriculture.* New York: McGraw-Hill.

Hamilton, N. D. 1995. Property rights, takings issue oversold to agriculture. *Feedstuffs* (January 23):14–16.

Hansen, J. M. 1991. *Gaining access: Congress and the farm lobby, 1919–1981.* Chicago: University of Chicago Press.

Harrison, G. G., T. Moon, E. J. Graves, et al. 1988. *Health related factors affecting dietary intakes.* Final report for USDA Cooperative Agreement #58–319R-7–010. Cited by Expert Panel on Nutrition Monitoring, 1989.

Harrison, R. 1964. *Animal machines: The new factory farming industry.* London: Vincent Stuart.

———. 1993. Since animal machines. *J. Agric. Environ. Eth.* 6(spec. supp. 1):4–14.

Hart, R., K. Keenan, A. Turtorro, K. Abdo, J. Leakey, and B. Lyn-Cook. 1995. Caloric restriction and toxicity. *Fund. App. Toxic.* 25:184–95.

Hays, V. W. 1997. Past and present use of antibiotics in animal food production. Implications of bacterial resistance to antibiotics for livestock producers and the animal health industry. *J. Anim. Sci.* 75(supp. 1):141.

Hays, V. W., and C. A. Black. 1989. *Antibiotics for animals: The antibiotic resistance issue. Comments from CAST, 1989–2.* Ames, Ia.: CAST.

Heady, H. F. 1994. Summary: Ecological implications of livestock herbivory in the West. In *Implications of livestock herbivory in the West*, eds. M. Vavra, W. A. Laycock, and R. D. Pieper. Denver: Society for Range Management.

Heaney, R. P. 1993. Nutritional factors in osteoporosis. *Annu. Rev. Nutr.* 13: 287–316.

Hecht, S. B. 1993. The logic of livestock and deforestation in Amazonia. *BioScience* 43:687–95.

Hegsted, D. M. 1980. Nationwide food consumption survey—implications. *Fam. Econ. Rev.* (Spring):20.

———. 1986. Calcium and osteoporosis. *J. Nutr.* 116:2316–19.

Heimbach, J. T. 1986. Changing public beliefs about diet and health. Speech delivered at the National Food Editor's Conference, New York.

———. 1987. Risk avoidance in consumer approaches to diet and health. *Clin. Nutr.* 6:159–62.

Heitschmidt, R. K., R. E. Short, and E. E. Grings. 1996. Ecosystems, sustainability, and animal agriculture. *J. Anim. Sci.* 74:1395–1405.

Herbert, V. D., and N. Coleman. 1988. Folic acid and vitamin B_{12}. In *Modern nutrition in health and disease*, 7th ed., eds. M. E. Shils and V. R. Young. Philadelphia: Lea and Febiger.

* Hightower, J. 1973. *Hard tomatoes, hard times: A report of the Agribusiness Accountability Project on the failure of America's land grant college complex.* Cambridge, Mass.: Schenkman.

Hildreth, R. J. 1982. Normative information, positive information, and policy. In *Agriculture, change, and human values*, eds. R. Haynes and R. Lanier. Gainesville: University of Florida, Humanities and Agriculture Program.

Hobbes, T. 1651. *Leviathan*, ed. C. B. McPherson. Baltimore: Pelican, 1968.

Hoffmann, B., and P. Evers. 1986. Anabolic agents with sex hormone-like activities: Problems of residues. In *Drug residues in animals*, ed. A. G. Rico, 111–46. New York: Academic Press.

Honduis, F. W. 1980. Toward a European law for animals. *Anim. Reg. Stud.* 3:159.

Honeyman, M. S. 1996. Sustainability issues of U.S. swine production. *J. Anim. Sci.* 74:1410–17.

Hornig, S. 1993. Reading risk: Public response to print media accounts of technological risk. *Pub. Understand. Sci.* 2:95–109.

Horwich, G. 1989. Response to Bishop O'Rourke. In *Food, policy, and politics: A perspective on agriculture and development*, eds. G. Horwich and G. J. Lynch, 274–78. Boulder, Colo.: Westview Press.

Horwich, G., and G. J. Lynch, eds. 1989. *Food, policy, and politics: A perspective on agriculture and development.* Boulder, Colo.: Westview Press.

Houghton, J. T., L. G. Meiro Filho, B. A. Callander, N. Harris, A. Kattenburg, and K. Maskell, eds. 1996. *Climate change 1995—the science of climate change: Contribution of Working Group I to the second assessment report of the Intergovernmental Panel on Climate Change.* New York: Cambridge University Press.

Hu, J.-F., X.-H. Zhao, J.-B. Jia, B. Parpia, and T. C. Campbell. 1993. Dietary calcium and bone density among middle-aged and elderly women in China. *Am. J. Clin. Nutr.* 58:219–27.

Hurnik, J. F. 1993. Ethics and animal agriculture. *J. Agric. Environ. Eth.* 6(spec. supp. 1):21–35.

Hyde, W. F., G. S. Amacher, and W. Magrath. 1996. Deforestation and forest land use: Theory, evidence, and policy implications. *World Bank Res. Obs.* 11(2):223–48.

IARC (International Agency for Research on Cancer). 1993. *IARC monographs on the evaluation of carcinogenic risks to humans. Some naturally occurring sub-*

stances: Food items and constituents, heterocyclic aromatic amines, and myco-toxins. Vol. 56. Lyon, France: IARC.

ICMSF (International Commission on Microbiological Specifications for Foods). 1988. *Microorganisms in foods. IV. Application of the hazard analysis critical control point (HACCP) system to ensure microbiological safety and quality.* Cambridge, Mass.: Blackwell Scientific.

IOM (Institute of Medicine). 1989. *Human health risks with the subtherapeutic use of penicillin or tetracyclines in animal feed.* Committee on Human Health Risk Assessment of Using Subtherapeutic Antibiotics in Animal Feeds. Washington, D.C.: National Academy Press.

———. 1991a. *Improving America's diet and health: From recommendation to action.* Committee on Dietary Guidelines Implementation, Food and Nutrition Board. Washington, D.C.: National Academy Press.

———. 1991b. *Cattle inspection.* Committee on Evaluation of USDA Streamlined Inspection System for Cattle (SIS-C), Food and Nutrition Board. Washington, D.C.: National Academy Press.

IPCC (Intergovernmental Panel on Climate Change), United Nations (UN). 1990. *Climate change: The IPCC scientific assessment.* New York: Cambridge University Press.

Ip, C., M. Singh, H. J. Thompson, and J. A. Scimeca. 1994. Conjugated linoleic acid suppresses mammary carcinogenesis and proliferative activity of the mammary gland in the rat. *Cnc. Res.* 54:1212–15.

Jackson, W. 1980. *New roots for agriculture.* San Francisco: Friends of the Earth.

———. 1987. *Altars of unhewn stone: Science and the earth.* San Francisco: North Point Press.

Jacobs, C., and J. T. Dwyer. 1988. Vegetarian children: Appropriate and inappropriate diets. *Am. J. Clin. Nutr.* 48:811–18.

Jamison, W. V., and W. M. Lunch. 1992. Rights of animals, perceptions of science, and political activism: Profile of American animal rights activists. *Sci. Technol. Hum. Val.* 17(4):438–58.

Jarvis, W. F. R. 1994. Preventing spread of vancomycin resistance. *Lancet* 344:119.

* Jasper, J. M., and D. Nelkin. 1992. *The animal rights crusade: The growth of a moral protest.* New York: Free Press, Macmillan.

Jensen, P., and A. Algers. 1984. An ethogram of piglet vocalizations during suckling. *Appl. Anim. Ethol.* 11:2357.

Johnson, G. L., J. T. Bonnen, D. Fienup, C. L. Quance, and N. Schaller. 1991. *Social science agricultural agendas and strategies.* East Lansing: Michigan State University Press.

Johnson, K. A., and D. E. Johnson. 1995. Methane emissions from cattle. *J. Anim. Sci.* 73:2483–92.

Kaiser, J. 1997. When a habitat is not a home. *Science* 276:1636–38.

Kalter, R. J., R. Milligan, W. Lesser, W. Magrath, and D. Bauman. 1984. *Biotechnology and the dairy industry: Production costs and commercial potential of the bovine growth hormone.* A. E. Research 84–22 (December). Ithaca, N.Y.: Cornell University, Department of Agricultural Economics.

Kant, A. K., A. Schatzkin, T. B. Harris, R. G. Ziegler, and G. Block. 1993. Dietary diversity and subsequent mortality in the first national health and nutrition examination survey epidemiologic follow-up study. *Am. J. Clin. Nutr.* 57:434–40.

Kant, I. 1788. *Critique of Practical Reason.* L. W. Beck, trans. Indianapolis, Ind.: Bobbs-Merrill, 1956.

Kay, J. 1993. On the nature of ecological integrity: Some closing comments. In *Ecological integrity and the management of ecosystems*, eds. S. Woodley, J. Kay, and G. Francis, 201–12. Boca Raton, Fla.: St. Lucie Press.

Keeney, D. 1996. Can sustainable agriculture landscapes accommodate corporate agriculture? In *Environmental enhancement through agriculture*, ed. W. Lockeretz. Medford, Mass.: Tufts University.

Kellert, S. R. 1988. Human–animal interactions: A review of American attitudes to wild and domestic animals in the twentieth century. In *Animals and people sharing the world*, ed. Andrew Rowan, 137–75. Hanover, N.H.: University Press of New England.

Kellogg Commission on the Future of State and Land-Grant Universities. 1997. *Returning to our roots: The student experience*. Washington, D.C.: National Association of State Universities and Land-Grant Colleges.

Kenney, J., and D. Fallert. 1989. Livestock hormones in the United States. *Natl. Food Rev.* 12(3):21–24.

Kessler, D. A., M. R. Taylor, J. H. Maryanski, E. L. Flamm, and L. S. Kahl. 1992. The safety of foods developed by biotechnology. *Science* 256:1747–49, 1832.

Kirkendall, R. S. 1987. Up to now: A history of American agriculture from Jefferson to revolution to crisis. *Agri. Hum. Val.* 4(1):4–26.

Kitchell, R. L., and H. E. Erickson. 1983. *Animal pain: Perception and alleviation*. Bethesda: American Physiological Society.

Kleiner, A. M., D. H. Constance, and J. S. Rikoon. 1997. Pig tales from the hog trail: An exploration into industrialization of the pork industry in Missouri. Paper presented at the meeting of the Agriculture, Food, and Human Values Society, Madison, Wisconsin, June 7–9.

Kothmann, M. M. 1995. Rangeland ecosystems in the Great Plains: Status and management. In *Conservation of Great Plains ecosystems*, eds. S. R. Johnson and A. Bouzaher, 199–209. Boston: Kluwer Academic.

Kreeger, K. Y. 1996. Researchers homing in on mechanisms of encephalopathic diseases. *Scientist* (June 10):13, 16.

Krissoff, B. 1989. The European ban on livestock hormones and implications for international trade. *Natl. Food Rev.* 12(3):34–36.

Krohn, W., and W. Schäfer. 1982. Agricultural chemistry: A goal-oriented science. In *Science in Context: Readings in the Sociology of Science*, eds. B. Barnes and D. Edge, 196–211. Cambridge, Mass.: MIT Press.

Kuchler, F., and J. McClelland. 1988. *Issues raised by new agricultural technologies: Livestock growth hormones*. Agricultural economic rept. no. 608. Washington, D.C.: USDA, Resources and Technology Division, Economic Research Service.

Kuchler, F., J. McClelland, and S. E. Offert. 1989. Regulating food safety: The case of animal growth hormones. *Natl. Food Rev.* 12(3):25–30.

Kuhn, T. S. 1996. *The structure of scientific revolution*, 3d ed. Chicago: University of Chicago Press.

Kunkel, H. O. 1992. Overview. In *National Research Council: Agriculture and the undergraduate*, 1–15. Washington, D.C.: National Academy Press.

———. 1996. Interests and values in the recommended dietary allowances and nutritional guidelines for Americans. *J. Nutr.* 126:2390S–97S.

Kunkel, H. O., and G. R. Hagevoort. 1994. Construction of science for animal agriculture. *J. Anim. Sci.* 72:247–53.

Kunkel, H. O., and P. B. Thompson. 1988. Interests and values in national nutritional policy in the United States. *J. Agri. Eth.* 1:243–56.

———. 1996. Thinking through higher education in agriculture: Content, values, and purpose. In *Revolutionizing higher education in agriculture: Framework for change*, eds. H. O. Kunkel, I. L. Maw, and C. S. Skaggs. Ames: Robson and Associates and Iowa State University Press.

Kunkel, H. O., I. L. Maw, and C. L. Skaggs, eds. 1996. *Revolutionizing higher education in agriculture: Framework for change*. Ames: Robson and Associates and Iowa State University Press.

Kunkel, H. O., P. B. Thompson, B. A. Miller, and C. L. Skaggs. 1998. Use of competing conceptions of risk in animal agriculture. *J. Anim. Sci.* 76:706–13.

Kushi, L. H., E. B. Lenert, and W. C. Willett. 1995. Health implications of Mediterranean diets in the light of contemporary knowledge. I. Plant foods and dietary products. *Am. J. Clin. Nutr.* 61:1407S–15S.

Ladd, J. 1978. Ethics. In *Encyclopedia of bioethics,* Vol. 1, 400–406. New York: Free Press.

Lal, R., J. Kimble, E. Levine, and B. A. Stewart, eds. 1995. *Soil management and the greenhouse effect.* Boca Raton, Fla.: Lewis Publishers.

Lancet. 1991. Should trials carry a health warning? *Lancet* 338:1496.

Lang, T. 1999. The complexities of globalization. The UK as a case study of tensions within the food system and the challenge to food policy. *Agri. Hum. Val.* 16(2):169–83.

* Lappé, F. M. 1975. *Diet for a small planet,* rev. ed. New York: Ballantine Books.

———. 1982. *Diet for a small planet,* 10th anniv. ed. New York: Ballantine Books.

* Lappé, F. M., and J. Collins. 1977. *Food first: Beyond the myth of scarcity,* 378. Boston: Houghton Mifflin.

———. 1986. *World hunger: Twelve myths.* New York: Grove Press.

Lappé, F. M., J. Collins, and P. Rosset. 1998. *World Hunger: 12 myths,* 2d ed. Oakland, Calif.: Grove/Atlantic and Food First Books.

Latta, S. 1999. Debate heats up over antibiotic resistant foodborne bacteria. *The Scientist.* (July 3):4–5.

Lawrence, P. 1986. Introduction. In *World recession and the food crisis in Africa,* ed. P. Lawrence, 1–8. Boulder, Colo.: Westview Press.

Leavitt, E. S., and D. Halverson. 1978. The evolution of anti-cruelty laws in the United States. In *Animals and their legal rights,* 3d ed. Washington, D.C.: AWI.

Lee, K. N., D. Kritchevsky, and M. W. Pariza. 1994. Conjugated linoleic acid and atherosclerosis in rabbits. *Atherosclerosis* 108:19–25.

Lenfant, C. 1996. Integrative physiology: You must plant trees before you can have a forest. *Physiologist* 39:4.

Leopold, A. 1949. *A sand county almanac.* London: Oxford University Press.

Letson, D., and N. Gollehon. 1996. Confined animal production and the manure problem. *Choices* (3d quar.):18–24.

Levenstein, H. 1988. *Revolution at the table: The transformation of the American diet.* New York: Oxford University Press.

Lewis, S. 1991. *The hamburger connection revisited: The status of tropical deforestation and conservation in Central America and southern Mexico.* San Francisco: Rain Forest Action Network.

———. 1994. An opinion on the global impact of meat consumption. *Am. J. Clin. Nutr.* 59 (supp.):1099S–1102S.

Library of Congress, Congressional Research Service. 1984. *Feeding the world's population: Developments in the decade following the World Food Conference of 1974.* Washington, D.C.: Government Printing Office.

Liebhardt, W. C. 1993. *The dairy debate: Consequences of bovine growth hormone and rotational grazing technologies.* Oakland, Calif.: ANR Publ., University of California.

Liebig, J. 1840. Die organische Chemie in ihrer Anwendung auf Agricultur und Physiologie. Braunschweig: Vieweg.

Lockeretz, W., ed. 1997. *Agricultural production and nutrition.* Medford, Mass.: Tufts University.

Loew, F. M. 1993. Turning plowshares into Volvos: Changing American attitudes toward livestock. *J. Agric. Environ. Eth.* 6(spec. supp. 1):105–109.

Loker, W. M. 1996. Cowboys, Indians and deforestation: Ethical and environmental issues associated with pastures research in Amazonia. *Agri. Hum. Val.* 13(1): 52–58.

Lowrance, W. W. 1976. *Of acceptable risk: Science and the determination of safety.* Los Altos, Calif.: William Kaufman.

Lucas, M. L. 1988. *Progres techniques et scientifiques dans la transformation agro-alimentaire, au seuil du 3éme millenaire.* Proceedings of the 11th International Colloquium of the Agricultural Fair of Verona, Italy, March 12. Verona, Italy: Agricultural Fair.

Lundgren, M. H. 1987. Tweeten as exorcist: A response to "sector as personality." *Agri. Hum. Val.* 4(4):47–53.

Lyman, F., I. Mintzer, K. Courrier, and J. MacKenzie. 1990. *The greenhouse trap: What we're doing to the atmosphere and how we can slow global warming.* Boston: Beacon Press.

Lynam, J. K., and R. W. Herdt. 1989. Sense and sensibility: Sustainability as an objective in international agricultural research. *Agric. Econ.* 3:381–98.

Madden, P., and P. B. Thompson. 1987. Ethical perspectives on changing agricultural technology in the United States. *Notre Dame J. Law, Eth., Pub. Pol.* 3(1):85–116.

Malone, T. F. 1994. *Sustainable human development: A paradigm for the 21st century.* Research Triangle Park, N.C.: Sigma Xi Center.

Marberry, S. 1995. Iowa governor signs livestock waste law. *Feedstuffs* (June 5):5, 8.

Marcus, A. I. 1985. *Agricultural science and the quest for legitimacy.* Ames: Iowa State University Press.

Martin, L. L., and K. D. Zering. 1997. Relationship between industrialized agriculture and environmental consequences: The case of vertical coordination in broilers and hogs. *J. Agric. Appl. Econ.* 29:25–50.

Maslow, A. H. 1970. *Motivation and personality.* New York: Harper and Row.

Mason, J., and P. Singer. 1980. *Animal factories.* New York: Crown Publishers.

Mason, J. B., J.-P. Habicht, J. P. Greaves, U. Jonsson, J. Kevany, R. Martorell, and B. Rogers. 1996. Letters to the editor: Public nutrition. *Am. J. Clin. Nutr.* 63: 399–400.

Matson, P. A., W. J. Parton, A. G. Power, and M. J. Swift. 1997. Agricultural intensification and ecosystem properties. *Science* 277:504–509.

Matsuzaki, T. 1992. Longevity, diet, and nutrition in Japan: Epidemiological studies. *Nutr. Rev.* 12:355–59.

Matthews, J. T., ed. 1991. *Preserving the global environment: The challenge of shared leadership.* The American Assembly, Columbia University, and World Resources Institute, Washington, D.C. New York: W. W. Norton and Co.

Maxwell, N. 1992. What kind of inquiry can best help us create a good world? *Sci. Technol. Hum. Val.* 17:205–27.

Mayer, J. 1990. Hunger and undernutrition in the United States. *J. Nutr.* 120:919–23.

Mayr, E. 1982. *The growth of biological thought.* Cambridge, Mass.: Harvard University Press.

McDowell, R. E. 1980. The role of animals in developing countries. In *Animals, feed, food, and people,* ed. R. L. Baldwin, 105–20. Boulder, Colo.: Westview Press.

———. 1984. The need to know about animals. In *World food issues, 2d ed.,* ed. M. Drosdoff, 39–46. Ithaca, N.Y.: Cornell University.

———. 1991. *A partnership for humans and animals.* Raleigh, N.C.: Kinnic Publishers.

McElfish, J. M., Jr. 1994. Property rights, property roots: Rediscovering the basis for legal protection of the environment. In *Environmental law reporter* (May). Washington, D.C.: Environmental Law Institute.

McGlone, J. J. 1993. What is animal welfare? *J. Agric. Environ. Eth.* 6(spec. supp. 2):26–36.

McIntosh, W. A., and M. Zey-Ferrell. 1988. Predicting intent to reduce the consumption of beef among Texas women. Unpublished manuscript. College Station: Texas A&M University.

* Meier, K. J. 1985. *Regulation: Politics, bureaucracy, and economics.* New York: St. Martin's Press.

Mellor, J. 1989. World food situation in historical perspective. In *Food policy and politics: A perspective on agriculture and development,* ed. G. Horwich and G. J. Lynch, 50–64. Boulder, Colo.: Westview Press.

Mench, J. A. 1993. Assessing animal welfare: An overview. *J. Agric. Environ. Eth.* 6(spec. supp. 2):68–75.

Mersmann, H. J. 1998. Overview of the effects of β-adrenergic receptor agonists on animal growth including mechanisms of action. *J. Anim. Sci.* 76:160–72.

Meyers, N. 1981. How Central America's forests become North America's hamburgers. *Ambio* 10:1, 3–8.

Michaels, P. J. 1990. The greenhouse effect and global change: Review and reappraisal. *Int. J. Environ. Stud.* 36:55–71.

Mill, J. S. 1863. *Utilitarianism.* Reprinted in *Ethical Theories,* ed. A. I. Melden, 270–89. Englewood Cliffs, N.J.: Prentice-Hall.

Miller, D., and J. Reilly. 1995. Making an issue of food safety: The media pressure groups and the public sphere. In *Eating agendas: Food and nutrition as social problems,* eds. D. Maurer and J. Sobol, 305–36. New York: Aldine de Gruyter.

Miller, D. R., B. L. Specker, N. L. Ho, and E. J. Norman. 1991. Vitamin B_{12} status in a macrobiotic community. *Am. J. Clin. Nutr.* 53:524–29.

Miller, H. I. 1994. A need to reinvent biotechnology at the EPA. *Science* 266: 1815–18.

Miller, N. E. 1985. The value of behavioral research on animals. *Am. Psychol.* 40:423.

Mintzer, I., W. R. Mooman, and M. C. Trexler. 1989. Reducing the risks: A preliminary investigation of strategies to reduce the risk of rapid climate change. In *The full range of responses to anticipated climatic change.* Nairobi: UN Environment Program and the Beyer Institute.

Moberg, G. P. 1993. Using risk assessment to define domestic animal welfare. *J. Agric. Environ. Eth.* 6(spec. supp. 2):1–7.

Montgomery, E., and J. W. Bennett. 1979. Anthropological studies of food and nutrition: The 1940s and the 1970s, the uses of anthropology. *Am. Anthropol. Assoc. Spec. Publ.* 11:127–44.

Morgan, M. G. 1990. Choosing and managing technology-induced risks. In *Readings in risk,* eds. T. S. Glickman and M. Gough, 5. Washington, D.C.: Resources for the Future.

Murphy, W., J. Silman, L. McCrory, S. Flack, J. Winstein, D. Hoke, A. Schmidt, and B. Pillsbury. 1996. Environmental, economic, and social benefits for feeding livestock on well-managed pasture. In *Environmental enhancement through agriculture,* ed. W. Lockeretz, 125–35. Medford, Mass.: Tufts University.

Narang, H. 1996. Origin and implications of bovine spongiform encephalopathy. *Proc. Soc. Exp. Biol. Med.* 211:306–22.

Nathanson, N., J. Wilesmith, and C. Griot. 1997. Reviews and commentary: Bovine spongiform encephalopathy (BSE): Causes and consequences of a common source epidemic. *Am. J. Epidemiol.* 145:959–69.

National Advisory Committee on Microbiological Criteria for Foods. 1990. *Hazard analysis and critical control point system.* Washington, D.C.: USDA Food Safety and Inspection Service.

———. 1994. The role of the regulatory agencies and industry in HACCP. *Int. J. Food Microbiol.* 21:187–95.

———. 1997. Hazard analysis and critical point principles and applications guidelines, adopted Aug. 19, 1997. Washington, D.C.: Food Processors Institute.

National Livestock and Meat Board. 1992. *Vegetarianism: Definition, scope, and impact on the meat industry.* Res. rept. no. 100–3. Chicago: National Livestock and Meat Board.

Nations, J., and J. Leonard. 1986. Grounds of conflicts in Central America. In *Bordering in trouble: Resources and politics in Latin America,* eds. A. Maguire and J. W. Brown. Bethesda: Adler and Adler.

Nicholson, S. E. 1983. Sub-Saharan rainfall in the years 1976–80: Evidence of continued drought. *Mthly. Wea. Rev.* 111:1646.

Nicol, W. M. 1991. Free circulation of foods within the European community. *Food Saf. Notebk.* 2:49–50.

NIH (National Institutes of Health). 1985. *Guide for the care and use of laboratory animals.* NIH publ. no. 85–230. Bethesda: NIH, PHS, DHHS.

Norton, B. G. 1991a. *Toward unity among environmentalists.* New York: Oxford University Press.

———. 1991b. Making the land ethic operational: Toward an integrated theory of environmental management. In *Beyond the large farm: Ethics and research goals for agriculture,* eds. P. B. Thompson and B. A. Stout, 147–59. Boulder, Colo.: Westview Press.

———. 1991c. Sustainability, human welfare, and ecosystem health. *Environ. Val.* 1:97–111.

NRC (National Research Council). 1985. *An evaluation of the role of microbiological criteria for foods and food ingredients.* Washington, D.C.: National Academy Press.

———. 1989a. *Alternative agriculture.* Board on Agriculture. Washington, D.C.: National Academy Press.

———. 1989b. *Designing foods: Animal product options in the marketplace.* Board on Agriculture. Washington, D.C.: National Academy Press.

———. 1989c. *Diet and health: Implications for reducing chronic disease risk.* Washington, D.C.: National Academy Press.

———. 1989d. *Investing in research.* Board on Agriculture. Washington, D.C.: National Academy Press.

———. 1989e. *Recommended dietary allowances.* Washington, D.C.: National Academy Press.

———. 1993a. *Rangeland health: New methods to classify, inventory, and monitor rangelands.* Washington, D.C.: National Academy Press.

———. 1993b. *Sustainable agriculture and the environment in the humid tropics.* Washington, D.C.: National Academy Press.

———. 1996a. *Carcinogens and anticarcinogens in the human diet.* Committee on Comparative Toxicity of Naturally Occurring Carcinogens, Board on Environmental Studies and Toxicology, Commission on Life Sciences. Washington, D.C.: National Academy Press.

———. 1996b. *Use of reclaimed water and sludge in food crop production.* Washington, D.C.: National Academy Press.

———. 1998. *The use of drugs in food animals: Benefits and risks.* Washington, D.C.: National Academy Press.

Nuffield Council on Bioethics. 1999. Genetically modified crops: The ethical and social issues. Nuffield, UK.

O'Brien, M. N. 1993. Being a scientist means taking sides. *BioScience* 43:706–708.

Oltjen, J. W., and J. L. Beckett. 1996. Role of ruminant livestock in sustainable agricultural systems. *J. Anim. Sci.* 74:1406–1409.

Ornish, D., S. E. Brown, L. W. Scherwitz, J. H. Billings, W. T. Armstrong, T. A. Ports,

S. M. McLanahan, R. L. Kirkeeide, R. J. Brand, and K. L. Gould. 1990. Can lifestyle changes reverse coronary heart disease? *Lancet* 336:129–33.

Orr, J. B. 1936. *Food, health, and income.* London: Macmillan.

OTA (Office of Technology Assessment). 1987. *Aid to developing countries: The technology/ecology fit,* 8–9. Staff pap., June. Washington, D.C.: OTA, Food and Renewable Resources Program.

Outlaw, J. L., D. P. Anderson, and D. I. Padberg. 1997. Relationships between market price signals and production management: The case of fed beef. *J. Agric. Appl. Econ.* 29:37–44.

Padberg, D. I. 1986. Using market forces to improve U.S. nutrition. Unpublished paper, September 8. NAS, Committee on Technological Options to Improve the Nutritional Attributes of Animal Products, Washington, D.C.

Paden, R. 1990. Moral metaphysics, moral revolutions, and environmental ethics. *Agri. Hum. Val.* 7(3–4):70–79.

Palmer, M. 1990. The encounter of religion and conservation. In *Ethics of environment and development,* eds. J. R. Engel and J. G. Engel, 50–62. Tucson: University of Arizona Press.

Palmer, T. 1993. A nonlinear dynamical perspective on climate change. *Weather* 48:314–16.

Pan, W.-H., C.-J. Chin, C.-T. Shen, and M.-H. Lee. 1993. Hemostatic factors and blood lipids in young Buddhist vegetarians or omnivores. *Am. J. Clin. Nutr.* 58:354–59.

Parikh, K. S., and W. Tims. 1989. Food consumption, dietary status, and chronic hunger: An assessment of its extent and policy options. In *1988 World Food Conference proceedings. II. Issue papers,* eds. J. W. Helmuth and S. R. Johnson, 3–44. Ames: Iowa State University Press.

Parodi, P. W. 1997. Cow's milk fat components as potential anticarcinogenic agents. *J. Nutr.* 127:1055–60.

Patterson, F. F., and E. Linden. 1981. *The education of Koko.* New York: Holt, Rinehart and Winston.

Peto, R. 1992. Statistics of disease control. *Nature* 356:557–58.

Pfeffer, M. J. 1992. Sustainable agriculture in historical perspective. *Agri. Hum Val.* 9(4):4–12.

Physicians Committee for Responsible Medicine (PCRM). 1991. The new four food groups. PCRM Update: 1–11. Washington, D.C.

Pimentel, D. L., E. Hurd, A. C. Bellotti, M. J. Forster, I. N. Oka, O. D. Sholes, and R. J. Whitman. 1973. Food production and the energy crisis. *Science* 182:443–49.

Pimentel, M. 1990. Food as a resource. In *Food and natural resources,* eds. D. Pimentel and C. Hall, 409–37. San Diego: Academic Press.

Pinstrup-Anderson, P., R. P. Pandya-Lorch, and M. W. Rosegrant. 1997. The world food situation: Recent developments, emerging issues and long-term prospects. *Food policy report,* International Food Policy Research Institute, Washington, D.C.

Plough, A., and S. Krimsky. 1987. The emergence of risk communication studies: Social and political context. *Sci. Tech. Hum. Val.* 12:4–10.

Pluhar, E. 1990. Utilitarian killing, replacement, and rights. *J. Agric. Environ. Eth.* 3:147–71.

———. 1992. Who can be morally obligated to be a vegetarian? *J. Agric. Environ. Eth.* 5:189–215.

———. 1994. Vegetarianism, morality, and science revisited. *J. Agric. Environ. Eth.* 7:77–82.

Popkin, B. M., P. S. Haines, and R. E. Patterson. 1992. Dietary changes in older Americans, 1977–1987. *Am. J. Clin. Nutr.* 55:823–30.

Popkin, B. M., M. K. Richards, and C. A. Montiero. 1996. Stunting is associated with overweight in children of four nations that are undergoing the nutrition transition. *J. Nutr.* 126:3009–16.

Popper, K. 1959. *The logic of scientific discovery* (originally published as *Logik der Forschung;* Springer [1934]). New York: Harper and Row.

Pothukuchi, K., and J. L. Kaufman. 1999. Placing the food system on the urban agenda: The role of municipal institutions in food systems planning. *Agri. Hum. Val.* 16(2):213–24.

Price, D. K. 1954. *Government and science: Their dynamic relationship in American democracy.* New York: New York University Press.

Putnam, J. J., and J. E. Allshouse. 1996. Food Consumption, Prices and Expenditures, 1996: Annual Data, 1970–94. Economic Research Service, USDA Statistical Bulletin No. 928. Washington, D.C.

Quijandra, B. 1989. Role of animal agriculture in farm enterprises/household production and linkage to regional and national economies. In *Summary report of the Animal Agriculture Symposium: Development priorities toward the year 2000.* U.S. Agency for International Development, Washington, D.C. Rome: FAO.

Rachels, J. 1977. Vegetarianism and "the other weight problem." In *World hunger and moral obligation,* eds. W. Aiken and H. Follette. Englewood Cliffs, N.J.: Prentice-Hall.

Rappaport, R. A. 1967. Ritual regulation of environmental relations among a New Guinea people. *Ethnology* 6:17–30.

Rathje, W. L., and E. E. Ho. 1987. Meat fad madness: Conflicting patterns of meat fat consumption and their public health implications. *J. Am. Diet. Assoc.* 87: 1357–62.

Rawitscher, M., and J. Mayer. 1977. Nutritional outputs and energy inputs in seafoods. *Science* 198:261.

Rawls, J. 1971. *A theory of justice.* Cambridge, Mass.: Harvard University Press.

Recker, R. R., K. M. Davies, S. M. Hinders, R. P. Heaney, R. P. Stegman, and D. B. Kimmel. 1992. Bone gain in young adult women. *J. Am. Med. Assoc.* 268:2403–2408.

Regan, T. 1980. Utilitarianism, vegetarianism, and animal rights. *Philos. Pub. Aff.* 9:305–24.

* ———. 1983. *The case for animal rights.* Berkeley: University of California Press.

Repetto, R. 1990. *Promoting environmentally sound economic progress: What the North can do.* Rept., April. New York: World Resources Institute.

Rescher, N. 1983. *Risk: A philosophical introduction to the theory of risk evaluation and management.* Washington, D.C.: University Press of America.

Richards, P. 1989. Agriculture as a performance. In *Farmer first: Farmer innovation and agricultural research,* eds. R. Chambers, A. Pacey, and L. A. Thrupp, 39–42. London: Intermediate Technology Publications.

Rifkin, J. 1983. *Algeny.* New York: Viking Press.

———. 1992. *Beyond beef: The rise and fall of the cattle culture.* New York: Dutton.

Riggs. B. L., H. W. Wahner, L. J. Melton III, L. S. Richelson, H. L. Judd and W. M. O'Fallon. 1987. Dietary calcium intake and rates of bone loss in women. *J. Clin. Invest.* 80:979–82.

Riley, L. W., M. L. Cohen, J. E. Seals, M. J. Blaser, K. A. Birkness, N. T. Hargett, S. M. Martin, and R. A. Feldman. 1984. Importance of host factors in human salmonellosis caused by multiresistant strains of *Salmonella. J. Infect. Dis.* 149: 878–83.

Robbins, J. 1987. *Diet for a new America.* Walpole, N.H.: Stillpoint Publishing.

Roberts, W. O., and H. Lansford. 1979. *The climate mandate.* San Francisco: W. H. Freeman and Co.

Rodgers, P. 1997. Risk reduction—an ounce of prevention. *Shepherd* 42(2):16.

Rollin, B. E. 1989. *The unheeded cry: Animal consciousness, animal pain, and science.* New York: Oxford University Press.

———. 1990. Animal welfare, animal rights, and agriculture. *J. Anim. Sci.* 68: 3456–61.

———. 1993. Animal welfare, science, and value. *J. Agric. Environ. Eth.* 6(spec. supp. 2):44–50.

———. 1994. Animal production and the new social ethic for animals. *J. Anim. Sci.* 72(supp. 1):150.

———. 1995. *The Frankenstein syndrome: Ethical and social issues in the genetic engineering of animals.* New York: Cambridge University Press.

———. 1996. Bad ethics, good ethics, and the genetic engineering of animals in agriculture. *J. Anim. Sci.* 74:535–41.

Rose, S. 1988. Reflections and reductionism. *Trends Biochem. Sci.* 13:160–65.

Rossiter, M. W. 1979. The organization of the agricultural sciences. In *The organization of knowledge in modern America, 1920–1960,* eds. A. Oleson and J. Voss, 211–48. Baltimore: Johns Hopkins University Press.

Russell, M. G., R. J. Sauer, and J. M. Barnes. 1982. *Enabling interdisciplinary research: Perspectives from agriculture, forestry, and home economics.* Minnesota Agricultural Experiment Station Misc. Publ. 19. St. Paul, Minn.

Ruttan, V. W. 1987. Commentary: Agricultural scientists as reluctant revolutionaries. *Choices* (3d quar.):3.

———. 1990. Alternative agriculture: Sustainability is not enough. In *Alternative agriculture scientists' review,* 130–34. Ames, Ia.: CAST.

Ryder, C. J. 1990. Foodborne illness: UK food legislation. *Lancet* 336:1559–62.

Ryder, R. D. 1989. *Animal revolution: Changing attitudes towards speciesism.* New York: Basil Blackwell.

Sachs, C. 1992. Reconsidering diversity in agriculture and food systems: An ecofeminist approach. *Agri. Hum. Val.* 9(3):4–10.

Sagoff, M. 1993. Environmental bedfellows. *Hastings Ctr. Rept.* (March–April): 42–43.

———. 1995. Carrying capacity and ecological economics. *BioScience* 45:610–20.

Sanders, S., and J. M. Jasper. 1994. Civil politics in the animal rights conflict: God terms versus casuistry in Cambridge, Massachusetts. *Sci. Technol. Hum. Val.* 19(2):169–88.

Sanders, T. A. B. 1988. Growth and development of British vegan children. *Am. J. Clin. Nutr.* 48:822–25.

Sanders, T. A. B., and S. Reddy. 1994. Vegetarian diets and children. *Am. J. Clin. Nutr.* 59(supp. 5S):1176S–81S.

Sapolsky, H. M. 1986. Introduction. In *Consuming Fears,* ed. H. M. Sapolsky, 3–18, New York: Basic Books.

Satchell, M. 1996. Hog heaven—and hell. *U.S. News World Rept.* (January 22):55–59.

Savell, J. W., J. J. Harris, H. R. Cross, D. S. Hale, and L. C. Beasley. 1991. National beef market basket survey. *J. Anim. Sci.* 69:2883–93.

Savell, J. W., H. R. Cross, J. J. Francis, J. W. Wise, D. S. Hale, D. L. Wilkes, and G. C. Smith. 1989. National consumer retail beef study: Interaction of trim level, price, and grade on consumer acceptance of beef steaks and roasts. *J. Food Qual.* 1:251.

Schlesinger, W. H., J. Reynolds, G. Cunningham, L. F. Huenneke, W. M. Jarrell, R. A. Virginia, and W. Whitford. 1990. Biological feedbacks in global desertification. *Science* 247:1043–48.

Schmitz, J. D., and O. Capps. 1993. A complete systems analysis of nutritional awareness and food demand. *Texas Agr. Expt. Sta. Pub. B-1712.* College Station, Tex.

Schneider, S. H. 1988. The whole earth dialogue. *Iss. Sci. Technol.* (Spring):93–99.

Schultz, S. G. 1996. Homeostasis, Humpty Dumpty, and integrative biology. *News Physiol. Sci.* 11:238–46.

Schulz, T. W. 1964. Economic growth from traditional agriculture. In *Agricultural sciences for the developing nations,* ed. A. H. Moseman, 185–205. Publ. no. 76. Washington, D.C.: American Association for the Advancement of Science.

———. 1971. *Investment in human capital: The role of education and research.* New York: Free Press.

Schumacher, E. F. 1973. *Small is beautiful: Economics as if people mattered.* London: Blond and Briggs.

Science Council of Canada. 1992. *Sustainable agriculture: The research challenge.* Rept. 13. Ottawa, Ontario: Science Council of Canada.

Scrimshaw, N. S. 1991. Iron deficiency. *Sci Am.* (October):46–52.

Select Committee on Nutrition and Human Needs, U.S. Senate. 1977. *Dietary goals for the United States—supplemental views.* Washington, D.C.: U.S. Government Printing Office.

Selye, H. 1952. *The story of the adaptation syndrome.* Montreal: Acta.

Sen, A. K., and J. Dréze. 1990. *Hunger and public action.* Oxford: Clarendon Press.

Senauer, R. 1986. Economics and nutrition. In *What is America eating?: Proceedings of a symposium,* 46–57. Washington, D.C.: National Academy Press.

Serafin, R., and R. S. Steedman. 1991. *Working group report: Measuring integrity at the municipal level.* Workshop on Ecological Integrity and the Management of Ecosystems. Heritage Resource Center, University of Waterloo, Waterloo, Ontario, Canada.

Seragoldin, I. 1999. Biotechnology and food security in the 21st century. *Science* 285:387–91.

Shackley, S., and B. Wynne. 1996. Representing uncertainty in global climate change science and policy: Boundary-ordering devices and authority. *Sci. Technol. Hum. Val.* 21(3):275–302.

Shepherd, R., and L. Stockley. 1987. Nutrition knowledge, attitudes, and fat consumption. *J. Am. Diet. Assoc.* 87:615–19.

Shilling, F. 1997. Do habitat conservation plans protect endangered species? *Science* 276:1662–63.

Shogren, J. F., and T. D. Crocker. 1995. Valuing ecosystems and diversity. In *Conservation of Great Plains ecosystems,* eds. S. R. Johnson and A. Bouzaher, 33–46. Boston: Kluwer Academic.

Shrader-Frechette, K. 1991. *Risk and rationality: Philosophical foundations for populist reforms.* Berkeley: University of California Press.

Sinclair, A. R. E., and M. P. Wells. 1989. Population growth and poverty cycle in Africa. In *Food and natural resources,* eds. D. Pimentel and C. W. Hall. San Diego: Academic Press.

Sinclair, U. 1906. *The jungle.* New York: Doubleday, Page & Company.

Singer, M. 1986. Ethics, science, and moral philosophy. In *New directions in ethics,* eds. J. P. DeMarco and R. M. Fox, 282–98. New York: Routledge and Kegan Paul.

Singer, P. 1975. *Animal liberation.* New York: Random House.

———. 1979. Killing humans and killing animals. *Inquiry* 22:145–56.

———. 1980. Utilitarianism and vegetarianism. *Philos. Pub. Aff.* 9:325–37.

Slater, E. C. 1988. Is biochemistry irreducible to chemistry? *Trends Biochem. Sci.* 13:378.

Slattery, M. L., and E. E. Randall. 1988. Trends in coronary heart disease mortality and food consumption in the United States between 1909 and 1980. *Am. J. Clin. Nutr.* 47:1060–67.

Smallwood, D. 1989. Consumer demand for safer foods. *Natl. Food Rev.* 12(3):9–11.

Smil, V. 1997. *Cycles of life: Civilization and the biosphere.* Scientific American library. San Francisco: W. H. Freeman and Co.

Smith, D. J. 1998. The pharmacokinetics, metabolism and tissue residues of β-adrenergic agonists in livestock. *J. Anim. Sci.* 76:173–94.

Smith, G. C., J. W. Savell, R. P. Clayton, T. G. Field, D. B. Griffin, D. S. Hale, M. F. Miller, T. H. Montgomery, J. B. Morgan, J. D. Tatum, and J. W. Wise. 1992. Improving the consistency and competitiveness of beef: A blueprint for total quality management in the fed-beef industry. Report of the National Beef Quality Audit. Fort Collins and College Station: Colorado State University and Texas A&M University.

Smith, H. 1988. *The power game.* New York: Random House.

Snaydon, R. W., and J. Elston. 1976. Flows, cycles, and yields in agricultural ecosystems. In *Food production and consumption,* eds. A. N. Duckham, J. G. W. Jones, and E. H. Roberts, 44–60. New York: American Elsevier.

Snowdon, D. A. 1988. Animal product consumption and mortality because of all causes combined: Coronary heart disease, stroke, diabetes, and cancer in Seventh-Day Adventists. *Am. J. Clin. Nutr.* 48:739–48.

Spedding, C. R. W. 1984. Uses, products, and roles of the animal. In *Development of animal production systems.* Amsterdam: Elsevier.

———. 1993. Animal welfare policy in Europe. *J. Agric. Environ. Eth.* 6(spec. supp. 1):110–17.

Starr, C., and C. Whipple. 1980. Risks of risk decision. *Science* 208:1114–18.

Steinbeck, J. 1939. *The grapes of wrath.* New York: Viking Press.

Steinhart, C. E., and J. S. Steinhart. 1974. Energy use in the U.S. food system. *Science* 184:307–16.

Stenholm, C. W., and D. B. Waggoner. 1989. A Congressional perspective on food safety. *J. Am. Vet. Med. Assoc.* 195:916–20.

Stevenson, K. E., and D. T. Bernard. 1995. *HACCP: Establishing hazard analysis critical control point programs.* Washington, D.C.: Food Processors Institute.

Stone, N. D., P. B. Siegel, C. S. Admission, and W. B. Gross. 1984. Socializations and behavior of two commercial stocks of chickens. *Poul. Sci.* 63:616.

Stout, B. A. 1990. *Handbook of energy for world agriculture.* New York: Elsevier Applied Science.

———. 1996. Energy for agriculture in the 21st century. Paper presented at the International Symposium on Feeding a World Population of More than Eight Billion People: A Challenge to Science, December 6–9, Ferndown, Dorset, UK.

Stout, J. 1996. The Missouri Anti-Corporate Farming Act: Reconciling the interests of the independent farmer and the corporate farm. *UMKC Law Rev.* 64:835–60.

Strange, M. 1988. *Family farming: A new economic vision.* Lincoln: University of Nebraska Press.

Stuth, J. W., C. J. Scifres, W. T. Hamilton, and J. R. Conner. 1991. Management systems analysis as guidance for effective interdisciplinary grazingland research. *Agric. Syst.* 36:43–63.

Suppe, F. 1987. The limited applicability of agricultural research. *Agri. Hum. Val.* 4(Fall):4–14.

Taiganides, E. P., ed. 1977. *Animal wastes.* London: Applied Science.

Tarrant, J. R. 1987. Variability in world cereal yields. *Trans. Inst. Brit. Geogr.* (N.S.) 10:315–26.

———. 1989. An analysis of variability in Soviet grain production. In *Variability in grain yields*, eds. J. R. Anderson and P. B. R. Hazell, 60–77. Baltimore: Johns Hopkins University Press.

———. 1991. *Farming and food*. New York: Oxford University Press.

Tauson, R. 1993. Research approaches for improving the physical welfare and environment of laying hens. *J. Agric. Environ. Eth.* 6(spec. supp. 2):76–85.

Telzak, E. E., L. D. Budnick, M. S. Zweig-Geenberg, S. Blum, M. Shayengi, C. E. Benson, and S. Schultz. 1990. A nosocomial outbreak of *Salmonella enteritidis* infection due to the consumption of raw eggs. *N. Engl. J. Med.* 323:394–97.

Thompson, P., P. A. Salsbury, C. Adams, and D. L. Archer. 1990. Foodborne illness: U.S. food legislation. *Lancet* 336:1557–59.

Thompson, P. B. n.d. The moral significance of land. Unpublished manuscript. Texas A&M University.

———. 1985. The nature of ethics and values with particular application to agricultural issues. Paper presented at the Workshop on Ethics and Values in Agricultural and Natural Resource Education, Gainesville, Florida, February 28–March 2.

———. 1986. The social goals of agriculture. *Agri. Hum. Val.* 3(4):32–42.

———. 1990a. Agrarianism and the American philosophical tradition. *Agri. Hum. Val.* 7(1):3–8.

———. 1990b. Risk: Ethical issues and values, agricultural biotechnology, food safety, and nutritional quality for the consumer. *Natl. Agric. Biotechnol. Counc.* 2:204–17.

———. 1992. The varieties of sustainability. *Agri. Hum. Val.* 9(3):11–19.

———. 1993a. Animals in the agrarian ideal. *J. Agric. Environ. Eth.* 6(spec. supp. 1):36–49.

———. 1993b. *Food labels and biotechnology: The ethics of safety and consent*, disc. No. 93-1. College Station: Texas A&M University, Center for Biotechnology Policy and Ethics.

———. 1995. Risk and responsibilities in modern agriculture. In *Issues in agricultural bioethics*, T. B. Mepham, G. A. Tucker and J. Wisemore, 5. Nottingham, UK: Nottingham University Press.

———. 1997a. The cloning debate. Center for Science and Technology Policy Center. *Tex. A&M Univ. Newsl.* 6(6):1–3.

———. 1997b. *Food biotechnology in ethical perspective*. London: Chapman and Hall.

———. 1997c. From a philosopher's perspective, how should animal scientists meet the challenge of contentious issues? Paper presented at the annual meeting of the American Society of Animal Science, Nashville, Tennessee, July 31.

Thompson, P. B., and W. Dean. 1996. Competing conceptions of risk. *Risk: Hlth. Saf. Environ.* 7:361–84.

* Thompson, P. B., and B. A. Stout, eds. 1991. *Beyond the large farm: Ethics and research goals for agriculture*. Boulder, Colo.: Westview Press.

* Thompson, P. B., R. Matthews, and E. O. Van Ravenswaay. 1994. *Ethics, public policy, and agriculture*. New York: Macmillan.

Thrupp, L. A., B. Cabarle, and A. Zazueta. 1994. Participatory methods in planning and political processes: Linking the grassroots and policies for sustainable development. *Agri. Hum. Val.* 11(2–3):77–84.

Thurow, A. P., and J. Holt. 1997. Induced policy innovation: Environmental compliance requirements for dairies in Texas and Florida. *J. Agric. Appl. Econ.* 29: 17–36.

Toufexis, A. 1990. Red alert on red meat. *Time* (December 24):70.

Trenkle, A., and R. L. Wilham. 1977. Beef production efficiency. *Science* 198: 1009–15.

Tudge, C. 1977. *The famine business*. New York: St. Martin's Press.

Tweeten, L. 1987. Sector as personality: The case of farm protest movements. *Agri. Hum. Val.* 4(1):66–74.

———. 1993. Public policy decisions for farm animal welfare. *J. Agric. Environ. Eth.* 6(spec. supp. 1):87–104.

Tweeten, L., and C. Zulauf. 1998. Post-industrial agriculture. *Choices* (2d quar.): 30–33.

UN (United Nations). 1978. *United Nations Conference on Desertification: Round-up, plan of action, and resolutions, August 20–September 9, 1977*. New York: UN.

UN (United Nations) Administrative Committee on Coordination—Subcommittee on Nutrition. 1992. Second report on the world nutrition situation. I. Global and regional results. Geneva: UN ACC/SCN.

Upton, P., and J. E. Cola. 1994. Outbreak of *Escherichia coli* 0157 infection associated with pasteurized milk supply. *Lancet* 344:1015.

USDA (United States Department of Agriculture) and DHHS (Department of Health and Human Services). 1995. *Nutrition and your health: Dietary guidelines for Americans*, 4th ed. Washington, D.C.: U.S. Government Printing Office.

USDA, Food Safety and Inspection Service (FSIS). 1997. Pathogen reduction: Hazard analysis and critical control point (HACCP) systems. Final rule. *Fed. Reg.* 62(92):26211–19. Washington, D.C.: U.S. Government Printing Office.

U.S. Department of Health, Education and Welfare (DHEW). 1979. *Healthy people: The Surgeon General's report on health promotion and disease prevention*. Washington, D.C.: U.S. Government Printing Office.

van Dusseldorp, M., I. C. W. Arts, J. S. Bergsma, N. de Jong, P. C. Dagnelie, and W. A. van Staveren. 1996. Catch-up growth in children fed a macrobiotic diet in early childhood. *J. Nutr.* 126:2977–83.

van Staveren, W. A., and P. C. Dagnelie. 1988. Food consumption, growth, and development of Dutch children fed on alternative diets. *Am. J. Clin. Nutr.* 48:819–21.

Varner, G. E. 1992. *Facts, values, and hunting: The prospects for consensus and convergence in the animal rights debate*. CBPE 92–2. College Station: Texas A&M University, Center for Biotechnology Policy and Ethics.

———. 1994a. In defense of the vegan ideal: Rhetoric and bias in the nutrition literature. *J. Agric. Environ. Eth.* 7:29–40.

———. 1994b. The prospects for consensus and convergence in the animal rights debate. *Hastings Ctr. Rept.* 24(1):24–28.

———. 1994c. Rejoinder to Kathryn Paxton George. *J. Agric. Environ. Eth.* 7:83–86.

Vaughn, G. F. 1994. Ever-changing property rights. University of Missouri, Columbia, University Extension. *Econ. Pol. Info. Mo. Agri.* 37(2).

Vavra, M. 1996. Sustainability of animal production systems: An ecological perspective. *J. Anim. Sci.* 74:1418–23.

Vitousek, P. M., C. M. D'Antonio, L. L. Loope, and R. Westbrooks. 1996. Biological invasions as global environmental change. *Am. Sci.* 84:468–78.

Vitousek, P. M., P. R. Ehrlich, A. H. Ehrlich, and P. A. Matson. 1986. Human appropriation of the products of photosynthesis. *BioScience* 36:368–73.

Waggoner, P. E. 1994. *How much land can ten billion people spare for nature?* Task force rept. 121, February. Ames, Ia.: CAST.

Walker, J. L., Jr. 1991. *Mobilizing interest groups in America: Patrons, professions, and social movements*. Ann Arbor: University of Michigan Press.

Ward, G. M. 1982. Economic and resource cost of production of foods by ruminants. In *Animal products in human nutrition*, eds. D.C. Beitz and R. G. Hansen, 35–56. New York: Academic Press.

Ward, G. M., P. L. Knox, and B. W. Hobson. 1977. Beef production options and requirements for fossil fuel. *Science* 198:266–71.

Washburn, S. P., R. J. Knook, J. T. Green Jr., G. D. Jennings, G. A. Benson, J. C. Barker, and M. H. Poore. 1996. Enhancement of communities with pasture-based dairy production systems. In *Environmental enhancement through agriculture*, ed. W. Lockeretz, 137–43. Medford, Mass.: Tufts University.

Watson, R. T., M. C. Zinyowera, and R. C. Moss. 1996. *Climate change 1995. Impact, adaptations, and mitigation of climate change: Scientific-technical analysis.* Cambridge, UK: Cambridge University Press. Published for the International Panel on Climate Change (IPCC).

Watson, T. 1993. Animal regulations overturned. *Science* 259:1389.

Weber, P. 1995. Protecting oceanic fisheries and jobs. In *Worldwatch Institute, State of the World, 1995*, 21–37. New York: W. W. Norton and Co.

Weise, R. W. 1997. The Dolly dilemma. *Luth. Witn.* 116(6):6–9.

West, P. C. 1982. *Natural resource bureaucracy and rural poverty: A study in the political sociology of natural resources.* Monograph no. 2. Ann Arbor: University of Michigan, Natural Resource Sociology Research Laboratory.

Whelan, E. M. 1993. *Toxic terror: The truth behind the cancer scares*, 2d ed. Buffalo: Prometheus Books.

Whittlesey, N. K., R. G. Huffaker, and W. R. Butcher. 1993. Grazing policy on public lands. The authors reply. *Choices* (4th quar.):44–45.

Will, J. A. 1987. The case for the use of animals in science. In *Advances in animal welfare sciences 1986/87.* Washington, D.C.: Humane Society of the United States.

Willett, W. C., M. J. Stampfer, G. A. Colditz, B. A. Rosner, and F. E. Speizer. 1991. Relation of meat, fat, and fiber to the risk of colon cancer in a prospective study among women. *N. Engl. J. Med.* 323:1664–72.

Willett, W. C., F. Sacks, A. Trichopoulos, G. Drescher, A. Gerro-Luzzi, E. Helsing, and D. Trichopoulos. 1995. Mediterranean diet pyramid: A cultural model for healthy eating. *Am. J. Clin. Nutr.* 61:1402S–1406S.

Williams, B., C. Campbell, and R. Williams. 1995. Broken houses: Science and development in the African savannahs. *Agri. Hum. Val.* 12(2):29–38.

Williams, N. 1997. Biologists cut reductionist approach down to size. *Science* 277:476–77.

Wilmut, I., A. E. Schnieke, J. McWhir, A. J. Kind, and K. H. S. Campbell. 1997. Viable offspring derived from fetal and mammalian cells. *Nature* 385:810–13.

Wilson, J. Q. 1980. *The politics of regulation.* New York: Basic Books.

Wilson, K., and G. E. B. Morren. 1990. *Systems approaches for improvement in agriculture and resource management*, 109–13. New York: Macmillan.

Witte, W. 1998. Medical consequences of antibiotic use in agriculture. *Science* 279:996–97.

Wohlgenant, M. 1986. Effects of changing composition of beef consumption on the elasticities for beef and poultry. Paper presented at the S-165 Symposium, The demand for meat: What do we know and what does it mean? Charleston, South Carolina, October 20–21.

World Bank. 1989. *The challenge of hunger in Africa: A call to action.* Washington, D.C.: World Bank.

———. 1990. *World development report 1990.* Oxford: Oxford University Press.

World Food Council. 1977. A programme of action to eradicate hunger and malnutrition. Report to the UN General Assembly, 32d session.

World Resources Institute, United Nations Environment Program, United Nations Development Program, and the World Bank. *World resources 1996–97.* New York: Oxford University Press.

Wunderlich, Gene. 1990. Agricultural technology, wealth, and responsibility. *J. Agric. Environ. Eth.* 3:21–35.

Young, V. R., and P. L. Pellett. 1994. Plant proteins in relation to human protein and amino acid nutrition. *Am. J. Clin. Nutr.* 59(supp. 5S):1203S–12S.

Zeckhauser, R. J., and W. K. Viscusi. 1990. Risk within reason. *Science* 248:559–64.

Ziegler, R. G. 1991. Vegetables, fruits, and carotenoids and the risk of cancer. *Am. J. Clin. Nutr.* 53 (supp.):251S–59S.

Zock, P. L., and M. B. Katan. 1998. Linoleic acid intake and cancer risk: A review and meta-analysis. *Am. J. Clin. Nutr.* 68:142–53.

Zurer, P. S. 1991. Economic considerations enter fray over global climate change policies. *Chem. Eng. News* (April 1):1–13.